The Prose *Brut:*

The Development

of a

Middle English Chronicle

MEDIEVAL & RENAISSANCE TEXTS & STUDIES

VOLUME 180

The Prose *Brut:*

The Development of a Middle English Chronicle

by

Lister M. Matheson

MEDIEVAL & RENAISSANCE TEXTS & STUDIES
Tempe, Arizona
1998

© Copyright 1998

Arizona Board of Regents for Arizona State University

Library of Congress Cataloging-in-Publication Data

Matheson, Lister M.
    The prose Brut : the development of a Middle English chronicle / edited by Lister M. Matheson.
        p. cm. — (Medieval & Renaissance texts & studies ; v. 180)
    Includes bibliographical references (p.) and indexes.
    ISBN 0-86698-222-1 (alk. paper)
    1. Chronicles of England — Manuscripts. 2. Great Britain — History — To 1485 — Sources — Manuscripts. 3. English language — Middle English, 1100–1500 — Texts. 4. Brutus the Trojan (Legendary character). 5. Middle Ages — Sources — Manuscripts. 6. Manuscripts, Medieval — England. 7. Manuscripts, English (Middle). I. Title. II. Series.
DA130.M38 1998
942—dc21   98-11574
                                                                                                CIP

This book is made to last.
It is set in Caslon,
smythe-sewn and printed on acid-free paper
to library specifications.

Printed in the United States of America

Table of Contents

Preface   ix

Abbreviations and Short Titles   xi

Location Lists of Manuscripts and Early Printed Editions   xvii

Introduction

I.	The Prose *Brut:* Contents and Overview of the Versions	1
II.	Cultural and Historical Influence	8
III.	The Anglo-Norman *Brut*	30
IV.	The Latin *Brut*	37
V.	The Middle English *Brut*	47
VI.	Methods of Classification	49
	Appendix 1: The Text of the Cadwallader Episode	57
	Appendix 2: The Text of Queen Isabella's Letter	62
	Appendix 3: The Text of an Extended Version Exordium (Group B)	64

Classification of the Texts of the Middle English *Brut*

Synoptic Inventory of Versions   67

I. The Common Version

The Common Version to 1333 (CV–1333)   79
The Common Version to 1377 (CV–1377)   87
The Common Version to 1419, ending "and manfully countered with our English men" (CV–1419[men])   97

	The Common Version to 1419, ending "in rule and governance" (CV–1419[r&g])	106
	The Common Version to 1419, with "Leyle" for Lear (CV–1419 [Leyle])	128
	The Common Version to 1419, ending in "men" or (?) "in rule and governance" (CV–1419[men/?r&g])	131
	Continuation to a CV–1377 f.c. Stage 3 text from a Common Version text ending in 1419(r&g)	132
	The Common Version beyond 1419, including John Page's poem "The Siege of Rouen" (CV–JP)	133
	The Common Version to 1461 (CV–1461)	157
	Manuscripts containing the *Polychronicon* 1461 continuation and associated with "Warkworth's" *Chronicle* (Poly. 1461 W.C.)	166
II.	**The Extended Version**	
	The Extended and Abbreviated Versions	173
	The Extended Version to 1377 (EV–1377)	174
	The Extended Version to 1419, Group A (EV–1419:A)	177
	The Extended Version to 1419, Group B (EV–1419:B)	188
	The Extended Version to 1419, Group C (EV–1419:C)	197
III.	**The Abbreviated Version**	
	The Abbreviated Version to 1419, Group A (AV–1419:A)	204
	The Abbreviated Version to 1419, Group B (AV–1419:B)	215
	The Abbreviated Version to 1419, Group C (AV–1419:C)	228
	The Abbreviated Version to 1419, Group D (AV–1419:D)	230
	Remarks on the Extended and Abbreviated Versions	234
IV.	**Peculiar Texts and Versions**	256
	Reworked Texts and Versions	257
	Sections of Longer *Brut* Texts	311
	Very Brief Works Based on the *Brut*	314
	Texts Containing Brief King-Lists	318
	Appendages to Other Works	322
	The Translation Attributed to John Mandeville (JM–1333)	328
V.	**Unclassified Texts**	335

| TABLE OF CONTENTS | vii |

VI. The Early Printed Editions   339

Bibliography   349

Index of Manuscripts and Early Printed Editions   366

Index of Persons, Places, and Texts Associated with
   Manuscripts and Early Printed Editions   378

Preface

The Middle English prose *Brut* survives in more manuscripts than any other Middle English work except the two Wycliffite translations of the Bible. The present study classifies and groups the Middle English manuscripts and early printed editions and comments on the relationships that developed among them from the late fourteenth through the fifteenth centuries (and, in some cases, beyond the end of the latter century).

This book is the product of many years of intermittent engagement with the manuscripts and texts of the *Brut*, in the course of which I have incurred many pleasurable debts to scholars, librarians, and owners of manuscripts around the world.

For information on manuscripts, I acknowledge my gratitude above all to Michael L. Samuels, A. I. Doyle, and A. S. G. Edwards, as well as to Eugene J. Crook, Norman Davis, Marcel Dikstra, Caroline D. Eckhardt, Margaret H. Engel, Arthur Henne, Edward Donald Kennedy, Erik Kooper, Lan Lipscomb, Felicity Riddy, Christine M. Rose, Kathleen L. Scott, Barbara A. Shailor, Linda Ehrsam Voigts, Charlotte Wulf, and the librarians, keepers of manuscripts, and archivists of the many far-flung institutions, listed on pages xviii–xxi, xxiii–xxxi that hold manuscripts of the *Brut*. For information on early printed editions, I thank Katharine F. Pantzer.

For access to and microfilms of manuscripts in their care, I again thank those librarians and keepers, particularly Jack Baldwin (University of Glasgow Library), Hans E. Braun (Bibliotheca Bodmeriana), C. R. Cheney (Corpus Christi College, Cambridge), William O'Sullivan (Trinity College, Dublin, Library), and R. I. Page (Corpus Christi College, Cambridge). I mention especially those private owners, Mrs. P. G. Gordan, Mr. Robert Heyneman, and Professor Toshiyuki Takamiya, who generously accommodated, in one way or another, my requests to inspect their manuscripts. I am grateful to the staff of Special Collections at Edinburgh University Library for providing access to microfilms of Professor Takamiya's manuscripts that were made for the Middle English Dialect Project and to Margaret Laing for facilitating my examination of these.

Rachel Whitaker and Michael Grisinger were of great help in transferring information from paper to computer disk.

For funding in support of this study, I am much indebted to the National Endowment for the Humanities and the Rackham Foundation of the University of Michigan.

As always, I owe my deepest personal gratitude to my parents, Margaret A. and Charles Matheson, who supported in so many ways my early work at the University of Glasgow. I am grateful to my partner and fellow toiler in the vineyard, Tess Tavormina, who read earlier drafts of the present volume and who made many invaluable editorial suggestions on style and details of content. I also thank my son, Calum Matheson, for his patient tolerance of my frequent disappearances into manuscript reading rooms or into my study, where the microfilm reader resides. He (and I) might well echo the heartfelt sentiments expressed by the scribe of New College, Oxford, MS. 121 in a colophon on fol. 376v:

¶ Explicit...longissima prolixissima & tediosissima scribenti. Deo gratias. Deo gratias. & iterum Deo gratias.

L.M.M.

Abbreviations and Short Titles

General Abbreviations

a	column a
Addit.	Additional
App.	Appendix
b	column b
Bibl. Nat.	Bibliothèque Nationale (Paris)
BL	British Library (London)
Bodl.	Bodleian Library (Oxford)
ca.	circa
cat.	catalogue
CCCC	Corpus Christi College, Cambridge
Coll.	College
CUL	Cambridge University Library
EETS	Early English Text Society
e.s.	Extra Series
EUL	Edinburgh University Library
fol(s).	folio(s)
HMSO	Her Majesty's Stationery Office
MS(S).	manuscript(s)
NLS	National Library of Scotland (Edinburgh)
NLW	National Library of Wales (Aberystwyth)
n.s.	New Series
o.s.	Original Series
PRO	Public Record Office (London)
r	recto
Soc.	Society
TCC	Trinity College, Cambridge
TCD	Trinity College, Dublin
v	verso
vol(s).	volume(s)

Taxonomic Abbreviations Used in Classifying Middle English Brut *Texts*

CV	Common Version
EV	Extended Version
AV	Abbreviated Version
PV	Peculiar Version
JM	the translation attributed to John Mandeville, rector of Burnham Thorpe, Norfolk
f.c.	full continuation from 1333 to 1377
s.c.	short continuation from 1333 to 1377
–[year]	to [year] (e.g., CV–1333 = Common Version to 1333)
men, "men"	ending "and manfully countered with our English men" (applied to texts to 1419 that end with these words)
r&g, "r&g"	ending "in rule and governance" (applied to texts to 1419 that end with these words)
Leyle	with "Leyle" for Lear (applied to texts to 1419 that refer to King Lear as "Leyle")
JP	including John Page's poem "The Siege of Rouen" (found in certain texts that extend beyond 1419)
Poly. 1461	containing the *Polychronicon* continuation from 1419 to 1461
W.C.	"Warkworth's" *Chronicle*
Cad	the Cadwallader episode
QIL	Queen Isabella's letter
"5w"	"fifth ward" (an intrusive heading frequently found in the account of the battle of Halidon Hill)
A, B, C, etc.	group A, B, C, etc.
(a), (b), (c)	subgroup (a), (b), (c)

Abbreviations Used in Textual Citations and Apparatus

add.	added (in)
corr.	corrected, corrector
del.	deleted (in)

ABBREVIATIONS AND SHORT TITLES

xiii

etc.   et cetera
foll.   followed
ins.   inserted (in)
marg.   (in) margin
om.   omitted (in)
orig.   originally
poss.   possibly
vr(r).   variant reading(s)

Short Titles

Frequently cited catalogues, studies, and editions are referred to on their first occurrence by full name of author and title (with basic bibliographical information) and thereafter by surname and abbreviated title. The following short titles should, however, be particularly noted: they refer to (a) editions, bibliographical works, and important studies and (b) works that are cited only by short title. Full bibliographical and publishing details are found in the Bibliography.

Brie: Friedrich W. D. Brie, ed., *The Brut or The Chronicles of England*, EETS o.s. 131, 136 (1906, 1908).

Brie, *Geschichte und Quellen*:
     Friedrich W. D. Brie, *Geschichte und Quellen der mittelenglischen Prosachronik The Brute of England oder The Chronicles of England* (Marburg, 1905).

"Davies's" *Chronicle*:
     John Silvester Davies, ed., *An English Chronicle of the Reigns of Richard II, Henry IV, Henry V, and Henry VI Written Before the Year 1471*, Camden Society o.s. 64 (1856).

DNB: *The Dictionary of National Biography.*

Gairdner, ed., *Chronicles*:
     James Gairdner, ed., *Three Fifteenth-Century Chronicles*, Camden Society n.s. 28 (1880).

Gairdner, ed., *Hist. Collections*:
     James Gairdner, ed., *Historical Collections of a Citizen of London in the Fifteenth Century*, Camden Society n.s. 17 (1876).

Gransden, *Historical Writing II*:
: Antonia Gransden, *Historical Writing in England. II. c. 1307 to the Early Sixteenth Century* (Ithaca, 1982).

Kennedy, *Manual*:
: Edward Donald Kennedy, "Chronicles and Other Historical Writing," *A Manual of the Writings in Middle English 1050–1500*, ed. Albert E. Hartung, vol. 8 (Hamden, 1989).

Ker, *MMBL I*:
: N. R. Ker, *Medieval Manuscripts in British Libraries. I. London* (Oxford, 1969).

Ker, *MMBL II*:
: N. R. Ker, *Medieval Manuscripts in British Libraries. II. Abbotsford–Keele* (Oxford, 1977).

Ker, *MMBL III*:
: N. R. Ker, *Medieval Manuscripts in British Libraries. III. Lampeter–Oxford* (Oxford, 1983).

Kingsford, ed., *Chrons. London*:
: Charles L. Kingsford, ed., *Chronicles of London* (Oxford, 1905).

Kingsford, *English Historical Literature*:
: Charles L. Kingsford, *English Historical Literature in the Fifteenth Century* (Oxford, 1913).

LALME:
: Angus McIntosh, M. L. Samuels, and Michael Benskin, *A Linguistic Atlas of Late Mediaeval English*, 4 vols. (Aberdeen, 1986).

Marx, "Middle English Manuscripts":
: C. W. Marx, "Middle English Manuscripts of the Brut in the National Library of Wales," *The National Library of Wales Journal* 27 (1991–92): 361–82.

Matheson, "Historical Prose":
: Lister M. Matheson, "Historical Prose," in *Middle English Prose: A Critical Guide to Major Authors and Genres*, ed. A. S. G. Edwards (New Brunswick, 1984). Pp. 209–48.

Matheson, "Printer and Scribe":
> Lister M. Matheson, "Printer and Scribe: Caxton, the *Polychronicon*, and the *Brut*," *Speculum* 60 (1985): 593–614.

SC: Falconer Madan, H. E. Craster, Noel Denholm Young, et al., *A Summary Catalogue of Western Manuscripts in the Bodleian Library*, 7 vols. (Oxford, 1895–1953).

Short English Metrical Chronicle (see Zettl).

Smith, ed., *Kalendar*:
> Lucy Toulmin Smith, ed., *The Maire of Bristowe Is Kalendar, by Robert Ricart, Town Clerk of Bristol, 18 Edward IV*, Camden Society n.s. 5 (1872).

STC: A. W. Pollard and G. R. Redgrave, comps., *A Short-Title Catalogue of Books Printed in England, Scotland and Ireland, and of English Books Printed Abroad, 1475–1640*, 2nd ed., rev. and enlarged by W. A. Jackson, F. S. Ferguson, and Katharine F. Pantzer, 2 vols. (London, 1976, 1986).

Taylor, *English Historical Literature*:
> John Taylor, *English Historical Literature in the Fourteenth Century* (Oxford, 1987).

Zettl, ed., *Metrical Chron.*:
> Ewald Zettl, ed., *An Anonymous Short English Metrical Chronicle*, EETS o.s. 196 (1935).

Location Lists of Manuscripts and Early Printed Editions

The Anglo-Norman *Brut*

The Anglo-Norman prose *Brut* survives in at least forty-nine manuscripts (containing fifty texts). The following list includes those texts traditionally assigned to the Anglo-Norman work that formed the basis for the Middle English translation. (The manuscripts listed below have been subsumed in a general list of manuscripts and rolls of French historical texts published by Diana B. Tyson under the title of "the French prose *Brut* chronicle." Tyson has, however, defined "*Brut*" as an umbrella term for a genre rather than as the title of an identifiably separate work; accordingly, her list includes without differentiation many texts and sections of texts that have been excluded here, although they may well have drawn upon or been influenced by the Anglo-Norman prose *Brut*.[1])

---

[1] See Diana B. Tyson, "Handlist of Manuscripts Containing the French Prose *Brut* Chronicle," *Scriptorium* 98 (1994): 333–44. Tyson's criteria are given on p. 333; it should be noted that she has chosen to ignore distinctions between the Short and Long Versions and among the continuations, as well as whether *Des Grantz Geanz* is in verse or prose (p. 334). The present list supersedes those given in Friedrich W. D. Brie, *Geschichte und Quellen der mittelenglischen Prosachronik The Brute of England oder The Chronicles of England* (Marburg, 1905), pp. 1–2, and Johan Vising, *Anglo-Norman Language and Literature* (London and Oxford, 1923), pp. 74f., 88ff. For partial lists, see Georgine E. Brereton, ed., *Des Grantz Geantz. An Anglo-Norman Poem*, Medium Ævum Monographs 2 (Oxford, 1937), pp. vi–xi (manuscripts containing the introductory poem); Wendy R. Childs and John Taylor, eds., *The Anonimalle Chronicle, 1307 to 1334, From Brotherton Collection MS 29*, Yorkshire Archæological Society, Record Series 147 (Leeds, 1991), pp. 74–75 (manuscripts containing the short continuation). See also M. Dominica Legge and Georgine E. Brereton, "Three Hitherto Unlisted MSS. of the French Prose *Brute* Chronicle," *Medium Ævum* 7 (1938): 113–17; James P. Carley and Julia Crick, "Constructing Albion's Past: An Annotated Edition of *De Origine Gigantum*," *Arthurian Literature XIII*, ed. James P. Carley and Felicity Riddy (Cambridge, 1995), p. 46 n. 18; Ruth Dean's forthcoming catalogue of Anglo-Norman literature (noted in Carley and Crick). A single leaf was listed in Quaritch cat. 1147, *Bookhands of the Middle Ages: Part V, Medieval*

England
Cambridge, Cambridge University Library
    Ee.1.20, fols. 78v–142
    Gg.1.15, fols. 1–80v
    Ii.6.8, fols. 1–183v
    Mm.1.33, fols. 1–62v

Cambridge, Corpus Christi College
    98 (roll on 16 skins)

Cambridge, Trinity College
    R.5.32, fols. 1–59
    R.7.14, fols. 1–147v

Leeds, University of Leeds Library
    Brotherton Collection 29, fols. 23–26, 248v–271 (formerly Bradfer-Lawrence, Ingilby)

London, British Library
    Additional 18462(a), fols. 8–101v
    Additional 18462(b), fols. 103–204v
    Additional 35092, fols. 5–144
    Additional 35113, fols. 2–92
    Cotton Cleopatra D.iii, fols. 74–182v

Manuscript Leaves (1991), item 101; see H. R. Woudhuysen, "Manuscripts at Auction January 1991 to December 1991," in *English Manuscript Studies 1100–1700*, ed. Peter Beal and Jeremy Griffiths, 4 (London and Toronto, 1993), p. 297. The present list does not contain BL MS. Additional 10622, fols. 1–62v, which agrees with the first part of BL MS. Royal 20.A.xviii (the text is similar to that found as the first section of Leeds MS. Brotherton 29); there can be no certainty, however, that the Additional manuscript ever included the long continuation from the *Brut* that is appended in a different hand in the Royal manuscript. Vising lists Trinity College, Cambridge, MS. R.4.26, which contains a text of the *Brut abrégé*; see Ewald Zettl, ed., *An Anonymous Short English Metrical Chronicle*, EETS o.s. 196 (1935), pp. xxxi–xxxiv (description of CUL Gg.1.1), 92–107 (text of CUL Gg.1.1). Other manuscripts of the *Brut abrégé* include Trinity College, Cambridge, R.7.23; Trinity College, Cambridge, R.14.9; Harvard Law School 1; Trinity College, Cambridge, R.4.26; Public Record Office, Exchequer 164/24; BL Royal 20.C.vi; Bodleian Selden Supra 74; Corpus Christi College, Cambridge, 53; see Marcia L. Maxwell, "The Anglo-Norman Prose *Brut*: An Edition of British Library MS Cotton Cleopatra D.iii," Ph.D. diss., Michigan State University, 1995, pp. 7, 12–13, and, for further manuscripts, Tyson, "Handlist of Manuscripts Containing the French Prose *Brut* Chronicle," pp. 338–44.

Cotton Cleopatra D.vii, fols. 76–79v (hand 2), 80–139v (hand 1), 140–182v (hand 2)
Cotton Domitian x, fols. 14–87v
Cotton Julius A.i, fols. 51–53v (fragment)[2]
Cotton Tiberius A.vi, fols. 121–142
Harley 200, fols. 4–79v
Harley 6359, fols. 1–84
Royal 19.C.ix, fols. 1–155
Royal 20.A.iii, fols. 121–236
Royal 20.A.xviii, fols. 311–335v
Royal App. 85, fols. 15–22 (fragment)

London, College of Arms
Arundel 31, fols. 1–186v

London, Lambeth Palace Library
504, fols. 1–77v

London, Library of the Honourable Society of the Inner Temple
511, Vol. XIX, fols. 7v–147v

London, Lincoln's Inn
88, fols. 9–76v

London, Westminster Abbey Chapter Library
25, fols. 1–92v

Oxford, Bodleian Library
Ashmole 1804 (SC 25174), fols. 49–104v
Douce 120 (SC 21694), fols. 1–64v
Douce 128 (SC 21702), fols. 60–163v
e Musaeo 108 (SC 3697), fols. 1–119
Lyell 17, fols. 58v–121v (formerly Wrest Park 33)
Rawlinson D.329 (SC 13117), fols. 8–122v
Wood empt. 8 (SC 8596), fols. 1–57v

Oxford, Corpus Christi College
78, fols. 3–214
293, fols. 21–87v

---

[2] Misnumbered as "A.VI" in John Taylor, *English Historical Literature in the Fourteenth Century* (Oxford, 1987), p. 121, and Childs and Taylor, eds., *Anonimalle Chronicle*, p. 74.

Scotland
Edinburgh, University of Edinburgh Library
    181 (Laing 51), fols. 47–201v

Ireland
Dublin, Trinity College
    500, pp. 13–199
    501, fols. 51–125

France
Paris, Bibliothèque de l'Arsenal
    3346, fols. 84–156

Paris, Bibliothèque Mazarine
    1860, fols. 1–108

Paris, Bibliothèque Nationale
    fonds français 12155, fols. 2–233
    fonds français 12156, fols. 3–126
    fonds français 14640, fols. 1–49v
    nouvelles acquisitions françaises 4267, fols. 9–14 (fragment)

Paris, Bibliothèque Ste. Geneviève
    935, fols. 1–208

United States of America
New Haven, Beinecke Library, Yale University
    86, fols. 1–12v (fragments; formerly Fletcher, Lyell)
    405, fols. 1–74v (formerly Brudenell; Sotheby 10 July 1967, no. 48; H. A. Levinson, cat. 60 [1969], no. 765)
    593, fols. 1–118v (formerly Phillipps 3338)

The Latin *Brut*

The Latin *Brut* is known to survive, in whole or in part, in the nineteen manuscripts below, although this list is almost certainly incomplete.

England
Cambridge, Corpus Christi College
    311, fols. 1–101

Cambridge, Gonville and Caius College
    72, fols. 1–51

London, British Library
    Cotton Domitian iv, fols. 2–57v
    Cotton Galba E.vii, fols. 119v–120 (15th-century interpolation)
    Cotton Julius B.iii, fols. 51v–101v
    Harley 941, fols. 1–3v
    Harley 3884, fols. 227–228v (2 extracts)
    Harley 3906, fols. 2–108
    Lansdowne 212, fols. 2–171v

London, College of Arms
    Arundel 5, fols. 120–168v

London, Lambeth Palace Library
    99, fols. 1–22v

Oxford, Bodleian Library
    Rawlinson B.147, fols. 1–43v
    Rawlinson B.169, fols. 1–88
    Rawlinson B.195, fols. 1–54 (16th century)
    Rawlinson C.234, fols. 1–72v
    Rawlinson C.398, fols. 1–51

Oxford, Magdalen College
    200, fols. 40–56

Oxford, St. John's College
    78, fols. 2–55v

United States of America
San Marino, Henry E. Huntington Library
    HM 19960, fols. before fol. 175 (extract)

The Middle English *Brut*

The following list of manuscripts and early printed editions consolidates the list published by the present writer in 1979 (supplemented in 1984 and 1985) with those in the *Index of Printed Middle English Prose* (1985) and the *Manual of the Writings in Middle English* (1989).[3] Some minor

---

[3] Lister M. Matheson, "The Middle English Prose *Brut*: A Location List of the

corrections have been made, and the only completely new addition to the corpus is the Brogyntyn MS. (on deposit in the National Library of Wales). Welbeck Abbey MS. 29/331, previously on deposit at the British Library, has now been incorporated into the Additional manuscripts as BL Additional 70514.

In addition to English texts of or directly descended from the main translation of the Anglo-Norman *Brut*, the present list also includes manuscripts of works derived from or textually related to the *Brut*, namely:

(a) the manuscripts of John Mandeville's English translation of the Anglo-Norman work (BL Harley 4690, Coll. of Arms Arundel 58, and the seventeenth-century transcript of Arundel 58 in Magdalene College, Cambridge, Pepys 2833);

(b) Bodl. Digby 196, which includes a short king-list and a brief chronicle derived from the main *Brut*, catalogued separately by Kennedy (*Manual*, p. 2637);

(c) CUL Ff.1.6 and Folger Shakespeare Library V.a.198, a brief king-list/chronicle, again partly based on the main *Brut*, catalogued separately by Kennedy as *The Cronekelys of Seyntys and Kyngys of Yngelond* (*Manual*, p. 2637);

(d) Bodl. Ashmole 791, Holkham 669, Columbia Plimpton 261, and the brief seventeenth-century extracts in Bodl. Ashmole 1139.iv.2, translated from a Latin *Brut*, provisionally classified separately by Kennedy as *The New Croniclys Compendyusly Idrawn of the Gestys of the Kynges of England* (*Manual*, pp. 2638–40);

(e) Mayor's Calendar, City of Bristol Record Office, no. 04720 (1) (the *Bristowe Chronicle*), the first part of which is an abridgement of the *Brut* (unrecognized as such in *Manual*, p. 2655).

In the following list, alternate or former shelfmarks or catalogue numbers are given in parentheses. Kennedy's information on former,

---

Manuscripts and Early Printed Editions," *Analytical and Enumerative Bibliography* 3 (1979): 254–66; Matheson, "Historical Prose," in *Middle English Prose: A Critical Guide to Major Authors and Genres*, ed. A. S. G. Edwards (New Brunswick, 1984), pp. 232–33; Matheson, "Printer and Scribe: Caxton, the *Polychronicon*, and the *Brut*," *Speculum* 60 (1985): 593 n. 3; Robert E. Lewis, N. F. Blake, and A. S. G. Edwards, *Index of Printed Middle English Prose* (New York and London, 1985), pp. 132–34; and Edward Donald Kennedy, "Chronicles and Other Historical Writing," *A Manual of the Writings in Middle English 1050–1500*, ed. Albert E. Hartung, vol. 8 (Hamden, 1989), pp. 2818–21.

modern owners of manuscripts and his references to sale catalogues have been incorporated and, where possible, expanded. Texts and transcripts that were undoubtedly written after 1500 are so indicated; some represent useful witnesses to the medieval manuscript tradition.

England
Bristol, City of Bristol Record Office
    Mayor's Calendar, no. 04720 (1), fols. 3v–15v

Cambridge, Cambridge University Library
    Additional 2775, fols. 10–255 (formerly Charlemont [Sotheby 1865], Harwood [Sotheby 1883])
    Ee.4.31, fols. 203–276v
    Ee.4.32, fols. 24–207v
    Ff.1.6, fols. 110–113 ("Findern MS.," formerly John Moore 60)
    Ff.2.26, fols. 2–104 (formerly More 611)
    Hh.6.9, fols. 1–183v
    Kk.1.3, 10 unnumbered folios inserted near end of MS.
    Kk.1.12, fols. 1–129
    Ll.2.14, fols. 143–225v

Cambridge, Corpus Christi College
    174, fols. 1–198v
    182, fols. 1–179v

Cambridge, Fitzwilliam Museum
    McClean 186, fols. 2–198

Cambridge, Magdalene College
    Pepys 2833, pp. 1–3, fols. 485–518 (ca. 1685 copy of Coll. of Arms Arundel 58 [Mandeville translation])

Cambridge, Peterhouse
    190, fols. 1–214v, ("Warkworth's" *Chronicle*) 214v–225

Cambridge, Trinity College
    O.9.1 (1413), fols. 49–227 (including London chronicle from fol. 198v)
    O.10.34 (1486), fols. 1–160
    O.11.11, fols. 3v–130v (formerly Loscombe, Ashburnham Appendix CIX, Leighton, Dunn, Murray)
    R.5.43 (731), Part II, fols. 39–199v

Leicester, University of Leicester Library
   47, fols. 1–106v (formerly Ashburnham; Sotheby 1 May 1899, lot 57)

Lincoln, Lincoln Cathedral Chapter Library
   70 (C.5.12), fols. 1–59v
   98 (A.4.6), fols. 174–181v

London, Bedford Estates Office, 29A Montague St., London WC1B 5BL
   Woburn Abbey 181, fols. [100v–202v]

London, British Library
   Additional 6915, fols. 1–141 (transcript of BL Harley 63 by J. H. Hindley, made 1785–1827)
   Additional 10099, fols. 1–203
   Additional 12030, fols. 1–167v
   Additional 24859, fols. 1–149
   Additional 26746, fols. 1–371v (16th century?)
   Additional 33242, fols. 1–164
   Additional 70514, fols. [1–38v] (formerly Welbeck Abbey 29/331, Duke of Portland, BL Deposit, MS. Loan 29)
   Cotton Claudius A.viii, fols. 1–12 (7–18 in alternative foliation)
   Cotton Galba E.viii, fols. 29–148
   Egerton 650, fols. 2–114v (including London chronicle from fol. 111v)
   Harley 24, fols. 1–220v
   Harley 53, fols. 14–164v
   Harley 63, fols. 1–44v
   Harley 266, fols. 1–151v
   Harley 753, fols. 1–191v
   Harley 1337, fols. 1*, 1–105
   Harley 1568, fols. 1–182, 183v
   Harley 2182, fols. 1–185
   Harley 2248, fols. 1–290v
   Harley 2256, fols. 1–202
   Harley 2279, fols. 3–146
   Harley 3730, fols. 2–119v
   Harley 3945, fols. 1–117v
   Harley 4690, fols. 4–108 (Mandeville translation)

Harley 4827, fols. 1–157
Harley 4930, fols. 1–111v
Harley 6251, fols. 1–105v
Harley 7333, fols. 1–24v
Royal 11.B.ix, fols. 133–134v
Royal 17.D.xxi, fols. 1–197
Royal 18.A.ix, fols. 8–132v
Royal 18.B.iii, fols. 1–275v (misbound; begins on fol. 5; fols. 1–4 should follow fol. 8, though some leaves have been lost after fol. 4)
Royal 18.B.iv, fols. 1–169
Sloane 2027, fols. 96v–97v, 170–188v
Stowe 68, fols. 1–189v
Stowe 69, fols. 2–195v (including London chronicle from fol. 192)
Stowe 70, fols. 3–139v
Stowe 71, fols. 3–84v

London, College of Arms
Arundel 8, fols. 1–68
Arundel 58, fols. 5–6, 76, 302v–334 (Mandeville translation)
Vincent 421, fols. [1–143v]

London, Lambeth Palace Library
6, fols. 1–257
84, fols. 1–202v
259, pp. 1–229
264, fols. 1–168v
306, fols. 1–17v
331, fols. 1–117v
491, fols. 1–205v
738, fols. 1–228v

London, Library of the Honourable Society of the Inner Temple
Petyt 511, Vol. XI, fols. 66–169v

London, Sion College
Arc. L.40.2/E.42, fols. 1–186v

London, Society of Antiquaries
93, fols. 1–97v
223, fols. 1–45v

Manchester, John Rylands University Library
    Eng. 102, fols. 1–101v (formerly Wasey, Leighton)
    Eng. 103, fols. 1–130v (formerly Leighton)
    Eng. 104, fols. 1–133v (formerly Tomlynson, Leighton)
    Eng. 105, fols. 3–136v (formerly Phillipps 9486)
    Eng. 206, fols. 3–104v (formerly Coke, Dunn)
    Eng. 207, fols. 1–103v, 104–124v (two MSS. combined before 1749; formerly Quentock, Dunn)

Norfolk, Holkham Hall
    669, pp. 1–185
    670, fols. [1–125v] (formerly Coke)

Northumberland, Alnwick Castle
    457A, fols. 1–47v, 48–69

Nottingham, Nottinghamshire County Council
    DDFS 3/1, fols. 1–83v (formerly Stanhope)

Oxford, Bodleian Library
    Ashmole 791 (SC 7430), fols. 1–59v
    Ashmole 793 (SC 7433), fols. 1–148v
    Ashmole 1139.iv.2, fol. 80r–v (transcript of 1672 of excerpts from Bodl. Ashmole 791)
    Bodley 231 (SC 2174), fols. 1–198v
    Bodley 754 (SC 27653), fols. 2–154
    Bodley 840 (SC 27654), fols. 1–166v
    Digby 185 (SC 1786), fols. 1–79v
    Digby 196 (SC 1797), fols. 26–27, 156v–158
    Douce 290 (SC 21864), fols. 157–280v
    Douce 323 (SC 21897), fols. 1–101v
    e Musaeo 39 (SC 3634), fols. 1–182v
    Hatton 50 (SC 4112), fols. 2–130
    Laud Misc. 550 (SC 1375), fols. 1–120v
    Laud Misc. 571 (SC 1493), fols. 1–142v
    Laud Misc. 733 (SC 1129), fols. 18–168v
    Lyell 34, fols. 1–214v
    Rawlinson B.166 (SC 11535), fols. 1–131v
    Rawlinson B.171 (SC 11539), fols. 1–201v
    Rawlinson B.173 (SC 11541), fols. 1–221v
    Rawlinson B.187 (SC 11548), fols. 1–135v

AND EARLY PRINTED EDITIONS xxvii

    Rawlinson B.190 (SC 15500), fols. 1–163v
    Rawlinson B.196 (SC 11556), fols. 1–109
    Rawlinson B.205 (SC 15506), fols. 1–68v
    Rawlinson B.216 (SC 11568), fols. 1–125
    Rawlinson C.155 (SC 12019), fols. 89–94v (transcript of 1606 by Henry Spelman)
    Rawlinson C.901 (SC 12735), fols. 1–130
    Rawlinson poet. 32 (SC 14526), fols. 55v–168
    Tanner 11 (SC 9831), fols. 1–211
    Tanner 188 (SC 10014), fols. 1–127

Oxford, Jesus College
    5, fols. 1–216v

Oxford, Lincoln College
    Lat. 151, fols. 1–177v (numbered to fol. 176 [fol. 26 was omitted]; formerly Norris, gift to Norwich Castle Museum 1830; Sotheby 11 Dec. 1961, lot 159)

Oxford, Trinity College
    5, fols. 1–216v

Oxford, University College
    154, fols. 1–121v

Wiltshire, Longleat House
    183A, fols. 1–137v

Scotland

Edinburgh, National Library of Scotland
    6128, fols. 1–142v (formerly Borthwick)

Edinburgh, University of Edinburgh Library
    184 (Laing 217), fols. 1–25v
    185 (Laing 196), fols. 1–125

Glasgow, University of Glasgow Library
    Hunterian 61 (T.2.19), fols. iv–147v (123 fols. in MS.; several folios missing)
    Hunterian 74 (T.3.12), fols. 1–114v
    Hunterian 83 (T.3.21), fols. 15–140v, ("Warkworth's" *Chronicle*) 141–148v

Hunterian 228 (U.3.1), fols. 1–151v
Hunterian 230 (U.3.3), fols. 2–246
Hunterian 443 (V.5.13), fols. 2–173v

Wales
Aberystwyth, National Library of Wales
    442D (Williams 241), fols. 1–342v
    21608D, fols. 1–189v (formerly Llannerch-Gwysaney, acquired in 1978)
    Brogyntyn 8, fols. 1–18v (Lord Harlech MS., 1934 deposit)
    Peniarth 343A (Hengwrt 257), pp. 1–45, 58 (16th/17th century)
    Peniarth 396D (Hengwrt 429 Appendix and Hengwrt 429), pp. 1–16, fols. 3–212v (two texts)
    Peniarth 397C (Hengwrt 115), pp. 1–538
    Peniarth 398D (Hengwrt 320), pp. 3–274

Ireland
Dublin, Trinity College
    489, pp. 35–213
    490, fols. 3–177v
    505, pp. 87–285
    506, fols. 1–93v
    5895, fols. 3–133v (formerly Ware, Henniker MS.)

Belgium
Brussels, Bibliothèque Royale
    IV.461, fols. 1–75v (formerly Baynes, Sotheby 12 Dec. 1966, lot 183)

France
Paris, Bibliothèque Nationale
    fonds anglais 30, fols. 1–42v (Gough sale, 1810)

Germany
Hamburg, Staats- und Universitätsbibliothek Hamburg
    Cod. 98 in scrin, pp. 1–398

Switzerland
Cologny-Genève, Bibliotheca Bodmeriana
 Cod. Bodmer 43, fols. 1–2v (formerly Aldenham, Sotheby 22 March
  1937, lot 107)

United States of America
Ann Arbor, Hatcher Library, University of Michigan
 225, fols. 1–135

Berkeley, Bancroft Library, University of California at Berkeley
 152, fols. 1–138v (formerly Bute 47; Sotheby 13 June 1983, lot 12,
  H. P. Kraus Cat. 180, Dec. 1988, lot 44)

Bethlehem, Pennsylvania, Lehigh University Library
 3 fragments from 1 MS.

Cambridge, Mass., Houghton Library, Harvard University
 Eng. 530, fols. 59–211v
 Eng. 587, fols. 1–151v (formerly Ashburnham Appendix CX)
 Eng. 750, fols. 10–71v, 84–103 (two texts; formerly Wrest Park 18)
 Eng. 938, fols. 91–101v
 Richardson 35, fols. 2–94v

Chapel Hill, Robert G. Heyneman, 1108 Sourwood Circle, Chapel
  Hill, North Carolina 27514
 1 MS., fols. 1–167v (formerly Earl of Inchiquin, Wangenheim)

Charlottesville, University of Virginia Library
 38–173, fols. 1–229v (formerly von Scherling)

Chicago, University of Chicago Library
 253, fols. 1–132v (Quaritch cat. 303 [1911], no. 882, Sotheby 20
  Nov. 1912, lot 127, Quaritch cat. 344 [1916], no. 8)
 254, fols. 1–149v (formerly Phillipps 2706)

Cleveland, Cleveland Public Library
 W q091.92-C468, fols. 13 (2nd leaf so numbered)–75v (formerly
  Aldenham, Sotheby 22 Mar. 1937, lot 108; E. P. Goldschmidt,
  cat. 44 [April 1938], no. 4, cat. 50 [Jan. 1939], no. 59, cat. 59
  [Sept. 1940], no. 49; bought in 1944)

New Haven, Beinecke Library, Yale University
 323, fols. 3–157v (formerly Lord Amherst of Hackney, Jones,

Anderson Galleries, New York, 23 January 1923, cat. 1699, no. 125, Sinderen)
494, fols. 3–103 (formerly Segar, Frewen, H. P. Kraus)

New York, Columbia University Library
Plimpton 261, fols. 1–133v (formerly Phillipps 191)
Plimpton 262, fols. 1–134v (formerly Phillipps 2307)

New York, Mrs. J. D. Gordan, 113 East 78th St., New York, NY 10021
63, fols. 1–175v (formerly Duke of Newcastle, probably Rennie 733 before 1829; Clumber sale, Sotheby 15 Feb. 1938, lot 1140; obtained from Maggs, 1938)

Philadelphia, Free Library of Philadelphia
Lewis 238, fols. 1–126 (formerly 2nd Tollemache copy, Helmingham Hall; Sotheby 14 June 1965, lot 18)

Princeton, Princeton University Library
Garrett 150, fols. 1–157v
Taylor Medieval 3, fols. 40–131v (formerly Wrest Park 5)

San Marino, Henry E. Huntington Library
HM 113, fols. 1–171v (formerly Phillipps 8857)
HM 131, fols. 1–154v (formerly Duke of Buccleuch, White, Jones, Smith)
HM 133, fols. 1–110v (formerly Hellman, Smith)
HM 136, fols. 1–172v (formerly Phillipps 8858)

University Park, Pennsylvania State University Library
PS. V–3A, fols. 1–197 (formerly Hale, Sotheby 8 Dec. 1981, lot 81)

Urbana, University of Illinois Library
82, fols. 1–218v (formerly Haslewood)
116, fols. 1–206v (formerly Duke of Buccleuch, Lord Amherst of Hackney, Harmsworth, Sotheby 15 Oct. 1945, lot 1951, Halliday)

Washington, D.C., Folger Shakespeare Library
V.a.198 (1232.3), fols. [1–3v] (formerly Phillipps 9613)
V.b.106 (725.2), fols. 1–92v (formerly Phillipps 3784)

Australia
Corio, Victoria, Geelong Church of England Grammar School
    1 MS., fols. 1–76v (formerly Baynes; gift to school in 1938 by C. A. S. Hawker; now missing)
Sydney, University of Sydney Library
    Nicholson 13, fols. 1–177v (formerly Cochrane, Nicholson)

Japan
Tokyo, collection of Toshiyuki Takamiya, Dept. of English, Keio University, Mita, Minatoku, Tokyo 108
    12, fols. 1–222v (formerly Fairfax of Cameron; Clumber sale, Sotheby 15 Feb. 1938, lot 1142; Dawsons of Pall Mall, 1975)
    18, fols. 1–71v (formerly 1st Tollemache copy, Helmingham Hall; Sotheby 8 July, 1970, lot 66)
    29, fols. 1–150v (formerly Hughlock, Duke of Newcastle; Clumber sale, Sotheby 15 Feb. 1938, lot 1141; Sotheby 14 Dec. 1977, lot 50)
    67, fols. 1–203v (formerly Bradfer-Lawrence 11, Ingilby; formerly on deposit in the Fitzwilliam Museum, Cambridge; sold to Quaritch ca. 1980)

Unlocated Manuscripts

As Kennedy notes, "All but five of the manuscripts listed by Brie have been located with certainty," and of these five, Brie's Rennie 733 is probably the present Gordan 63 (*Manual*, p. 2635); the manuscripts listed below may also correspond to texts in the list above. The erstwhile owners of other manuscripts listed by Brie (but unseen by him) are[4]

1. John Edwards, Glasgow. A manuscript containing a CV heading and ending, perhaps imperfectly, with the death of Edward III.[5] Edwards

---

[4] Brie, *Geschichte und Quellen*, p. 5; see Kennedy, *Manual*, pp. 2635–36, 2821. The following corrections to Brie's list of English manuscripts should also be noted: Laud 550 and 571 are erroneously listed under the British Museum, as well as under the Bodleian Library; Lambeth 751 is an error (possibly confused with Laud 571); four manuscripts are listed at Holkham Hall: 210, 236, 670, and 672—the correct references should be Holkham 669 and 670.

[5] See Brie, *Geschichte und Quellen*, p. 59; John Edwards, "History in the 'Chronicle of the Brute'," *Proceedings of the Royal Philosophical Society of Glasgow* 34 (1903): 272–81.

records the heading as "Here may a man heren how Engeland was first called Albion and thurgh whom it hadde the name." Edwards's citations from his manuscript show that it was not an Extended Version, and his description suggests that it included the Cadwallader episode. It is very possible that the text actually ended in 1377 with the death of Edward III and that Edwards described it as "imperfect" because he was primarily aware, from his comparisons with manuscripts in the Hunterian collection at the University of Glasgow, of texts ending in 1419. If so, then this text was probably similar to the important text found as the first part of Princeton University Library, Taylor Medieval MS. 3 (item 20). Fortunately, Edwards included in the printed form of his paper a good facsimile of a page, the text of which recounts Merlin's establishment of Stonehenge; the manuscript (which probably still survives) may therefore be easily identifiable at some future time.

2. Sir Edward Lechmere, Rhydd Court, Upton-on-Severn, Worcestershire. Brie lists two manuscripts, while the Report of the Historical Manuscripts Commission records only one.[6]

3. Sir John Lawson, Brough Hall, Yorkshire. A seventeenth-century transcript of 183 pages.[7]

To these should be added:
4. Gurney MS. 116.13, Keswick Hall, Norfolk, fols. 139–150.[8] Gurney manuscripts were sold in 1920 and at Sotheby in 1936.

5. Foyle, Beeleigh Abbey, Maldon, Suffolk, bought a manuscript with Durham names at Sotheby 24 Jan. 1944, lot 126.[9]

6. Bradfer-Lawrence MS. 11, formerly deposited in the Fitzwilliam Museum, Cambridge, is now Takamiya MS. 67; I have used a microfilm copy supplied by the Museum before the sale of the manuscript.

---

[6] *Fifth Report of the Royal Commission on Historical Manuscripts* (London, 1876), Appendix, p. 299. Cf. *Guide to the Location of Collections Described in the Reports and Calendars Series 1870–1980*, Guides to Sources for British History 3 (London, 1982), p. 36.

[7] *Third Report of the Royal Commission on Historical Manuscripts* (London, 1872), Appendix, p. 255. Cf. *Guide to the Location of Collections*, p. 36.

[8] *Twelfth Report of the Royal Commission on Historical Manuscripts* (London, 1891), Appendix, Part 9, pp. 153–55. Cf. *Guide to the Location of Collections*, p. 28.

[9] I am indebted for this information to A. I. Doyle.

Early Printed Editions

The STC list of locations has been supplemented from William W. Bishop, *A Checklist of American Copies of 'Short-Title Catalogue' Books*, 2nd ed. (Ann Arbor, 1950) and David Ramage, *A Finding-List of English Books to 1640 in Libraries in the British Isles* (Durham, 1958); the present list is not, however, exhaustive. I have not indicated which copies are imperfect, though where a "copy" consists of only a few leaves this has been noted.

1. William Caxton, Westminster, 1480 (STC 9991).
   Copies: (a) Great Britain: British Library, London; Lambeth Palace Library, London; London University Library; Bodleian Library, Oxford; University Library, Cambridge; John Rylands University Library, Manchester; Liverpool University Library; University of Glasgow Library; (b) United States: Folger Shakespeare Library, Washington, D.C.; Huntington Library, San Marino; Library of Congress, Washington, D.C.; New York Public Library; Pierpont Morgan Library, New York; Garrett Collection, Johns Hopkins University Library, Baltimore.

2. William Caxton, Westminster, 1482 (STC 9992).
   Copies: (a) Great Britain: British Library, London; Bodleian Library, Oxford; University Library, Cambridge; Pepysian Library, Magdalene College, Cambridge (5 leaves); John Rylands University Library, Manchester; (b) United States: Cornell University Library, Ithaca; Mellon Collection, Yale Center for British Art, New Haven; Newberry Library, Chicago; New York Public Library (1 leaf); Pierpont Morgan Library, New York.

3. [Schoolmaster-Printer,] St. Albans, [?1483] (STC 9995).
   Copies: (a) Great Britain: British Library, London; Bodleian Library, Oxford (3 copies); University Library, Cambridge; University of Glasgow Library; John Rylands University Library, Manchester; (b) United States: Huntington Library, San Marino; University of Chicago Library; Newberry Library, Chicago; Pierpont Morgan Library, New York; Beinecke Library, Yale University, New Haven.

4. [William de Machlinia, London, ?1486] (STC 9993).
   Copies: (a) Great Britain: British Library, London; Bodleian

Library, Oxford (2 copies); Pepysian Library, Magdalene College, Cambridge; Pembroke College Library, Cambridge; John Rylands University Library, Manchester; (b) United States: Chapin Library, Williams College, Williamstown; Mrs. J. D. Gordan, New York; University of Illinois Library, Champaign-Urbana; Pierpont Morgan Library, New York; Beinecke Library, Yale University, New Haven; Eric H. L. Sexton, Rockport, Maine.

5. Gerard de Leew, Antwerp, 1493 (STC 9994).
Copies: (a) Great Britain: British Library, London; Bodleian Library, Oxford; University Library, Cambridge; John Rylands University Library, Manchester; Peterborough Cathedral (on deposit at the University Library, Cambridge); Ripon Cathedral Library; (b) Ireland: Trinity College Library, Dublin; (c) United States: Newberry Library, Chicago.

6. Wynkyn de Worde, Westminster, 1497 (STC 9996).
Copies: (a) Great Britain: British Library, London; Bodleian Library, Oxford; University Library, Cambridge; King's College Library, Cambridge; John Rylands University Library, Manchester (2 copies); (b) United States: Folger Shakespeare Library, Washington, D.C.; Huntington Library, San Marino (1 leaf); Mellon Collection, Yale Center for British Art, New Haven; Newberry Library, Chicago (1 leaf); Pierpont Morgan Library, New York; University of South Carolina Library, Columbia; (c) Australia: State Library of Victoria, Melbourne (1 leaf).

7. Wynkyn de Worde, London, 1502 (STC 9997).
Copies: (a) Great Britain: British Library, London; Bodleian Library, Oxford; Wadham College Library, Oxford; Chetham's Library, Manchester; (b) Ireland: Marsh's Library, Dublin; (c) United States: Boston Public Library; Carl H. Pforzheimer Library, New York; Library Company of Philadelphia; Pierpont Morgan Library, New York (25 leaves, interleaved with the 1515 W. de Worde edition); Princeton University Library.

8. Julyan Notary, London, 1504 (STC 9998).
Copies: Great Britain: British Library, London; University Library, Cambridge; Trinity College Library, Cambridge.

9. Richard Pynson, London, 1510 (STC 9999).

Copies: (a) Great Britain: British Library, London; Bodleian Library, Oxford; University Library, Cambridge; John Rylands University Library, Manchester (2 copies); Peterborough Cathedral (on deposit at the University Library, Cambridge); (b) United States: Folger Shakespeare Library, Washington, D.C.; Annmary Brown Library, Brown University, Providence.

10. Julyan Notary, London, 1515 (STC 10000).
   Copies: (a) Great Britain: British Library, London; Bodleian Library, Oxford; University Library, Cambridge; John Rylands University Library, Manchester; Blackburn Public Library; National Library of Scotland, Edinburgh; (b) United States: Folger Shakespeare Library, Washington, D.C.; Huntington Library, San Marino; Lehigh University Library, Bethlehem; Pierpont Morgan Library, New York; Beinecke Library, Yale University, New Haven; (c) Japan: Imperial University Library, Tokyo.

11. Wynkyn de Worde, London, 1515 (STC 10000.5, formerly 9985).
   Copies: (a) Great Britain: British Library, London; London University Library; University of Liverpool Library; John Rylands University Library, Manchester; (b) United States: Folger Shakespeare Library, Washington, D.C.; Huntington Library, San Marino; Houghton Library, Harvard University, Cambridge; Pierpont Morgan Library, New York; Annmary Brown Library, Brown University, Providence; St. Vincent College Library, Latrobe (1 leaf).

12. Wynkyn de Worde, London, 1520 (STC 10001).
   Copies: (a) Great Britain: Bodleian Library, Oxford (2 copies); All Souls College Library, Oxford; Edward Clark Library, Napier College of Science and Technology, Edinburgh; Ely Cathedral (on deposit at the University Library, Cambridge); National Library of Wales, Aberystwyth; (b) United States: Chapin Library, Williams College, Williamstown; Mellon Collection, Yale Center for British Art, New Haven; Newberry Library, Chicago; University of Notre Dame Library, Notre Dame; Pierpont Morgan Library, New York (1 leaf); (c) Japan: Toshiyuki Takamiya, Keio University, Tokyo.

13. Wynkyn de Worde, London, 1528 (STC 10002).
   Copies: (a) Great Britain: British Library, London; King's College Library, Cambridge; University of Glasgow Library; University of Leeds Library; John Rylands University Library, Manchester; Wor-

cester Cathedral Library; (b) Ireland: Trinity College Library, Dublin; (c) United States: Library of Congress, Washington, D.C.; Princeton University Library; Beinecke Library, Yale University, New Haven (2 copies); (d) Japan: Toshiyuki Takamiya, Keio University, Tokyo.

Introduction

I. The Prose *Brut:*
Contents and Overview of the Versions

Contents

The chronicle known as the prose *Brut* is a comprehensive account of the history of England from its first discovery and settlement to what were, to its writers, continuators, and audience, modern times.[1] It occurs in over 240 manuscripts, written in the three major literary languages of medieval England; it was the first chronicle of England to be printed, going through thirteen early printed editions, and in both the Middle Ages and the early Renaissance it served as the standard account of English history.

The original Anglo-Norman form of the work, written in the reign of Edward I, attributes the discovery of Britain to Brut (Brutus in Latin, Latin-based, or Latinate texts, the form of the name henceforward adopted in this book), the great-grandson of the Trojan Eneas, who is directed to the Isle of Albion by the goddess Diana. Brutus and his Trojan comrades

---

[1] Extracts from the Anglo-Norman *Brut* are published in Paul Meyer, "De quelques chroniques anglo-normandes qui ont porté le nom de Brut," *Bulletin de la société des anciens textes français* (1878): 104–45. Middle English texts are printed in Friedrich W. D. Brie, ed., *The Brut or The Chronicles of England*, EETS o.s. 131, 136 (1906, 1908). For comments on Brie's edition and details of editions of variant texts, extracts, and unpublished dissertations, see Matheson, "Historical Prose," pp. 212–14 and 233; Kennedy, *Manual*, pp. 2631–33, 2824–25.

defeat the indigenous giants and their leader Gogmagog and settle the entire island, including Scotland and Wales. To Brutus's lieutenant Coryn, who kills Gogmagog in a wrestling match, is given a land that he calls Cornwall after himself. In honor of the Troy to which he and his people trace their lineage, Brutus founds the city of New Troy (London) on the banks of the Thames. Forests are felled, agriculture is established, and the land is apportioned to the settlers. The country itself is named Britain after Brutus, while Scotland is named Albanye after Brutus's son Albanac, and Wales is called Cambre after a second son, Cambre. After a reign of twenty years, Brutus dies and is buried at New Troy, to be succeeded by his son Lotryn.

The majority of the texts of the Anglo-Norman *Brut* are prefaced by a second foundation story that accounts for the presence of the giants whom Brutus defeats. The source for this addition was an Anglo-Norman poem, *Des Grantz Geanz*, a version of which was originally prefixed to the Anglo-Norman prose *Brut* chronicle.[2] This verse prologue was subsequently reduced to prose (with some alterations in content), in which form it occurred in the texts that formed the bases for the two Middle English translations of the chronicle.

In its prose version, this prologue recounts how King Dioclician of Syria weds his thirty-three headstrong, ungovernable daughters to thirty-three kings. At the instigation of the eldest daughter, Albine (Albina in Latin, Latin-based, or Latinate texts, the form of the name henceforward adopted in this book), the sisters murder their husbands. The sisters are banished forever, and after a long sea voyage they arrive on an isle that is all wilderness. Albina names the country Albion after herself, and the sisters take the land. In time, the women are consumed by sexual desire, which is satisfied by the devil, who appropriates human shape and semen to impregnate them. The result is a brood of giants, among whom Gogmagog and Laugherigan are named, who inhabit Albion until their destruction by Brutus.

After Brutus and his sons, the narrative continues with the history of the British kings, including such notables as Leir, Lud (the eponym of "Ludstan," since "chaungede þrouȝ variance of lettres" to "London" [Brie 31/20, 21, 22], and builder of Ludgate), Kembelyn (in whose time Christ was born), Coel (the founder of Colchester), Constance (a Roman), Constantine

---

[2] See Brereton, ed., *Des Grantz Geanz*; Lesley Johnson, "Return to Albion," *Arthurian Literature XIII*, ed. Carley and Riddy, pp. 19–40. For a Latin version, see Carley and Crick, "Constructing Albion's Past," pp. 41–114; *Des Grantz Geanz* is discussed on pp. 45–48.

(son of Constance and St. Helena, later emperor of Rome), Vortiger (in whose time Engist and his Saxons arrive and establish a brief heptarchy), Aurilambros (the slayer of Vortiger and Engist), Uther Pendragon, Arthur (conqueror and overlord of much of Europe, whose reign is recounted at length), and Curan (son of Havelok).

Saxon supremacy is reestablished through the help of Gurmond, the mercenary son of the king of Africa, at which time the names of the country and its people are changed to England and Englishmen (after the name of Engist), and the heptarchy is reintroduced. A number of the Middle English texts (though not all) include an account of Cadwallader, the last British king. The histories of the Anglo-Saxon and Danish kings end with the death of Harold.

The chronicle continues with accounts of the reigns of the Norman and Plantagenet kings, narrated at greater length and with considerably more historical detail than are the reigns of the pre-Conquest monarchs, except for Arthur.

The original Anglo-Norman text probably ended with the death of Henry III in 1272 but was continued in later versions to the death of Edward I in 1307 and then to 1333. The two Middle English translations ended originally in 1333; the first and by far more important of these received continuations to the death of Edward III in 1377 and then to the siege of Rouen in 1419, in which year many texts end. Subsequent major continuations carried the narrative to the death of Henry V in 1422 (with a further continuation to 1437) and to 1430. William Caxton's *Chronicles of England* ended with the death of Henry VI in 1461.

These dates, however, only represent salient ending points for major continuations. Various minor or individual continuations also exist, the latest of which, in Lambeth Palace MS. 84, closes in 1479/82. Throughout the fifteenth century, continuations were frequently supplied to texts that originally ended at an earlier point. Even after the Anglo-Norman text was translated into Middle English, copies in the original language continued to be made. A version of the Middle English text itself was translated into Latin and then translated back into English. Combinations of texts of different types were made and extracts were used to supplement other historical works.

Overview of the Versions

As the preceding paragraphs suggest, the development and interrelationships of the texts of the Anglo-Norman, Latin, and English *Brut* are complicated, and any description of the many versions and numerous subgroups must inevitably be complex. The present section provides a general overview, synthesized from the fuller descriptions and arguments that form the bulk of this study—a simplified roadmap that points out the major landmarks and most significant features ahead. Subgroups, minor groups, and nuances of classification that require extended discussion are not adduced at this point. As a further aid to negotiating the highways and byways of the texts of the Middle English *Brut*, a Synoptic Inventory of all English versions and groups, with a complete listing of their manuscripts, appears at the beginning of the classification of those texts.

A. THE ANGLO-NORMAN *BRUT*

The Anglo-Norman *Brut* survives in forty-nine known manuscripts, one of which contains two texts of the work. The major versions and their primary features can be summarized as follows:

Common Text
    Stage 1: the Anglo-Norman *Brut* to 1272 (the original form of the text).
    Stage 2: the common text, stage 1, with a continuation to 1307.

Revisions and continuations made ca. 1350 (two major recensions):
    Short Version
        Stage 1: the common text to 1307 plus the "short continuation" to 1333 (ending with an English raid on Haddington Fair in Scotland).
        Stage 2: the Short Version, stage 1, plus the Albina verse prologue.
    Long Version: the common text to 1307, much revised (including the addition of Merlin's prophecies and many factual details), plus the Albina prose prologue and the "long continuation" to 1333 (ending with the battle of Halidon Hill).

The original form of the Anglo-Norman *Brut* covered the history of England from Brutus to the death of Henry III in 1272. This first stage received a continuation to the death of Edward I in 1307; the resulting text from Brutus to 1307 formed a common text that is at the core of the two subsequent versions, both of which were made around the mid-fourteenth century and which together comprise the great majority of the extant texts.

The first of these, the so-called Short Version, went through two stages. The first stage consisted of the common text to 1307, to which was added a continuation to 1333 that ends with an account of an English raid on the fair at Haddington in southern Scotland. The second stage of the Short Version was formed by the addition of a verse prologue telling the story of Albina and her sisters.

The core of the Long Version was a thorough revision of the common text to 1307, including the interpolation of a set of prophecies by Merlin concerning the five kings to follow King John. A prose prologue on Albina and her sisters and a continuation to 1333 that ends with the English victory over the Scots at the battle of Halidon Hill were also added, probably at the same time as the core text was revised. The former addition may not have been derived directly from the verse prologue found in the Short Version; rather, it may have been based on a common original. The continuation from 1307 to 1333 is independent of the continuation to the same year that occurs in the Short Version, though it is possible that the Long Version continuator was aware of the other narrative. In the late fourteenth century, the Long Version to 1333 was translated into English, thus giving rise to the entire family of Middle English *Brut* texts, except for a second translation made in 1435 by the priest John Mandeville, which survives in only two manuscripts. The first English translation and its textual descendants eventually superseded the popularity of the Anglo-Norman texts, for although the latter continued to be copied through the fifteenth century, only two Anglo-Norman texts contain continuations beyond 1333.

B. THE LATIN *BRUT*

The nineteen known texts of the Latin *Brut* fall into two major versions that are not immediately related except for their use of the same form of the Albina prologue. (A third, minor "version" consists solely of a short, unique translation into Latin of the prose prologue from the Long Version of the Anglo-Norman *Brut*.)

The first version is based on the second stage of the Anglo-Norman Short Version (with the verse prologue translated into Latin prose), which is followed to the year 1066. Thereafter, two of the three manuscripts of this version continue with a Latin chronicle not based on the vernacular *Brut*s, ending in 1367.

The second version of the Latin *Brut* is a sophisticated historical compilation whose basic framework and some of whose content (especially from 1377) derives from a version of the Middle English *Brut* ending in 1437. The Albina prologue has been borrowed from the first version of the Latin *Brut*. There are, however, significant additions and adaptations drawn from many other sources. This second Latin version has two subgroups, with longer and shorter treatments of the reign of Henry V, of which the longer is probably the earlier. The subgroup with the longer treatment was itself retranslated into English, thereby creating a second, later class of Middle English *Brut*s ending in 1437.

C. THE ENGLISH *BRUT*

The English *Brut* has survived in 181 medieval and post-medieval manuscripts (three of which contain two discrete texts of the work) and in thirteen early printed editions. Many of the manuscripts contain recognizably composite texts cobbled together from texts of different types, whose component parts must be considered separately. Accordingly, the total number of entries in the classification comes to 215.

The English texts can be divided into four major categories, labeled the Common Version (CV), the Extended Version (EV), the Abbreviated Version (AV), and a looser grouping of Peculiar Texts and Versions (PV).

The Common Version is based on the Anglo-Norman Long Version ending in 1333 with the battle of Halidon Hill; it gives rise to all other English *Brut* texts, aside from John Mandeville's independent translation from the Anglo-Norman Long Version.

The texts of the Common Version developed primarily through a process of accretion, in which the narrative was brought more up to date through the acquisition of continuations. The numerous groups belonging to this version are classified in the first instance by the date at which the texts end (1333, 1377, 1419, 1430, 1461; abbreviated CV–1333, CV–1377, etc.). The classification can be refined by considering sets of textual variations within the date-defined groups. For example, a narrative on the reign of Cadwallader (Cad) and the text of a letter sent by Queen Isabella (QIL) to the citizens of London, neither of which is found in the Anglo-Norman Long Version and its original English translation to 1333, appear in successive groups of the Common Version that ended in 1377 (see Methods of Classification below). The absence or presence of one or both of these narratives is a powerful factor in (a) determining the provenance of the text to 1333 in texts that proceed past that date and (b) assessing the relationships among groups.

Similarly, Common Version texts ending in 1419 can be divided into those that end in the midst of the siege of Rouen with the phrase "and manfully countered with our English men" and those that end at the successful conclusion of the siege with "in rule and governance"—the CV–1419(men) and the CV–1419(r&g) groups, respectively. Some groups, such as the CV–1419 (Leyle), are distinguished not only by their formal contents but also by their verbal changes. Other variations generate further subgroups, as summarized in the Synoptic Inventory of Versions below. The final group of the Common Version (the CV–1461) includes a continuation from 1419 to 1461 that was almost certainly written by William Caxton for his 1480 edition of the *Brut* as *The Chronicles of England*. When this continuation occurs in manuscripts, it was copied from a printed edition. Caxton's *editio princeps* served as the base for the twelve subsequent early printed editions, which fall into two types according to whether certain interpolations have been added.

The initial identification of texts of the Extended and Abbreviated Versions depends on three primary features: (1) the presence of an added exordium, of one or another particular type, describing the historical origins of the *Brut* itself; (2) the words "Some time..." at the beginning of the Albina prologue; (3) the inclusion in the prologue and early parts of the narrative of details borrowed from the *Short English Metrical Chronicle*. The exordium is of particular interest in that it reflects contemporary understanding of the genesis of English chronicle writing.

Although all surviving complete texts of the Extended and Abbreviated Versions end in 1419 (though sometimes with subsequent continuations), the language of the exordium shows that the original Extended Version was based on a text of a Common Version group with the full continuation to 1377. It is even possible that the Cadwallader episode was first interpolated in this original Extended Version and subsequently introduced into the Common Version.

Based on three distinct forms of the exordium, the wording of the additions from the *Short English Metrical Chronicle*, and verbal differences elsewhere in the general narrative, three groups within the Extended Version (EV–1419:A, B, C) can be identified.

Similarly, the Abbreviated Version presents different recensions of the exordium, three of which correspond to those in the Extended Version and one of which presents a text unparalleled among extant Extended Version texts. Despite this correspondence, however, there is not a simple one-to-one relationship between the groups of the Abbreviated and the Extended Versions. Four primary groups (the AV–1419:A, B, C, D) can be distinguished in the Abbreviated Version. The first of these comprises three subgroups, connected primarily by the presence of the same exordium as is found in the EV–1419:A; otherwise, however, these AV–1419:A subgroups are not immediately related. Textual analyses of various Abbreviated Version groups show correspondences and differences *vis-à-vis* the Extended Version that can be best explained by a complex development, the precise details of which may now be irrecoverable, that included the crossing of texts of the Common and Extended Versions. Some features that are particularly distinctive of individual Abbreviated Version groups are the omission of material after King Arthur (who is thus succeeded by Conan rather than Constantine) in the AV–1419:A(a), the AV–1419:B, and the AV–1419:C; the sharing of a common chapter on Constantine in the AV–1419:A(c) and the AV–1419:D; and the omission of material around the battle of Halidon Hill in the AV–1419:B.

Finally, there is an amorphous, heterogeneous category of Peculiar Texts and Versions, often of historical and literary importance, consisting of individual reworkings of *Brut* texts, works based on or adapted from the *Brut*, and combinations of the *Brut* with adaptations of other works. Many such texts are unique, but a number fall into recognizable groups. Of particular interest are the PV–1437:A (a sizable group) and the PV–1437/1461, which are related to the second version of the Latin *Brut*, and the PV–1437:B, which represents a translation back into English from that Latin version. Also included, for convenience, under Peculiar Texts and Versions are John Mandeville's translation of the Anglo-Norman *Brut* to 1333 (JM–1333) and three skimpy king-lists possibly drawn, at least in part, from English *Brut* texts.

II. Cultural and Historical Influence

Circulation

The result of this massive scribal activity is that the *Brut* survives, in whole or in part, in at least forty-nine Anglo-Norman manuscripts, almost 180 English manuscripts (including a few post-medieval transcripts), and about twenty Latin manuscripts. Its dissemination spread even wider when, under the title *The Chronicles of England*, the *Brut* became the first chronicle printed in England, passing through thirteen editions between 1480 and 1528. As I have remarked elsewhere, such "a number of manuscripts of a Middle English work [is] exceeded only by that of the manuscripts of the two Wycliffite translations of the Bible."[3] In comparison, the *Prick of Conscience* is found, in whole or in part, in 115 manuscripts, Chaucer's *Canter-*

---

[3] Matheson, "Historical Prose," p. 210; see Conrad Lindberg, "The Manuscripts and Versions of the Wycliffite Bible," *Studia Neophilologica* 42 (1970): 333–47.

bury Tales in eighty-three, Gower's *Confessio Amantis* in sixty-four, and Langland's *Piers Plowman* in sixty-one.[4] If the *Prick of Conscience* was "the most popular English poem of the Middle Ages," then the Middle English prose *Brut* was "the most popular secular work of the fifteenth century in England."[5]

The amount of time and labor that went into the production of such a number of manuscripts—let alone the probably greater number that have failed to survive—must have made the *Brut* omnipresent for those engaged or interested in the book trade in the fifteenth century, whether as scribes, illuminators, binders, and booksellers or as librarians, readers, hearers, and owners. It is no exaggeration to say that in the late Middle Ages in England the *Brut* was the standard historical account of British and English history. It is clear that it occupied a central position in fifteenth- and sixteenth-century historical writing and was a major influence in shaping national consciousness in medieval and post-medieval England.

Ownership and Audience

The extent of the *Brut*'s contemporary influence is indicated by the social and geographical range of its medieval ownership.

The style, content, and chivalric tone of the Anglo-Norman work suggest that it was originally aimed at an upper-class, lay audience.[6] Among the twenty-seven books given in 1305 by Guy Beauchamp, earl of Warwick, to Bordesley Abbey, Worcestershire, occurs "Un Volum del Romaunce deu

---

[4] These figures include fragmentary and excerpted texts. See Robert E. Lewis and Angus McIntosh, *A Descriptive Guide to the Manuscripts of the Prick of Conscience*, Medium Ævum Monographs n.s. 12 (Oxford, 1982), p. 1; Helen Cooper, *The Canterbury Tales* (Oxford, 1989), p. 6; John H. Fisher, R. Wayne Hamm, Peter G. Beidler, and Robert F. Yeager, "John Gower," *A Manual of the Writings in Middle English*, ed. Albert E. Hartung, vol. 7 (Hamden, 1986), pp. 2408–2409; Ralph Hanna III, *William Langland*, Authors of the Middle Ages 3 (Aldershot, Hants., 1993), p. 37.

[5] Lewis and McIntosh, *Descriptive Guide*, p. 1; Matheson, "Historical Prose," p. 210. Cf. Charles L. Kingsford, *English Historical Literature in the Fifteenth Century* (Oxford, 1913), p. 113: "the most popular and widely diffused history of the time"; Taylor, *English Historical Literature*, p. 110: "the most popular retelling of the Arthurian legend in late medieval England... the most widely diffused history of the day." See also Carol M. Meale, "Patrons, Buyers and Owners: Book Production and Social Status," in *Book Production and Publishing in Britain 1375–1475*, ed. Jeremy Griffiths and Derek Pearsall (Cambridge, 1989), pp. 215–16.

[6] See Antonia Gransden, *Historical Writing in England. II. c. 1307 to the Early Sixteenth Century* (Ithaca, 1982), pp. 75–76.

Brut, e del Roy Costentine," perhaps an Anglo-Norman *Brut* to 1272.[7] An early, variant text of the *Brut*, known as *Le Petit Bruit* (BL MS. Harley 902), was an abridgement made in 1310 by Ralph de Bohun for Henry de Lacy, earl of Lincoln.[8] Isabella of France (died 1358) bequeathed a French *Brut* to her son, Edward III.[9] A French *Brut* is listed in an inventory made in 1388 of the books of Sir Simon Burley, knight of the royal household and tutor of Richard II.[10] In 1391 John Percyhay of Swynton, rector of St. Edward's in York, left "unum Brutum in gallico, quod est in manibus Thomæ Slegill" (a knight from Leeds) to Master John de Scardeburgh, notary public, canon of York, and rector of Tickmarsh; this book reappears in an inventory of the latter's goods in 1395 as "Bruyt in Gallico, pret. ij s., non vend."[11] Sir Thomas Ughtred (died 1401) of Yorkshire left his wife "unum Romauns quod vocatur Bruyt" in his will, dated 1398.[12] John Man-

---

[7] See Madeleine Blaess, "L'abbaye de Bordesley et les livres de Guy de Beauchamp," *Romania* 78 (1957): 513; Blaess suggests that this was either a prose *Brut* or a copy of Wace (p. 518 n. 2).

[8] Diana B. Tyson, ed., *Le Petit Bruit of Rauf de Boun*, Anglo-Norman Text Society (London, 1987). See also M. Dominica Legge, *Anglo-Norman Literature and Its Background* (Oxford, 1963), pp. 280–83; Gransden, *Historical Writing II*, p. 74; Taylor, *English Historical Literature*, p. 118.

[9] See Edith Rickert, "King Richard II's Books," *The Library* 4th. ser., 13 (1932): 144–45; Richard F. Green, "King Richard II's Books Revisited," *The Library* 5th. ser., 31 (1976): 235–39. The inventory of Isabella's books made on her death lists "Unus liber qui vocatur Tresor et Bruyt in fine"; see Juliet Vale, *Edward III and Chivalry: Chivalric Society and Its Context 1270–1350* (Woodbridge, 1982), p. 170. This volume may be connected with books listed in a roll of issues and receipts from the privy wardrobe (1322–1341), which includes "j libro romanc' . . . vocato Tresor" (possibly the *Tresor* of Brunetto Latini) and a very ambiguous work that is called both "De Bricton in latino" and "De Brittonibus in latino"—in other words, a copy of either Britton's legal treatise or, perhaps, a Latin *Brut*—that was issued to John de Bohun, earl of Hereford (died 1336); see Vale, *Edward III and Chivalry*, pp. 49, 127 n. 101, 169.

[10] See John Scattergood, "Two Medieval Booklists," *The Library* 5th ser., 23 (1968): 237 (printed from PRO E154/1/19); for another copy in Bodleian MS. Eng. hist. b. 229, fol. 3, see Vale, *Edward III and Chivalry*, p. 131 n. 155. See also Maude V. Clarke, *Fourteenth-Century Studies*, ed. L. S. Sutherland and M. McKisack (Oxford, 1937), pp. 120–21.

[11] James Raine Jr., ed., *Testamenta Eboracensia*, vol. 1, Surtees Society 4 (1855), p. 164; vol. 2, Surtees Society 45 (1865), p. 6. See also Jo Ann Hoeppner Moran, *The Growth of English Schooling 1340–1548: Learning, Literacy, and Laicization in Pre-Reformation York Diocese* (Princeton, 1985), p. 203.

[12] Raine, ed., *Testamenta Eboracensia*, 1: 243; cf. M. G. A. Vale, *Piety, Charity and Literacy among the Yorkshire Gentry, 1370–1480*, Borthwick papers 50 (1976), p. 30. The short continuation of the Anglo-Norman *Brut* makes honorable mention of an earlier Sir

deville, rector of Burnham Thorpe, Norfolk, must have had access to an Anglo-Norman text to 1333 when he made his translation thereof in 1435. Among other chronicles listed in a catalogue of 1450, Sir John Fastolf owned a French *Cronicles d'Angleterre*.[13] Also in the fifteenth century, Trinity College, Cambridge, MS. R.7.14 belonged to Robert Isham, the seneschal of the count of Weedon Bec.[14]

Various religious houses also possessed copies of the French *Brut*. BL MS. Cotton Vitellius A.x belonged to the Cistercians of Fountains Abbey, Yorkshire; the Cistercian abbey of Hailes, Gloucestershire, owned BL MS. Cotton Cleopatra D.iii; and Trinity College, Dublin, MS. 500 was owned in 1385 by the priory of the Knights Hospitallers of St. John in Clerkenwell, London.[15] In addition to the *Anonimalle Chronicle* (Leeds, Brotherton Collection MS. 29), which incorporates a *Brut* continuation from 1307 to 1333, St. Mary's Abbey, York, acquired Bodleian MS. Lyell 17 in the fifteenth century, "de perquisicione" of John Graystock, the librarian.[16]

Several manuscripts of the Anglo-Norman *Brut*, all of the fifteenth century, are of continental origin: Bibliothèque de l'Arsenal, Paris, MS. 3346,

---

Thomas Ughtred, "noble chivaler et vaillant," especially in the defense of the bridge at Roxsburgh in late 1332; see Childs and Taylor, eds., *Anonimalle Chronicle*, pp. 146, 152, 156. Cf. Joel Rosenthal, "Down the Up Staircase: Quondam Peers and Downward Mobility in Late Medieval England," *Medievalia* 15 (1993, for 1989): 309, 318 n. 43 (I am indebted to Professor Rosenthal for this reference).

[13] Noted in H. S. Bennett, *The Pastons and Their England: Studies in an Age of Transition*, 2nd ed. (1932; rpt. Cambridge, 1970), p. 111.

[14] Taylor, *English Historical Literature*, p. 120. The manuscript also belonged in the fifteenth century to John Gardenere; see Montague Rhodes James, *The Western Manuscripts in the Library of Trinity College, Cambridge. A Descriptive Catalogue*, 3 vols. (Cambridge, 1901–1903), 2: 229.

[15] N. R. Ker, *Medieval Libraries of Great Britain: A List of Surviving Books*, 2nd ed. (London, 1964), pp. 88, 94, xxxii (addendum to p. 126); Brereton, ed., *Des Grantz Geanz*, p. ix. It may have been for the loan of a French *Brut* ("pro uno libro Brute vocato") that in the fourteenth century John Phelippus of Mansell gave first as security ("caucio") and then as a bequest a manuscript, now Hereford Cathedral MS. O.v.12, to the Franciscan convent at Hereford; see R. A. B. Mynors and R. M. Thomson, *Catalogue of the Manuscripts of Hereford Cathedral Library* (Cambridge, 1993), p. 37.

[16] See Childs and Taylor, eds., *Anonimalle Chronicle*, pp. 12–15, 21–22; Taylor, *English Historical Literature*, p. 121 and n. 66; Ker, *Medieval Libraries*, pp. 217, 321; Albinia de la Mare, *Catalogue of the Collection of Medieval Manuscripts Bequeathed to the Bodleian Library, Oxford, by James P. R. Lyell* (Oxford, 1971), p. 42.

written in Lorraine[17]; Bibliothèque Nationale, Paris, MS. fonds français 12156, written in France[18]; Bibliothèque Nationale, Paris, MS. fonds français 12155, written in Flanders, perhaps for the seigneur de la Gruthuyse or the dukes of Burgundy[19]; BL MS. Royal 19.C.ix, written in northern France[20]; Bibliothèque Geneviève, Paris, MS. 935, written in France.[21]

The major Middle English translation of the *Brut*, with its derivative groups and versions, was even more popular than its Anglo-Norman forebear. It retained the audience that had already been established and expanded it among the merchant class in the fifteenth century. (The following discussion of ownership of the Middle English manuscripts is abstracted from the full Classification of Texts that follows this Introduction, and readers are referred to the individual entries there for further factual and bibliographical details.)

Among the landowning gentry, Glasgow MS. Hunterian 74 belonged to the Wauton family of Great Staughton, Huntingdonshire, and Basmead, Bedfordshire; Bodleian MS. Digby 185 was owned and possibly commissioned by the Hopton family of Swillington, near Leeds, in Yorkshire; BL MS. Harley 53 has been ascribed to the Stokes family; and BL MS. Royal 18 B.iii contains the signatures of members of the Gaynesford family of Surrey. BL MS. Additional 70514 probably belonged to the Hill family of Nettlecombe, Somersetshire. Glasgow MS. Hunterian 230 seems to have belonged to the Willoughby and Zouche families of Nottinghamshire and Derbyshire. Princeton MS. Garrett 150 probably belonged to Sir John Sulyard (died 1488), justice of the King's Bench, before passing to Sir Thomas Bourghier (died 1492; the son of Henry Bourghier, earl of Essex), the constable of Leeds Castle, who married Sulyard's widow, Anne. CUL MS. Ff.1.6, which contains a brief king-list, belonged to the Findern family in Derbyshire and is associated with other local gentry families. Coats of arms in Bodleian MSS. Rawlinson B.171 and Douce 323 suggest armigerous ownership, as does, perhaps, the inclusion of a treatise on arms in Bodleian

---

[17] See Legge and Brereton, "Three Hitherto Unlisted MSS.," pp. 114–15. The *Brut* forms a sequel to the *Geste des Loherains*, an account of the dukes of Lorraine.

[18] See Legge and Brereton, "Three Hitherto Unlisted MSS.," p. 115; Brie, *Geschichte und Quellen*, p. 21; Meyer, "De quelques chroniques," p. 117.

[19] See Meyer, "De quelques chroniques," p. 126 n. 1; Brie, *Geschichte und Quellen*, p. 29.

[20] See Brie, *Geschichte und Quellen*, p. 30.

[21] See Brie, *Geschichte und Quellen*, p. 30.

MS. Laud 733 and of a catalogue of shields in Harvard MS. Richardson 35 (an owner of which was Richard Thomas of Neath, Glamorganshire). An owner of Yale MS. Beinecke 323 was particularly interested in the fortunes of the Clare family. William Braundon of Knowle, Warwickshire, who owned BL MS. Sloane 2027, and John Willeys, probably of Berkshire, who owned Lambeth Palace MS. 264, were minor provincial landowners.

As in the case of the Anglo-Norman texts, several religious houses possessed copies. The Augustinian priory of St. Bartholomew in Smithfield, London, owned BL MS. Royal 17.D.xxi, and the Dominican priory of the Virgin Mary and St. Margaret in Dartford, Kent, owned Trinity College, Dublin, MS. 490. Yale MS. Beinecke 494 is associated with a Dominican convent in Suffolk or at Chelmsford in Essex (see below). It has been suggested that BL MS. Harley 7333 was compiled at the Augustinian abbey of St. Mary de Pratis in Leicester.

Ecclesiastics who owned personal copies were John Neuton, prior of Battle Abbey in Sussex (Chicago MS. 254), and John Warkworth, master of Peterhouse, Cambridge (Peterhouse, Cambridge, MS. 190). William Trouthe, vicar in the close of Salisbury, left Bodleian MS. Laud Misc. 571 to his niece, Isabel Alen.

Among women owners and readers, Isabel is joined by "Domina" Alice Brice, who owned Longleat MS. 183A. The name of Elizabeth Dawbne appears on the first flyleaf of Bodleian MS. Laud Misc. 733. Huntington MS. HM 136 seems to have belonged in the late fifteenth century or early sixteenth century to John Leche of Nantwich, Chester, and to Dorothy Helbartun, whose name, either alone or in more extended annotations, appears more than sixty times throughout the volume.

In the fifteenth century the Middle English *Brut* increasingly appealed to a mercantile audience, in addition to the gentry and the religious. The standard continuation that carried the narrative from 1377 to 1419 and succeeding continuations to 1430 and 1461 are heavily indebted to London civic chronicles. In the case of these continuations, the material has been adapted into a narrative format that is generally consistent with the preceding text. In a number of instances, however, appended material is left in the typical annalistic civic chronicle format, as in MSS. Trinity College, Cambridge, O.9.1, CUL Hh.6.9, BL Egerton 650, Bodleian Rawlinson B.173, and BL Stowe 69. Lambeth Palace MS. 306 contains both an abbreviated *Brut* and a London chronicle. Presumably such manuscripts were usually produced or augmented for London merchant-owners. The appended civic chronicle material in Trinity College, Cambridge, MS. O.9.1, is followed by a copy of a

London mercantile indenture. (On the other hand, Rawlinson B.173 has strong West Herefordshire connections and omits some material of local London interest that is found in the related BL Egerton 650.) Various manuscripts can be linked with mercantile owners, such as Lambeth Palace MS. 259, which contains shields with a merchant's mark. Yale MS. Beinecke 494 (also associated with a Dominican convent; see above) was bought by William Nasby, skinner of London, in 1464 (another note records its earlier purchase from S. Belamy in 1455). Among other names, that of Thomas Northlond, grocer, possibly the alderman and sheriff of London in 1483 who died in 1484, appears in Woburn Abbey MS. 181, which includes regulations on cooks' fees in London. The sumptuous Lambeth Palace MS. 6 may have belonged to William Purchas, mercer, who was mayor of London in 1497–98. Outside London, an abbreviated *Brut* text forms the beginning of the official *Bristowe Chronicle*, begun in the late fifteenth century by Robert Ricart, the town clerk, for the use of the civic officers of Bristol. William Caxton, mercer, probably possessed a copy ending in 1419 that formed the basis for his *Chronicles of England*, published in 1480. This edition (and the twelve subsequent printed editions to 1528) undoubtedly served to spread further ownership of the work, especially in the London merchant class.[22] The evidence of sixteenth-century names suggests that mercantile acquisition of existing manuscripts also expanded.

Irrespective of their dialect or place of writing, the widespread geographical availability of Middle English *Brut* texts is suggested by the identified owners noted above: in the north, the West Riding of Yorkshire; in the West Midlands and Wales, Cheshire, Derbyshire, Warwickshire, Herefordshire, Gloucestershire, and Glamorganshire; in the East Midlands, Nottinghamshire, Leicestershire, Huntingdonshire or Bedfordshire, Cambridgeshire, and Suffolk or Essex; in the south, Wiltshire, Berkshire, Surrey, Kent, and Sussex; and, of course, London. Possibly English copies were bequeathed by Sir Thomas Chaworth of Wiverton, Nottinghamshire (1459), John Hamundson of York (1472), and John Fell of York (1506).[23]

---

[22] See Matheson, "Printer and Scribe," pp. 593–94. Caxton indicates the popularity and circulation of *Brut* manuscripts in his prologue to the *Description of Britain* (1480): "Hit is so that in many and diuerse places the comyn cronicles ben had and also now late enprinted at Westmynstre."

[23] See R. M. Wilson, *The Lost Literature of Medieval England*, 2nd ed. (London, 1970), pp. 150–51; cf. Kate Harris, "Patrons, Buyers and Owners: The Evidence for Ownership and the Rôle of Book Owners in Book Production and the Book Trade," in

Given the sheer amount of copying, combining, and recopying of texts, the lateness of the majority of the manuscripts, and the associations with metropolitan London, it is not surprising that many of the manuscripts are written in language that is dialectally mixed or "colorless."[24] Those scribes whose dialectal origins can be determined parallel and supplement the geographical information provided by owners of the *Brut* (though it should be recalled that scribes need not have worked in or even near the places where they had learned their letters). The scribes of the following manuscripts can be localized: from the north, Bodleian Digby 185 (West Riding of Yorkshire), Glasgow Hunterian 83; from the West Midlands, CUL Ff.1.6 (basically Derbyshire), Bodleian Rawlinson B.166 (Staffordshire), Bodleian Rawlinson B.171 (South-West Herefordshire), Bodleian Rawlinson B.173 (West Herefordshire), CUL Kk.1.12 (Central Herefordshire), BL Sloane 2027 (Warwickshire); from the East Midlands, Pennsylvania State PS. V–3A (possibly Northamptonshire, with central West Midlands elements), Bodleian Bodley 840 (Essex, with Herefordshire relicts), Glasgow Hunterian 74 (North-West Essex; Central South Essex, with some Kentish or East Sussex relicts; South-East Suffolk, Ipswich area); from the south, Glasgow Hunterian 443 (Central Surrey), Bodleian Lyell 34 (Surrey), BL Harley 7333 (Hampshire), and College of Arms Arundel 58 (Wiltshire). CUL MS. Ff.2.26 is written in Central Midland Standard.

As might be expected in the fourteenth and fifteenth centuries, the Latin prose *Brut* appealed to the more educated segment of the potential reading public, primarily to a monastic audience, though there is some evidence of lay interest.

Among those texts that have been called Latin *Brut*s, Lambeth Palace MS. 99 (late fourteenth century) belonged to St. George's Chapel, Wind-

---

Book Production and Publishing in Britain 1375–1475, ed. Griffiths and Pearsall, pp. 164 and 184 n. 5. John Hamundson was an Oxford B.A. in 1455, headmaster of the Howden Schools in 1456, and grammar-master at St. Peter's School in York from 1465 to his death; see Jo Ann Hoeppner Moran, *Education and Learning in the City of York 1300–1560*, Borthwick Papers 55 (1979), p. 40.

[24] On the types of language mixtures in Middle English texts, see *LALME*, 1: 13, 19–23. On the growth of standardization, see M. L. Samuels, "Some Applications of Middle English Dialectology," *English Studies* 44 (1963): 81–94; M. L. Samuels, "Spelling and Dialect in the Late and Post-Middle English Periods," in *So Meny People Longages and Tonges: Philological Essays in Scots and Mediaeval English Presented to Angus McIntosh*, ed. Michael Benskin and M. L. Samuels (Edinburgh, 1981), pp. 43–54.

sor.[25] BL MS. Cotton Julius B.iii may be associated with William Rede, Oxford scholar and bishop of Chichester.[26] BL MS. Lansdowne 212 (fifteenth century), a text of the *Noua Cronica*, was at Glastonbury Abbey in Somerset.[27] St. John's College, Oxford, MS. 78 (mid-fifteenth century) was either owned or written by the monk John Shyrburne.[28] BL MS. Harley 3906 was almost certainly written soon after 1456 at the Benedictine abbey of Sherborne in Dorset.[29] In several instances, the *Brut* is followed by monastic annals of more local interest to the religious house.[30]

Kingsford suggests that a continuation in BL MS. Harley 3884 was written before 1460 by an Oxford scholar.[31] College of Arms MS. Arundel 5 ends with a continuation written between 1471 and 1480 by someone familiar with London civic chronicles.[32] Sir John Fortescue (died 1476), chief justice of the King's Bench, owned Bodleian MS. Rawlinson C.398 (mid-fifteenth century), which attributes the work to Richard Rede, who may have been, however, an earlier owner or the scribe.[33]

Use and Influence

Further indications of the popularity, authority, and textual availability of the prose *Brut* are found in its widespread use as a source (or possible source or influence) first by medieval historical writers of the fourteenth and fifteenth centuries and then by sixteenth-century historians. As with owners of *Brut* manuscripts, a range of social backgrounds is found among writers who used them as sources—noble, gentry, ecclesiastical (especially monastic), and merchant. The houses of monastic chroniclers who used the *Brut* presumably owned or were able to borrow copies of the work. Until near the end of the fourteenth century, the only text available was the Anglo-Norman; after that time, it is often uncertain whether the text being used was in Anglo-

---

[25] See Ker, *Medieval Libraries*, p. 203; the time of ownership may, however, be late.
[26] See p. 42.
[27] See Ker, *Medieval Libraries*, p. 91.
[28] See Kingsford, *English Historical Literature*, p. 311: "Frater Johannes Shyrburne me fecit fieri" (fol. 156).
[29] See Kingsford, *English Historical Literature*, pp. 158, 346–47.
[30] See Gransden, *Historical Writing II*, pp. 412–13.
[31] Kingsford, *English Historical Literature*, pp. 158, 310, 342–43.
[32] See Kingsford, *English Historical Literature*, p. 159; James Gairdner, ed., *Three Fifteenth-Century Chronicles*, Camden Society n.s. 28 (1880), pp. xx–xxvi.
[33] See Kingsford, *English Historical Literature*, p. 311.

Norman, English, or Latin, unless the material occurs in texts found in only one of these languages. The following is a representative listing of such works that either used or may have used the *Brut* as a source, arranged by approximately chronological date of composition, or, in the case of works that underwent revision, the date of the final revision.

A. FOURTEENTH-CENTURY USE AND INFLUENCE

In the mid-fourteenth century the *Chronicon* (covering the period 1303 to 1356) of Geoffrey le Baker, a secular clerk from Swinbrook, Oxfordshire, has points of similarity to details in the *Brut*. It is perhaps significant that Baker was connected with the Bohun family, since the preparer of an earlier abridgment of the *Brut* was a Master Ralph de Bohun (see above).[34]

The close connection between the civic chronicles of London and the *Brut* began early: an Anglo-Norman *Brut* with the short continuation to 1333 (see below) was a major source for the anonymous French *Croniques de London* (1259 [probably originally 1189] to 1343), written around the middle of the fourteenth century in London.[35]

John, vicar of Tynemouth in Northumberland, seems to have used the short continuation to 1333 (see below) of the Anglo-Norman *Brut* for the text of Queen Isabella's letter to the citizens of London (1326), translated into Latin in his massive *Historia Aurea* (origins to 1347).[36]

Sir Thomas Gray of Heaton in Northumberland began his Anglo-Norman prose *Scalacronica* (Creation to 1363) during his captivity in Edinburgh

---

[34] Edward Maunde Thompson, ed., *Chronicon Galfridi le Baker de Swynebroke* (Oxford, 1889). See Gransden, *Historical Writing II*, pp. 37–39, 74; Legge, *Anglo-Norman Literature*, pp. 280–83. Baker was also connected with the Augustinian abbey of Osney in Oxfordshire.

[35] George J. Aungier, ed., *Croniques de London depuis l'an 44 Hen. III jusqu'à l'an 17 Edw. III*, Camden Society o.s. 28 (1844); Edmund Goldsmid, trans., *The Chronicles of London from 44 Hen. III to 17 Edw. III*, 3 vols. (Edinburgh, 1885–1886). See Childs and Taylor, eds., *Anonimalle Chronicle*, pp. 62–63; D. C. Cox, "The French Chronicle of London," *Medium Ævum* 45 (1976): 201–208; Gransden, *Historical Writing II*, p. 71; Taylor, *English Historical Literature*, p. 123.

[36] See V. H. Galbraith, "The *Historia Aurea* of John, Vicar of Tynemouth, and the Sources of the St. Albans Chronicle," in *Essays in History Presented to Reginald Lane Poole*, ed. H. W. C. Davis (Oxford, 1927), pp. 379–93; V. H. Galbraith, "Extracts from the Historia Aurea and a French 'Brut' (1317–47)," *English Historical Review* 63 (1928): 203–206, 208–15 (text of Queen Isabella's letter on pp. 211–12). On the *Brut* source, see Childs and Taylor, eds., *Anonimalle Chronicle*, pp. 62, 124 and 126 (text of the letter); Cox, "French Chronicle of London," p. 207 n. 12.

Castle from 1355 to 1359, utilizing a large number of Latin, French, and English chronicles that he found there, possibly including the prose *Brut*.[37]

The fifth book of the *Eulogium Historiarum*, written at the Benedictine abbey of Malmesbury in Wiltshire, treats the history of England from Brutus to 1366. To 1333 its narrative uses the *Brut* as a major source.[38]

For a brief continuation (1348 to 1360) to his English translation of Ranulph Higden's *Polychronicon*, completed in 1387, John Trevisa, vicar of Berkeley in Cornwall, may have drawn upon the London chronicles and the *Brut*.[39]

There are some similarities between Ralph de Bohun's *Le Petit Bruit* and the *Chronicon* (tenth century to 1395) of Henry Knighton (died ca. 1396), canon of the Augustinian abbey of St. Mary's in Leicester. Wendy Childs and John Taylor suggest that he may have found the short continuation to the Anglo-Norman *Brut* incorporated in a text of Walter de Guisborough's *Chronicle*.[40]

---

[37] Found in Corpus Christi College, Cambridge, MS. 133. The later part (1066 to 1362) is published in Joseph Stevenson, ed., *Scalacronica: By Sir Thomas Gray of Heton, Knight*, Maitland Club (Edinburgh, 1836); translated in Herbert Maxwell, trans., *Scalacronica. The Reigns of Edward I, Edward II, and Edward III As Recorded by Sir Thomas Gray* (Glasgow, 1907). See Legge, *Anglo-Norman Literature*, pp. 283–87; Gransden, *Historical Writing II*, p. 93; Lister M. Matheson, "King Arthur and the Medieval English Chronicles," in *King Arthur through the Ages*, ed. Valerie M. Lagorio and Mildred Leake Day, 2 vols. (New York and London, 1990), 1: 257–58. Gray's inspiring Sibyl instructs him to consult Geoffrey of Monmouth ("le Brut"), the *Historia Aurea*, and a number of standard sources, including "Bruyt en Engles,—'þat Cadwaladre sal on Conan cal,' etc.—per ditz de Merlyn"; it seems likely that Gray used some form of the prose *Brut*, either directly or through his sources (Stevenson, ed., *Scalacronica*, pp. 2–4).

[38] Frank S. Haydon, ed., *Eulogium Historiarum sive Temporis: Chronicon ab Orbe condito usque ad Annum Domini M.CCC.LXVI, a Monacho quodam Malmesburiensi exaratum*, 3 vols., Rolls Series 9 (London, 1858–1863), 2: 205–385, 3: 1–201; see also Gransden, *Historical Writing II*, pp. 103–104. Among the compiler's major sources is Geoffrey of Monmouth, from whom the Cadwallader episode is taken (1: 379–85), as well as a version of the Latin tag appended to the name of Blegabred in certain groups of the Extended Version of the English *Brut* (1: 248).

[39] Joseph R. Lumby, ed., *Polychronicon Ranulphi Higden Monachi Cestrensis*, vol. 8, Rolls Series 41 (London, 1882), pp. 339–52. Lumby suggests (p. xxviii) that Trevisa translated his continuation from the manuscript of Higden that he used, but see Gransden, *Historical Writing II*, p. 221.

[40] Joseph R. Lumby, ed., *Chronicon Henrici Knighton vel Cnitthon Monachi Leycestrensis*, 2 vols., Rolls Series 92 (London, 1889, 1895). See Childs and Taylor, eds., *Anonimalle Chronicle*, p. 65; Gransden, *Historical Writing II*, p. 179 and n. 125; Taylor, *English Historical Literature*, p. 119; Legge, *Anglo-Norman Literature*, p. 282.

Among many other sources, Thomas Burton of the Cistercian abbey of Meaux in Yorkshire (abbot from 1396 to 1399, died 1437), used the Anglo-Norman *Brut*, with the short continuation to 1333 (see below), as a subsidiary source for the general history subsections in his chronicle of the abbey (1150 to 1396), written and revised between 1388 and 1402.[41]

B. FIFTEENTH-CENTURY USE AND INFLUENCE

Compiled in the early fifteenth century, the early part of the Latin chronicle (Creation to 1413) of the Cistercian abbey of Louth Park in Lincolnshire may be based, at least in part, on the *Brut*; some material in the later part of the chronicle is reminiscent of the English *Brut*.[42]

The chronicle (Brutus to 1420) ascribed to Thomas of Otterbourne, probably a northerner and perhaps rector of Chingford in Essex in 1393, was written after 1423 and has some similarities to the *Brut*.[43]

John Strecche, a canon of the Augustinian priory of St. Mary's at Kenilworth, Warwickshire, compiled a collection of romances and histories in the first quarter of the fifteenth century. It includes a *Historia Regum Anglie* from Anglo-Saxon times to 1422, to which is prefixed a brief history from Brutus to A.D. 827. Gransden notes that the early part is derived from the *Brut*.[44]

---

[41] Edward A. Bond, ed., *Chronica Monasterii de Melsa, a Fundatione usque ad Annum 1396, Auctore Thoma de Burton, Abbate*, 3 vols., Rolls Series 43 (London, 1866–1868). The catalogue of the abbey's library (BL MS. Cotton Vitellius V.vi, fols. 241v–245), printed by Bond (3: lxxxiii–c) includes "Brutus, et aliæ multæ chronicæ Angliæ" (p. xcvii); Bond suggests that either this work included the *Brut* or that Burton kept his own (or the monastery's) copy in his chamber (1: lxxx). See also Childs and Taylor, eds., *Anonimalle Chronicle*, pp. 64–65; Gransden, *Historical Writing II*, p. 358–59.

[42] The text from 1066 is printed in Edmund Venables, ed., with a trans. by A. R. Maddison, *Chronicon Abbatie de Parco Lude: The Chronicle of Louth Park Abbey*, Lincolnshire Record Society (Horncastle, 1891). The manuscript still belongs to the Allison family, now of Flackwell Heath, Buckinghamshire. The text begins imperfectly during an account of the ages of the world, before proceeding to the history of England, which begins with Brutus; Venables notes that "[t]he earlier portion appears to be derived from Geoffrey of Monmouth, Henry of Huntingdon, and Florence of Worcester, and possibly Simeon of Durham" (xi). See also Gransden, *Historical Writing II*, p. 412.

[43] Printed in volume 1 of Thomas Hearne, ed., *Duo Rerum Anglicarum Scriptores Veteres viz. Thomas Otterbourne et Johannes Whethamstede*, 2 vols. (Oxford, 1732). See Kingsford, *English Historical Literature*, pp. 21–22, 116; Gransden, *Historical Writing II*, p. 196 n. 18.

[44] Gransden, *Historical Writing II*, p. 405. See also Kingsford, *English Historical Literature*, pp. 39–40 and n. 2. Strecche's collection is found in BL Additional MS.

Two related mid-fifteenth-century lives of Henry V use the *Brut* to different degrees. Titus Livius's *Vita Henrici Quinti* was written before 1438 or 1439 at the behest of Humphrey, duke of Gloucester. The Latin *Brut* ending in 1437 formed an important source and is frequently quoted almost verbatim. Kingsford suggests that the Italian humanist might also have been acquainted with the English *Brut*.[45] The *Vita et Gesta Henrici Quinti* by pseudo-Elmham survives in two recensions, the first of which was dedicated to Walter Lord Hungerford (died 1449) and the second of which, written between 1445 and 1446, was dedicated to John Somerset (died 1455), who had been physician to Henry VI from 1428 to about 1432 and who remained in royal employ until 1450. The earlier part of the work is based closely on Titus Livius and thus echoes Livius's use of the Latin *Brut*.[46]

The Latin annals (1066 to 1447) of the Augustinian abbey of Waltham, Essex, are a compilation from several sources, including the English *Brut*, from which the narrative for the reigns of Henry IV and Henry V is chiefly derived.[47]

The work known as *Giles's Chronicle* is a compilation of individual Latin narratives on the reigns of Richard II through Henry VI. The first part of the narrative of Henry VI's reign (1422 to 1438), composed about 1460, is based mainly on the *Brut* or on a London chronicle.[48]

John Hardyng's English verse *Chronicle* survives in two versions. The first (Brutus to 1437) was completed by 1457 and intended for presentation to Henry VI; the second (Brutus to 1464) was revised first for Edward, duke of York, and then twice re-revised for final presentation to Edward IV in

---

35295; a large section of the fifth book is printed in Frank Taylor, "The Chronicle of John Strecche for the Reign of Henry V (1414–1422)," *Bulletin of the John Rylands Library* 16 (1932): 137–87.

[45] Thomas Hearne, ed., *Titi Livii Foro-Juliensis Vita Henrici Quinti* (Oxford, 1716). See Kingsford, *English Historical Literature*, pp. 53–54; Gransden, *Historical Writing II*, p. 212. Livius also uses John Page's poem on the siege of Rouen, which was itself used by compilers of the English *Brut*.

[46] Thomas Hearne, ed., *Thomae de Elmham Vita et Gesta Henrici Quinti* (Oxford, 1727). See Kingsford, *English Historical Literature*, pp. 56, 59–61; Gransden, *Historical Writing II*, p. 215.

[47] Found in BL MS. Cotton Titus D.xv, fols. 7–57. Selections from 1403 to 1447 are printed in Kingsford, *English Historical Literature*, pp. 350–54; see also pp. 160–61; Gransden, *Historical Writing II*, pp. 412–13.

[48] John A. Giles, ed., *Incerti Scriptoris Chronicon Angliae de Regnis Trium Regum Lancastrensium Henrici IV, Henrici V, et Henrici VI* (London, 1848); the narrative on Richard II is omitted. See Kingsford, *English Historical Literature*, pp. 156–57, 338; Gransden, *Historical Writing II*, p. 160 n. 17.

1464. Hardyng probably used a Peculiar Version of the *Brut* ending in 1437, in either Latin or English, as a source for the story of Joseph of Arimathea's settling in Britain and for his general scheme of history from 1399 to 1437 (in which year Hardyng's first version ends). Kingsford suggests that Hardyng's marginal references to the chronicle of Master Norham, doctor of theology, which occur in BL MS. Lansdowne 204, a copy of the first version, refer to a copy of the Latin *Brut* owned by Norham. It is possible that in the second version of his *Chronicle* Hardyng made additional use of another copy of the *Brut*.[49]

The first continuation (1149 to 1470) to the chronicle of the Benedictine abbey of Crowland, Lincolnshire, was written in Latin by the prior. Its primary focus up to 1460 is local, and some of its general information, such as the story of Henry V and the tennis-balls, may have been derived from the *Brut*.[50]

The first part of the *Chronicle* (creation to 1462) attributed to John Benet and perhaps written between 1462 and 1468, is based on the *Polychronicon*, Geoffrey of Monmouth, and Florence of Worcester, though the compiler may have used the *Brut* for the period 1333 to 1377. A version of the *Brut* similar to that in *"Davies's" Chronicle* (see items 168 and 169) underlies the narrative for 1422 to 1440. Benet was vicar of Harlington in Bedfordshire (1443–1471) at the time of writing his chronicle and subsequently rector of Broughton in Bedfordshire (1471 to his death in 1474); it is possible that he was able to borrow books from the Augustinian priory in Dunstable or from the chapel and hospital at nearby Toddington in Bedfordshire.[51]

The Latin compilation attributed in a fifteenth-century note to John Tiptoft, earl of Worcester (ca. 1427–1470), contains a section drawn from the version of the Latin *Brut* that ends in 1437.[52]

---

[49] Henry Ellis, ed., *The Chronicle of Iohn Hardyng* (London, 1812). See Charles L. Kingsford, "The First Version of Hardyng's *Chronicle*," *English Historical Review* 27 (1912): 476–78; Kingsford, *English Historical Literature*, pp. 147–48; Gransden, *Historical Writing II*, p. 283 and n. 267; Kennedy, *Manual*, pp. 2645, 2647.

[50] The first continuation is printed in William Fulman, ed., *Rerum Anglicarum Scriptorum Veterum Tom. I* (Oxford, 1684), pp. 451–546. See Kingsford, *English Historical Literature*, p. 179; Gransden, *Historical Writing II*, pp. 265 n. 110, 411.

[51] The later part of the chronicle is published, with introduction, in G. L. Harriss and M. A. Harriss, eds., *John Benet's Chronicle for the Years 1400 to 1462*, Camden Miscellany 24 (1972), pp. 151–252; see pp. 157–58 for biographical details and pp. 161–63 for the *Brut* sources. See also Gransden, *Historical Writing II*, p. 255.

[52] Gransden, *Historical Writing II*, p. 253; Gransden examined the manuscript when it was in the hands of Maggs Bros. (Cat. no. 838, item 44, 1956) and reproduces her

In the second half of the fifteenth century the version of British and English history presented in the *Brut* was made available to the nobility of Burgundy through the *Recueil des Croniques et Anchiennes Istories de la Grant Bretaigne* by Jean de Waurin, lord of Forestal, which was begun at the request of Waurin's nephew Waleran, lord of Waurin. He completed the first four volumes in 1455, from Albina to the death of Henry V in 1422, but subsequently added two volumes that brought the narrative down to 1443 (written after 1461) and to Edward IV's restoration to the throne in 1471. For the earlier part and the history of England to the beginning of the fourteenth century Waurin relied very heavily on the *Brut*. For the fourteenth century he turned primarily to Jean Froissart's *Chroniques* (1327 to 1400) and for 1400 to 1443 he drew either on Enguerran de Monstrelet's *Chronique* (1400 to 1444) or on a common source. For his last volume, in addition to personal observation and oral information, Waurin used such official English narratives as the *Arrival of Edward IV* and the *Chronicle of the Rebellion in Lincolnshire*, probably consulted in the ducal library of Burgundy. Waurin may well have been able to use a copy of the Anglo-Norman *Brut* in the same library (see the manuscripts written in France noted above, especially Bibliothèque Nationale, Paris, MS. fonds français 12155). The inclusion of the Cadwallader episode and material in his fifteenth-century history, however, suggests strongly that he also had knowledge of an English text of the type of BL MS. Harley 53 and Lambeth Palace MS. 6 (the latter of which was illuminated by a Flemish artist). Waurin's work was directed at the highest of noble audiences: the surviving manuscripts are all sumptuous *de luxe* productions with fine illustrations. A presentation copy was possibly made for Philip the Good, duke of Burgundy from 1419 to 1467; another was probably made for Philip's successor to 1477, Charles the Bold, who had aided Waurin's work and married Margaret of York. Other copies were owned by Edward IV of England, Louis de Bruges, seigneur de Gruthuyse (and earl of Winchester), the counts of Marche, and a marquis whose

---

report on p. 480. The manuscript, formerly Phillipps MS. 11301, is now Huntington Library MS. HM 19960; see C. W. Dutschke, *Guide to Medieval and Renaissance Manuscripts in the Huntington Library*, 2 vols. (San Marino, 1989), 2: 618–20. The fifteenth-century attribution to Tiptoft (fol. iiii), signed by "Sheldwych," is accepted in Rosamond J. Mitchell, *John Tiptoft, 1427–1470* (London, 1938), pp. 9–10, 195–96 (cf. also pp. 242, 243), but is rejected in R. Weiss, *Humanism in England during the Fifteenth Century*, 3rd ed., Medium Ævum Monographs n.s. 4 (Oxford, 1967), pp. 118–19 and n. 11.

INTRODUCTION 23

coronet and arms appear in Bibliothèque Nationale MS. fonds français 6761.[53]

When William Caxton undertook the preparation of a *Liber ultimus* (1358 to 1461) for his edition of John Trevisa's translation of Higden's *Polychronicon* (1482), bringing the narrative more up to date, he turned to his 1480 edition of the *Chronicles of England* as a major source for his material.[54]

The *Historia Regum Anglie* (creation to 1485) of the bibliophile and antiquary John Rous (died 1491), a chantry priest at Guy's Cliff in Warwickshire, was written between 1480 and 1486. Rous used numerous sources, including the *Brut*, to which he may refer when he cites Geoffrey of Monmouth.[55]

C. SIXTEENTH-CENTURY USE AND INFLUENCE

In the sixteenth century the *Brut* continued to be used, in both its manuscript and printed forms, as a principal source for historical works.[56] It should also be noted that the *Brut* text itself, under its printed title as the *Chronicles of England*, remained salable in the early sixteenth century: there were seven reprinted editions by various publishers between 1502 and 1528. Sixteenth-century names and annotations in the medieval manuscripts attest that these were read, but such texts were increasingly the province of the antiquary or the casual owner.

---

[53] The text from Albina to 688 and from 1399 to 1471 is printed in William Hardy and E. L. C. P. Hardy, eds., *Recueil des Croniques et Anchiennes Istories de la Grant Bretaigne*, 5 vols., with an English translation in 3 vols., Rolls Series 39 (London, 1864–1891); the text from 1325 to 1471 is printed in L. M. E. Dupont, ed., *Anchiennes Cronicques d'Engleterre par Jehan de Wavrin*, 3 vols., Société de l'Histoire de France (Paris, 1858–1863). See Kingsford, *English Historical Literature*, pp. 136–37; Gransden, *Historical Writing II*, pp. 288–92.

[54] See Matheson, "Printer and Scribe," pp. 601–607.

[55] Thomas Hearne, ed., *Joannis Rossi Antiquarii Warwicensis Historia Regum Angliae* (Oxford, 1716). See Gransden, *Historical Writing II*, pp. 321–22 and n. 86. Rous cites Geoffrey of Monmouth as his source for the story of Brutus (pp. 18, 26); however, as noted by Charles Ross, a comment in Rous's roll history of the earls of Warwick suggests that he knew Geoffrey through the medium of the "comen Brute": see John Rous, *The Rous Roll*, introd. Charles Ross (Gloucester, 1980), p. viii n. 10 and cap. 7. The *Historia* includes the Albina and her sisters narrative (pp. 10–14); on Rous's treatment, see T. D. Kendrick, *British Antiquity* (London, 1950), pp. 24–25.

[56] For an account of the activities of sixteenth-century antiquaries, manuscript collectors, and historians, see May McKisack, *Medieval History in the Tudor Age* (Oxford, 1971); see also William R. Trimble, "Early Tudor Historiography 1485–1548," *Journal of the History of Ideas* 11 (1950): 30–41.

The *New Chronicles of England and France* (creation to 1485) by Robert Fabyan, draper, alderman, and sheriff of London in 1493–94 (died 1513), were completed in 1504 and published posthumously and anonymously in 1516. For much of the later part of his work Fabyan alternates chapters on French and English history. The earlier history of Britain and England is modeled on the *Brut*, from which Fabyan borrows extensively; the French material is mainly based on Robert Gaguin's *Compendium super Francorum Gestis*, printed in 1497 at Paris. From 1189 the English material constitutes a London chronicle (Fabyan was almost certainly the author of the later section of Guildhall Library, London, MS. 3313, *The Great Chronicle of London*).[57]

The so-called Translator of Livius compiled his English life of Henry V in 1513–1514. His principal source was, of course, Titus Livius's *Vita Henrici Quinti*, which had itself used the *Brut* (see above), supplemented by Enguerran de Monstrelet and by reminiscences ultimately derived from the earl of Ormonde. However, the Translator also used the version of the *Brut* prepared by Caxton for his *Liber ultimus* to the *Polychronicon* edition.[58]

The Italian humanist Polydore Vergil offered a new response to the version of history presented in the *Brut*. He began his *Anglica Historia* (Roman times to, originally, 1509) at the command of Henry VII; the first printed edition, dedicated to Henry VIII, appeared in Basle in 1534. Vergil is highly skeptical about the historicity of Brutus and Arthur as presented by Geoffrey of Monmouth (and thus in the *Brut*). For the fifteenth century, Vergil relied on some version of the London chronicle, perhaps supplemented by the printed editions of Fabyan and the *Chronicles of England*.[59] Vergil was not

---

[57] Henry Ellis, ed., *The New Chronicles of England and France, by Robert Fabyan, Named by Himself the Concordance of Histories* (London, 1811). See Kingsford, *English Historical Literature*, p. 105; McKisack, *Medieval History in the Tudor Age*, pp. 95–97; Gransden, *Historical Writing II*, p. 246; Matheson, "Historical Prose," p. 221; Kennedy, *Manual*, p. 2654; Lister M. Matheson, "English Chronicle Contexts for Shakespeare's Death of Richard II," in *From Page to Performance: Essays in Early English Drama*, ed. John A. Alford (East Lansing, 1995), p. 230.

[58] Charles L. Kingsford, ed., *The First English Life of King Henry the Fifth* (Oxford, 1911). See Kingsford, *English Historical Literature*, p. 64; Gransden, *Historical Writing II*, p. 217.

[59] Sections from an English translation of Henry VIII's time are printed in Henry Ellis, ed., *Three Books of Polydore Vergil's English History, Comprising the Reigns of Henry VI, Edward IV, and Richard III*, Camden Society o.s. 29 (1844); Henry Ellis, ed., *Polydore Vergil's English History, From an Early Translation. Vol. 1, Containing the First Eight Books, Comprising the Period Prior to the Norman Conquest*, Camden Society o.s. 36 (1846). The later, original narrative is printed in Denys Hay, ed. and trans., *The Anglica*

entirely alone in doubting the veracity of Geoffrey of Monmouth; his nationality and suspect religion did, however, single him out for vehement attack, and although a sign of things to come, his skepticism about evidence did not affect other popular English histories of the sixteenth century.[60]

The scope of Edward Hall's *Union of the Two Noble Families of Lancaster and York* (first edition published posthumously in 1548), recounting the reigns of Henry IV to Henry VIII, circumvented the problems of the historical assessment of early British history that attended Vergil's *Anglica Historia*. Hall borrowed from Vergil and was influenced by his style, but he also turned to a wide range of medieval chronicles for his material. Among his English sources Hall notes Trevisa, Fabyan, and Caxton, whose *Liber ultimus* is much used; in his preface, Hall acknowledges "one with out name, whiche wrote the common English Chronicle," that is, the *Brut*.[61]

Hall's *Union* was a major source for fifteenth-century English history in the collaborative work known as Holinshed's *Chronicles of England, Scotland, and Ireland*, first published in 1577. Raphael Holinshed (died ca. 1580) was the principal compiler of the first edition; the lengthy "Names of the Authors" used as sources for the history of England (creation to 1577), compiled as two books of the whole work, includes "Caxtons Chronicles," Hardyng, Fabyan, and Hall, as well as "diuers other bookes and treatises of historicall matter" by anonymous authors. The revised and expanded edition of 1587 contains supplementary material contributed by John Hooker, Francis Thynne, Abraham Fleming, and John Stow, whose "diligent collected summarie" is acknowledged in the first edition and whose *Chronicles* are used in the second.[62]

Historia of Polydore Vergil A.D. 1485–1537, Camden Society, 3rd ser., 74 (1950). See also Kingsford, *English Historical Literature*, pp. 254–55; McKisack, *Medieval History in the Tudor Age*, pp. 99–103; Gransden, *Historical Writing II*, pp. 436–37, 442.

[60] See Hugh A. MacDougall, *Racial Myth in English History: Trojans, Teutons, and Anglo-Saxons* (Montreal and Hanover, 1982), pp. 19–20; Gransden, *Historical Writing II*, pp. 442–43.

[61] Henry Ellis, ed., *Hall's Chronicle* (London, 1809); *The Union of the Two Noble Families of Lancaster and York, 1550* (Menston, Yorkshire, 1970) (a facsimile of Richard Grafton's second edition of 1550). See Kingsford, *English Historical Literature*, pp. 262, 265; McKisack, *Medieval History in the Tudor Age*, pp. 105–11; Gransden, *Historical Writing II*, p. 223. Hall also seems to have known Lambeth Palace MS. 84 directly; see Matheson, "English Chronicle Contexts for Shakespeare's Death of Richard II," pp. 226, 232.

[62] The edition of 1587 is the basis of Henry Ellis, ed., *Holinshed's Chronicles*, 6 vols. (London, 1807–1808; rpt., with an introduction by Vernon Snow, New York, 1965); for

John Stow (?1525–1605), originally a London tailor by trade and a freeman of the Merchant Taylors' Company, owned manuscripts of the *Brut* and also used *Brut* material in his historical works, all of which went through numerous editions. The earliest of these works, *A Summarie of Englyshe Chronicles* (1565), contains a section listing the names of all the kings of England since Brutus. Stow's major sources for the *Summarie* were Hardyng, Fabyan, and Hall; in subsequent, much enlarged editions he added the Translator of Livius. His *Chronicles of England* (1580) covered the period from Brutus to the year of publication; this work reappeared in 1592 in an enlarged and restructured form under the new title *Annales of England*. Stow utilized Thomas Walsingham's chronicles, Fabyan, Hall, the Translator of Livius, and many other chronicle, record, and literary sources. He incorporated material from the Peculiar Version of the *Brut* known as *"Davies's" Chronicle* from the manuscript that is now Bodleian MS. Lyell 34, which he owned (it was later in the possession of John Speed, who used it in his *Historie of Great Britaine* [1611]; see item 168 below). Stow also owned Lambeth Palace MS. 306, which contains a much abbreviated Peculiar Version of the *Brut*, a London chronicle, and other works, including a number of memoranda and transcriptions by Stow himself (some of which were inserted by Abraham Fleming in the 1587 edition of Holinshed's *Chronicles*).[63]

---

an overview, see McKisack, *Medieval History in the Tudor Age*, pp. 116–20. On the influence of the *Brut*, cf. Kingsford, *English Historical Literature*, pp. 113, 118; on the revised edition, see Annabel Patterson, *Reading Holinshed's* Chronicles (Chicago and London, 1994), pp. 9–10, 56. Although he also recounts the Albina story, Holinshed adopts as his primary account of the first inhabiting of Britain the version devised by John Bale in which Samothes, son of Japhet, son of Noah, is the first king of Britannia and Gaul. The giant Albion is later given Britain (which he renames after himself) by his father Neptunus, who is descended from Noah's wicked son Ham, thus accounting for the giants whom Brutus and his men defeat upon their arrival; see Kendrick, *British Antiquity*, pp. 69–73.

[63] Stow's *Chronicles* (or *Annales*) have not been reprinted in modern times; on the *Summarie*, the *Chronicles*, and the *Annales*, see McKisack, *Medieval History in the Tudor Age*, pp. 112–14. On Stow's indefatigable collecting of manuscripts, one may note that a search of Stow's house in 1569 revealed, among other books, "a great Parcell of old M.S. Chronicles, both in Parchment and Paper": see A. H. Thomas and I. D. Thornley, eds., *The Great Chronicle of London* (London and Aylesbury, 1938; microprint rpt. Gloucester, 1983), p. xvi. On Fleming's additions from Stow's Lambeth Palace MS. 306, see Patterson, *Reading Holinshed's 'Chronicles'*, p. 283 n. 6.

D. SEVENTEENTH-CENTURY USE AND INFLUENCE

Manuscripts of the *Brut* continued to be used by late sixteenth- and seventeenth-century antiquaries: the name of Sampson Erdeswicke (died 1603) appears in Glasgow MS. Hunterian 83; Bodleian MS. Rawlinson C.155 contains extracts made by Sir Henry Spelman in 1606 from an English text ending in 1333; Bodleian MS. Ashmole 1139.iv.2 contains passages transcribed in 1672 from Bodleian MS. Ashmole 791; Magdalene College, Cambridge, MS. Pepys 2833 contains a copy from College of Arms MS. Arundel 58 of John Mandeville's English translation of the *Brut*, made ca. 1685 for Sir William Hayward; NLW MS. Peniarth 343A contains a much abbreviated Peculiar Version of the English *Brut* written by William White in the seventeenth century.

However, the last printed edition of the *Chronicles of England* appeared in 1528, suggesting that as the standard popular narrative of the history of England the *Brut* had been replaced by the works of the sixteenth-century historians such as Stow and Holinshed, which were regularly reprinted into the seventeenth century. Since these had in fact utilized the *Brut* as a source, its indirect influence on conceptions of the past survived. Increasingly, though, the version of early British history presented in the *Brut* (and in its ultimate source, Geoffrey of Monmouth's *Historia Regum Britannie*) was challenged and ridiculed.[64]

Declared skeptics of Geoffrey's *Historia*, either in whole or in part, had existed from its first appearance but were in a small minority until the sixteenth and seventeenth centuries.[65] The major points of attack on the *His-*

---

[64] A full account of the debate is found in Kendrick, *British Antiquity*; see also MacDougall, *Racial Myth*, pp. 17–27, and Stuart Piggott, *Ancient Britons and the Antiquarian Imagination: Ideas from the Renaissance to the Regency* (New York, 1989), pp. 59–60.

[65] For active skeptics of all or part of the British History, see Kendrick, *British Antiquity*, pp. 11–14 (Alfred of Beverley, Giraldus Cambrensis, William of Newburgh, Ranulph Higden), 34–35 (John Whethamstede, Thomas Rudborne), 41–44 (Robert Fabyan, John Rastell, John Twyne, George Lily, Thomas Lanquet, Thomas Elyot, John Harington, Philip Sidney), 78–85 (John of Fordun, John Major, Polydore Vergil, George Buchanan), 105–11 (John Twyne, William Camden, John Clapham, John Selden, Walter Raleigh, John More, Samuel Daniel, Digory Whear, Matthias Prideaux, William Temple, James Tyrrell); MacDougall, *Racial Myth*, p. 22 (Edward Ayscu, John Speed). See also Laura Keeler, *Geoffrey of Monmouth and the Late Latin Chroniclers, 1300–1500*, University of California Publications in English 17.1 (Berkeley and Los Angeles, 1946), pp. 29–46, 76–85; Matheson, "King Arthur and the Medieval English Chronicles," pp. 263–65.

toria and its chronicle descendants were the accounts of Brutus and of Arthur, though the non-Galfridian stories of Albina and of St. Joseph of Arimathea were also doubted. Counter-attacks in defense of the "British History" were vigorous, especially those directed against Polydore Vergil's discounting of King Arthur.[66] Full-scale scholarly support, however, grew ever feebler in the face of developments in Renaissance historiographical methodology, embryonic anthropological studies resulting from the discovery of the Americas, and the rise of Anglo-Saxon studies.[67] Kendrick also distinguishes a middle party "that did not countenance total belief or total disbelief in the British History, but preferred a position that may be described as that of the institutionalist."[68] While pointing out the historical inconsistencies and illogicalities in the foundation and other stories, including that of King Arthur, the institutionalists suggested that there might be grains of truth contained therein that had been overlaid by the fabulous. Thus Milton in his *History of Britain . . . From the first Traditional Beginning, Continu'd to the Norman Conquest* (1670; 2nd ed., 1677) summarily dismisses Samothes but is less skeptical about Albion, son of Neptune. The Albina story is dismissed out of hand—"too absurd, and too unconscionably gross is that fond invention that wafted hither the fifty Daughters of a strange Dioclesian King of Syria." Brutus and his line cannot, however, "so easily be discharg'd"—*faute de mieux*, Milton's first book records Geoffrey's British kings up to Cassibelan, at which point the much relieved author is able to switch

---

[66] For active defenders of all or part of the British History, see Kendrick, *British Antiquity*, pp. 14 (John Trevisa's rebuttal of Higden), 85–98 (attacks on Polydore Vergil by John Leland, Arthur Kelton, David Powel, Humphrey Lluyd, John Price), 99 (attack on George Buchanan by Richard Harvey), 100 (attack on Camden by Henry Lyte; general defenses by John Ross and John Lewis; attack on Polydore Vergil by Edmund Howes), 101–102 (defense on linguistic grounds by Robert Sheringham; uncritical use by Bulstrode Whitelock and Winston Churchill); MacDougall, *Racial Myth*, pp. 23–25 (general defense by Edmund Bolton; attack on Polydore Vergil by Silas Taylor; general defense by Nathaniel Crouch). For Caxton's defense of Arthur's historicity, see Eugène Vinaver, ed., *The Works of Sir Thomas Malory*, 3 vols. (Oxford, 1947), 1: cxii–cxiii. See also James P. Carley, "Polydore Vergil and John Leland on King Arthur: The Battle of the Books," *Interpretations* 15 (1984): 86–100.

[67] See Kendrick, *British Antiquity*, pp. 114–15, 120–25; George P. Gooch, *A History of Historical Writing*, 2nd rev. ed. (New York, 1962), pp. 114–17; Ernst Breisach, *Historiography: Ancient, Medieval, and Modern* (Chicago and London, 1983), pp. 165–66, 173–77; MacDougall, *Racial Myth*, pp. 31–50.

[68] Kendrick, *British Antiquity*, p. 125; for members, see pp. 126–32 (Edmund Spenser), 126 (John Milton), 101 and 125 (Daniel Langhorne), 102 and 125 (William Wynne).

to Roman sources, though his "disease" over verifiable historicity returns during the Arthurian period.[69]

Modern Value

By the end of the seventeenth century only a few diehards continued to support the veracity of Geoffrey of Monmouth. However, despite the general exploding of the British history related in the *Brut*, its later sections, especially from 1307 on, and the individual late medieval continuations have remained valuable for political and social historians.[70]

As a cultural artifact the *Brut* is of the first importance. Its popularity and circulation in the fourteenth and fifteenth centuries and its influence in the sixteenth century gave it the status of a standard history that defined and created a sense of England's past, its national identity, and its destiny. Besides providing continuity with an ancient Trojan past, the Brutus story (and the Albina story) served a useful political and legal purpose in English claims to the overlordship of Scotland.[71] The central figure of King Arthur, conqueror of much of Europe, was a potent political icon used by and on behalf of monarchs from Henry II to the Tudors to the Stuarts.[72] Both in its own right and as a source for later writers, the account of Henry V in the English *Brut* was central in creating the cult surrounding that king and his exemplary victories in France.[73]

---

[69] See the facsimile of the second edition (1677) in John Milton, *The History of Britain*, introd. Graham Parry (Stamford, 1991), pp. 8–38, 143–49.

[70] See, for example, the assessments in Kingsford, *English Historical Literature*, pp. 113–35; Childs and Taylor, eds., *Anonimalle Chronicle*, pp. 35–61; Edgar B. Graves, ed., *A Bibliography of English History to 1485* (Oxford, 1975), pp. 409 (item 2811), 413 (item 2829).

[71] See Susan Reynolds, "Medieval *Origines Gentium* and the Community of the Realm," *History* 68 (1983): 375–90; Carley and Crick, "Constructing Albion's Past," pp. 42–43, 54–67. For a detailed examination of earlier (pre-*Brut*) stages in the development of English national consciousness, see Thorlac Turville-Petre, *England the Nation: Language, Literature, and National Identity, 1290–1340* (Oxford, 1996).

[72] See Gordon H. Gerould, "King Arthur and Politics," *Speculum* 2 (1927): 33–51; Kendrick, *British Antiquity*, pp. 35–39, 42; R. S. Loomis, "Edward I, Arthurian Enthusiast," *Speculum* 28 (1953): 114–27; Sydney Anglo, "The British History in Early Tudor Propaganda," *Bulletin of the John Rylands Library* 44 (1961–62): 21–44; MacDougall, *Racial Myth*, pp. 13–19, 21–26; Vale, *Edward III and Chivalry*, pp. 67–69, 93–94; Sharon L. Jansen, "Prophecy, Propaganda, and Henry VIII," in *King Arthur through the Ages*, ed. Lagorio and Day, 1: 275–91; Carley and Crick, "Constructing Albion's Past," p. 68.

[73] See Christopher Allmand, *Henry V* (Berkeley and Los Angeles, 1992), pp. 426–35.

III. The Anglo-Norman *Brut*

Development and Sources

For present purposes, the main outlines of textual development and the sources of the Anglo-Norman *Brut* seem reasonably clear.[74] However, a comprehensive and detailed catalogue, description, and textual classification of the Anglo-Norman and continental French manuscripts remain a matter for future study, and the following discussion makes no attempt to classify or account for every text.

In its earliest form, the Anglo-Norman *Brut* related the history of England from Brutus to the death of Henry III in 1272, at which point end MSS. Bibliothèque Nationale, fonds français 14640; Bibliothèque Nationale, nouvelles acquisitions françaises 4267; BL Additional 35092; and BL Cotton Tiberius A.vi.[75] The work must have been composed between 1272 and ca. 1300 (the date of the earliest manuscript, Bibliothèque Nationale, fonds français 14640); the author of this first stage is anonymous.

For his narrative from Brutus to what corresponds to the beginning of Cadwallader's reign, the writer used primarily Wace's *Roman de Brut*, apparently in a form closer to its source in Geoffrey of Monmouth's *Historia* than is found in the surviving manuscripts.[76] The Cadwallader episode, the ending point of both Geoffrey of Monmouth and Wace, is omitted. This omission is either a deliberate, politically motivated decision, as C. W. Marx has

---

Cf. also Kennedy, *Manual*, pp. 2633–34. "The cronycle of kyng Henry the v" in BL MS. Cotton Claudius A.viii is an extract from Caxton's *Chronicles of England*.

[74] See Meyer, "De quelques chroniques anglo-normandes," pp. 113–44; Brie, *Geschichte und Quellen*, pp. 13–51; Vising, *Anglo-Norman Language and Literature*, nos. 378(a)–(i); Brereton, ed., *Des Grantz Geanz*, pp. xiv–xviii; Taylor, *English Historical Literature*, pp. 117–18, 120–27, 274–84; Childs and Taylor, eds., *Anonimalle Chronicle*, pp. 15–17.

[75] Brie, *Geschichte und Quellen*, pp. 13–15. Vising, *Anglo-Norman Language and Literature*, no. 378a, lists Trinity College, Cambridge, MS. R.4.26, but this is a text of the *Brut abrégé*. See also Taylor, *English Historical Literature*, p. 117; ambiguous phrasing in Childs and Taylor, eds., *Anonimalle Chronicle*, p. 15, seems to suggest that the original ended in 1307. Brie argues that the original text ended in 1066 (*Geschichte und Quellen*, pp. 13–14, 37, 42), partly since the pre- and post-1066 sources seem of very different sorts and partly from the evidence of some of the Latin *Brut* texts, but these arguments are far from convincing.

[76] Ivor Arnold, ed., *Le Roman de Brut de Wace*, 2 vols. (Paris, 1938, 1940); see Brie, *Geschichte und Quellen*, pp. 38–40, who adduces convincing parallel passages to support this view.

speculated,[77] or it reflects some loss of text or dislocation of narrative at this point in the source text or in the writer's transition from one source to another. The material from what should have been the death of Cadwallader to Harold's death in 1066 seems to be derived from Geffrei Gaimar's *Estoire des Engleis*, though more loosely than from the previous source in Wace.[78] A version of the Havelok story, which occurs near the beginning of Gaimar, is inserted in the *Brut* soon after Arthur (though it is not simply derived from Gaimar).[79] The direct source for the narrative from 1066 to 1100, covering the reigns of William the Conqueror and William Rufus, is not known; for the remainder of the text to 1272, the writer used the annals (A.D. 1 to 1291) written at the Cistercian abbey of Waverley in Surrey (or perhaps, as Brie suggests, an intermediary Anglo-Norman work based on them).[80]

There are some indications that in the early fourteenth century the basic text to 1272 received a continuation covering the reign of Edward I and ending with his death in 1307, though this stage must have been quickly subsumed into later recensions. Among complete manuscripts, only CUL MS. Ee.1.20, a text of the later Long Version (see below), ends in 1307.[81] The first part of Corpus Christi College, Oxford, MS. 78 is a text of the basic version to 1307, with an Anglo-Norman prose translation from a Latin version of the Albina prologue and some additions, to which a second scribe

---

[77] See C. W. Marx, "Middle English Manuscripts of the Brut in the National Library of Wales," *The National Library of Wales Journal* 27 (1991–92): 377–80.

[78] Alexander Bell, ed., *L'Estoire des Engleis: By Geffrei Gaimar*, Anglo-Norman Text Society 14–16 (Oxford, 1960); see Brie, *Geschichte und Quellen*, pp. 40–42. The parallel passages from the *Brut* and Gaimar cited by Brie on p. 41 are very close, but much of Gaimar's text, at least as it now survives, is omitted or altered. Thus the tedious series of minor wars among the heptarchy kingdoms (that occur in Gaimar up to the parallel passages quoted by Brie) are reduced to a short, general statement (cf. the English version in Brie 102/24–28). Gaimar's occasional confusions of persons with the same or similar names could not have helped the composer of the *Brut*. Brie suggests that the *Brut* writer might have used an earlier, simpler version of Gaimar (p. 42).

[79] See Friedrich W. D. Brie, "Zum Fortleben der Havelok-Sage," *Englische Studien* 35 (1905): 360–64. The heroine is called "Goldeburgh" in BL Cotton Domitian x (fol. 45), a Short Version text; "Argentil" in BL Cotton Cleopatra D.iii (fol. 108), a Long Version text.

[80] Printed in Henry R. Luard, ed., *Annales Monastici*, vol. 2, Rolls Series 36 (London, 1865), pp. 127–211.

[81] Bodl. Wood empt. 8, a text of the Short Version, breaks off just after the beginning of the reign of Edward I.

has added a unique continuation to 1398.[82] College of Arms MS. 31, a text of the Short Version with the metrical prologue (see below) that ends incompletely in 1329, leaves half a page blank after the death of Edward I.[83] Bodleian MS. Wood empt. 8, which does not contain the metrical prologue, breaks off soon after the beginning of the reign of Edward I. It could, therefore, represent a text that originally ended in 1307, though it could belong to the Short Version with a continuation to 1333 (see below), depending on how much text has been lost. Most convincingly, however, Brie notes that the majority of texts extending beyond 1307 fall into three groups that essentially agree up to that point and then diverge independently thereafter.[84]

The source of the material from 1272 to 1307 is an unedited version of Langtoft's verse *Chronicle* that is exemplified in MSS. College of Arms Arundel 14, CUL Gg.1.1, and Bodleian Fairfax 24.[85]

Major additions and revisions to the basic text of the Anglo-Norman *Brut* occurred between 1333 and the middle of the fourteenth century, resulting in the two major recensions known as the Short and Long Versions.

The first stage of the Short Version was formed by the addition of a continuation from the accession of Edward II in 1307, known as the short continuation, which survives in various states of fullness or abbreviation. The precise conclusion of this first stage is somewhat unclear since none of the manuscripts is unambiguously complete. Yale MS. Beinecke 405 apparently ends at some point in the year 1333, but the "final folio [is] only partially legible, with end of text totally obscured."[86] Other manuscripts of the group end incompletely: BL Additional 35113 breaks off in 1324; CUL

---

[82] See Brie, *Geschichte und Quellen*, pp. 16, 25. Brie mistakenly believed the prose prologue to have been based on the Anglo-Norman *Des Grantz Geanz*; see Brereton, ed., *Des Grantz Geanz*, p. xxxvi, and Carley and Crick, "Constructing Albion's Past," pp. 45, 86–87.

[83] Brie, *Geschichte und Quellen*, p. 16.

[84] Brie, *Geschichte und Quellen*, p. 16; cf. Taylor, *English Historical Literature*, p. 117. Brie includes among these three groups Corpus Christi College, Oxford, 78, whose evidence I have mentioned above; the remaining texts really fall into two major groups, with subgroups.

[85] See Brie, *Geschichte und Quellen*, pp. 44–46, for a comparison of readings. The *Brut* continuation presents some omissions and alterations and a number of misunderstandings.

[86] Barbara A. Shailor, *Catalogue of Medieval and Renaissance Manuscripts in the Beinecke Rare Book and Manuscript Library, Yale University*, 3 vols., Medieval & Renaissance Texts & Studies 34, 48, 100 (Binghamton, 1984–1992), 2: 293.

INTRODUCTION 33

Mm.1.33 in 1326; Corpus Christi College, Oxford, 293 in 1329; while BL Cotton Julius A.i contains only a fragment from the reign of Edward II. Nevertheless, the evidence of the next stage in the development of the Short Version suggests strongly that the end point was the English raid on Haddington fair in Scotland that occurred in 1333, shortly before the battle of Halidon Hill.

In view of the London interest of the earlier part of the continuation, coupled with the amount and the detail of the material on Edward III's Scottish campaigns, Taylor suggests that the writer may have been a clerk of the Exchequer who accompanied the administration to York in the 1330s and that the continuation may have been an originally independent work that became attached to the *Brut*.[87]

The next stage in the development of the Short Version was the addition of a metrical prologue that recounts the story of Albina and her sisters, the thirty daughters of an unnamed king of Greece who, exiled after plotting unsuccessfully to murder their husbands, are the first settlers of Albion and the mothers of giants, whose descendants Brutus and his men were to slay.[88] This prologue is an abbreviated redaction of an Anglo-Norman poem, *Des Grantz Geanz*, that is found in full in BL MS. Cotton Cleopatra D.ix, a manuscript that has been dated by Carley and Crick between 1332 and 1334.[89] All but two of the *Brut* manuscripts that contain *Des Grantz Geanz* also include a short linking passage in Latin or French between the prologue and the main text that summarizes the Albina story and the future contents up to the arrival of the Saxons. College of Arms, MS. Arundel 31 (breaks off in 1329) and Bodleian MS. e Musaeo 108 (breaks off in 1327) contain no linking passage.

The following manuscripts contain the linking summary in Latin: BL

---

[87] See John Taylor, "The French Prose *Brut*: Popular History in Fourteenth-Century England," in *England in the Fourteenth Century: Proceedings of the 1985 Harlaxton Symposium*, ed. W. M. Ormrod (Woodbridge, 1986), pp. 253–54 and n. 30; Taylor, *English Historical Literature*, pp. 122–24, 146; Childs and Taylor, eds., *Anonimalle Chronicle*, pp. 19–20.

[88] See Brereton, ed., *Des Grantz Geanz*, p. v.

[89] "Constructing Albion's Past," p. 45 and n. 17. For the following account of the manuscripts of the Short Version, see Brie, *Geschichte und Quellen*, pp. 17–24; Brereton, ed., *Des Grantz Geanz*, pp. vi–xi, xii–xviii (classification of the manuscripts), and xxxvi; Legge and Brereton, "Three Hitherto Unlisted MSS.," pp. 113–17; Taylor, *English Historical Literature*, pp. 120–24; Childs and Taylor, eds., *Anonimalle Chronicle*, pp. 20–22; Carley and Crick, "Constructing Albion's Past," pp. 45–47.

Harley 6359 (breaks off in 1330); BL Additional 18462(b) (breaks off in the first chapter of Edward I's reign); Lambeth Palace 504 (ends in 1333 with Haddington raid); Inner Temple Library, London, 511, Vol. XIX (to 1333, Haddington); Trinity College, Dublin, 500 (to 1333, Haddington); Bodleian Rawlinson D.329 (to 1333, Haddington); Bodleian Lyell 17 (to 1333, Haddington); CUL Gg.1.15 (breaks off in 1326); Trinity College, Cambridge, R.7.14 (breaks off in 1333 with Archibald Douglas's raid into England); EUL 181 (to 1333, Haddington); Yale Beinecke 593 (to 1333, Haddington); Westminster Abbey 25 (ends in 1330); Bibliothèque de l'Arsenal, Paris, 3346 (ends in 1330 at the same point as the preceding, related text). BL Cotton Domitian x (to 1333, Haddington) contains the Latin summary but not the prologue, which has either been lost or was deliberately omitted despite its presence in the exemplar. The Latin summary follows *Des Grantz Geanz* in Leeds Brotherton 29 (*The Anonimalle Chronicle*). It occurs also in BL Cotton Cleopatra D.vii as part of the fifteenth-century augmentation of the original fourteenth-century text. In Bibliothèque Nationale, fonds français 12156, a fifteenth-century continental French manuscript (possibly from Picardy), the prologue is completely recast into laisses of monorhyme alexandrines and precedes a Short Version text (to 1333, Haddington). Three fifteenth-century manuscripts form a distinct group in which the linking passage is in Anglo-Norman: BL Harley 200, Bodleian Douce 128, and Trinity College, Cambridge, R.5.32 contain the metrical prologue, the Short Version of the *Brut* to 1332, followed by the Latin chronicle of Robert of Avesbury (died 1359).[90]

The Long Version was also generated between 1333 and 1350, though its less circumspect account of Edward II's murder suggests that it may have been compiled slightly later than the Short Version.[91]

All but two of those manuscripts of the Long Version that are complete at the beginning contain a prose prologue that recounts a version of the Albina story. The two exceptions are CUL Ee.1.20 and Lincoln's Inn 88, each of which possesses individual textual peculiarities; their texts cannot, therefore, represent the initial stage of the Long Version, though it is just possi-

---

[90] Avesbury's work survives in these three manuscripts only. It is printed in Edward Maunde Thompson, ed., *Adae Murimuth Continuatio Chronicorum. Robertus de Avesbury de Gestis Mirabilibus Regis Edwardi Tertii*, Rolls Series 93 (London, 1889), pp. 279–471. See also Gransden, *Historical Writing II*, pp. 67–71; Taylor, *English Historical Literature*, p. 127.

[91] See Childs and Taylor, eds., *Anonimalle Chronicle*, p. 22.

ble that they are descended from an original Long Version that did not include the prologue.[92]

The prose prologue that is generally found in the Long Version represents a different version of the Albina story from that found in the metrical prologue to the Short Version; for example, Albina is now one of thirty-three daughters of King Dioclisian of Syria who succeed in murdering their husbands, rather than one of thirty daughters of an unnamed king of Greece who fail in their homicidal plot. It is uncertain whether the prose version is derived directly from the metrical version or whether both versions had a common source, possibly in Latin.[93]

The text to the death of Edward I in 1307 is a much revised version of the basic, standard text described above.[94] There are many changes in the names of the towns in which the British kings are buried and in the lengths of their reigns. Some factual details are changed: for example, Gorbodian's four brothers become his sons, in the Havelok story Goldeburgh becomes Argentille, and a long story recounts the poisoning of King John by a monk in Swineshead rather than the short report of the king's death from illness. Some small omissions are found, such as the notice of Malgo, the successor to Conan Meriadoc, and the names of the bishops present at Henry III's coronation. A number of minor additions also are made, and an important new section of narrative, the lengthy set of Merlin's prophecies concerning the five kings to follow King John (cf. Brie 72–76), appears. Many additional historical details appear in the account of the reign of Edward I.

This revised text proceeds with a continuation from 1307 to the battle of Halidon Hill in 1333, ending with the words "saunz chalenge de ascuny. Amen. Deo gracias." (BL Cotton Cleopatra D.iii). The narrative is independent of the short continuation and is known as the long continuation. It covers the reign of Edward II and the early years of Edward III in much fuller detail and at greater length than any preceding reign. The notion that it was written by William Pakington, who served as a clerk in the households of the Black Prince and Richard II and whose career is recorded from

---

[92] See Brie, *Geschichte und Quellen*, pp. 28 and 30–31, for a description of these manuscripts. Despite its verbal peculiarities, Lincoln's Inn 88 can be associated with a subgroup of Long Version texts that do include the prologue (see below).

[93] See Brereton, ed., *Des Grantz Geanz*, pp. xxxv–xxxvii.

[94] For a fuller and more detailed account of the differences up to 1307 between the Short and the Long Versions, see Brie, *Geschichte und Quellen*, pp. 26–27.

1364 to 1390, has been successfully refuted by John Taylor.⁹⁵ Instead, Childs and Taylor suggest that, like the short continuation, the long continuation, which shows marked knowledge of northern events, may have been written by a clerk attached to the central administration and stationed at York during the 1330s who was aware of the short continuation.⁹⁶ Indeed, it is possible that the continuator was also responsible for the entire compilation and revision of the Long Version.

Thirteen of the fourteen manuscripts of the Long Version (BL Royal App. 85 is a fragment) can be divided into three primary subgroups: (a) CUL Ee.1.20 (breaks off in 1307 during the interpretation of Merlin's prophecy on Edward I) lacks the prologue and abbreviates heavily; (b) BL Royal 20.A.iii; Trinity College, Dublin, 501; CUL Ii.6.8; BL Additional 18462a; (c) BL Cotton Cleopatra D.iii; Bibliothèque Mazarine 1860; Bibliothèque Nationale, fonds français 12155; BL Royal 19.C.ix; Bibliothèque Ste. Geneviève 935; Bodleian Ashmole 1804; Lincoln's Inn 88; BL Royal 20.A.xviii.⁹⁷

Brie reports that his comparisons of readings in Long Version manu-

---

⁹⁵ See Taylor, *English Historical Literature*, pp. 277–83 (originally printed as part of "The French *Brut* and the Reign of Edward II," *English Historical Review* 76 [1957]: 423–37). The attribution to Pakington began with John Leland and was accepted by Brie, who thought he had discovered Pakington's original chronicle in BL MS. Cotton Tiberius A.vi: see Friedrich W. D. Brie, "Recovery of an Anglo-Norman Chronicle," *Notes and Queries* 10th ser., 2 (1904): 41; *Geschichte und Quellen*, pp. 47–51. Taylor shows that this text is, in fact, a composite chronicle derived from various sources, including the Anglo-Norman *Brut* (pp. 278–81).

⁹⁶ Childs and Taylor, eds., *Anonimalle Chronicle*, pp. 22–23.

⁹⁷ See Brie, *Geschichte und Quellen*, p. 32. I paraphrase Brie's further distinctions among the texts: in group (b), BL Royal 20.A.iii and Trinity College, Dublin 501 agree almost word for word, while CUL Ii.6.8 and BL Additional 18462a have deviations in common; in group (c), Bibliothèque Nationale, fonds français 12155, BL Royal 19.C.ix, and Bibliothèque Ste. Geneviève 935 stand against BL Cotton Cleopatra D.iii, Bibliothèque Mazarine 1860, Bodleian Ashmole 1804, Lincoln's Inn 88, and BL Royal 20.A.xviii; furthermore, BL Royal 19.C.ix and Bibliothèque Ste. Geneviève 935 stand against Bibliothèque Nationale, fonds français 12155, while BL Cotton Cleopatra D.iii and Bodleian Ashmole 1804 agree almost word for word against Bibliothèque Mazarine 1860, Lincoln's Inn 88, and BL Royal 20.A.xviii. Also within group (c), BL Royal 20.A.xviii contains variations from the normal continuation to 1333, such as a concluding section that recounts rumors that Edward II was still alive, followed by the prophecies of Merlin, which have been accorded chapter numbers to fit in at the end of the appropriate reign; see Taylor, "The French Prose *Brut*: Popular History in Fourteenth-Century England," in *England in the Fourteenth Century*, ed. Ormrod, p. 250, and Childs and Taylor, eds., *Anonimalle Chronicle*, p. 18.

scripts show that a text of the type of MSS. Bibliothèque Nationale, fonds français 12155, BL Royal 19.C.ix, and Bibliothèque Ste. Geneviève 935 formed the basis for the Middle English translation that was made in the second half of the fourteenth century.[98] The work of supplying continuations to the Anglo-Norman text essentially ceased, though it continued to be copied and read in the fifteenth century. But, apart from the three manuscripts that append Robert of Avesbury's Latin chronicle, only two surviving manuscripts contain continuations beyond 1333. Leeds MS. Brotherton 29 adds two French continuations that bring the narrative to 1381.[99] Corpus Christi College, Oxford, MS. 78 originally ended in 1307 but subsequently received two continuations. The first, in a fourteenth-century hand, recounts the reigns of Edward II and Edward III; the second, in a fifteenth-century hand, covers the period from 1377 to 1397.[100]

IV. The Latin *Brut*

The definition—let alone the affiliations—of the so-called Latin *Brut* texts has been subject to debate by those few scholars who have considered them.

Brie identified three manuscripts—Magdalen College, Oxford, 200; Lambeth Palace 99; and BL Cotton Julius B.iii—as constituting a close and accurate translation from the Anglo-Norman *Brut*, though the last of these contained abbreviations and additions from other Latin sources that were not found in the other two texts.[101] However, to account for instances where he considered that the Latin text agreed better with Geoffrey of Monmouth's *Historia Regum Britannie*, Brie posited that the translation had been made from an earlier form of the Anglo-Norman *Brut* than now survives, one that corresponded more closely to Geoffrey and that ended in 1066, the date of the conclusion of the *Brut* texts in the three Latin manuscripts (two of which then append continuations). To account for the presence of the Albina prologue, not found in the earliest extant Anglo-Norman

---

[98] Brie, *Geschichte und Quellen*, pp. 54–55.

[99] See V. H. Galbraith, ed., *The Anonimalle Chronicle 1333–1381* (Manchester, 1927); Taylor, *English Historical Literature*, pp. 133–53.

[100] See Galbraith, "Extracts from the Historia Aurea and a French 'Brut' (1317–47)," pp. 206–207 (description), 215–17 (extract from the first continuation).

[101] For these, and Brie's other comments that are summarized below, see his *Geschichte und Quellen*, pp. 127–30.

texts ending in 1272, Brie suggested that either there had once existed Anglo-Norman texts to 1272 that included the prologue or the prologue was an individual addition to a text ending in 1066.

Brie remarked further the presence of the same prologue in an anonymous Latin chronicle in Bodleian MSS. Rawlinson B.169, B.195, C.398, "u. a. m." (that is, "and many others"), but felt that this work had nothing otherwise to do with the *Brut*. He also noted the interpolated presence of the prologue in BL MS. Cotton Galba E.vii of the *Eulogium Historiarum* and a second translation of the prologue (from the Anglo-Norman Long Version), with an original preface, in BL MS. Harley 941.

Kingsford, however, regarded the anonymous Latin chronicle rejected by Brie as the fully developed form of the Latin *Brut*, ending with the murder of James I of Scotland in 1437, and added a further eight texts to the three specifically mentioned by Brie. He noted frequent textual variations, perhaps "due in part to independent translations from the English original," but concluded from his comparison of three texts for the reign of Richard that "all three are obviously translated (though with much abbreviation) from the common English text."[102] Kingsford accepted the three manuscripts described by Brie as the Latin *Brut* as representatives of the original work, to which, presumably, the material translated from the English *Brut* had subsequently been appended.

Kingsford assigned nine of his eleven texts to two main classes, according to whether they contain brief or full accounts of the reign of Henry V, and commented on the contents of the remaining two texts.[103]

Most recently, Kennedy has raised the possibility, at least for the texts discussed by Kingsford, that "they are not translations but original compositions in Latin that drew upon the English *Brut*s and other works as sources," since there is material in Bodleian MS. Rawlinson C.398 that

---

[102] Kingsford, *English Historical Literature*, pp. 310, 311.

[103] The text from 1399 to 1437, designated "The Common Version," is printed from manuscripts containing the brief account in Kingsford, *English Historical Literature*, pp. 312–23; the text of "The Longer Version for the Reign of Henry V" is printed on pp. 323–37. Despite textual variations, Kingsford considered (presumably on account of content) that all the texts were very similar for the reigns of Henry IV and Henry VI (p. 310). The narrative from 1422 to 1437 (and a continuation to 1471) in College of Arms Arundel 5 is printed in Gairdner, ed., *Chronicles*, pp. 164–66 (*Brut*), 166–85 (continuation). The imperfect text of Bodleian Rawlinson C.234 is printed under the title "Chronicon (Anonymi) Godstovianum" as an appendix in Thomas Hearne, ed., *William Roper's Vita Thomae More* (Oxford, 1716), pp. 180–246.

Kennedy did not find in the English texts ending in 1437.[104]

It is almost certain that a number of texts remain unidentified in sketchily catalogued manuscripts.[105] It would, therefore, be premature to try to resolve all outstanding problems connected with the Latin *Brut*s, the texts of which require a more detailed and extensive treatment than is either necessary or possible in the present context. The following comments attempt to address the opinions and concerns of the scholars noted above, especially insofar as they relate to the relationship between the Latin texts and the English *Brut*.

As noted earlier, those texts that have been called Latin *Brut*s fall into two major versions and a minor "version" represented by a single text. The two major versions are connected only by their use of a common form (with variations) of the Albina prologue.

The First Version of the Latin Brut

The first version consists of the texts found in MSS. Magdalen College, Oxford, 200 and Lambeth Palace 99, with which can be associated the text of BL MS. Cotton Julius B.iii.

Both Magdalen College, Oxford, 200 (fols. 40–56) and Lambeth Palace 99 (fols. 1–22v) contain a short prefatory passage, beginning "Adam & Eua in agro Damasceno formati virgines exierunt de paradiso" and ending "Computantur igitur ab Adam usque ad passionem anni quinque milia ducentesimo & viginti octo" (Lambeth Palace 99).

The work that follows immediately is based on the Short Version of the Anglo-Norman *Brut* and is headed "Incipit Brute de gestis Anglorum" (Magdalen Coll. 200), "Incipit Bruto de gentes Anglorum & de omnibus regibus Anglie" (Lambeth Palace 99). The Albina prologue begins "Anno [a] creacione mundi M¹M¹M¹ DCCCC erat in Grecia quidem rex potentissimus super ceteros reges optinens principatum" and ends "& sic gigantes expulsi C x annis terram Anglie tenuere in pace" (Lambeth Palace 99); as Brie

---

[104] *Manual*, pp. 2638–39.
[105] The present discussion includes those manuscripts noted in Brie, *Geschichte und Quellen*, p. 5; Kingsford, *English Historical Literature*, pp. 310–12; Carley and Crick, "Constructing Albion's Past," pp. 48–49 and n. 32 (CCCC 311 and Gonville and Caius Coll., Cambridge, 72); and Dutschke, *Guide*, 2: 618–19 (Huntington HM 19960). *Brut*-like texts such as those found in Lambeth Palace 386, BL Egerton 672, and Chicago 224, fols. 7–24v (see Mary E. Giffin, "A Wigmore Manuscript at the University of Chicago," *The National Library of Wales Journal* 7 [1951–52]: 316–25) have not been included.

noted, this text is a slightly shortened translation into Latin prose of the introductory poem found in many Anglo-Norman Short Version texts.

The first chapter of the narrative proper is entitled "De ciuitate magne [noue *Lambeth*] Troie que est ciuitate London" and begins "In ciuitate magne [noue *Lambeth*] Troie erat quidam miles fortissimus nomine Eneas" (Magdalen Coll. 200). The succeeding text is a close translation of the Anglo-Norman Short Version and shares the features thereof, such as the omission of Merlin's prophecies and the Cadwallader episode and the inclusion of King Malgo (see pp. 32–35 above). The *Brut* text ends in 1066 with the death of Harold: "Et isto modo rex Haroldus perdidit regnum Anglie cum regnasset ab Epiphania dum vsque ad festum sancti Kalixti xl septimanas & mortuus est in bello vt predicatur & iacet humatus aput Waltham. Explicit Bruto [Brute *Magdalen Coll.*] de gestis Anglorum" (Lambeth Palace 99).

Magdalen College 200 ends at this point, but Lambeth Palace 99 continues with a chronicle entitled "Conquestus regni Anglie per Willelmum ducem Normannorum" (fol. 22v), which begins by recounting William's reasons for the Conquest. This work ends in 1367 with a full list of those captured at the battle of Nájera: "& alij multi vsque ad numerum quinque M^l vel vj Mill. bonarum gencium armatarum exceptis Ienetorijs Panisorijs & seruentibus sine numero" (fol. 56v).

Besides the *Brut* text and its continuation, Lambeth Palace 99 contains a number of other works, all written by the same scribe, that bear on the development of this first version of the Latin *Brut*. The manuscript includes a chronicle of popes to Gregory XI (mistakenly called "Vrbanus"), elected in 1370 and died 1378 (fols. 60–112v); a chronicle of Roman and Holy Roman emperors from Julius Caesar to Charles IV, elected in 1355 and died 1378 (fols. 113–127v); a chronicle of archbishops of Canterbury from Augustine to William Whittesley, archbishop from 1368 to 1374 (fols. 129–150); a list of bishoprics (fols. 153–155v); a *Cosmographia* attributed to "Rogerum monachum Cestrensis," extracted from Ranulph Higden's *Polychronicon* (fols. 158–186); a catalogue of saints in England (fols. 187–196); a text on Scottish history from the time of King Westmer to 1368 (fols. 203–206); the *Ymago mundi* of Honorius of Autun (fols. 207–218, ending imperfectly); and a tractate and three epitaphs on William the Conqueror (fols. 219–224v). The dates associated with the various works suggest that the manuscript was compiled soon after 1377.[106]

---

[106] At some point the manuscript belonged to St. George's Chapel at Windsor; see Ker, *Medieval Libraries*, p. 203.

Versions of several of the works found in Lambeth Palace 99 also occur in BL MS. Cotton Julius B.iii: the chronicles of the popes (fols. 3–25v), emperors (fols. 26–31), and archbishops of Canterbury (fols. 31v–42) and the list of bishoprics (fols. 42v–50v). Clearly, the two manuscripts are closely related.

Nevertheless, the version of the *Brut* is not identical to that found in Lambeth Palace 99. The short preface from Adam is omitted, but the text of the Albina story is similar to that in Lambeth Palace 99; it begins "A principio mundi iij^M ix^C erat in Grecia quidam rex potentissimus super [*repeated*] ceteros reges optinens principatum" and ends "et sic gigantes sunt expulsi." The following narrative, however, is largely a selective adaptation of Geoffrey of Monmouth's *Historia Regum Britannie*, the language of which is sometimes paraphrased, sometimes followed verbatim. Thus, Brutus's questions and Diana's reply are given in Geoffrey's verse form, and Merlin's prophecies are included, with the kings being identified in the margins. Additions are also made, as, for example, in the inclusion of an extended account of Sts. Alban and Amphiball. Considerable omissions from Geoffrey are also made, and one principle of omission may have been the absence of corresponding material in the *Brut* so as to follow generally the narrative structure of that work. After Cadwallader occurs an extended account of the kings of the Anglo-Saxon heptarchy. Thereafter, the text turns to the *Brut* for the remainder of the narrative to 1066; it then proceeds with the third chapter of the chronicle to 1367 found in Lambeth Palace 99, thus avoiding a overlap between the two works. The changeover (fol. 101v) is as follows:

> Et isto modo rex Haroldus perdidit regnum Anglie cum regnasset ab Epiphania dum vsque ad festum sancti Kalixti per xl septimanas & mortuus est in bello vt predicatur & iacet humatus apud Waltham.
>
> Explicit Bruto de gestis Anglorum. Conquestus regni Anglie per Willelmum ducem Normannie et de coronacione dicti Willelmi regis Anglie.
>
> Anno domini M lxvj dux Normannorum Willelmus vrbem London adiens in multo exultacione a clero & populo susceptus

The succeeding text is abbreviated, especially in lists of names, and ends after a much truncated account of the captured at Nájera: "& alij multi vsque ad numerum v Mill. bonarum gencium armatorum exceptis Ienetorijs Panisorijs & seruentibus sine numero" (fol. 115v).

BL MS. Cotton Julius B.iii appears to have been directly based on Lambeth Palace MS. 99 and contains a contemporary note in the lower margin of fol. 3 that reads: "Istum librum compilauit magister Willelmus Rede iij^{us} episcopus Cirestrensis." William Rede was indeed bishop of Chichester from 1368 to his death in 1385; why the annotator designates him as "third" is mysterious (the see was first established in 1075 and only one of Rede's predecessors was named William). Emden accepts his authorship of the chronicle of the popes and emperors, the chronicle of the archbishops of Canterbury, and the *Brut* and its continuation to 1367 in BL Cotton Julius B.iii.[107] Rede's dates fit, and he was certainly qualified to have compiled such a manuscript. He was a noted scholar of Merton College and the author of several astronomical tables and works. He was also a collector who made major donations of books to Merton College and New College and lesser gifts to several other Oxford colleges and religious institutions outside Oxford. Numbered among his books were historical works, including Bede's *De Gestis Anglorum*, Henry of Huntingdon's *De Historia Anglorum*, and Ailred of Rievaulx's *Liber de Genealogia regum Anglorum*, and several saints' lives, including two lives of Thomas Becket. But questions remain. Does the annotator refer to all or part of the particular compilation of works in BL Cotton Julius B.iii? Does he refer to authorship and revision as well as compilation? Does he include the much altered *Brut* text and its continuation? How should one account for Lambeth Palace 99, which was the source for BL Cotton Julius B.iii? Without corroborating evidence, the attribution to Bishop Rede must remain possible but not proven.

The Second Version of the Latin Brut

The second version includes the eleven texts listed by Kingsford but rejected by Brie and questioned by Kennedy, with the addition of two subsequently identified texts. Both Kennedy and Kingsford are partially correct: as the former suspected, this is not a simple translation from an English *Brut* but is a compilation; Kingsford, though, whose primary interest was in the later section of the text, is also correct in saying that that part is derived from an English *Brut*. Kingsford also noted that there was much textual variation in

---

[107] For Rede's career and books, see A. B. Emden, *A Biographical Register of the University of Oxford to A.D. 1500*, 3 vols. (Oxford, 1957–1959), 3: 1556–60. Emden accepts the evidence of the note on pp. 1556 and 1560.

the manuscripts and suggested that this might be due in part to independent translation from the English texts.

In its complete form, the second version covers the period from Albina to the murder of James I of Scotland in 1437. As we have seen, Kingsford divides the texts of the second version into two main classes, depending on whether they contain a brief or a full account of the reign of Henry V. Manuscripts containing the brief account are Bodleian Rawlinson C.398 (except for the battle of Agincourt, which is of the full account type), BL Cotton Domitian iv, BL Harley 3906 (with a continuation to 1456), College of Arms Arundel 5 (with a continuation to 1471), and Bodleian Rawlinson B.195 (sixteenth century). The full account is found in MSS. BL Lansdowne 212, St. John's College, Oxford, 78, Bodleian Rawlinson B.169, and BL Harley 3884 (the *Brut* narrative from 1415 to 1437, with a continuation from 1445 to 1455).[108] The text found in Bodleian Rawlinson C.234 (the so-called *Godstow Chronicle*, imperfect at both beginning and end) is similar to that in BL Cotton Domitian iv but contains the full account for 1415 to 1421. Kingsford notes distinctive peculiarities in the final part of the text of Bodleian Rawlinson B.147, but it appears to be a variant of the second version rather than a separate version. The text of Corpus Christi College, Cambridge, 311 can be assigned to the longer class, while that of Gonville and Caius College, Cambridge, 72 remains to be assigned to one or the other class.[109]

As mentioned above, the Albina prologue is interpolated from this version in BL MS. Cotton Galba E.vii, a text of the *Eulogium Historiarum*.[110] The historical compilation in Huntington MS. HM 19960 completes its narrative with material from the second version, ending in 1437 with the murder of James I.[111]

The second version of the Latin *Brut* appears to be a deliberate and sophisticated compilation whose purpose was to improve upon the historical narrative presented in the English *Brut* to 1437 (the PV–1437:A and the corresponding part of the PV–1437/1461). The Latin text replaces, adopts,

---

[108] See Kingsford, *English Historical Literature*, pp. 310–11.

[109] See Montague Rhodes James, *A Descriptive Catalogue of the Manuscripts in the Library of Corpus Christi College, Cambridge*, 2 vols. (Cambridge, 1912), 2: 111–12, and *A Descriptive Catalogue of the Manuscripts in the Library of Gonville and Caius College*, 2 vols. (Cambridge, 1907, 1908), 1: 65–66.

[110] Printed in Haydon, ed. *Eulogium Historiarum*, 2: 216–18.

[111] See Dutschke, *Guide*, 2: 618–20.

or supplements at will the material found in the English text, using a variety of sources while generally following the outline of the English *Brut*. A fuller and more detailed analysis than is possible here is required to establish the identities and range of the sources; what follows should be regarded as a preliminary and provisional account of the text.

Some of the Latin texts have a heading similar to that found in the English PV–1437:B, for example:

> Nova cronica de gestis regum Anglorum cum aliis incedenciis rerum notabilium et mirabilium eorum temporibus contingencium a primo rege Bruto usque ad annum XIIII regis Henrici sexti sub compendio congesta. [CCCC 311: James, *Descriptive Catalogue... Corpus Christi College*, 2: 111]

> Noua Cronica de gestis regum Anglorum a primo rege Bruto usque ad annum xiiij regis Henrici sexti sub quodam compendio compilata. [Bodl. Rawlinson C.398]

Corpus Christi College, Cambridge, MS. 311 and Bodleian MS. Rawlinson B.169 continue with a short introduction, beginning "Britannia que nunc Anglia dicitur," again corresponding to the English PV–1437:B.

The first section of the text proper is the Albina prologue, apparently taken from the corresponding text in the first version of the Latin *Brut* (or perhaps from a text of the *Eulogium Historiarum* in which it occurred as an interpolation), beginning "Anno a creacione Mundi III^m nongentesimo erat in grecia Rex potentissimus super ceteros Reges" (Gonville and Caius Coll. 72: James, *Descriptive Catalogue... Gonville and Caius College*, 1: 65).

The succeeding narrative opens with a short genealogy from Jupiter and Juno to Brutus (descended from the union of Jupiter and Electra); this corresponds to part of the genealogy from Noah to Brutus represented in the English text of Bodleian MS. Lyell 34 (*"Davies's" Chronicle*) and National Library of Wales MS. 21608D but has been improved by comparison with some other text, possibly the *Eulogium Historiarum*.[112]

The immediately following narrative, from Brutus to Cadwallader, is mainly based on Geoffrey of Monmouth's *Historia Regum Britannie*, with which there are frequent verbal correspondences. However, additional material shows that the compiler either supplemented Geoffrey from other

---

[112] See Haydon, ed. *Eulogium Historiarum*, 2: 203–205.

sources (such as Higden's *Polychronicon*, itself indebted to Geoffrey for early British history), or used an intermediate chronicle that had already done so. Gildas and William of Malmesbury are cited by name. There are also correspondences with the English PV–1437/61, such as the arrival in England of Joseph of Arimathea with two vials of Christ's blood and his establishment of a church at Glastonbury, where he is buried. Considerable abbreviation also occurs: for example, Merlin's prophecies are omitted and the reign of Arthur is recounted in one short chapter.

As in the English PV–1422:A, the PV–1437:A, and the PV–1437/61 (as represented by Bodleian MS. Lyell 34), the Cadwallader episode is followed by a lengthy account of the kingdoms of the heptarchy.

The following narrative, from Alfred to a point near the end of the reign of Edward III, is largely extracted from the corresponding narrative found in those texts of the AB version of the *Polychronicon* that append to Higden's work a continuation to 1377, combined with material from the English PV–1437:A.[113] The compiler appears to have also used other sources, including the *Eulogium Historiarum*, from which he probably took, for example, William the Conqueror's dream concerning the foundation of Battle Abbey, Becket's vision of the ampulla containing the consecration oil (related under the reign of Henry II), and the poisoning of King John by a monk of Swineshead. The reigns of Henry III, Edward I, and Edward II are relatively brief, as they are in the English PV–1422:A and some texts of the PV–1437:A. The last recorded event taken from the *Polychronicon* continuation is the creation of Richard of Bordeaux as prince of Wales, duke of Cornwall, and earl of Chester; unfortunately, the compiler has moved this notice forward to a point before the record of the death of Edward, prince of Wales. The reign of Edward III closes with a notice of Wyclif and his followers, taken from the continuation, an account of Edward's wife Philippa and their children, and a note of the king's death.

---

[113] See John Taylor, *The 'Universal Chronicle' of Ranulf Higden* (Oxford, 1966), pp. 98–100 (on the almost seventy copies of the AB version), 118–19 and 178–81 (on the compilation of the continuation). Two forms of the continuation are printed in Lumby, ed., *Polychronicon*, 8: 407–28 (from Gonville and Caius College, Cambridge, MS. 82), and Thomas Hog, ed., *Adam Murimuthensis Chronica Sui Temporis... cum eorundem Continuatione (ad M.CCC.LXXX) a Quodam Anonymo* (1846; rpt. Vaduz, 1964), pp. 174–227 (pp. 171–73 represent Higden's text). For an example of the combination of texts, see the passage quoted from the English translation of the Latin text on p. 306 below, where the account of the battle of Halidon Hill is based on the *Brut* while the following notice of the Holy Roman Emperor comes from the *Polychronicon*.

The final section of narrative, from the accession of Richard II to the death of James I in 1437, is closely associated with the English PV–1437:A, probably in some form that underlies the PV–1437/61 as exemplified by *"Davies's" Chronicle*.[114] The Latin text with the fuller account of the reign of Henry V (the briefer account is seemingly a secondary development) is based on the English text but abbreviates it considerably to the year 1416, after which abbreviation decreases though it does not cease. In the reign of Richard II the abdication speeches and references to the coronation ampulla do not appear. Some minor additions are also made that are not always accurate; for example, the conclusion of the text names the murderer of James I as William (rather than the correct Robert) Graham.

In Bodleian MS. Rawlinson C.398, a Latin text, and Columbia MS. Plimpton 261, an English PV–1437:B text translated from the Latin (see below and item 174), the chronicle is attributed to a Richard Rede. Rede may have been either the compiler or just the scribe of the former manuscript, whose name was then taken to be that of the compiler by the English translator and thus introduced into the latter manuscript. The identity of the surname with that of William Rede, who is associated with the unrelated first version of the Latin *Brut*, is probably coincidental.

The precise relationship of the second version of the Latin *Brut* to the English PV–1422:A, PV–1437:A, and PV–1437/61 remains problematical. The final portion of the Latin text seems to be clearly based on the English text to 1437. But the opening words of the Albina prologue and the presence in the section abstracted from the *Polychronicon* of all the additional material from that work found in the English texts, together with the extended account of the heptarchy, might suggest that the Latin text formed the source for those additions. It is more likely, however, that the compiler of the Latin text used an English text as a template to guide his selection of material from the *Polychronicon* and, when he came across passages borrowed from that source in the English text, he included them as a matter of course, as well as the account of the heptarchy.

The English PV–1437:B is a translation of a text from the second class of the Latin *Brut* and thus includes the longer account of the reign of Henry V.[115]

---

[114] See Kingsford, *English Historical Literature*, pp. 127–28.

[115] For further comments on the source of the English translation, see pp. 305–306. Kennedy slips in saying that the translation is from the shorter type (*Manual*, p. 2639).

INTRODUCTION 47

The Third Version of the Latin Brut

The final "version" consists of a short narrative in BL MS. Harley 941, which contains on fols. 1–3v a unique translation into Latin of the prose adaptation of the Albina prologue from the Anglo-Norman Long Version of the *Brut*.[116] It seems quite likely that this was a one-time exercise, rather than an extract from some longer translation of the *Brut* into Latin.

V. The Middle English *Brut*

The preeminent translation into English of the Anglo-Norman Long Version with the long continuation was made at some point between 1333, the ending point of the basic text, and ca. 1400, the probable date of the earliest English manuscripts. Brie chose the middle years of 1350 to 1380 as the most likely period of translation, while Kingsford dated it "[t]owards the end of the fourteenth century," and the present writer has used the date "about 1400."[117] A date late in the fourteenth century seems preferable for several reasons: (1) a number of the Anglo-Norman manuscripts of the Long Version belong to the late fourteenth and early fifteenth centuries, suggesting that the French text remained popular at that time; (2) the earliest extant manuscripts in English were written ca. 1400 and are still very close to their French original (though it is clear that there were texts antedating those that survive); (3) the dialect of the earliest surviving texts is still relatively pure; (4) the work may be seen as analogous to what Ralph Hanna has characterized as "the Ricardian translation project."[118] Accordingly, some point be-

---

[116] See Brie, *Geschichte und Quellen*, p. 130; Carley and Crick, "Constructing Albion's Past," pp. 48, 49–50.

[117] *Geschichte und Quellen*, p. 54; *English Historical Literature*, p. 114; and "Historical Prose," p. 210, respectively. A recent, general account of the English *Brut* and of selected episodes therein is found in Robert A. Albano, *Middle English Historiography* (New York, 1993), pp. 37–89. Extracts of historical and social interest, often with commentary, are given *passim* in Basil Cottle, *The Triumph of English 1350–1400* (London, 1969).

[118] See Ralph Hanna III, "Henry Daniel's *Liber Uricrisiarum* (Excerpt)," in *Popular and Practical Science of Medieval England*, ed. Lister M. Matheson (East Lansing, 1994), pp. 185–86. Beside the *Liber Uricrisiarum*, translated by Henry Daniel between 1376 and 1379, Hanna notes the translation of Macer's *De virtutibus herbarum* by John Lelamour, a Hereford schoolmaster, in 1373 and also adduces Trevisa, Chaucer, and the Wycliffite translators, all from the 1380s and 1390s.

tween 1380 and 1400 would, perhaps, be a safe date for the original English translation of the *Brut*.

The translator is anonymous, but the dialects of the earliest manuscripts and relict forms in later ones suggest that he came from Herefordshire.[119] The ensuing fifteenth-century textual development of the work and the standardized language of many texts show increasing ties with London and its environs. The first continuation, to 1377, is associated with the work of Westminster chroniclers, and subsequent continuations are closely linked with the civic chronicles of London. Their contents often reveal a marked interest in metropolitan affairs, which would have appealed to an audience that expanded to include members of the merchant class. The major center of production for both texts and manuscripts was undoubtedly the London area, and the first printed edition, by William Caxton, was published at Westminster.

As we have seen, the numerous surviving manuscripts and texts fall into four broad categories (here designated by the Roman numerals used in the Classification of Texts below) within which many smaller groups can be distinguished:

I. The Common Version, which originally took the narrative to 1333 but to which numerous additions were made, eventually bringing one group (which includes the first of the early printed editions) to the year 1461.
II. The Extended Version, which adds an exordium and includes details taken from the *Short English Metrical Chronicle*.
III. The Abbreviated Version, which is a shortened cross between the Common and Extended Versions.
IV. Peculiar Texts and Versions, which is an amorphous grouping of (1) reworked texts and versions of all or part of a *Brut* text, sometimes abbreviated or expanded by interpolations from other works and sometimes containing continuations; (2) material of an individual nature forming a section of a longer *Brut* text that belongs to an otherwise distinct group; (3) appendages to some work other than the *Brut*; (4) very brief works that have used the *Brut* as a primary source; (5) the second translation of the Anglo-Norman *Brut*, made in 1435 by John

---

[119] See, for example, Bodleian Rawlinson B.171, one of the earliest manuscripts (South-West Herefordshire), and the later Bodleian Rawlinson B.173 (West Herefordshire), CUL Kk.1.12 (Central Herefordshire), and Bodleian Bodley 840 (Essex, with Herefordshire relicts).

Mandeville, rector of Burnham Thorpe in Norfolk, contained in two manuscripts.

A small number of incomplete or fragmentary texts have proved resistant to classification and are grouped below as "Unclassified Texts" (V). Additions made subsequent to the first printed edition (derived from the Common Version) allow the early printed editions to be identified as belonging to two types (VI).

VI. Methods of Classification

The system of classification employed in the present study is partially indebted to that used by Friedrich W. D. Brie in his *Geschichte und Quellen der mittelenglischen Prosachronik The Brute of England oder The Chronicles of England* (1905), but represents a considerable expansion and refinement of that work. Although a pioneering effort, Brie's study contains many flaws and errors.[120] He knew only a limited number of manuscripts and was unable to examine all of these personally. His method of classifying manuscripts almost exclusively by the type of continuations they contained, seldom taking account of textual differences, prevented him from identifying a number of groups and resulted in oversimplified views of the complex relationships among the texts. Neither the intrusive Cadwallader episode nor Queen Isabella's letter are used as criteria for classification. Furthermore, Brie discounted the many manuscripts of the Extended and Abbreviated Versions of the *Brut* as worthless.

The criteria and factors used in the present classification are several, and classification depends upon a combination of features. The most important are a formal examination of each text to determine its contents and continuations (reflected in the layout of each entry, with additional commentary, if necessary, in the Remarks). This formal analysis is combined with textual comparison of selected test passages that show consistent, definitional variation in particular groups (that is, passages demonstrating that some process of conscious revision has taken place as opposed to simple scribal variation between texts). Textual comparison is also used extensively in the case of texts that are imperfect at either beginning or end. The starting point for all comparisons is the Anglo-Norman Long Version of the *Brut* and the initial translation thereof into English.

---

[120] For detailed criticism, see Matheson, "Historical Prose," pp. 210–12.

The texts of the Middle English Common Version developed primarily through a process of accretion, through the acquisition of certain added sections of text and of continuations, though some groups (for example, the CV–1419 [Leyle]) are distinguished not only by their formal contents but also by their verbal changes. However, the process of accretion does conceal some potential complexities, since apparent additions need not always be *later* accretions. In theory at least, an early type of text might contain an extra feature which, in the normal course of scribal transmission, was omitted from a stage of the copying process and was then naturally absent from all texts descending from that stage. Conversely, as Dobson has remarked with regard to the texts of the *Ancrene Wisse*:

> When the case is one of additions to a basic text... it must be apparent that the author of the additions may well have taken steps to circulate them to the known owners of copies; and scribes or owners who became aware that additions were in existence would be likely to seek to acquire copies. In the result the same additions might be inserted into manuscripts that were otherwise not at all closely related; and the affiliations of the manuscripts in the added portions may be quite different from those in the basic text.[121]

Given the large number of primary and related texts in circulation, the situation of the *Brut* is not quite as contained as in the case of the *Ancrene Wisse*. I have tried to exercise sufficient caution by regularly using the textual collation of selected portions of text as a control and double-check, especially in the case of doubtful or complex relationships where scribal cross-collation has apparently occurred. In general, however, in the case of the absence of a recognized later accretion to the basic text where there is no contrary or conflicting evidence, I have assumed that the additional matter was not present in the exemplar of a specified group of texts.

The classification of texts of the Extended and Abbreviated Versions depends primarily on which of four recensions of the exordium is present, on distinctive verbal differences among the several textual groups, and, for some Abbreviated Version groups, on the handling of the chapter that includes the battle of Halidon Hill in 1333.

---

[121] E. J. Dobson, "The Affiliations of the Manuscripts of *Ancrene Wisse*," in *English and Medieval Studies Presented to J. R. R. Tolkien*, ed. Norman Davis and C. L. Wrenn (London, 1962), p. 129.

Texts included under "Peculiar Texts and Versions," whether singletons or members of groups, require detailed examination both of formal contents and continuations and of verbal treatment to determine their likely antecedents and affiliations.

That so many texts of a work that went out of fashion in the sixteenth century are extant implies that an even greater number have not survived, a conclusion that is borne out by textual comparisons. It is rare, though not unknown, that direct links between manuscripts can be established, and each manuscript remains its own cultural artifact and textual witness. In addition, the age of a manuscript cannot be used as an absolutely defining criterion, since a late but accurately copied manuscript may preserve well an early form of the text. Accordingly, assignment to a particular group does not imply total identity among the texts of that group, and some variation and differences must be allowed.

Test Factors and Passages

The following principal test factors were regularly examined and, if appropriate, recorded for texts of the Common Version to serve as the basis for classification of groups and subgroups within the version. Through factor 13, they are listed in the order in which they would appear (if present) in the narrative. Combinations of these factors provide a set of criteria whereby texts have been classified.

1. The heading (if any) and the opening words of the text, whether complete or imperfect.[122]
2. A comparison of the Albina prologue and the Lear story (especially the form of the king's name—"Leyl(e)" instead of "Leir") with the lexically altered texts represented by Glasgow Hunterian 74.[123]

---

[122] The beginning and ending of any table of contents, usually derived from the chapter headings, is also noted. Such tables appear randomly among the Anglo-Norman and English manuscripts and the printed editions. They are of limited classificatory use since they could be generated easily, naturally, and independently, and just as easily omitted. They are, however, of great use in determining or confirming the original ending point of texts that are now imperfect at the end or of texts to which continuations have been subsequently added.

[123] This is the only case in which the form of a proper name has been used as a major distinguishing feature. Especially in the earlier sections of the texts, the manuscript spellings of proper names are highly variable and often idiosyncratic. Standardized forms based either on the CV-1333 or on commonly found spellings are adopted conventionally

3. The presence or absence of the Cadwallader episode, which does not occur in the Anglo-Norman Long Version or in the original English translation. See Appendix 1 below.
4. The presence or absence of Queen Isabella's letter to the citizens of London, which does not occur in the Anglo-Norman Long Version or in the original English translation. See Appendix 2 below.
5. The presence or absence of the intrusive heading to the fifth ward of the battle of Scotland—that is, the fifth division in the battle array of the Scottish army—in the chapter recounting the battle of Halidon Hill ("5w" heading; cf. Brie 284/28, and see pp. 86–87). Where the wording of the heading differs significantly from that of the standard heading, then it is recorded in the description of the text.
6. The final words of the account of the battle of Halidon Hill, which is the conclusion of the Anglo-Norman Long Version and the original English translation (cf. Brie 286/8–9).
7. The changeover between the battle of Halidon Hill and any continuation to 1377, which can be of a long or a short type.[124]
8. The presence or absence of the poem on the battle of Halidon Hill, found only in John Mandeville's translation of the Anglo-Norman Long Version (Brie 287–89).
9. The presence or absence of the chapter describing the character of Edward III, which occurs sporadically after the continuation to 1377 (Brie 333–34; see p. 92).
10. The presence (if any) of a continuation from 1377 to 1419 (Brie 335–91) and to which of two major types it belongs, depending on the closing words of the continuation, whether "and manfully countered with our English men" or "in rule and governance."
11. The presence (if any) of a continuation beyond 1419 that includes John Page's poem on the siege of Rouen (cf. Brie 394–439) and to which of three recensions it belongs.

---

below: thus, Coryn, Ebrak, Blegabred (one of the thirty-three kings), Lud, Engist (the modern Hengest or Hengist), Vortiger, Cadwallader—but (under Shakespeare's influence) Lear rather than "Leir." As noted above, the Latinized forms Albina and Brutus are generally adopted instead of the Anglo-Norman and Middle English "Albine" and "Brut(e)" respectively. The modern form Isabella (Edward II's queen) is used in preference to manuscript "Isabel," and other modern forms are used for names that remain current, e.g., Alfred for "Alurede," William the Conqueror for "William Bastard," Henry for "Harri," and so on.

[124] The long continuation to 1377 is printed in Brie 291–332.

12. The presence (if any) of a continuation from 1419 to 1461 (Brie 491–533).
13. The concluding words of the text, whether complete or imperfect, and any colophon.
14. Any unique contributions, continuations, or other distinguishing textual features.
15. The comparison of selected passages of text, as deemed appropriate, both within and outside putative groups.
16. Any changes of hand or ink at potentially significant points in the text, for example, at the onset of a continuation.
17. Any spaces or blank leaves at potentially significant points in the text, especially at the onset of a continuation.

Many of the factors significant for the Common Version are not useful for the Extended and Abbreviated Versions; for example, the Cadwallader episode and Queen Isabella's letter are consistently present in complete texts of the Extended and Abbreviated Versions. Nevertheless, as a matter of course, the seventeen factors above should be checked in the preliminary examination of any unclassified *Brut* text. The main additional test factors for the identification and classification of the Extended and Abbreviated Versions and their groups are:

1. The presence of one of several distinctive headings to the whole work.
2. The presence of one of four distinctive recensions of the added exordium and prologue heading that characterize these versions. See Appendix 3 below for the most common of these recensions.
3. The opening words of the text proper, whether complete or imperfect.
4. The distinctive treatments of the description of the giants in the Albina narrative, which incorporates details derived from the *Short English Metrical Chronicle*, especially the inclusion of extra named giants and the giants' sizes ("first giants passage"; see pp. 184–85, 237–38).
5. The distinctive treatments of the description of the giants' mode of existence in Diana's prophecy to Brutus ("second giants passage"; see pp. 185–86).
6. The designation of Coryn's beloved as his "paramour" or his "leman," and whether her name is given ("Coryn's paramour passage"; see pp. 186–87).
7. The omission of the names of King Ebrak's numerous sons and daughters (Brie 15/15–24).

8. The treatment of the chapter recounting the reigns of thirty-three kings of Britain (Brie 30/20–31/13), specifically (a) the type of linkage ("after him" type, enumeration, or simple listing); (b) abbreviation, including the loss of some names; and (c) the presence or absence of an intrusive Latin tag after King Blegabred (see p. 176).
9. The distinctive wording of the chapter on King Lud's building projects in London and the change of the city's name ("Lud passage"; cf. Brie 31/18–24, and see pp. 238–40).
10. The wording of the passage recounting the establishment of Engist's heptarchy (Brie 54/33–55/14), including confusions between "Winchester"/"Worcester" and "Derbyshire"/"Devonshire."
11. The substitution (if any) of a single chapter for the four chapters recounting the reign of King Arthur's successor, Constantine.
12. The omission of material after the death of King Arthur, whereby he is succeeded by Conan rather than Constantine.
13. An examination of the chapter on the battle of Halidon Hill and of the surrounding chapters, specifically to determine (a) the number of wards of the Scottish army that are listed and (b) the omission or reworking of material around the battle of Halidon Hill, including loss of the entire narrative on the battle.
14. The end of the continuation to 1419, such as the concluding words "in rule and good governance. (Deo gracias.)," or some variation thereof that includes "good."
15. The presence (if any) and type of a continuation beyond 1419.
16. The concluding words of the text, whether complete or imperfect, and any colophon.
17. Any unique contributions, continuations, or other distinguishing textual features.
18. The comparison of selected passages of text, as deemed appropriate, both within and outside putative groups.
19. Any changes of hand or ink at potentially significant points in the text, for example, at the onset of a continuation.
20. Any spaces or blank leaves at potentially significant points in the text, especially at the onset of a continuation.

The two sets of test factors listed above were also applied to texts that have been classified as Peculiar Texts and Versions, though by their nature such texts usually require additional individualized criteria and commentary.

INTRODUCTION 55

Layout and Style of Entries

Although there are 181 manuscripts and thirteen early printed editions, the Classification of Texts contains 215 items due to the not uncommon scribal practice of combining texts. At its simplest level, such combination consisted of the addition to an existing text of a continuation taken from another exemplar by a different scribe. The resulting text could then be copied as a whole by a single scribe. At more complex levels, texts from several exemplars could be combined to form a unified text, or additions from another *Brut* text or from some unrelated historical work could be made to or interpolated into a copy as it was being compiled. Where a manuscript can be subdivided into distinct textual items—for example, from the evidence of the hands or the cobbling together of texts from otherwise distinct groups—such items have been distinguished by (1), (2), etc., immediately following the manuscript shelfmarks in the Classification of Texts below. Accordingly, different sections of one manuscript can appear as independent entries (with appropriate cross-references to the other items) in different groups.

Typically, the description of each group begins with a list of its manuscripts and any subgroups, usually accompanied by some contextual comments on the group's place in the general scheme of development. Individual entries on each of the items then record the formal features—heading, opening words, contents, omissions, changeovers between continuations, concluding words—that form the essential basis for classification. Where appropriate, an optional Remarks section comments on these textual features and on physical aspects of the manuscript that bear on classification, including explanations of details marked in the formal description by a parenthetical "(but) see below." In some instances, these Remarks quote sections of text that support the classification. Also included under Remarks (or notes thereto) is information on other contents of the manuscript, early ownership and names, the dialect of the text, and further points of interest specific to the item under discussion. Where no Remarks are given for an individual item, the omission reflects a judgment on my part that further available evidence, if any, is not illuminating for the immediate purposes of this study.

Again where appropriate or necessary, groups and subgroups of individual entries are followed by a Remarks section on the group or subgroup, which contains comments on the textual character and contents of the group as a whole and on its internal and external affiliations and relationships, sometimes supported by textual comparisons. (For minor modifications in this general procedure for the Extended and Abbreviated Versions, see pp. 173–74.) In the case of unique texts included under Peculiar Texts and Versions, commentary on the wider affiliations of the texts has been placed under the item-specific Remarks.

For ease of reference in a system as complex and lengthy as that which follows, notes to each of the entries (including the entry-specific Remarks) are placed at the end of the entry; similarly, notes to the group-specific Remarks are placed directly after those Remarks. Readers who are not specialists in manuscript or medieval chronicle studies may wish to glance through the introductory and Remarks sections where they exist (that is, for the majority of versions, groups, and subgroups, and many of the individual items) before plunging into the more formal textual descriptions, especially when there are more than three or four descriptions in a row.

Page and line references to Brie's standard edition of the *Brut* (and occasionally to other relevant editions) occur liberally throughout this study to aid comparison with the modern edition. Accordingly, those readers who wish to pursue textual details and comparisons in depth should, if possible, use Brie as a *vade mecum*.

In all quotations from manuscripts and texts (except those cited from modern editions), word division, capitalization, and (light) punctuation are editorial. Abbreviations and contractions have been silently expanded according to conventional or manuscript-local use; when in doubt, possibly otiose marks and curls have been ignored. Word-initial *ff* has been capitalized as *F* in proper names and at the beginning of sentences; *ʒ* has been resolved as *ʒ* or as *z* as etymologically necessary. Chapter headings have been set off from their surrounding text. Editorial emendations, comments, and notes of scribal alterations and insertions are enclosed in square brackets. Missing or illegible letters or words are similarly noted; if one or two letters only are concerned, this is indicated by [.] or [. .], while anything longer is indicated by [. . .].

Appendix 1:
The Text of the Cadwallader Episode

The intrusive Cadwallader episode regularly appears in texts other than those representing or directly derived from the original translation from the Anglo-Norman Long Version. When present, it occurs between two chapters. The first recounts how King Oswold of Northumberland was killed by King Cadwalyn of Leicester and his brother-in-law Peanda and how Oswy, Oswold's brother, killed Peanda, became king of Northumberland, and then killed Oswyn, Peanda's cousin, who was buried at Tynemouth (Brie 101/4–102/20). The next chapter in the CV–1333 (and directly derivative texts) describes how King Offa (or "Ossa"), Oswold's brother, conquered the continually warring minor kings of England and thus became their overlord; it ends by recording how certain monastic chronicles were written that later came into the possession of King Alfred (Brie 102/21–103/8).

The following text of the Cadwallader episode is edited from Staats- und Universitätsbibliothek Hamburg MS. 98 in scrin (designated H below), a text of the Common Version to 1377 with full continuation, Stage 2, which is possibly the earliest group to include the interpolated material (see pp. 92–93). However, a comparison with the source in Geoffrey of Monmouth's *Historia* and with other *Brut* texts shows that the Hamburg text contains some small modifications in wording that must be subsequent to the original form of the episode. Thus the date of Cadwallader's death has fallen away, and some phrases from the beginning of the following chapter are anticipated in the opening lines (cf. Brie 102/26–28) and then reworked slightly for their reappearance. Accordingly, the text has been compared with that found in Columbia University Library MS. Plimpton 262 (designated P below), which belongs to one group of the mainstream Common Version that ends in 1419 (see pp. 98–100). It represents well forms of the heading and text that are commonly found in the extant manuscripts, and selected variant readings of significant or interesting material difference are recorded below. Significantly, the Hamburg and Plimpton texts (like a number of other texts) do not accord separate chapter numbers to the intrusive episode;

the first, preceding chapter described above is numbered "Capitulo Centesimo Primo" while the second, succeeding chapter is numbered "Capitulo Centesimo ijᵒ" or "Capitulo C ijᵒ." In later texts, the episode is more fully assimilated by according its chapters separate numbers.

[p. 111] How Cadwaladre regned after his fader Cadwaleyn and how for þe grete pestylence derthe of vitaylles and hunger he wente to the kyng of Litel Britaigne & after to Rome & þere deide.

[How kyng Cadwaladre þat was Cadwaleyns sone regnede aftere his fadere & was þe last kyng of Brittons. P]

After þe deth of Cadwaleyn regned his sone Cadwaladre wel & nobly and his moder was [p. 112] the suster of þe kyng Peanda & whan he had regned xij ȝeer he fel in a grete sykenesse & þan was þere so grete discord bytwene the lordes of þe londe þat euery werred vpon other and he þat was þe strenger & more myghty toke þe londe & kyngdome fro hym þat was þe more feble [and . . . feble *om*. P].

And ȝit in þat tyme þer felle so grette derthe [and scarcete *add*. P] of corne and of other vitailles in þis lond þat a man myghte wel gone thre or foure dayes fro toun to toun þat he shulde not fynde to bigge of vitaille for gold [ne for gold *del*. H] ne for siluer breed wyne ne none other vitaille wherwith man myght lyuen but only [þe peple leuede *add*. P] by rootes of herbes ffor other lyvynge hadde þei none so moche was the londe bareyne and failled al aboute and of fysshe & wylde bestes and of all oþer thinges so þat of þis mysauenture come so grete mortalite and pestilence among þe peple by þe corrupcioun of þe eyre þat þe peple lyvinge sufficed not to burye the dede ffor þei deyed so sodenly bothe olde & ȝonge [olde & ȝonge *om*. P] grete & smale lord and servaunt etynge goynge and spekynge so þat neuere was herd of more sodeyn deth among þe peple ffor he þat wende to burye þe dede body with þe same dede body was buryed.

Thei þat myghte fleen fledden & leften her londes houses and tenementz [fledden and hire londes and houses P] as wel for þe grete hunger and derthe [hunger derth and scarcete P] of corn as for the horrible mortalite & pestilence in the londe and wenten into othre landes forto sauen her lyues and lefte þe londe al deserte and waast so þat þer was not left eny man to trauayle and tilye þe londe ne to eren ne sowen so þat þe londe was bareyne of tyliers and of cornes.

And þis mysauenture durede xj ȝeer and more þat [p. 113] no man myghte eren ne sowe.

How Cadwaladre wente out of Engelond [þis lond P] into Litel Brytaigne.

Cadwaladre sawh the grete hunger and mortalite [hunger mortalite and pestilence P] and þe lande al pouere & failynge cornes & other vitailles & his folk perisshed and sawh þe moste partye of his land al wasted & voyde of peple. He apparaylled him and his folk þat were lefte on lyue and passed ouer into Britaygne with a litel navye vnto kyng Aleyn þat was his cosyn whom his fader had moche loued [in his tyme *add*. P].

And as þey seyled in the see he made grete lamentacioun and alle they þat were with hym sayenge "Dedisti nos domine tanquam oues escarum et in gentibus dispersisti nos." And þan bygan Cadwaladre to compleyne him to his folk pitously and saide "Allas" seide he "to vs wrecches or caytyues fforwhy for oure grete synnes of þe whiche we wolden not amenden vs while we hadde space of repentaunce is now comen vpon vs þis mysauenture whiche chasith vs out of oure reawme and propir londe [soyle P]. Fro and out of whiche londe somtyme Romayns Scottes ne Saxons ne Danes ne myght not exilen vs. But what availleþ it now to vs þat byfore tymes oftesithes haue geten & wonne manye oþere regiouns and londes sithen it is not the wille of God þat we abide & dwelle in oure owne lond. God þat is verray iuge þat alle thynges knoweth byfore þey be done or made he seeth þat we wolde not cessen of oure synnes and þat oure enemyes myght not vs ne oure lynage out of oure rewme exilen he wolde þat we amende vs of oure folyes and þat we seen oure owne propre defautes. Þerfore [p. 114] haþ he shewed to vs his wratthe and wole chasticen vs of oure mysdedes sithen þat he dooth vs withoute bataille & strengthe of oure enemyes by grete companyes & copyouse multitude of peple [& copyouse... peple *om*. P] wrecchedly to leuen oure rewme and propre soyle [londe P].

"Turne ageyn ȝe [þe P] Romaynes [*phrase repeated* P]; turne ageyn ȝe [þe P] Scottes; turne ageyn ȝe [þe P] Saxons; turne ageyn ȝe Frensshe men [þe Frauncoys P]—now sheweþ to ȝow Brytaigne al deserte the whiche ȝoure power myght neuere make deserte [the... deserte *om*. P]. Ne ȝoure power now haþ not putte vs in exile but only þe power of þe kyng almyghti whom we haue ofte offended by oure folyes þe whiche we wolde not leuen til he had chasticed vs by his dyvyne power."

Among þe wordes & lamentaciouns þat kyng Cadwaladre made to his folk they arryued in Lytel Britaigne and come to kyng Aleyn byforesaid and þe kyng recyued hym wiþ grete ioye and dide hym be serued wonder nobly and þere he dwellid longe tyme after.

Þe Englisshe peple þat were lefte alyue and were escaped þe grete hunger and pestilence [mortalite P] lyueden in þe beste wise þat þei myghten and moche peple sprong of hem and þei senten to Saxoun where þey were born to here frendes forto haue men wommen & children to restore þe citees and oþre townes þat were al desolate & [desolate & *om.* P] voyde of peple and forto laboren and [trauaylen and *add.* P] tilyen þe erthe.

Whan þe Saxons hadde herde þat they come wonder thikke with many companyes and grete multitude of peple hadde þis tithinge þei comen into þis lande wonder thik in grete companyes and laggede [*sic*] and herberwed hem in þe cuntree al aboute where þey wolde ffor þei fond no man hem to lette [ne withstonde *add.* P] and so thei [woxen and *add.* P] multiplyed gretly and vsed þe customes [p. 115] of þe cuntrees wherof þei were comen and þe lawes and þe langages of her owne land and þei chaunged þe names of citees townes castelles and borghes and ȝaue hem names & called hem as þei be now called and þei helden the countees baronages lordshipes and cuntrees in manere as þe Britouns byfore tyme hadden compased hem.

And am[on]g oþer companyes grete þat come fro Germanye into þis lond cam þe noble queene þat was called Sexburga with men and wommen wiþoute noumbre and she arryued in þe counte of Northumberlond and toke þe lond of [fro P] Albanye into Cornewayle for hir and for hir folk ffor þere was noon þat myght lette hem for al was desolate & voyde of folk but it were a fewe pouere Brytouns þat leften [were lefte P] in mountaynes & wodes [& wodes *om.* P] vnto þat tyme.

And fro þat tyme forth losten Brytouns þis lond [reame P] for alle dayes and þe Englisshe bygonne to regne and departed þe land bytwene hem and they maden many kynges aboute by dyuers parties in þe londe as here ben dyvised: þat is to say the [deuysede and P] ferste of Westsex; the secounde of Merchenriche; thridde of Estangle; the iiij^{te} of Kent; the v^{te} of Southsex and alle thise kynges regnede [regnedne H] in this londe after þat Cadwaladre passed out of þis lande & dwelled in Lytel Brytaigne with kyng Aleyn his cosyn and trewe frend.

And whan he had longe dwelled þere and hadde knowynge þat þe mortalite [and pestilence *add.* P] was ouerpassed and þat þe land was replenysshed & ful [& ful *om.* P] of alien peple he þoughte forto turne ageyn into his owne lande and prayed kyng Aleyn of socour and helpe þat he myghte be restored to his propre rewme and his firste dignyte. And kyng Aleyn graunted [p. 116] him his prayer.

Than dede he apparaillen hym to take his way and viage into Engelond [this lande P] & prayed God devoutly þat he wolde make to [him (to him P)] demonstacioun ʒif his repeyre into Engelond [his lande P] were plesaunce to him or noght for ageyn þe wille of God he wolde no þing done.

Whan he in þis wise had made devoutly his prayer a voyce fro heuene to him saide þat he [saide and bade him P] leue þat iournay & way into Engelond and þat he goo to þe pope of Rome and counsail þere with him [and counsail...him *om.* P] for it was not þe wille of God þat Brytouns regne more in Engelond [Brutaigne P] [ne (ne P)] neuere recouere þe londe vnto þe tyme þat þe prophecie þat Merlyn saide [saide before P] be fulfilled & þat shulde neuere be vnto þe tyme were come þat þe relykes of his body shulde be broght fro Rome and translated in Brytaigne. And þan whan þe relikes of oþre seintes þat were [haue bene P] hidde for þe persecucioun of þe paynymes shal be founden and openly schewed þan shal þei recouere ferst [recouere *add.* H] her londe þat þei shal haue so longe tyme by þe deserte of her good feith [haue so longe tyme loste thurgh hire desertes P].

Whan Cadwaladre had herd þis answere he meruailled greetly & tolde it to kyng Aleyn al þat he hadde iherd [al...iherd *om.* P]. Than kyng Aleyn sent after þe clergie of his land and diden bryngen forth þe bookes of [and made ham to bringe þe P] stories [and prophecies *add.* P] & serchen forto preuen ʒif it were so as Cadwaladre had seid to him; so þei acorded wiþ the prophecies þat Merlyn & Sibille had seide in her prophecies. And whan kyng Aleyn had knowynge þat the prophecie þat Fescome had prophecied of þe egle and the othere prophecies accorde [acordede P] to þe dyvine answere þat Cadwaladre had herd he counseilled hym [p. 117] to leue his folk and his navie and submitten him to þe disposicioun of God & done all þat the aungel had comaunded hym.

Than Cadwaladre called Ynor [*or* Yuor] his sone and Ynory [*or* Yuory] his cosyn þat was his suster sone and saide to him: "Taketh" seide he "my folk and my navie þat is here al redy and passith into Walys and beth ʒe lordes of Britouns þat no dishonour come to hem by irrupcioun of þe paynyme folk for defaute of lordes."

And so he himself lefte his rewme of Britaigne and his folk for euermore and toke his way to Rome and come [and come *om.* P] to þe pope Surgius whiche dede hym moche worship and so he dede him be confessed of his synnes [Sergious þe whiche worshiped him moche and so he was confessede P] and toke penaunce for his synnes. And he ne hadde not longe tyme soiourned þere þat he ne fil into grete sikenesse and sithen deide and his soule passed to God. Amen. [and he hadde nought longe dwellede þere þat he ne deide þe xij kalendes of May the yere of grace vjC lxxix. P]

Appendix 2:
The Text of Queen Isabella's Letter

The intrusive text of a letter by Queen Isabella to the citizens of London in 1326, with a short narrative frame, is again regularly found in texts other than those representing or descended from the original form of the translation of the Anglo-Norman Long Version, in which it is not found. When it occurs, the letter appears regularly after Brie 236/28 (following Isabella's landing at Harwich), although in Folger Shakespeare Library MS. V.b.106 it appears exceptionally in the following chapter.[125] The text is here printed from Columbia University Library MS. Plimpton 262.

[fol. 83] And þe quene and sire Edwarde here sone sente lettres to þe meyre and the cominalte of London requiryng hem [fol. 83v] þat þey shulde bene helpyng in þe quarel and cause þat þey had begonne þat is to seye to destroye þe traytours of þe reame but none answer was sente ayene. Wherfore þe quene and sire Edwarde hire sone senten anoþer patente letter vndere here seales hangyng the tenure of whiche lettre here folowith in this maner:

"Isabell by the grace of God quene of Engelond ladie of Ireland and countesse of Pountiff and we Edwarde þe eldest sone of þe kyng of Engelond duke of Guyen erle of Chestre and of Pountif and of Monsterell to þe mayer and to alle þe cominalte of þe cite of London senden gretyng. For as moche as we haue before this tyme sente to yow by oure lettres how we be come into this lande with good aray and in good maner for the honoure and profite of holi churche and of our right dere lorde þe kynge and alle þe reame with alle oure myght and poer to kepe and mayntene as we and alle þe good folk of þe saide reame are halden to do and vppon þat we prayed yow þat ye wolde bene helpyng to vs in as moche as ye coulde now in this querell þat is for þe comon profite of alle [the] reame and we haue had into þis tyme non answere of þe saide lettres ne knowe nouȝt your wille in þat partie. Wherfore we sende to yow agayne and praye and charge yow but þat

---

[125] See item 60 below.

ye bene to vs helpyng by alle the wayes that ye may or shall knowen or mowen. For weteth well in certeyn þat we and alle þo þat beth comen with vs into this reame ne thenke not to done if hit like God eny thynge but that shal be for the comon profite of al þe reavme but onely to distroye Hugh Spencer oure enemy ande enemy to alle þe reame as ye wel knowe. Wherfore we prey yow and charge yow in þe feith that ye owith vnto oure lorde þe kyng and to vs and vppon alle that ye shullen forfete ayenste vs that if þe seide Hugh Spencer oure enemye come within youre power þat ye done hym hastely be taken and saufly kept vnto we haue ordeyned of him oure wille and þat ye leue hit not in no maner as ye desire honour and profite of vs alle and of alle þe reavme. Vnderstondyng well þat if ye done our preyer and maundemente we shul þe more be holden to yow and also ye shal gete yow worshep and profite if ye sende vs hastely answer of alle your wille. Yeuen atte Baldok þe vj day of Octobre."

Whiche lettre erly in þe dawnyng of þe day of Seint Denys was takked vppon the nywe crosse in the Chepe and mony copies of þe same lettre were takked vppon wyndowys and dores and vppon other places in the citee that alle men passyng by the way myght seen and reden.

The original letter sent by Isabella to the city of London was written in French.[126] It appears, with introductory material, in the Short Version of the Anglo-Norman *Brut*, which probably used a copy of the original letter.[127] The English translation was made from this source for incorporation in the English *Brut* and the introductory material was reordered to form the narrative frame.[128] At the same time, the interpolator of the letter took the opportunity to correct the date of Isabella's landing at Harwich to September 24, 1326, as reported in the Anglo-Norman Short Version, from the erroneous date of October 10 given in the Long Version and its immediate Middle English descendants (see Brie 236/27–28).

---

[126] A copy of the original is found in Guildhall, London, Roll A 1b, membrane 10(12), and is calendared in Arthur H. Thomas, ed., *Calendar of Plea and Memoranda Rolls Preserved among the Archives of the Corporation of the City of London at the Guildhall, A.D. 1323–64*, vol. 1 (Cambridge, 1926), pp. 41–42; a further letter and reply are also found in the Guildhall roll (p. 42).

[127] The text is printed, with translation, in Childs and Taylor, eds., *Anonimalle Chronicle*, pp. 124–27.

[128] Copies of the letter in the London civic chronicles are derived from the English *Brut*; see Cox, "The French Chronicle of London," p. 204. A Latin translation from the Anglo-Norman *Brut* appears in the *Historia Aurea* and is printed in Galbraith, "Extracts from the Historia Aurea and a French 'Brut' (1317–47)," pp. 211–12.

Appendix 3:
The Text of an Extended Version Exordium
(Group B)

The most immediately distinctive feature of the Extended and Abbreviated Versions, in texts that are complete at the beginning, is an exordium describing the genesis and scope of the *Brut*. This exordium survives in three recensions in the Extended Version and in four in the Abbreviated Version, three of which match those of the Extended Version. Printed here are a representative exordium text, the Albina prologue heading, and the first words of the prologue itself from the most common EV group, the EV–1419:B, whose corresponding AV group is likewise the most numerous group within its version. It should be noted that even within the distinct recensions there are minor variations in layout and wording, details of which will be found in the description of individual texts in the Classification of Texts.

The base text is that of BL MS. Harley 4827, collated selectively with NLW MS. Addit. 442D (EV–1419:B; designated N) and with Bodl. MS. Hatton 50 (AV–1419:B; designated H).

[fol. 1] Here bigynneth a book whiche is callid Brute [of *add.* H] the Cronicles of Englond. Capitulo primo. [Capitulo primo *om.* H]

This boke treteth and telleþ of [all *add.* H] þe kynges & principal lordes þat euer were in þis londe & of auentures & wondreful þinges and [of *add.* H] batailles & [of *add.* H] oþer notable actes werres conquestes þat bifelle in þis [þat N] same [*om.* H] londe. And this lande is [was N, H] callid Bretaigne aftir him þat first enhabited it whos name was callid [*om.* H] Brute; & þis same [*om.* H] Brute biganne first þe citee of Londoun þe whiche he lete calle þat tyme [London & lete call it H] Newe Troye in þe [*om.* N, H] remembraunce of þe olde Troye ffrom whens he & all his lynage weren come. And þis boke made & compiled men of religioun & oþer good clerkes þat wreten [weren N] þat [what N, H] bifell in her tymes [tyme H] and made þerof grete bokes and remembraunce [remembraunsis H] to men þat comen

EXTENDED VERSION EXORDIUM

aftir hem to heere [rede H] and to see what bifell in þe londe afore tyme [tofore hem H] and callid hem Cronycles. And in þis londe haue been from Brute to [vnto N, onto H] kynge Edward þe thridde aftir þe [*om.* N] conquest C xxxij kynges whos lyues and actes ben compiled shortly in þis boke þe whiche conteyneth CC xxxviij [CC xxxxiiij N] chapiters wiþoute þe prothogoll or prolog [þe whiche... prolog *om.* H; The Prologg *add.* H].

The prolog of þis book declareth hou this lande was callid Albioun aftre þe eldest doughtre of þe riall kyng [emperoure H] Dioclisian of Surry the which doughtre was callid Albyne and she wiþ hir xxxij sustres weren exiled oute of her owne londe for grete trespaces þat þei had doon and [thei *add.* H] arrived in this londe casuelly where-in [wher H] was no lyuyng creature but [save H] wilde beestes and hou vnclene spirites lay bi hem and þei brouȝt forth horrible geauntz and Brute killed hem. [Here begynnyth the first chaptir of this book of Croniculis *add.* H]

Somtyme in þe noble land of Surry þer was a man of grete [grete man of H] renoun callid Dioclisian whiche wele and worthily reulid him & all his realme [&... realme *om.* H] so þat almooste [*om.* H] all þe kynges not Cristen to him weren [kyngis abowt hym wer to hym H] contributours and obedient.

Classification of the Texts of the Middle English Brut

Synoptic Inventory of Versions

The following list of versions, groups within versions, and manuscripts of the Middle English prose *Brut* summarizes the findings reported in more detail in the descriptions and classification laid out in the remaining sections of this book. The texts are listed in the order in which they appear in the detailed classification and are prefaced by the item number that they bear there. Where texts have been separated into different items for purposes of classification, the items are indicated by (1), (2), etc., immediately following the shelfmark. Texts that are incomplete at beginning or end are sometimes difficult to classify; such "doubtful" texts are listed immediately after the main group (with associated subgroups) to which they most correspond and thus might belong. Those texts that have proved resistant to classification are listed as Unclassified Texts.

THE COMMON VERSION

CV–1333 The Common Version to 1333

1. Bodleian MS. Rawlinson B.171(1)
2. Bodleian MS. Douce 323
3. Mrs. J. D. Gordan MS. 63
4. Rylands MS. Eng. 103(1)
5. Yale University, Beinecke MS. 494

6. Society of Antiquaries MS. 93
  7. Bodleian MS. Rawlinson C.155
  8. BL MS. Harley 3945
  9. Rylands MS. Eng. 206
  10. NLW MS. Peniarth 398D

CV-1377 The Common Version to 1377

CV-1377 f.c. Stage 1 The Common Version to 1377 with full continuation, Stage 1
  11. Corpus Christi College, Cambridge, MS. 174
  12. Rylands MS. Eng. 102
  13. Free Library of Philadelphia MS. Lewis 238
  14. Rylands MS. Eng. 103(2)
  15. BL MS. Harley 2279
  16. BL MS. Stowe 68

CV-1377 s.c. The Common Version to 1377 with shortened continuation
  17. Bodleian MS. Rawlinson B.171(2)
  18. Lambeth Palace Library MS. 491

CV-1377 f.c. Stage 2 The Common Version to 1377 with full continuation, Stage 2
  19. Staats- und Universitätsbibliothek Hamburg MS. 98 in scrin

CV-1377 f.c. Stage 3 The Common Version to 1377 with full continuation, Stage 3
  20. Princeton University Library, Taylor Medieval MS. 3(1)
  21. National Library of Scotland MS. 6128
  22. BL MS. Harley 266(1)
  23. University of Chicago MS. 253

CV-1419 The Common Version to 1419

CV-1419(men) The Common Version to 1419, ending "and manfully countered with our English men"

CV-1419(men):A The Common Version to 1419, ending "and manfully countered with our English men": Group A

  Subgroup (a)
  24. Peterhouse, Cambridge, MS. 190(1)

25. Sion College MS. L40.2/E 42
26. Columbia University Library MS. Plimpton 262
27. Takamiya MS. 29
28. Lambeth Palace Library MS. 264(1)

Subgroup (b)
29. BL MS. Egerton 650(1)
30. Bodleian MS. Rawlinson B.173(1)
31. Bodleian MS. Rawlinson B.166
32. Pennsylvania State University MS. PS. V–3A(1)

Subgroup (c)
33. Lambeth Palace Library MS. 738

CV–1419(men):B The Common Version to 1419, ending "and manfully countered with our English men": Group B
34. BL MS. Stowe 69
35. BL MS. Additional 33242

CV–1419(r&g) The Common Version to 1419, ending "in rule and governance"

CV–1419(r&g):A The Common Version to 1419, ending "in rule and governance": Group A
36. Cambridge University Library MS. Kk.1.12
37. Longleat House MS. 183A
38. Trinity College, Cambridge, MS. O.10.34
39. BL MS. Harley 2248
40. BL MS. Royal 17.D.xxi
41. Yale University, Beinecke MS. 323
42. Fitzwilliam Museum MS. McClean 186
43. College of Arms MS. Vincent 421
44. Bodleian MS. Rawlinson B.216
45. University of Glasgow, MS. Hunterian 228(1)
46. Harvard University MS. Eng. 587
47. Takamiya MS. 67

Doubtful Manuscripts
48. Bodleian MS. Bodley 231
49. BL MS. Royal 18.B.iii
50. University of California at Berkeley MS. 152
51. BL MS. Additional 26746

52. University of Glasgow, MS. Hunterian 61
53. Rylands MS. Eng. 104
54. Bodleian MS. Douce 290
55. Bibliothèque Royale MS. IV.461

CV–1419(r&g):B The Common Version to 1419, ending "in rule and governance": Group B

Subgroup (a)
56. Bodleian MS. Bodley 840
57. Trinity College, Dublin, MS. 490

Subgroup (b)
58. Heyneman MS.
59. BL MS. Harley 1568
60. Folger Shakespeare Library MS. V.b.106 (725.2)

Subgroup (c)
61. Huntington MS. HM 136(1)

Doubtful Manuscripts
62. Bodleian MS. Rawlinson B.205
63. Cambridge University Library MS. Ee.4.32
64. Trinity College, Cambridge, MS. R.5.43, Part II
65. University of Leicester MS. 47
66. University of Sydney, MS. Nicholson 13
67. Huntington MS. HM 113

CV–1419 (Leyle) The Common Version to 1419, with "Leyle" for Lear
68. University of Glasgow, MS. Hunterian 74(1)
69. Bodleian MS. Rawlinson B.196
70. Lambeth Palace Library MS. 259
71. BL MS. Harley 4930

CV–1419(men/?r&g) The Common Version to 1419, ending in "men" or (?) "in rule and governance"
72. University of Chicago MS. 254(1)

Continuation to a CV–1377 f.c. Stage 3 text from a Common Version text ending in 1419(r&g)
73. Princeton University Library, Taylor Medieval MS. 3(2)

CV–JP The Common Version beyond 1419, including John Page's poem "The Siege of Rouen"

CV–1430 JP:A The Common Version to 1430, including John Page's poem "The Siege of Rouen": Group A
    74. BL MS. Cotton Galba E.viii
    75. BL MS. Harley 2256
    76. Holkham Hall MS. 670
    77. Cambridge University Library MS. Ee.4.31
    78. BL MS. Harley 266(2)

CV–1430 JP:B The Common Version to 1430, including John Page's poem "The Siege of Rouen": Group B
    79. BL MS. Harley 753
    80. Lambeth Palace Library MS. 331
    81. University of Illinois MS. 116(2)

JP:C Manuscripts containing John Page's poem "The Siege of Rouen": Group C
    82. Cambridge University Library MS. Hh.6.9(2)
    83. Trinity College, Cambridge MS. O.9.1(2)
    84. University of Chicago MS. 254(2)

CV–1461 The Common Version to 1461
    85. "The Cronicles of Englond" (Caxton, 1480)
    86. BL MS. Additional 10099
    87. University of Glasgow, MS. Hunterian 74(2)
    88. BL MS. Cotton Claudius A.viii
    89. University of Glasgow, MS. Hunterian 228(2)
    90. Bodleian MS. Rawlinson poet. 32(3)
    91. Lambeth Palace Library MS. 264(2)
    92. Huntington MS. HM 136(2)
    93. Harvard University MS. Eng. 530(2)

Poly. 1461 W.C. Manuscripts containing the *Polychronicon* 1461 continuation and associated with "Warkworth's" *Chronicle*
    94. University of Glasgow, MS. Hunterian 83(2)
    95. Peterhouse, Cambridge, MS. 190(2)
    96. BL MS. Harley 3730(2)

THE EXTENDED VERSION

EV–1377 The Extended Version to 1377

No extant manuscripts; inferred from exordia of surviving texts of the Extended and Abbreviated Versions ending in 1419.

EV–1419 The Extended Version to 1419

EV–1419:A The Extended Version to 1419: Group A
- 97. Rylands MS. Eng. 105
- 98. Harvard University MS. Richardson 35
- 99. BL MS. Harley 24
- 100. BL MS. Additional 12030
- 101. Bodleian MS. Rawlinson B.187
- 102. Takamiya MS. 12
- 103. Bodleian MS. Tanner 188

EV–1419:B The Extended Version to 1419: Group B
- 104. BL MS. Harley 4827
- 105. BL MS. Harley 2182
- 106. Edinburgh University Library MS. 185
- 107. University of Glasgow, MS. Hunterian 230
- 108. Cambridge University Library MS. Additional 2775
- 109. Cambridge University Library MS. Ff.2.26
- 110. Trinity College, Oxford, MS. 5
- 111. BL MS. Additional 24859
- 112. University of Virginia MS. 38–173
- 113. Lincoln Cathedral MS. 98
- 114. National Library of Wales MS. Additional 442D
- 115. Bodleian MS. Rawlinson poet. 32(1)

EV–1419:C The Extended Version to 1419: Group C
- 116. Corpus Christi College, Cambridge, MS. 182
- 117. Trinity College, Cambridge, MS. O.9.1(1)
- 118. Bodleian MS. Laud Misc. 571
- 119. Princeton University Library, Garrett MS. 150
- 120. University of Illinois MS. 116(1)
- 121. Society of Antiquaries MS. 223
- 122. Huntington MS. HM 133

THE ABBREVIATED VERSION

AV–1419 The Abbreviated Version to 1419

AV–1419:A The Abbreviated Version to 1419: Group A

>Subgroup (a)
>123. University of Glasgow, MS. Hunterian 83(1)
>124. BL MS. Harley 3730(1)
>125. Bodleian MS. Digby 185
>
>Subgroup (b)
>126. BL MS. Royal 18.B.iv
>
>Subgroup (c)
>127. BL MS. Royal 18.A.ix
>128. Huntington MS. HM 131

AV–1419:B The Abbreviated Version to 1419: Group B
>129. University of Glasgow, MS. Hunterian 443
>130. BL MS. Harley 1337
>131. Bodleian MS. Hatton 50
>132. BL MS. Harley 6251
>133. BL MS. Stowe 71
>134. Jesus College, Oxford, MS. 5
>135. Bodleian MS. Tanner 11
>136. University of Michigan MS. 225
>137. Alnwick Castle MS. 457A
>138. NLW MS. Peniarth 396D(2)
>139. Bodleian MS. Rawlinson C.901
>140. Bodleian MS. Rawlinson B.190

AV–1419:C The Abbreviated Version to 1419: Group C
>141. Bodleian MS. Ashmole 793
>142. University of Illinois MS. 82(1)

AV–1419:D The Abbreviated Version to 1419: Group D
>143. BL MS. Stowe 70
>144. University College, Oxford, MS. 154
>145. Cambridge University Library MS. Hh.6.9(1)

PECULIAR TEXTS AND VERSIONS

Reworked Texts and Versions

PV–1377/1419(r&g) The Peculiar Version to 1377, with a continuation to 1419 ending "in rule and governance"
    146. Harvard University MS. Eng. 530(1)

PV–1419:A and PV–1451/1460 The Peculiar Version to 1419: Group A and the Peculiar Version to 1451/1460
    147. Cleveland Public Library MS. John G. White Collection W q091.92–C468
    148. Trinity College, Dublin, MS. 489

PV–1419:B The Peculiar Version to 1419: Group B
    149. Rylands MS. Eng. 207

PV–1419:C The Peculiar Version to 1419: Group C
    150. BL MS. Additional 70514

PV–1419(r&g):A The Peculiar Version to 1419, ending "in rule and governance": Group A
    151. Bodleian MS. Laud Misc. 733

PV–1419(r&g):B The Peculiar Version to 1419, ending "in rule and governance": Group B
    152. Bodleian MS. e Musaeo 39

PV–1419(r&g):C The Peculiar Version to 1419, ending "in rule and governance": Group C
    153. Lincoln College, Oxford, MS. Lat. 151

PV–1419(r&g):D The Peculiar Version to 1419, ending "in rule and governance": Group D
    154. Trinity College, Dublin, MS. 5895
    155. BL MS. Harley 7333

PV–1422:A The Peculiar Version to 1422: Group A
    156. Bodleian MS. Laud Misc. 550
    157. College of Arms MS. Arundel 8
    158. Trinity College, Dublin, MS. 506
    159. BL MS. Sloane 2027
    160. Bodleian MS. Rawlinson poet. 32(2)

PV–1437:A and PV–1437/1461 The Peculiar Version to 1437: Group A and the Peculiar Version to 1437, with a continuation to 1461
    161. Nottingham County Council MS. DDFS 3/1
    162. Trinity College, Cambridge, MS. O.11.11
    163. Takamiya MS. 18
    164. Harvard University MS. Eng. 750 (first text)
    165. Harvard University MS. Eng. 750 (second text)
    166. University of Illinois MS. 82(2)
    167. Trinity College, Dublin, MS. 505
    168. Bodleian MS. Lyell 34 (*"Davies's" Chronicle*)
    169. National Library of Wales MS. 21608D

PV–1422:B The Peculiar Version to 1422: Group B
    170. NLW MS. Peniarth 397C
    171. Bodleian MS. Bodley 754

PV–1436:A The Peculiar Version to 1436: Group A
    172. BL MS. Harley 53
    173. Lambeth Palace Library MS. 6

PV–1437:B The Peculiar Version to 1437: Group B
    174. Columbia University Library MS. Plimpton 261
    175. Holkham Hall MS. 669
    176. Bodleian MS. Ashmole 791

PV–1437:C The Peculiar Version to 1437: Group C
    177. Inner Temple Library, Petyt MS. 511, Vol. XI

PV–1479/82 The Peculiar Version to 1479/82
    178. Lambeth Palace Library MS. 84

Sections of Longer *Brut* Texts

PV–1431 and PV–1422:C The Peculiar Version to 1431 and the Peculiar Version to 1422: Group C
    179. BL MS. Egerton 650(2)
    180. Bodleian MS. Rawlinson B.173(2)
    181. Pennsylvania State University MS. PS. V–3A(2)

Very Brief Works Based on the *Brut*

PV–1307 The Peculiar Version to 1307
      182. NLW MS. Peniarth 343A

PV–1400 The Peculiar Version to 1400
      183. Lambeth Palace Library MS. 306

PV–1427 The Peculiar Version to 1427
      184. BL MS. Harley 63
      185. Edinburgh University Library MS. 184
      186. Bibliothèque Nationale MS. fonds anglais 30

Texts Containing Brief King-Lists

PV–1396/1422 The Peculiar Version to 1396, with a further text to 1422
      187. Bodleian MS. Digby 196

PV–1436:B and PV–1475 The Peculiar Version to 1436: Group B and the Peculiar Version to 1475
      188. Cambridge University Library MS. Ff.1.6 (The Findern Manuscript)
      189. Folger Shakespeare Library MS. V.a.198 (1232.3)

Appendages to Other Works

PV–1066 The Peculiar Version to 1066
      190. Mayor's Calendar, City of Bristol Record Office, no. 04720(1)

PV–1419:D The Peculiar Version to 1419: Group D
      191. Cambridge University Library MS. Ll.2.14

PV–1419:E The Peculiar Version to 1419: Group E
      192. Harvard University MS. Eng. 938

PV–1419:F The Peculiar Version to 1419: Group F
      193. Woburn Abbey MS. 181

The Translation Attributed to John Mandeville

JM–1333 Mandeville's Translation of the Anglo-Norman Long Version, with a CV–1419(men) continuation
      194. BL MS. Harley 4690

Mandeville's Translation of the Anglo-Norman Long Version (excerpts)
195. College of Arms MS. Arundel 58

UNCLASSIFIED TEXTS

196. Bibliotheca Bodmeriana, cod. Bodmer 43
197. Lincoln Cathedral MS. 70 (C.5.12)
198. Cambridge University Library MS. Kk.1.3
199. NLW MS. Peniarth 396D(1)
200. Brogyntyn MS. 8 (Lord Harlech; on deposit at NLW)
201. BL MS. Royal 11.B.ix
202. Lehigh University (3 fragments)
203. Geelong Church of England Grammar School MS.

THE EARLY PRINTED EDITIONS

The following list is chronological by date of publication. The texts can, however, be divided into two types; for further discussion see pages 339, 341 below.

[85.] "The Cronicles of Englond." William Caxton, Westminster, June 10, 1480 (STC 9991). Type 1.
204. "The Cronycles of Englond." William Caxton, Westminster, October 8, 1482 (STC 9992). Type 1.
205. "The Croniclis of Englonde with the Frute of Timis." [Schoolmaster-Printer,] St. Albans, [?1483] (STC 9995). Type 2.
206. ["Chronicles of England."] [William de Machlinia, London, ?1486] (STC 9993). Type 1.
207. "Cronycles of the londe of Englond." Gerard de Leew, Antwerp, 1493 (STC 9994). Type 1.
208. "Cronycle of Englonde wyth the Frute of Tymes." Wynkyn de Worde, Westminster, 1497 (STC 9996). Type 2.
209. "Cronycle of Englonde wyth þe Fruyte of Tymes." Wynkyn de Worde, London, May, 1502 (STC 9997). Type 2.
210. "Cronycle of Englonde wyth þe Fruyte of Tymes." Julyan Notary, London, August, 1504 (STC 9998). Type 2.
211. "Cronycle of Englonde with the Fruyte of Tymes." Richard Pynson, London, December 19, 1510 (STC 9999). Type 2.

212. "Cronycle of Englonde with the Fruyte of Tymes." Julyan Notary, London, 1515 (STC 10000). Type 2.
213. "Cronycle of Englonde with the Fruyte of Tymes." Wynkyn de Worde, London, 1515 (STC 10000.5). Type 2.
214. "Cronycle of Englande with the Fruyte of Tymes." Wynkyn de Worde, London, 1520 (STC 10001). Type 2.
215. "The Cronycles of Englonde with the dedes of popes and emperours and also the descripcyon of Englonde." Wynkyn de Worde, London, April 9, 1528 (STC 10002). Type 2.

I. The Common Version

The Common Version to 1333 (CV–1333)

The earliest stage in the development of the English *Brut*, containing the basic text to 1333, is represented by MSS. Bodl. Rawlinson B.171(1), Bodl. Douce 323, Gordan 63, Rylands Eng. 103(1), Yale Beinecke 494, Soc. of Antiquaries 93, and probably by the imperfect MSS. BL Harley 3945, Rylands Eng. 206, and NLW Peniarth 398D. Bodl. MS. Rawlinson C.155 contains early seventeenth-century extracts from a manuscript of this group.

The first sections (to 1333) of MSS. Bodl. Bodley 840 (item 56) and TCD 490 (item 57) should also be considered as witnesses to this group. These manuscripts contain continuations beyond 1333, to 1419, apparently added by the same scribes who wrote the earlier sections but at a later date and from new exemplars. These composite texts are classified below as the CV–1419(r&g):B, subgroup (a).

1. BODLEIAN MS. RAWLINSON B.171(1)[1]

First scribe begins imperfectly: disport. And þo come Lotryn and Camber [Brie 13/4]
Omits: Cad, QIL, "5w" heading
First scribe ends on fol. 171v: wiþout eny chalange of eny man. Deo gracias.

Remarks: The writing of the first part of the manuscript is early, possibly ca. 1400. The text corresponds closely to the Anglo-Norman source (see below) and forms the base text to 1333 of Brie's edition. The dialect is that of South-West Herefordshire.[2]

After the continuation from 1333 to 1377, added by a second scribe in a mid-fifteenth-century secretary hand, occur three shields with clear but unidentified coats of arms on fol. 201v and a largely illegible name, "Sere I[.]h[.] T[. . .]l (?)," presumably that of an early owner (but cf. the name in the next manuscript).

[1] For (2), see item 17.
[2] *LALME*, 1: 150, 3: 167.

2. BODLEIAN MS. DOUCE 323[1]

Begins: In the noble lande of Surrye
Omits: Cad, QIL, "5w" heading
Ends on fol. 101v: withoute eny chalange of eny man. Amen. Deo gracias.

Remarks: Brie uses this manuscript for the beginning of his text to 1333 (Brie 1/5–14/16) and for collation thereafter (designated O).

At the end of the text, on fol. 101v, the late-fifteenth-century scribe has written the name "Ihannes Tubantisville" (cf. the preceding manuscript) and has drawn a shield with an unidentified coat of arms.

---

[1] See George Kane, ed., *Piers Plowman: The A Version*, rev. ed. (London and Berkeley, 1988), p. 3, for a description of the manuscript. Other contents are an A text of *Piers Plowman* (fols. 102–140); *The Charter of the Abbey of the Holy Ghost* (fols. 140v–159v); *Ipotis* (fols. 160–167v, imperfect at end). Watermarks date the paper to after 1410.

3. MRS. J. D. GORDAN MS. 63

Heading: Her may a man here how Engelond was first callede Albion and þoru3 whome it hade þe name.
Begins: In the noble lande of Syrrie þer was a noble kyng and my3ty and a man of grete renoun þat me callede Dyoclician
Omits: Cad, QIL, "5w" heading
Ends: withouten eny chalange of eny man. Deo gracias. [Deo gracias *erased*]

Remarks: The manuscript is early, perhaps written ca. 1400. The heading occurs in a number of the Anglo-Norman texts, such as BL Royal 20.A.iii: "Ci poet hom oir coment Engletere fust primes nome Albion & par qi la tere receust cel noun." The text does not correspond exactly to any other CV–1333 text but shows individual agreements in its readings. In the Halidon Hill passage the names of those in the second part of the Scottish army are omitted (Brie 284/9–12). In the same passage there is an agreement in error with Bodl. Rawlinson B.171(1) in misnumbering the fourth ward of the Scottish army: "In þe first warde..." (Brie 284/20 and n.).

A second, later hand has added a line at the end of the text: "after kyng E [*ins.*] þe iij^{de} reynyd kyng Richard ij^{de} amd [*sic*] in his."

4. RYLANDS MS. ENG. 103(1)[1]
Table of contents by first scribe begins: Here may a man hure Engelonde was ferst called Albyon and thorugh wham it hadde þe name.
Table of contents ends on fol. 7v: How king Edwarde gette aȝen vnto him graciousliche þe feautees and þe homages of Scotlande whereof he was pulte out þorugh þe false counceil of Isabelle his mooder and of ser Roger Mortymer þat was made erl of þe March. Capitulo CC^{mo} xxiij°.
Heading on fol. 9: Here may a man hure Engeland was first called Albyon and þoruȝ wham it hadde þe name.
Text begins: In the nobele lande of Syrrye
Omits: Cad, QIL, "5w" heading
First scribe ends on fol. 126v: withoute eny chalaunge of eny man.

Remarks: As in TCD 490 (item 57), there is a table of contents to 1333 (fols. 1–7). Although the "5w" heading is absent, a space was left in the text; the heading has been supplied by a modern hand from "MS B."

---

[1] For (2), see item 14. See Ker, *MMBL III*, p. 417; Geoffrey A. Lester, *The Index of Middle English Prose, Handlist II: A Handlist of Manuscripts Containing Middle English Prose in the John Rylands and Chetham's Libraries, Manchester* (Cambridge, 1985), p. 38; Moses Tyson, "Hand-List of the Collection of English Manuscripts in the John Rylands Library, 1928," *Bulletin of the John Rylands Library* 13 (1929): 172.

5. YALE UNIVERSITY, BEINECKE MS. 494[1]
Heading on fol. 3: Here may a man hure hov Engelonde was ferst callede Albyon and after wham hit hadde that name.
Begins: In þe noble lande of Syrrie þer was a noble king a stronge man & a miȝty of body and of gret name þat me called Dioclician
Omits: Cad, QIL, "5w" heading
Ends: wiþoute eny chalange.

Remarks: The text is further removed from the Anglo-Norman source than that of Bodl. Rawlinson B.171(1), but the verbal changes made in the early chapters can be partially paralleled in the CV–1419 (Leyle).[2] The Yale text cannot, however, underlie the later group, which shows agreements with the CV–1333 texts of Bodl. Rawlinson B.171(1) and Bodl. Douce 323 not paralleled in the Yale text, thus indicating that yet other texts of the same type existed.

The manuscript was written in the first quarter of the fifteenth century.[3] Fol. 1r–v is a bifolium of an obituary calendar of a Dominican convent, probably in Suffolk or Chelmsford. Among many notes and scribbles are two early notes of purchase: on the last leaf is a note of purchase from S. Belamy, dated 33 Henry VI (1455); on fol. 1v is recorded that William Nasby, skinner of London, bought the book for 150s. on April 12, 3 Edward IV (1464). "Robard Naysbe" was apparently a subsequent owner in the late fifteenth or early sixteenth century.

---

[1] For a full description, see Shailor, *Catalogue*, 2: 478–80.
[2] See pp. 128–31.
[3] See Shailor, *Catalogue*, 2: 479–80, for this information and for post-medieval names and modern autographs in the manuscript.

6. SOCIETY OF ANTIQUARIES MS. 93

Heading: Here may a man here how Engelonde was ferst callede Albyon and þoruȝ wham hit had ferste þat name.
Begins: In þe noble lande of Surrie
Omits: Cad, QIL, "5w" heading
Ends: wiþoute chalange of eny maner man. Deo gracias.

Remarks: Although containing the normal contents, the text must be regarded as secondary, for in phraseology it shows numerous differences from the other manuscripts of the group. The "5w" heading is not present; however, the three words ("Þe erl of") that immediately follow are written in red.

7. BODLEIAN MS. RAWLINSON C.155

Heading on fol. 89: Extracts from an old English Chronicle MS. coming down to 6 Ed. III 1332.
Begins: And this bataile, between K. Harold and Wm the bastard [cf. Brie 136, ca. line 26]

Ends on fol. 93v: in the yer of Incarnacioun of oure lord Jesus Crist mccc & xxx^ti. [Brie 272/5–6]

Remarks: The copiest dates the transcription and names himself at the end of the extracts: "A.D. 1606 ab Henrico Spelmanno conscriptus."[1]

---

[1] Sir Henry Spelman (?1564–1641), the historian and antiquary; see *DNB*, 53: 328.

8. BL MS. HARLEY 3945
Begins: In the noble lande of Surre
Omits: Cad, QIL
Fragmentary last folio ends during the chapter recounting the deposition of Edward II.

Remarks: The text is of normal CV type. Many folios are missing throughout.

9. RYLANDS MS. ENG. 206[1]
Heading: [H]ere may a man heren howe that Englonde was first called Albion and thurgh whom it had the name.
Begins: [I]n the noble londe of Surrey
Omits: Cad, QIL
Ends imperfectly: the goote shuld lese moch of his londe til that shame shuld hym ouercome. And then shuld he cloo[then hym in a *catchwords*] [Brie 244/16–18]

---

[1] See Ker, *MMBL III*, pp. 421–22; Lester, *Handlist*, p. 39; Tyson, "Hand-List," p. 185.

10. NLW MS. PENIARTH 398D[1]
Begins imperfectly: lete call hyt Loundres [Brie 31/23–24]
Omits: Cad (see below), QIL
Ends imperfectly: Tho was the quene so wroth towarde sir Edmunde erle of Kente & cessed never to praye vnto hur sone that he scholde [Brie 265/33–266/1]

Remarks: Among other missing folios are the folios that might have contained the Cadwallader episode.

---

[1] See Marx, "Middle English Manuscripts," pp. 369–71, for a description and an analysis of the missing folios.

Remarks on the CV–1333
Like the Anglo-Norman text, the CV–1333 does not contain the Cadwallader episode (see Introduction, Appendix 1) or Queen Isabella's letter (see Introduction, Appendix 2). The heading found in some texts and the practice of prefixing a table of contents are paralleled in certain of the Anglo-Norman texts.

None of the English manuscripts preserves the original translation, for, like the majority of extant manuscripts of the *Brut*, they represent copies written some time after the presumed date of composition of any portion of text. None of the three manuscripts that form the basis of Brie's edition preserves an exact copy of the original translation, as a comparison of readings with the Anglo-Norman text shows, although Bodl. Rawlinson B.171(1) preserves the original readings most faithfully. However, no one text has a monopoly of readings that correspond exactly to those found in the Anglo-Norman, as the textual variants printed by Brie indicate.

The following extract from Brie serves the double purpose of showing the closeness of the translation to the original Anglo-Norman as well as the variant readings that show that none of the English manuscripts contains the original translation. The base text is that of Bodl. Rawlinson B.171(1), collated with Bodl. Douce 323 (designated O) and TCD 490 (designated D):

How Engist and xj M^l men come into þis lande, to whom Vortiger ʒaf a place þat is callede [Called is O] Thongecastell. Capitulo lvj^{to}.	Coment Engist & xj Mille hommes viendrent en ceste terre a Vortiger as queux Vortiger dona vn place nosme Thowgcastell [*sic*]. Capitulo lvj^{to}.
And sone after þis sorw, tidynges [sorwe tydyng D, tydynge O]	En toute ceste anguise nouel luy vient qe graunt navie de estran-

come to Vortiger, þat a grete nauye [meny D, meyne O] of straungers were arryuede in [in the contre of D, in þe Cuntre of O] Kent; but þai wist nouȝt whens [what D] þai were, ne wherfore þai were comen. The Kyng sent anone messagers [a messanger DO] þider, þat somme of ham shulde come and speke wiþ him, forto wete what folc þai werne, and what þai axede, and into what contre þai wolde gone. Þere were ij breþerne, Prynces and maistres of þat straunge company: þat on me callede Engist, and þat oþere Horn. Engist went þo to þe kyng, & tolde to him encheson wher-fore þai were þere arryuede in his [þis O] lande, and saide: "sire! we beth of a contre þat is callede Saxoyne, þat is, þe Lande of Germayn, wherin is so [om. O] miche sorw, þat [þay yf O] þe peple is [be O] so myche þat þe lande may nouȝt ham [hem not O] sustene ne suffice. The maystres & Prynces þat haueþ þe lande to gouerne and rewele, shul done come bifore ham men and wymmen, þe [that bene D] boldest þat bene a-monges ham and best mowen [boldest amonges ham forto fiȝt þat best mow D, boldest þat ben among hem for-to fight þat best mow O] trauaille into diuerseȝ [diuerse D, diuers O] londes; and so þai shal ham ȝeue Horse and

gers furent ariuez en la pais de Kent mais ne sauoit qils furent ne pur quoi ils furent venuz. Le roi maunda illoeqes vn messanger qe ascun de eux venist a luy parler pur sauoir qe la gent ceo furent & quoi ils demandassent & en quele parte ils vousissent aler. Ils y auoient deux freres maistre & prince de eux gentz estrangers lun out noun Engest & lauter Horne. Engist ala al roy & luy dist lenchesoun pur quele ils furent ariues en sa terre. "Sire" fait il "nous sumez de vne pais qest appellee Saxsoine qest en le terre de Germaine ou il y ad vne tiel custume qe si le poeple soit si graunt que la terre ne poet suffrir a eux sustenir les princes qe ount la seignurie & le pais a gouernir ferroit venir deuaunt eux hommes & femmes les plus hardiz a combatre qe meux purrount trauailler en diuerses terres. Si lour dorrount chiuaux armes & quanque mistere lour serra et puis dirrount a eux qils se augent purchacer terre en autre pais ou ils purrount viure si come lour auncestres firent deuaunt." [BL Cotton Cleopatra D.iii, fol. 92v] harneyse, armure, and al þing þat ham nedeþ; and after þai [þai shul D, þay schul O] say to ham þat þai go into anoþer contre, wher þat [*om.* D] þai mowen leue, as here auncestres deden biforne ham." [Brie 50/7–29]

A specific point in chapter 223 (the battle of Halidon Hill) provides some physical evidence of the genesis of a reading which can be used as a supplementary factor in determining the group to which a text belongs.

During the description of the Scottish army, Bodl. Rawlinson B.171(1), Bodl. Douce 323, Gordan, Rylands Eng. 103(1), Yale Beinecke 494, Soc. of Antiquaries 93, and Bodl. Bodley 840 (item 56; a witness to the CV–1333 in its first part) agree with the Anglo-Norman text in prefacing the first four divisions ("wards") of the Scottish army by a heading, e.g., "In þe þridde ward of þe bataile of Scotland were þise Lordes" (Bodl. Rawlinson B.171(1): Brie 284/13–14). After the names of the lords in the fourth ward (misnumbered as "first" in Bodl. Rawlinson B.171[1] and Gordan) and the numbers of the soldiery, the CV–1333 manuscripts continue the text of the chapter without break, whereas TCD 490 (item 57; a witness to the CV–1333 in its first part) introduces a subheading:

> ... William Landy, Thomas de Boys, Rogere de Mortymer, with xxx bachilers, ix C men of Armes, and [*om.* O] xviij M^l communes [and iiij C of communes D, & iiij C of Comune O]. [In þe v^{te} warde of þe bataile of Scotlond were those lordis *add.* D] ¶ The Erl of Dunbarre, keper of þe castel of Berwik, halpe þe Scottis wiþ l. men of Armes ... [Bodl. Rawlinson B.171(1): Brie 284/26–30]

Rylands Eng. 103(1) perhaps represents an intermediate stage; it has no heading, but leaves a space. The ¶ of Bodl. Rawlinson B.171(1) is omitted in Soc. of Antiquaries 93, but "Þe erl of" is written in red ink. The reason for the introduction of the subheading (here designated the "5w" heading) can be seen by looking at the visual presentation of the passage in the Anglo-Norman text of BL Cotton Cleopatra D.iii. The layout takes the form of three contiguous rectangles; the left one contains the appropriate ward heading, the central one contains the names of the lords arranged as a list, and the right hand one contains the phrase enumerating the lesser soldiery:

| En le quarte garde del batailes dEscoce furent ceux sirs | Robert de Lawether William de Vipount William de Lonstoun .... William Landy Thomas de Boys Roger de Mortimer | ouesque xxx bachilers ix C hommes darmes xviij Mille & iiij C des comunes Luy counte de Dunbarre gardein del chastel de Berwik aida les Escotz oue l hommes darmes... [BL Cotton Cleopatra D.iii, fol. 182] |

A similar layout may have been employed in the original manuscript of the English translation (cf. the layout in BL Harley 4690, a text of John Mandeville's translation to 1333 [item 193]).

If the original translation reproduced the Anglo-Norman layout, then it is clear that the wards would be distinctly differentiated from the body of the text. In Bodl. Rawlinson B.171(1), Bodl. Douce 323, and Soc. of Antiquaries 93 the layout has merged the wards into the body of the text; in an attempt to mark off the resumption of the narrative, first a space was left, as in Rylands Eng. 103(1), in order to insert a heading, and a heading was subsequently inserted, as in TCD 490. The heading is actually erroneous, for there were originally only four wards, and the new layout of Bodl. Rawlinson B.171(1) and other CV–1333 texts, integrating the previous wards into the body of the narrative, probably confused the correct reading of the text.

Reflecting the complex textual tradition, later manuscripts include all the types exemplified in the CV–1333—the absence of any heading; the leaving of a space; the presence of the "5w" heading; or (as a new solution) the introduction of a substitute heading, either because an exemplar possessed a space or because it was noticed that the "5w" heading is wrong.

The Common Version to 1377 (CV–1377)

To the text ending in 1333 a continuation was added that brings to a close the reign of Edward III and ends with his death in 1377. The continuation appears in two versions, the longer of which forms the basis of the majority of succeeding texts; manuscripts to 1377 containing this full continuation can be further subdivided into two definite stages and probably another. The first of these stages contains neither the Cadwallader episode nor Queen Isabella's letter; a probable second stage contains the Cadwallader episode, while the third stage includes both the episode and the letter.

The Common Version to 1377 with full continuation,
Stage 1 (CV–1377 f.c. Stage 1)

The full continuation is found in its entirety in MSS. CCCC 174 and Rylands Eng. 102. Free Library of Philadelphia MS. Lewis 238 is imperfect at the beginning of the continuation, while MSS. Rylands Eng. 103(2), BL Harley 2279, and BL Stowe 68 are imperfect at the end but probably belong to this group. The majority of the manuscripts that carry the text beyond 1377 also contain or are based on this continuation.

11. CORPUS CHRISTI COLLEGE, CAMBRIDGE, MS. 174
Heading: Here may a man hure Engelande was fferst callede Albyon and þoruȝ wham hit had þe name.
Begins: In the noble lande of Syrrie
Omits: Cad, QIL, "5w" heading
Changeover, 1333 to 1377: wiþoute eny chalaunge of eny man. Ande so after þis gracious victorye þe king turnyd him aȝen vnto þe same seege of Berwyk
Ends: the xj kalend of Iuyn he deide att Shene and is beried worshipfully at Westmynster on whos soule God haue mercy. Amen.

Remarks: Brie prints this as his base text for the 1333 to 1377 continuation (Brie 291–332).

12. RYLANDS MS. ENG. 102[1]
Begins imperfectly: and our soueraiegne his doughter Gennogen to his wiff [Brie 7/24–25]
Omits: Cad, QIL, "5w" heading
Changeover, 1333 to 1377: withoute calenge of any man. Deo gracias dicamus omnes. Amen. And so after this gracious victorie
Ends: þe xj kalendes of Iune he deyde at Shene and is buryed wirschipfully at Westminster vppon whos soule God haue mercy. Amen.

Remarks: Leaves have been lost after fols. 38, 43, and 57; three inserted leaves, written in a hand of the late fifteenth or early sixteenth century, summarize some of the missing text.

---

[1] See Ker, *MMBL III*, pp. 416–17; Lester, *Handlist*, pp. 37–38; Tyson, "Hand-List," p. 171.

13. FREE LIBRARY OF PHILADELPHIA MS. LEWIS 238
Heading: Here may a man hure Engelande was first callede Albyon & þoruȝ wham hit hadde the name.
Begins: In þe noble lande of Syrrie
Omits: Cad, QIL, ("5w" heading)
Ends: he deide at Shene & is beried worschepfully at Westmester whos soule God haue mercy. Explicit.

Remarks: Some leaves are lost that would have contained the end of the 1333 text, including the Halidon Hill material, and the beginning of the 1377 continuation.

A mid-sixteenth-century note on the second from last leaf records that "William Vmnor of Sharryngton [Norfolk] gentleman owyth this cronycle." The note is in the same hand as a memorandum on the same page that recounts the betrayal in 1557 of Calais into French hands.

14. RYLANDS MS. ENG. 103(2)[1]
Second scribe begins on fol. 126v: And so after thys gracius victorye
Ends imperfectly: Therfor þe xxvj day of August kyng Edeward in a feld fast by Crescy [Brie 298/23–24]

Remarks: As the table of contents for the text to 1333 indicates, the continuation from 1333 to 1377 represents an independent, later addition to the manuscript.

---

[1] For (1), see item 4.

15. BL MS. HARLEY 2279
Heading: Here may a man here how Engelond was first called Albyon and thurgh whom hit had the name.

Begins: [I]n the noble lande of Syrrye
Omits: Cad, QIL
Ends imperfectly: wherfore if I shal knoweliche þe verrey treuth [Brie 293/33–34]

Remarks: The text ends just over two-thirds down fol. 146r, which suggests that the scribe did not complete his task. A sixteenth-century hand (which also writes the verses ascribing the second translation of the *Brut* to "John Maundevyle"; see pp. 333–34) has added several lines to complete the sentence, ending "the comen people weare strongeley igreued &c."

16. BL MS. STOWE 68
Heading: Here may a man here hou Engelond was ferst called Albioun and thurgh wham hit hadde the name.
Begins: In the noble lond of Sirrie
Omits: Cad, QIL, "5w" heading
Ends imperfectly: hit was told and certified to the king [Brie 305/12–13]

Remarks on the CV–1377 f.c. Stage 1
The method by which many of the *Brut* manuscripts developed is shown in this first group that possesses a continuation. The continuation was probably added to a manuscript of the CV–1333, as in Rylands Eng. 103, and the resulting text to 1377 was then copied, with the result that manuscripts in a single hand were produced. No significant changes have been made to the CV–1333 text.

The Common Version to 1377
with shortened continuation (CV–1377 s.c.)

The shortened continuation is based on the longer continuation described above, and is found in MSS. Bodl. Rawlinson B.171(2) and Lambeth 491; it also occurs in MSS. BL Harley 753 and Lambeth 331 of the CV–1430 JP:B.[1] Lambeth MS. 491 ends with "The Description of Edward III."

---

[1] See pp. 145–50.

17. BODLEIAN MS. RAWLINSON B.171(2)[1]

Second scribe begins on fol. 171v: [A]nd eftre þis gracius victorie þe kyng turnyd ageyn to þe siege of Berwyk

Ends: and was rially and worthely buryed at Westmynstre on whos soule Gode haue mercy. Amen.

---

[1] For (1), see item 1.

18. LAMBETH PALACE LIBRARY MS. 491[1]

Begins imperfectly on fol. 1: the qwene anone toke gold and sylvir grete plente [Brie 19/29–30]

Omits: Cad (see below), QIL, "5w" heading

Contains: Description of Edward III

Changeover, 1333 to 1377: wiþout eny chalangyng of any man. Aftir which wyctorie þe kyng turnyd aȝen into Englond and ordeynid ser Edward Bayllol with othir worthy lordis forto kepe Scotland.

How kyng Edward went aȝen into Scotland. Of þe bataill of Scluys and Seynt Omers and of the turnament of Dunstaple and of Seynt Georges feest at Wyndesore. Capitulo CC xxiiij°.

The seveneþe ȝeer of kyng Edward in the wyntir tyme he went into Scotland & reparaillid the castell of Kylbrig aȝens þe Scottis

Changeover, 1377 to Description of Edward III: deyd at his manere of Shene xj kalend of Iuyn and is buried atte Westminster.

Þe descripcion of kyng Edward. Capitulo CCxxix°.

Ends on fol. 205v: and vnprofitable harmes with meny evelis bygan forto spring and þe more harme is continuyd longe tyme aftir.

Colophon: Explicit quidam tractatus Anglicus de gestis Anglorum Brute vulgariter nuncupatus.

Remarks: Despite the later textual evidence of the CV-1430 JP:B, to which the text of Lambeth 491 is related (see pp. 149–50), it is unlikely that the Cadwallader episode was originally present. Although the relevant leaf is missing, the amount of text which is omitted would probably fit into one folio if the episode were not included and there is no indication from the chapter numbering that any extra chapters were originally present.

Textually, this is the earliest group in which "The Description of Edward III" (printed in Brie 333–34), a short chapter assessing the character of the late king, appears. It is a translation of a Latin eulogy that is found in the misnamed "Continuation of Murimuth," one of the continuations to the *Polychronicon*.[2] This section of text also appears in Lambeth 738, BL Harley 266(1), Huntington HM 136(1), BL Harley 753, Lambeth 331, and in Caxton's *Chronicles of England* and BL Addit. 10099.[3]

The sixteenth-century signatures of John and Thomas Pat(t)sall occur several times, together with numerous notes by them. They may have been members of a merchant family that acquired land in Essex.[4]

---

[1] See Montague Rhodes James, *A Descriptive Catalogue of the Manuscripts in the Library of Lambeth Palace: The Mediaeval Manuscripts* (Cambridge, 1932), pp. 681–84. See also Karl D. Bülbring, "Über die Handschrift Nr. 491 der Lambeth-Bibliothek," *Archiv* 86 (1891): 383–92; A. G. Hooper, "The Lambeth Palace MS. of the 'Awntyrs off Arthure'," *Leeds Studies in English* 3 (1934): 37–43; Robert J. Gates, ed., *The Awntyrs off Arthure at the Terne Wathelyne* (Philadelphia, 1969), pp. 15–16; Ralph Hanna III, ed., *The Awntyrs off Arthure at the Terne Wathelyn* (Manchester, 1974), pp. 4–6; Ralph Hanna III, *Pursuing History: Middle English Manuscripts and Their Texts* (Stanford, 1996), pp. 27–29. The first part of the manuscript also includes texts of *The Awntyrs off Arthure*, *The Siege of Jerusalem*, *The Three Kings of Cologne*, and a poem on hunting; Hanna, *Pursuing History*, pp. 99, 128, and 304 n. 3, notes that the scribe also wrote Huntington MS. HM 114 and was the first scribe in BL MS. Harley 3943, both of which contain copies of Chaucer's *Troilus and Criseyde*.

[2] The continuation is reprinted from an edition of Queen's College, Oxford, MS. 304 by Anthony Hall (Oxford, 1722) in Thomas Hog, ed., *Adam Murimuthensis Chronica Sui Temporis . . . cum eorundem Continuatione (ad M.CCC.LXXX) a Quodam Anonymo* (1846; rpt. Vaduz, 1964); the eulogy is contained in pp. 225–27. On further texts of the continuation, unknown to its earlier editors, see Taylor, *The 'Universal Chronicle' of Ranulf Higden*, pp. 118–19, 180–81.

[3] See items 22, 33, 61, 79, 80, 85, and 86.

[4] See Julia Boffey and Carol M. Meale, "Selecting the Text: Rawlinson C.86 and Some Other Books for London Readers," in *Regionalism in Late Medieval Manuscripts and Texts*, ed. Felicity Riddy (Cambridge, 1991), pp. 161–62 and n. 63.

The Common Version to 1377 with full continuation,
Stage 2 (CV–1377 f.c. Stage 2)

A group that used the full continuation to 1377 and that first included the Cadwallader episode can be posited from the evidence of Hamburg MS. 98, although the manuscript is unfortunately imperfect at both beginning and end.

19. STAATS- UND UNIVERSITÄTSBIBLIOTHEK HAMBURG MS. 98 IN SCRIN[1]

Begins imperfectly on damaged fol. 1: tolen [...] queene of þat land [Brie 14/10]

Contains: Cad

Omits: QIL, "5w" heading

Changeover, 1333 to 1377: wiþoute any chalynginge of eny man. And so after þis gracious victorie þe kyng turned hym aȝen vnto þe same sege of Berwyk

Ends imperfectly: the chaunceler & þe tresorer þat were bysshopes & þe clerk of the pryve seel were remeued & put out of her office & in here stede were [Brie 324/23–25]

Remarks: Although the manuscript is now incomplete at the end, it is probable that little has been lost and that in its original state the text ended in 1377. The omission of the "5w" heading in the Halidon Hill passage is normally suggestive of a textually early group, and the text to 1333 agrees well with the texts of the CV–1333 that are closest to the Anglo-Norman text. If the text did indeed originally end in 1377, then it is a representative of the earliest Common Version group to include the Cadwallader episode, which appears on fols. 111–117, and suggests that the additions of the Cadwallader episode and Queen Isabella's letter were independent of each other in the Common Version.

---

[1] See Tilo Brandis, *Die Codices in scrinio der Staats- und Universitätsbibliothek Hamburg, 1–110* (Hamburg, 1972), pp. 167–68. The text of the Cadwallader episode is printed from this manuscript as Appendix 1 of the Introduction.

The Common Version to 1377 with full continuation,
Stage 3 (CV–1377 f.c. Stage 3)

If the preceding text does in fact indicate a valid group that ended in 1377, then a succeeding stage in the development of the CV (though based on a text closer to the original CV–1333 wording) is exemplified by Princeton

MS. Taylor Medieval 3(1) and by NLS MS. 6128. Both use the full continuation to 1377 and include both the Cadwallader episode (Cad) and the text of a letter from Queen Isabella to the citizens of London (QIL), though the two manuscripts cannot be directly related (see Remarks on the CV–1377 f.c. Stage 3 below). BL MS. Harley 266(1) seems to be related to NLS 6128, although the former also includes "The Description of Edward III." Although at some textual remove, the unfinished Chicago MS. 253 may also be an offshoot of this rather fragmented group and is thus included here.

20. PRINCETON UNIVERSITY LIBRARY, TAYLOR MEDIEVAL MS. 3(1)[1]

Table of contents by first scribe begins on fol. 40: This is the kalender of this boke of cronyclys clepid Brute makyng mencyon of the kyngis that haue regnyd in this londe now callid Englond. And the prolog stondith in the begynnyng and aftirward folowen the chapiters by order as they stondyn here.
Prologus.
How Brute was bigeten and how he slough furst his modre and aftirward his fadir... Capitulo primo.

Table of contents ends on fol. 43v: Of the dethe of kyng Edward and how sir Iohn Mynstreworth knyght was drawen and hongid for his treson.

Heading on fol. 44: Here may a man hyre how Englonde was ffurst callyd Albyon and thorow whom hit had the name.

Begins: In the noble lande of Surrye there was a nobill kyng and a myghty and a man of grete renowne that men called Dioclysian

Contains: Cad, QIL, "5w" heading

Changeover, 1333 to 1377: withoute any chalange of any man. Deo gracias. And so aftir this gracious victory the kyng turnyd hym ayen to the same sege of Berwyk

First scribe ends on fol. 118v: he deide at Shene and is buryed worshipfully at Westminster on whos sowle God haue mercy. Amen.

Remarks: Besides the change of hand, the ending point of the table of contents, written by the first scribe, shows that the original text ended in 1377, to which a continuation to 1419 was subsequently added.

The *Brut* table of contents is preceded by an incomplete text of *Sidrak and Bokkus* (fols. 1–39v), also written by the first scribe.[2]

The signature of William Cecil, Baron Burghley (1520–1598) appears on the first page of the *Brut* text.

[1] For (2), see item 73. See Adelaide Bennett, Jean F. Preston, and William P. Stoneman, *A Summary Guide to Western Manuscripts at Princeton University* (Princeton, 1991), p. 55.
[2] See Karl D. Bülbring, "Sidrac in England," *Beiträge zur romanischen und englischen Philologie: Festgabe für Wendelin Foerster* (Halle, 1902), pp. 457–58; R. E. Nichols Jr., "Sidrak and Bokkus, Now First Edited from Manuscript Lansdowne 793," Ph.D. diss., University of Washington, 1965.

21. NATIONAL LIBRARY OF SCOTLAND MS. 6128

Original text begins imperfectly on fol. 1: but heo and hire sustres yfere; þo sayde þis Albyne "My fair sustres ful wel we knoweþ…" [Brie 3/14–15]
Contains: Cad, QIL
Omits: "5w" heading (see below)
Changeover, 1333 to 1377: wiþoute eny chalaunge of eny man. And so after þis gracious victorye þe kyng turnede hym aȝen vnto þe same sege of Berwyk
Ends: he deide atte Shene and is beried worchipfully at Westmynestre on whos soule God haue mercy. Amen.

Remarks: A space has been left where the "5w" heading might appear. Unusually, the subheading on the array of the Scottish army at Halidon Hill has been accorded a separate chapter number: "How þe Scottis comen in iij batailles aȝens þe too kynges of Engelonde and of Scotlande. In þe vauntwarde of Scotlande were þese lordes. Capitulo CC^{mo} xxiiij^{to}." [cf. Brie 283/24–26]

The missing first leaf of the original text has been supplied at a later date, presumably from another text. It begins with the heading: "Here begynneth þe crounycks of this lande Engelonde þat first was callede Albyon þorug whom hit hadde the name." The text begins: "In þe noble lande of Syrrie."

22. BL MS. HARLEY 266(1)[1]

Begins imperfectly (see below): After þe death of kyng Henre regned his sone Edward þe worthiest knyght of al þe honour [cf. Brie 179/3–4]
Contains: QIL, Description of Edward III
Omits: "5w" heading (see below)
Changeover, 1333 to 1377: without ony chalaunge of any man. Deo gracias. And so after þis gracious victory the kynge turned him aȝen vnto the sege of Berwike

End of text to 1377 and beginning of "The Description of Edward III": the xj kalend of Iuyn he deid at Shene and is buryed worshipfully at Westminster on whos soule God haue mercy. Amen.

This kyng Edward was passyng gode and full gracious

"The Description of Edward III" ends on fol. 91: and þe more harme is it þat hit contynued so longe tyme after.

Remarks: Judging from the quire signatures, the text may be as finished as it ever was, though the evidence is not conclusive.[2]

At the conclusion of "The Description of Edward III" a couple of lines are left blank at the foot of fol. 91 and fols. 91v and 92 are also left blank, indicating a change of exemplar at this point. The same scribe then proceeds on fol. 93 with a CV–1430 JP:A continuation, in the course of which a change of scribe occurs.

As in the previous manuscript, a space (approximately half a line) occurs in lieu of a "5w" heading. Similarly, a chapter number was originally accorded the subheading on the array of the Scottish army, which is partially visible despite erasure:[3] "This was the arrey of the Scottis how þat thei come in batailles aʒens the kynge of Engelond and of Scotlond; in þe vauntward of Scotland were þe lordes. Capitulo [Cap. 61 *in modern hand over erasure ending* simo xxiiij°]."

---

[1] For (2), see item 78.

[2] Many of the signatures have been fully or partially cropped. However, it appears that the existing text began with quire "a" and continued beyond the break marking the change of exemplars. A new series from "a" starts on fol. 128, the leaf on which a change in hand in the CV–1430 JP:A continuation occurs.

[3] An early modern hand has erased the original chapter numbers (though missed that for chapter 168) and replaced them from unity; the same hand also added a title, "A verie large chronicle from the beginning of E. i. perfect to a°. 9°. H. 6.," and folio numbers.

23. UNIVERSITY OF CHICAGO MS. 253

Heading: Here may a man he[. . .] Engelond was fyrst calle Albion and of whom it [. .]d his first name. Capitulo Primo.

Begins: In the noble lond of Surrye þer was a noble kyng of myght and a man of grete renoun þat men called Dioclysian

Contains: Cad, QIL

Omits: "5w" heading

Changeover, 1333 to 1377: and euery man caught what he myght take without chalenge. Deo gracias. And after þis gracious victorie þe kyng turned agein to þe seege of Berwyk

Ends imperfectly: And in þe xlix^{ty} yere of kyng Edwarde þe vjth day of Iuyn deide ser William Witelesy erchebisshop of Canterbury wherfore þe monkes of the same chyrche desirede a cardynall of Engelonde to be erchebisshoppe [Brie 327/18–21]

Remarks: The manuscript is probably complete as we have it, for the scribe ends about one-third down the last page.

In the Halidon Hill passage, the heading for the array of the Scottish army (Brie 283/24–26) is given a separate (though confused) chapter number: "Off þe aray and names of þe lordes of Scotlond þat came enbatailed in iiij wynges ayenst þe kyng of Engelond and þe kyng of Scotlond. Capitulo CC xxix^{mo} xxx."

The manuscript contains the early signatures of Edmund, Alexander, and Robert Trayfort.

Remarks on the CV–1377 f.c. Stage 3
None of the four texts assigned to the present group can be directly derived one from another. They fall into two general types, in which NLS 6128, BL Harley 266(1), and Chicago 253 stand against Princeton Taylor 3(1), which contains the "5w" heading and does not have the secondary development of the additional chapter heading in the Halidon Hill narrative. BL Harley 266(1) shows a further development in that "The Description of Edward III" occurs as the conclusion of this first section of the text. Chicago 253 is distinguished by verbal changes, as in the wording of the conclusion of the narrative to 1333 and of the additional chapter heading (quoted above). Both BL Harley 266(1) and Chicago 253 present incomplete texts: the former may have begun with the accession of Edward I, while the latter was left unfinished by its scribe.

The Common Version to 1419, ending "and manfully countered with our English men" (CV–1419[men])

The main line of development is through the CV–1377 f.c. Stage 3, which is the first group to use the Cadwallader episode and Queen Isabella's letter; more specifically, the development was probably through texts of the type of Princeton Taylor MS. 3, which also includes the "5w" heading. To a text of this type, ending in 1377 with the death of Edward III, a further continuation was added taking the narrative to the siege of Rouen in 1419, during which it ends with the words "and manfully countered with our English men" (Brie 390/28–29).

Among texts ending at this point two main groups can be distinguished, designated A (with three subgroups) and B. The key features of these groups are as follows. Subgroup A(a) carries on the main tradition, containing the same formal features as the CV–1377 f.c. Stage 3—the Cadwallader episode, Queen Isabella's letter, and the "5w" heading. Subgroup A(b) is distinguished by a rewritten and more accurate narrative for the years 1399 to 1401 and by the appearance of a substitute heading in place of the "5w" heading in the Halidon Hill passage. The single manuscript witness to subgroup A(c) omits the "5w" heading (but does not substitute the heading found in A[b]), and includes "The Description of Edward III," found in texts from a number of different groups. Group B omits the Cadwallader episode but includes Queen Isabella's letter.

A text of the continuations from 1333 to 1377 and 1377 to 1419(men) is also found in BL MS. Harley 4690, appended to John Mandeville's translation of the basic *Brut* text (see item 194). The Heyneman MS. (item 58) also combines texts copied from three exemplars by three scribes to form a skilfully assembled, composite text that now ends in 1419(men), the final section having been added to supply leaves that must have been lost at an early point in the manuscript's history.

The Common Version to 1419, ending "and manfully
countered with our English men": Group A (CV–1419[men]:A)
The texts of the manuscripts that comprise this general group can be further differentiated into three secondary subgroups: subgroup (a) exemplifies the main line of subsequent development of the Common Version and is represented by Peterhouse 190(1), Sion Coll. L40.2/E 42, Columbia Plimpton 262, Takamiya 29, and Lambeth 264(1); subgroup (b) comprises the first sections of BL Egerton 650, Bodl. Rawlinson B.173, and Pennsylvania State PS. V–3A, together with Bodl. Rawlinson B.166, and is in part used in the composite text of TCD 505 (see item 167); subgroup (c) designates the text of Lambeth 738.

Subgroup (a)
24. PETERHOUSE, CAMBRIDGE, MS. 190(1)[1]

Heading: Here may a man here how Engelonde was first callid Albyon and thorough whame hit hade þe name.

First scribe begins: In the noble londe of Syrrie there was a noble kynge and myghti and a man of grete renoun that men callyd Dyoclician

Contains: Cad, QIL, "5w" heading

First scribe ends on fol. 196v: and manfully countred with our Englyssh men.

---

[1] For (2), see item 95.

25. SION COLLEGE MS. L40.2/E 42[1]

Heading: Here may a man hure hou Englonde was ferst called Albion and thurgh wham hit hadde that name.

Begins: In the noble lande of Surrye

Contains: Cad, QIL, "5w" heading

Ends on fragmentary fol. 184: oure En[glischmen].

---

[1] See Ker, *MMBL I*, pp. 289–90.

26. COLUMBIA UNIVERSITY LIBRARY MS. PLIMPTON 262

Heading: [H]ere a man may hure hou Engelond was first callede Albion and thurgh wham hit hadde þat name.

Begins: In the noble lande of Surrye ther was a noble kynge and myghty and a man of grete renoune that me callede Dioclician

Contains: Cad, QIL, "5w" heading

Ends: and manfully countred with oure Englissh men. Deo gracias.

Remarks: Fols. 59, 105, 108, and 131 are supplied by a late-fifteenth- or sixteenth-century hand.

On an end flyleaf occurs a note of ownership: "Iste liber constat Ricardo Wolston" (possibly fifteenth century). A later owner, "Fraunces Button," adds his name in a pious colophon to the text.

27. TAKAMIYA MS. 29

Original text begins imperfectly on fol. 2: the lordes and the ladies wente to

bedde and anon as hire lordes were in slepe they cutten alle hir husbonde throtes [Brie 3/28–30]
Contains: Cad, QIL, "5w" heading
Ends: and manfully countrede with oure Englissh men.

Remarks: The missing first folio has been expertly supplied by a modern leaf copied from Caxton's *Chronicles of England* and written in a style similar to that of the original text. It is headed "How the lande of Englonde was first named Albyon and by what encheson yt was so named"; the text begins "In the noble lande of Sirrie there was a noble king and myhty and a man of grete renowne that men called Dioclisian." The verso ends "And when night was come."

28. LAMBETH PALACE LIBRARY MS. 264(1)[1]

Begins imperfectly: vj yer. And after hym regnyd Bledhaghe iij yere [Brie 31/5–6]
Contains: Cad, QIL, "5w" heading
Text to 1419 ends on fol. 142v: and manly countrid with our Englisshmen.

Remarks: This first part of the manuscript is written in a number of hands of varying degrees of carefulness. Transitions between hands are awkward, sometimes with overlapping material cancelled and sometimes requiring blank spaces on pages that precede a new hand. (It is possible that an original manuscript that had lost leaves has been extensively supplied at a later date.)

Fols. 169v–170 contain fifteenth-century copies of deeds, dated 49 Edward III, 11 Henry VI, 34 Henry VI, and 38 Henry VI, that deal with Berkshire properties in Cookham, Bray, and Winkfield and with persons from these places and from Maidenhead ("Maydenhithe"). On fol. 170v occurs an early note of ownership: "Iste liber constat Johanni Willeys."

---

[1] For (2), see item 91. See James, *Descriptive Catalogue... Lambeth Palace*, pp. 410–11.

Subgroup (b)
29. BL MS. EGERTON 650(1)[1]
Begins imperfectly: þat Mordered had begoten [Brie 91/10]
Contains: Cad

Omits: "5w" heading (see below)
Ends on fol. 111: and manfully countered with our Englysh men.
Colophon: Here is no more of the sege of Rone and þat is be cause we wanted þe trewe copy þerof bot who so euer owys þis boke may wryte it oute in þe henderend of þis boke or in þe forþer end of it whene he gettes þe trew copy when it is wryttyn wryte in þeis iij voyde lyns wher it may be foundyn.

Remarks: The folios that would have contained Queen Isabella's letter are missing.

A substitute heading for the "5w" heading occurs in the Halidon Hill account: "How erle of Dunbare help þe Scottes."

The *Brut* text to 1419 has occasional improvements in historical content, as seen, for example, in the history of Owen Glendower's rebellion (see Remarks on the CV–1419[men]:A[b] below). There are also some minor additions to the account of the battle of Agincourt.

One cannot tell whether in his colophon the scribe meant a *Brut* continuation or some other work to be "þe trewe copy," for no subsequent owner has added to the text. On the following leaf the original scribe adds a short London chronicle continuation to 1431 (see item 179).

---

[1] For (2), see item 179. A facsimile of fol. 111, showing the colophon, is printed in Mary-Rose McLaren, "The Textual Transmission of the London Chronicles," in *English Manuscript Studies 1100–1700*, ed. Peter Beal and Jeremy Griffiths, 3 (London and Toronto, 1992), p. 61. As McLaren notes (p. 60), the plural "we" in the colophon suggests commercial production; the comparison to "Ashmole 73" [read Ashmole 793] is, however, misleading (see item 141).

30. BODLEIAN MS. RAWLINSON B.173(1)[1]
Partially illegible heading ends: [...] throw whom hit had his name.
Begins: In the noble lond of Surre [...] a noble kynge of myght and a man of greete renowne that men called [...]
Omits: Cad (but see below), "5w" heading (see below)
Contains: QIL
Text to 1419 ends imperfectly on fol. 221v: withouten tho that were slayne in the felde. And so they redyn forth [þroughoute Fraunce *catchwords*] [Brie 372/6–7]

Remarks: Although it is poorly made, the text is apparently based either on that of BL Egerton 650 or on a common exemplar, as a comparison of readings and the inclusion of similar continuations (see pp. 313–14) show. Many chapters and passages have been omitted throughout, and thus the lack of the Cadwallader episode is not necessarily significant. Spaces are left for headings in the Halidon Hill chapter, including one where the substitute subheading might have occurred.

The text originally continued further than its present ending but some leaves have been lost at the end of the text to 1419 (including the account of Agincourt) and the beginning of the continuation to 1431, which now begins in 1421 on the folio immediately following the imperfect 1419 text.

The dialect of the two hands of the manuscript is that of West Herefordshire, near the Welsh border. Memoranda and notes refer to Bucklersbury, Ewyas-Lacy, the foundation of the monastery of Dore, Weobley, Snowdell, Breknor, Clifford, Kington, Caldicot, etc., which are all in Herefordshire.[2]

---

[1] For (2), see item 180.
[2] *LALME*, 1: 150, 3: 172–73.

31. BODLEIAN MS. RAWLINSON B.166

Begins imperfectly: hom scomfited and kylled. And kynge Leyre hade th[e]n his lond aȝayne in pees [Brie 20/17–18]

Contains: Cad, QIL

Omits: "5w" heading (see below)

Ends imperfectly: bytturly and manly foȝten aȝayne the duke of [Burgoyne *catchword*] [Brie 295/11–12]

Remarks: The text corresponds with that of BL Egerton 650; for example, in the passage on the battle of Halidon Hill the substitute heading occurs: "How the erle of Dunbarr holp the Skottes."

The dialect is that of Staffordshire.[1]

---

[1] *LALME*, 1: 150, 3: 457.

32. PENNSYLVANIA STATE UNIVERSITY MS. PS. V–3A(1)[1]

Heading: He [*sic*] may a man here how Englond was first called Albyon and thorogh whom it had is name.

Begins (first page rubbed): In the noble lond of Surre ther was [a] nob[le k]ing [...] and a man of gret renowne þat men called [Diocli]cion
Contains: Cad, QIL
Omits: "5w" heading (see below)
Text to 1419 ends on fol. 196: And so thei preved hem when thei issuet oute of the cite bothe on hors bak and on fote for thei come neuer oute at one gate allone but thei come oute at iij or iiij; and at euery gate iij or iiij M¹ of goode mennes bodies wel armed and manfully countred with oure Englissh men.

Remarks: Although the continuation beyond 1419, to 1422, is written without break by the same scribe, the text as a whole is based on a text of the type of BL Egerton 650 and Bodl. Rawlinson B.173, including the continuation to 1431 found in those manuscripts. Accordingly, the continuation has been included with those found in the latter manuscripts.

As in the other texts of the group, the substitute heading "How þe erle of Dunbar holp the Scottes" occurs in place of the "5w" heading.

An omission (of one folio?) occurs in the Arthurian material: "for þe Saxons in þat cite and thei have dispended all oure vitailes" (cf. Brie 77/6–79/9–10). Some omissions are also found in the later parts of the text, for example, in the narrative on Richard II.

The dialect is possibly that of Northamptonshire, "with markedly central W[est] Midland elements."[2] A coat of arms has been erased on fol. 1, and there are erased notes on fols. 10, 10v, and 11 that record the births of children to John Shirley (1535–1570) of Staunton Harold and Rakedale in Leicestershire.[3]

A text in a very similar hand, possibly from the same scriptorium, is the English commentary on the prophecies of Merlin in Pennsylvania State PS. V–3, which is highly indebted to the *Brut* for its content and to which the commentary makes references.[4] The *Brut* text in PS. V–3A ends with the quire signature "N iij," while PS. V–3 begins with the signature "p."[5] It is possible that the two texts were once bound in the same volume. The dialect of the commentary is that of Northamptonshire.[6]

---

[1] For (2), see item 181.
[2] *LALME*, 1: 154.
[3] See Kate Harris, "The Origins and Make-Up of Cambridge University Library MS. Ff.1.6," *Transactions of the Cambridge Bibliographical Society* 8 (1983): 306 and n. 47.
[4] See Caroline D. Eckhardt, ed., *The 'Prophetia Merlini' of Geoffrey of Monmouth: A Fif-*

teenth-Century English Commentary, Speculum Anniversary Monographs 8 (Cambridge, Mass., 1982), pp. 34–38.
[5] Eckhardt, *'Prophetia Merlini'*, p. 20.
[6] *LALME*, 1: 154, 3: 370.

Remarks on the CV–1419(men):A(b)
Since BL Egerton 650 is closely related to Bodl. Rawlinson B.173, there is agreement in the section of text printed by Brie as Appendix C (Brie 392–93), which gives a slightly fuller version of the time from 1399 to 1401, including a more accurate account of Owen Glendower's rising, which Brie thought to be unique to Bodl. Rawlinson B.173.[1] A text of this subgroup underlies the CV–1419 (Leyle), which also agrees with this section of text.[2] Pennsylvania State PS. V–3A must have been copied from a manuscript that was closely related to BL Egerton 650, since it includes an adaptation of the London chronicle material found as a continuation in that manuscript (see item 181).

---

[1] See Brie 1: vii.
[2] See pp. 128–31.

Subgroup (c)
33. LAMBETH PALACE LIBRARY MS. 738
Begins imperfectly: geaunte þat was mayster off ham all þat men called Gogmagog [Brie 11/7]
Contains: Cad, QIL, Description of Edward III
Omits: "5w" heading
Ends on fol. 228v: & manfully countred with our Englesh men.

Remarks: The manuscript stands apart in that it contains "The Description of Edward III," found also in Lambeth 491, BL Harley 266(1), Huntington HM 136(1), BL Harley 753, Lambeth 331, and, at a later textual stage, in Caxton's *Chronicles of England* and BL Addit. 10099.[1] Although of different groups, these manuscripts (and Caxton's print) must be connected. The simplest explanation is that an attentive scribe was aware of, and had access to, the extra material in some other manuscript that contained the "Description" and incorporated it into the copy that he was executing, either Lambeth 738 or a lost precursor.

Two scribes have written the *Brut* text; the changeover between them occurs at a point of no particular textual significance, but the combination of features (especially the omission of the "5w" heading) suggests that a change of exemplar may have occurred at some point.

After a break of three blank folios, the scribe who completed the *Brut* text recommences on fol. 232 with a copy of the English "Deposition of Richard II," ending on fol. 243v.[2]

---

[1] See items 18, 22, 61, 79, 80, 85, and 86.
[2] See Kennedy, *Manual*, 2714–15, 2939–40. A copy is also appended in Woburn Abbey 181 (item 193). The copy inserted into the London chronicle found in BL Cotton Julius B.ii is printed in Charles L. Kingsford, ed., *Chronicles of London* (Oxford, 1905), pp. 19–62. The Latin version, with additions by Thomas Walsingham, is printed in Chris Given-Wilson, trans. and ed., *Chronicles of the Revolution, 1397–1400* (Manchester and New York, 1993), pp. 168–89.

The Common Version to 1419, ending "and manfully countered with our English men": Group B (CV–1419[men]:B)

This small group, which omits the Cadwallader episode but includes Queen Isabella's letter, contains MSS. BL Stowe 69 and BL Addit. 33242, though the two texts are not close and may be unrelated.

34. BL MS. STOWE 69

Heading: Here may a man here howe thatt England was fyrst callydd Albyon and thorough whom hytt hadd the name.
Begins: In the noble londe of Sirrie ther was a noble and a myghty and a man of grete renoun that men callyd Dioclicion
Omits: Cad, "5w" heading (but see below)
Contains: QIL
Ends: & manfully countred with oure Englisch men.

Remarks: A blank line is left for what would presumably have been the "5w" heading. (Chapter headings cease after chapter 20, though spaces are left for them.)

After a blank folio at the end of the *Brut* text, the same hand writes a short series of historical notes in typical London chronicle form, from 1189/90 to 1272. On fol. 196r–v (now fragmentary) the scribe has written

Lydgate's popular verses on the kings of England.[1]

---

[1] See Henry N. MacCracken, ed., *The Minor Poems of John Lydgate*, Part 2, EETS o.s. 192 (1934), pp. 710–16; Linne R. Mooney, "Lydgate's 'Kings of England' and Another Verse Chronicle of the Kings," *Viator* 20 (1989): 256–63, 278–79.

35. BL MS. ADDITIONAL 33242
Begins imperfectly: Gracyan was aryved and all hys oste [Brie 45/14–15]
Omits: Cad
Contains: QIL, "5w" heading
Ends on rubbed leaf a few lines into the chapter on the Ratcote Bridge rising: [Brie 342/8]
Remarks: The "5w" heading is given in slightly truncated form: "In the v^{te} bateille of Scotlond were thes lordes."

Remarks on the CV–1419(men):B
Neither of the manuscripts presents a good text when compared to early CV texts. One must assume that the original of this group was a text of either the CV–1333 or the CV–1377 f.c. Stage 1, which do not contain the Cadwallader episode, to which the 1419(men) continuation was added, probably from the CV–1419(men):A. To explain the presence of Queen Isabella's letter one must suppose that the compiler of the original text noticed its presence in the CV–1419(men):A text with which he was working or that there was an earlier change of exemplar to a text containing it. It seems unlikely that the compiler would have consciously omitted the popular Cadwallader episode had it been present in the exemplar, especially as this tale was considered historical.

The Common Version to 1419, ending "in rule and governance" (CV–1419[r&g])

A substantial number of manuscripts (some eighteen described in this section) take the narrative a few lines further than the CV–1419(men) to the successful conclusion of the siege of Rouen, ending with the words "in rule and governance." There are also fourteen manuscripts, now incomplete, that may belong to groups of this type (classified below in two sets of "doubtful" manuscripts immediately following the main groups they most closely resemble and to which, in their complete state, they may have belonged). This particular conclusion, ending in 1419 with the words "in rule and governance," was a major point of closure across the whole corpus of *Brut* texts, as can be seen by its regular occurrence in the Extended and Abbreviated Versions and in several Peculiar Version texts.

Among these CV–1419(r&g) texts, two main groups can be distinguished, designated A and B, the latter with three subgroups. Group A is characterized by the presence of the Cadwallader episode, Queen Isabella's letter, and the "5w" heading; this group represents the main line of development for the CV tradition. Group B consists of a set of texts that, like Group A, conclude in 1419 with the "rule and governance" ending; however, their narratives to 1333 or to 1377 derive from different, usually earlier, forms of the *Brut* than that contained in Group A. More specifically, the three subgroups in Group B draw their texts to 1333 or 1377 from, respectively, the CV–1333, the CV–1377 f.c. Stage 1, and a form of the CV–1377 f.c. Stage 3 containing "The Description of Edward III" (not present in Group A).

The Common Version to 1419, ending "in rule and governance":
Group A (CV–1419[r&g]:A)
The main tradition is carried on in those manuscripts that possess both the Cadwallader episode and Queen Isabella's letter. This group contains MSS. CUL Kk.1.12, Longleat House 183A, TCC O.10.34, BL Harley 2248, BL Royal 17.D.xxi, Yale Beinecke 323, Fitzwilliam Museum McClean 186, Coll. of Arms Vincent 421, Bodl. Rawlinson B.216, Glasgow Hunterian 228(1), Harvard Eng. 587, and Takamiya 67. (The last six manuscripts are imperfect at the beginning, but enough of the opening text remains to show that they do not belong to the Extended Version [EV].[1])

---

[1] For signs that indicate the EV, see p. 173.

36. CAMBRIDGE UNIVERSITY LIBRARY MS. KK.1.12
Table of contents begins on fol. 1: How Englonde was firste callid Albyon and through whom hit hade the name in the prologe.

Table of contents ends on fol. 5: And how king Henry the v^the went þe secunde tyme ynto Normandye and of the sege of Roone. Capitulo CC xlv^to.
Heading on fol. 6: Here may a man here how Engelonde was callid first Albyon and through whom it had the name.
Begins: In the noble lande of Sirie
Contains: Cad, QIL, "5w" heading
Ends: And þanne þe king entred ynto þe toun & restyd hym in the castell tyll þe toun were sette yn rewle and gouernawnce.

Remarks: Brie prints this as his base text for the 1377 to 1419(r&g) continuation (Brie 335–91). The dialect is that of Central Herefordshire, which may indicate that there was a continuing interest in that area in the production of *Brut* manuscripts.[1]

---

[1] *LALME*, 1: 68, 3: 170.

37. LONGLEAT HOUSE MS. 183A

Heading on fol. 6: Here may a man here how England was furst callyd Albion and throgh whom it had the name.
Begins: In the noble lande of Surre ther was a noble kyng and a myghty and a man of grete renoun that men called Dioclician that wele and worthely hym gouerned and reuled thorgh his noble chiualrie
Contains: Cad, QIL, "5w" heading (in red)
Ends: And the kyng entred into the towne and restyd hym in the castell till the towne was sett in reulle and gouernaunce.

Remarks: The first item (fols. 3–4v) in the manuscript is a copy in French of the Battle Abbey Roll, headed "Ces sont les facciounes les linages des grans qui vindrent ou William le Conqueroure en Angleterre"; it ends "Explicit quod R D."

The manuscript belonged in the fifteenth century to Alice Brice ("Constat Aligus[?] Brice" [fol. 2v]; "Iste liber constat Domina Alicia Brice" [fol. 136v]). The name of Francis Thynne (died 1611) also appears on fol. 136v.

38. TRINITY COLLEGE, CAMBRIDGE, MS. O.10.34[1]

Heading: Here may a man here Engelande was first callede Albyon and thoruȝ whom it had the name.

Begins: In the noble land of Syreie
Contains: Cad, QIL, "5w" heading
Ends: in rewle and in gouernaunce.

---

[1] See Linne R. Mooney, *The Index of Middle English Prose, Handlist XI: Manuscripts in the Library of Trinity College, Cambridge* (Cambridge, 1995), p. 150.

39. BL MS. HARLEY 2248

Table of contents begins on fol. 1: The ffirst how Brute was getten & howe he slow ffirst his moder and afterward his fader and how he conquered Albion that after he nempned Bretayne after his owne name that now ys called Englonde after the name of Engyst of Saxoyne.

Table of contents ends on fol. 17: The CCxlij wher as begynneth the cronicle of kyng Henry the fyfte.

Heading on fol. 19: Here may a man here how Englonde was ffirst called Albion and through whom hit hadde that name.

Begins: In the noble land of Surrye

Contains: Cad, QIL, "5w" heading

Ends: in good rule & good gouernance. Deo gracias.

Remarks: On fol. 1 appears a note of ownership: "Iste lyber constat Wyllyam Thomas." Other early names include "Edmunde Knyvet," "John Symons," and "Wyllyam Frost" (fol. 17).

40. BL MS. ROYAL 17.D.XXI

Heading: Here may a man here how Engelonde was first callede Albion and thorowgh wham yt hadde þe name.

Begins: In þe noble land of Sirie

Contains: Cad, QIL, "5w" heading

Ends: in rewle and gouernaunce.

Remarks: N. R. Ker ascribes the early ownership of the manuscript to the Augustinian Priory of St. Bartholomew, Smithfield, London, presumably from the evidence of the following addition, which suggests that the manuscript was written in the priory.[1] It is written in the same hand as the text in a lower margin and is marked for insertion in the *Brut* text at a point corresponding to Brie 369, between lines 10 and 11:

And in þe same x ȝeer of kyng Henries regne þe iiij^t on Candilmasse Day ser Raynold Colyer priour of þe priorye of Seynt Bartymewes in Westsmythfeld of London was schorn chanon beeng of aage xviij ȝer full on Shrofe Sonday next foloenge. And þe xxx day of Ianvere þan Monday þe xiiij^t ȝer of kynges Henry þe vj^{te} þe said ser Raynold was chosen priour of þe saide pryorye and vpon Shrofe Sonday next foloenge þe xix^t day of Feuerȝere þe said ser Raynold was stalled and so conteneweth pryour vnto þe

---

[1] Ker, *Medieval Libraries*, p. 123.

41. YALE UNIVERSITY, BEINECKE MS. 323[1]

Heading on fol. 3: Her may a man hure Engelande was ferst callede Albyon and þoruȝ wham hit had þe na[me.]
Begins: In the noble lande of Syrrie
Contains: Cad, QIL, "5w" heading
Ends imperfectly on fragmentary fol. 158v: [. . .]ne þe kyng [. . .] toun was [Brie 391/14–15]

Remarks: The last leaf is a mere fragment, but the few words left show that the text ended in 1419(r&g).

The *Brut* text was perhaps written ca. 1440,[2] and the manuscript can be associated in the later fifteenth century with some Yorkist adherent who was particularly interested in the Clare family, the direct male line of which ended with Gilbert at Bannockburn (1314).

Fol. 1 contains a series of notes on Richard, earl of Gloucester (died 1217) and his wife Amice, countess of Gloucester, down to the Clare heiresses, Eleanor, Margaret, and Elizabeth, the sisters of Gilbert, earl of Gloucester (killed at "bello de Polles," that is, Bannockburn), and their respective husbands, Hugh le Despenser the younger; Hugh d'Audeley the younger; and Theobald de Verdun (first husband), Roger d'Amory (second), and John de Burgh (third).

In response to references in the text, marginal notes in several early hands mention Robert, first earl of Gloucester (ca. 1090–1147; fols. 60, 61v); Gilbert of Clare (ca. 1180–1230; fols. 72, 73v); the death of Gilbert of Clare (1291–1314) at Bannockburn (fol. 85); Roger d'Amory, Hugh d'Audeley, the late Gilbert de Clare (fol. 87v); and the death of Roger d'Amory (fol.

88v). The primary focus is on the Clare family rather than the earldom of Gloucester, for there are no sidenotes for Thomas of Woodstock, duke of Gloucester, or for Thomas le Despenser, earl of Gloucester.

In the mid-fifteenth century, Richard Plantagenet, duke of York (1411–1460), the father of Edward IV, possessed extensive properties, especially in East Anglia, of the honour of Clare.[3] The strong Yorkist connections of the manuscript are further exhibited on fol. 2, which contains a set of genealogical roundels showing the claim of Edward IV to the crowns of England and France, whereas "Henricus Derby" and his successors are said to have usurped the throne.

---

[1] See Shailor, *Catalogue*, 2: 135–36.
[2] So dated by Kathleen L. Scott on the basis of the style of illumination (reported in Shailor, *Catalogue*, 2: 136).
[3] See Joel T. Rosenthal, "The Estates and Finances of Richard, Duke of York (1411–1460)," *Studies in Medieval and Renaissance History* 2, ed. W. M. Bowsky (Lincoln, 1965), p. 194. I am indebted to Professor Rosenthal for this reference.

42. Fitzwilliam Museum MS. McClean 186

Begins imperfectly on fol. 2: and vnto hem he seide that if thei wolde not be chastised thei shulde his loue lese for euermore [Brie 3/7–9]
Contains: Cad, QIL, "5w" heading
Ends: and than þe kyng entred the towne and restyd hym yn the castell tyll þe towne was sett yn rewle and gode gouernance.

43. College of Arms MS. Vincent 421

Begins imperfectly on fol. 2 (misbound after fol. 1):[1] to hem for half a yer and whan thys was doon alle the sustrys wenten ynto the shyp and saylid forth into the see [Brie 4/2–3]
Contains: Cad, QIL, "5w" heading
Ends: And thanne the kyng entryd ynto the toun and restid hym yn the castel tyl the toun was set yn rewle and yn governaunce.
Remarks: There are no EV signs.

That the manuscript was written before 1461 is clear, since Henry VI is called the current sovereign in a mnemonic poem on the kings of England that the scribe added in the bottom margin at the beginning of William the Conqueror's reign.

---

[1] Several folios have been bound in the wrong order at the beginning of the text.

44. BODLEIAN MS. RAWLINSON B.216[1]

Begins imperfectly: scomfited thise geauntes aboueseid. [Brie 4/33–34]
Contains: Cad, QIL
Omits: "5w" heading (but see below)
Ends on fol. 125: in rewle and in governaunce.

Remarks: The text shows no EV signs at the beginning.
    Instead of the "5w" heading occurs a chapter heading: "The batayle. Capitulo xxiiij^{to}," suggesting that a space had been left in the exemplar at this point for a rubricated heading.

---

[1] Described in M. C. Seymour, "The English Manuscripts of *Mandeville's Travels*," *Edinburgh Bibliographical Society Transactions* 4 (1966): 191–92. The *Brut* text is followed by an English copy of the Treaty of Troyes (1420) between Henry V and Charles VI of France (fols. 125–127v). The manuscript also contains texts of *Mandeville's Travels*, *The Proverbs of Solomon*, and Lydgate's *Life of St. Edmund*.

45. UNIVERSITY OF GLASGOW, MS. HUNTERIAN 228(1)[1]

First scribe begins imperfectly: done moche harme and sorow in many diuerse places [Brie 6/2–3]
Contains: Cad, QIL, "5w" heading
First scribe ends on fol. 149v: in rewle and in gouernaunce.

Remarks: The text shows no EV signs at the beginning.

---

[1] For (2), see item 89.

46. HARVARD UNIVERSITY MS. ENG. 587[1]

Begins imperfectly: Brute had the victory; neuertheles Brute made great sorow for his cosyn Turyn [Brie 10/17–18]

Contains: Cad (imperfect at start), QIL, "5w" heading
Ends: in rule and gouernaunce.
Colophon: Ita vita est hominum quasi cum ladas tesseris, si id quod maxime opus casu(?) non cadet: tunc idem quod cecidit forte, id arte ut coregas.

Remarks: There are no EV signs at the beginning.

The name "Ryther [*also* Rither] scriptor" occurs in several of the chapter headings when there remains room to add it. The early (possibly fifteenth-century) name "Edmond Goodwyn" appears in the top margin of fol. 96.

---

[1] See Linda Ehrsam Voigts, "A Handlist of Middle English in Harvard Manuscripts," *Harvard Library Bulletin* 33, no. 1 (Winter, 1985): 22–24.

47. TAKAMIYA MS. 67

Begins imperfectly on fragmentary fol. 203v (bound in at end):[1] for half ȝeer & whane þis was al i-done alle þe sustres wenten into a shippe [Brie 4/2–3]
Fol. 1 begins imperfectly: Newe Troye xx ȝeer aftir tyme þat þe cite was made and there he made þe lawes þat þe Bretouns helden [Brie 12/5–7]
Contains: Cad, QIL, "5w" heading
Ends imperfectly: Thane anon þey sente vnto þe kyng bisekynge him of grace & mercye & brouȝte [Brie 391/8–9]

Remarks: There are no EV signs.

The present ending-point occurs after the 1419(men) conclusion; probably one leaf, containing the few remaining lines to the 1419(r&g) ending, has been lost at the end.

---

[1] The original recto and verso have been reversed in the present numbering and binding. The fragmentary fol. 203 contains 6 lines of text: "Here endiþ the prolog of Albyon ... aftir the name of Engest of Saxoyne. Capitulo primo." [Brie 4/35–5/4]. At some point, the present verso lay against the present fol. 202v, on to which it bled considerably. Some of the opening words given here have been read from fol. 202v with the aid of a mirror.

Doubtful Manuscripts
Manuscripts with texts that are incomplete at either beginning or end, yet contain the Cadwallader episode and Queen Isabella's letter, can be difficult to classify with certainty depending on how much text has been lost.[1]

Some that are incomplete at the end—for example, MSS. Bodl. Bodley 231, BL Royal 18.B.iii, California-Berkeley 152, BL Addit. 26746, and Glasgow Hunterian 61—could belong to either the CV–1419(men):A or the CV–1419(r&g):A. Three texts, sufficiently incomplete at the beginning as to remove any possible EV signs, could belong to the CV or EV: Rylands Eng. 104 could belong to the CV–1419(men):A, the CV–1419(r&g):A, or the EV; Bodl. Douce 290 (which begins after the Cadwallader episode) belongs to either the CV or the EV; Bibliothèque Royale IV.461 (which is missing the relevant folios for the Cadwallader episode and Queen Isabella's letter) could belong to the CV–1419(men):A, the CV–1419(men):C, the CV–1419(r&g):A, the CV–1419(r&g):B, or the EV.

---

[1] See pp. 124–28 for further incomplete manuscripts that do not contain the Cadwallader episode or Queen Isabella's letter and that are similarly doubtful in classification.

48. BODLEIAN MS. BODLEY 231

Heading: Here may a man here howe Engelond was first callid Albyon and thorough whame hit hade þe name.
Begins: In the noble londe of Syrrie
Contains: Cad, QIL, "5w"
Ends imperfectly: the kyng of Fraunce & the dolphyn and the duke of Burgoyne wolde come adoun to rescue the citee of Rone with a [Brie 389/28–30]

Remarks: The text ends imperfectly before the 1419(men) or 1419(r&g) endings.

49. BL MS. ROYAL 18.B.III

Begins on fol. 5 (misbound after fols. 1–4): was alle wyldernesse. And whanne dame Al[. . .] comyn to that londe and all hyr susters [Brie 4/5–7]
Contains: Cad, QIL, "5w" heading
Ends imperfectly: And with him laye the erle of Southfolke and the lorde of Burgevenye wyth all here retenue [Brie 389/20–21]

Remarks: There are no EV signs, such as the extra giants, in the chapter on the thirty-three kings of Britain and in the description of Engist's heptarchy. The text ends imperfectly before the 1419(men) or 1419(r&g) endings.

The manuscript belonged to the Gaynesford family of Carshalton, Surrey, members of which can be connected with the ownership of a number of books.[1] Gaynesford names that appear are those of John, Mary, Erasmus, George, Ralph, and Thomas. Also in the sixteenth century, the manuscript belonged to Christopher Watson, whose note of ownership appears on fol. 160; a note on fol. 189 reads "To my louyd frynd Crystofer Wetson" and the name of Thomas Watson also occurs.

---

[1] See Julia Boffey, *Manuscripts of English Courtly Love Lyrics in the Later Middle Ages* (Woodbridge, 1985), p. 126 n. 42 (misnumbered as Royal 18.B.ii); Boffey and Meale, "Selecting the Text," p. 158 and n. 45.

50. UNIVERSITY OF CALIFORNIA AT BERKELEY MS. 152
Begins imperfectly: spousen Corynus doughter that men callid Guentolen. [Brie 13/22–23]
Contains: Cad, QIL, "5w" heading
Ends imperfectly: And anon þe kinge sente his heraudes to þe capteyne of Took to delyuer to þe kinge his castell and his toune and [.]llys he schulde [Brie 383/10–12]

Remarks: The leaves are missing that would have contained the chapter on the thirty-three kings of Britain and Lud's naming of London; there are, however, no EV signs in the passage on Engist's heptarchy. The text ends imperfectly before the 1419(men) or 1419(r&g) endings.

The manuscript belonged to Thomas London of Teberton, Suffolk, in 1627, as a note on fol. 1 attests. Other sixteenth-century names are those of Mary Whinkop and Timothy Thornborough.

51. BL MS. ADDITIONAL 26746
Begins imperfectly: them he saide thatt if thei wolde nought be chastisede thei schulde lese his loue for euermore [Brie 3/7–9]
Contains: Cad, QIL
Omits: "5w" heading (but see below)
Ends imperfectly: forto entere on the north side [Brie 389/31–32]

Remarks: There are no EV signs. The leaves are missing that would have contained the array of the Scottish army at Halidon Hill. The text ends imperfectly before the 1419(men) or 1419(r&g) endings.

The manuscript is a late (probably sixteenth-century), but handsome and careful, copy of the text. Some labor has gone into its production; proper names are written in different colors, chapter headings and initial letters of chapters are in red, and initials and numbers are tinged with yellow.

52. UNIVERSITY OF GLASGOW, MS. HUNTERIAN 61
Heading: Here begynneth þe cronnycles of þis lande Engelonde that first was callede Albyon þoru3 whom hit hadde þe name.[1]
Begins: In the noble lande of Syrrie
Contains: Cad, QIL, "5w" heading
Ends imperfectly: And Graunt Iackes a worþy [Brie 390/17]

Remarks: The text ends imperfectly before the 1419(men) or 1419(r&g) endings.

---

[1] Cf. BL Royal 19.C.ix, a text of the Anglo-Norman Long Version: "Cy commencent les croniqez d'Angleterre et premierement comment elle eut nom Albe et dont lui vint ce nom." The heading is also similar to the heading of certain EV texts.

53. RYLANDS MS. ENG. 104[1]
Fol. 1v begins (fol. 1r is illegible): Thanne kyng Aleyn did sende for the clergie of his londe [Cadwallader episode; see p. 61]
Contains: Cad, QIL, "5w" heading
Ends imperfectly: our king and his lordis atte þe dise & an [Brie 378/13–14]

Remarks: The text ends imperfectly before the 1419(men) or 1419(r&g) endings.

---

[1] See Ker, *MMBL III*, pp. 417–18; Lester, *Handlist*, p. 39; Tyson, "Hand-List," p. 172.

54. BODLEIAN MS. DOUCE 290
Begins imperfectly on fol. 157: Howe William Bastarde duke of Normandye come into Englonde and quelled kynge Harolde. Capitulo vj^{xx} iij d. [Brie 136/6–7]

Contains: QIL, "5w" heading
Ends imperfectly on fol. 280v: her londes & lordshypes þat þay helde in þe reame of [Brie 291/17–18]

Remarks: The incomplete text begins after the Cadwallader episode and ends at a point soon after the beginning of the 1377 to 1419 narrative.

55. BIBLIOTHÈQUE ROYALE MS. IV.461

Begins imperfectly: Afftre þe dethe of þis Eldrede Knoght þat was a Danoys bigan þo forto regne [Brie 119/5–6]
Omits: QIL (see below), "5w" heading (see below)
Ends imperfectly: many tovnes and poortes in Englonde [up]on þ[e] [Brie 365/18–19]

Remarks: The text begins after the point at which the Cadwallader episode would have appeared, and, among many others, the folios are missing that might have contained Queen Isabella's letter and the "5w" heading. Accordingly, the text could belong either to the CV–1419(men):A, the CV–1419(r&g):A, or the EV (if both features were originally present), or to the CV–1419(r&g):B (if both features were originally absent).

The Common Version to 1419, ending "in rule and governance":
Group B (CV–1419[r&g]:B)

Six manuscripts contain the complete 1419(r&g) continuation but reflect in their texts to 1333 or 1377 a different, usually earlier, form of the *Brut* than that found in manuscripts of Group A. Such composite texts are treated here if there are indications that they were deliberately conceived of as unified narratives by the scribes or their supervisors. Within the general type three subgroups can be distinguished, though the texts within each are not necessarily directly related and in most instances simply reflect similar methods of combination.

Subgroup (a) contains MSS. Bodl. Bodley 840 and TCD 490, unrelated composites of CV–1333 and CV–1419(r&g) texts. Subgroup (b) includes the Heyneman MS. and BL MS. Harley 1568, a combination of CV–1377 f.c. Stage 1 and CV–1419(r&g) texts, and Folger Shakespeare Library MS. V.b.106 (725.2), which was probably produced in the same way.

Subgroup (c) consists of Huntington MS. HM 136(1), apparently a combination of a CV–1377 f.c. Stage 3 text containing "The Description of

Edward III" and the CV–1419(r&g) text. Although only a single manuscript of subgroup (c) has survived, it is important in that a text of this type formed the basis for William Caxton's *Chronicles of England*. If Caxton's printed edition is seen as the culmination of the main tradition of the Common Version of the *Brut*, then its development is through this collateral subgroup of Group B rather than through the CV–1419(r&g):A, which can be regarded as the classic state of the pre-print manuscript tradition of the Common Version.

Subgroup (a)
56. BODLEIAN MS. BODLEY 840
Heading: Here may a man hure Engelande was fyrst callid Albyon and thorw wham hit hadde the name.
Begins: In the noble land of Syrrie
Omits: Cad, QIL, "5w" heading
Text to 1333 ends on fol. 117: wythoute any chalange of any man. Deo gracias.
Text from 1333 to 1419 begins on fol. 117: And so aftyr þis gracius victorye
Ends: in revle and gouernaunce.

Remarks: The text beyond 1333 continues in the same hand immediately after the narrative ending in that year. However, the ink used for the continuation is blacker, suggesting, in conjunction with the internal textual features, that a change of exemplar took place at this point and that the first part of the text was copied from a CV–1333, to which the 1419(r&g) continuation was added from another manuscript. Since it is possible that the scribe conceived of the complete narrative to 1419 as a unified text, it has been classified here rather than under the type represented by the second section of Princeton Taylor MS. 3 (item 73).

The dialect is that of Essex, with some Herefordshire relicts "probably to represent the flavour of the *Brut* original."[1]

---

[1] *LALME*, 1: 146, 3: 117.

57. TRINITY COLLEGE, DUBLIN, MS. 490
Table of contents begins on fol. 3: Here may a man here Engeland was first callede Albyon þorow3 wham hit hadde þe name.

THE COMMON VERSION   119

Table of contents ends on fol. 12: In þe ferþe warde of þe batayle of Scotland were þese lordes.
Heading on fol. 13: Here may a man hure how Engelande was ferst callede Albyon and through whome it hade the name.
Text begins: In the noble lande of Syrrie ther was a noble kyng and miȝty and a man of gret renoun that me callede Dyoclician
Omits: Cad, QIL
Contains: "5w" heading
Text to 1333 ends on fol. 132: withouten any chalange of any man. Deo gracias.
Text to 1419 begins on fol. 132: And so after þis gra[...] victorie king Edwarde turned hym aȝen toward þe same [...] [B]erewike
Text ends: And than the kinge entrid the toun and rested hym in the castelle tyll the tovne was sette in reule and goode gouernaunce.

Remarks: The inclusion of a table of contents is paralleled in several Anglo-Norman texts (for example, Bibl. Nat. fonds français 12155, BL Royal 19.C.ix, BL Addit. 18462a). The table shows that the original ending point, at least of the exemplar, was 1333, to which the continuation to 1419 was added. Brie seems to be mistaken in identifying a new hand as having continued the text beyond the 1333 ending; the continuation looks to be in the same hand but perhaps begun after some space of time with a new pen.[1]

The manuscript belonged to the Dominican priory of the Virgin Mary and St. Margaret at Dartford in Kent ("Iste liber constat religiosis sororibus de Dertfford," with an heraldic achievement of the Arma Christi drawn below [fol. 1v]; "IHC" and interlocked "Ave" and "Maria" appear on fol. 2.)[2]

---

[1] *Geschichte und Quellen*, p. 53. If there is indeed a second scribe, then the first section of the text should be reclassified under the CV–1333, to which the continuation to 1419(r&g) has been added.
[2] See Ker, *Medieval Libraries*, p. 57.

Subgroup (b)
58. HEYNEMAN MS.
Heading by first scribe: Here may a man heren how Engelande was first called Albyon and thorough whom it hadde the name.
Begins: In the noble londe of Syrrie
Omits: Cad, QIL, "5w" heading (see below)

Changeover, 1333 to 1377: withoute ony chalenge of ony man. Deo gracias. And so after this gracious victorie þe kynge turnede hym aȝen vnto þe same sege of Berwyke

First scribe ends text to 1377 on fol. 142r: he deyde at Shene and is entered worshipfully at Westmynstre on whos soule God haue mercy. Amen.

Second scribe begins continuation to 1419 on fol. 143r: And aftir þe king Eduuard þe thridde þat was born atte Wyndesore regned Richard of Burdeux

Second scribe ends imperfectly on fol. 165v: and there he kepte him longe tyme and at the last my [lord Powes *catchwords*] [Brie 386/16–17]

Third scribe begins on fol. 166: lorde Powes met with him and toke him [Brie 386/17–18]

Third scribe ends: and manfully countred with oure Englisshmen.

Remarks: The evidence of the following manuscript (see below) shows that, despite the present ending in 1419(men), the Heyneman MS. originally ended in 1419(r&g). It was designed as a composite text copied from a CV–1377 f.c. Stage 1 text with a continuation taken from a CV–1419(r&g). In addition to the change in hand, the blank page between the text to 1377 and the 1419 continuation indicates the change in exemplars. The illustrations, however, show that the text was treated as a whole. Its concluding leaves to 1419(r&g) must have been lost early in its history but were then supplied from a text ending in 1419(men).

The "5w" heading is not present, but a space of almost two full lines at the foot of the second column of a leaf occurs before the narrative continues.

This is a finely executed manuscript. There are decorated initials throughout; those at the beginnings of reigns contain portraits of rulers.[1]

There is evidence of care in the treatment of the continuation beyond 1377 in order to preserve the illustration program. In the chapter recounting the deposition of Richard II and the election of Henry Bolingbroke as king, a rubricated subheading (without separate chapter number) is introduced after Richard's death and burial for the first year of Henry's reign: "Here endeth the lief of king Richard with the materialle noticeon of his deposing. And now beginneþ the lief of kinge Henric' the iiij and the actes of his reign that folowen in this wise" (between Brie 360/26 and 360/27). This allows for a portrait of Henry IV within the following initial *A*. The chapter heading for the accession of Henry V is adapted to this model; Henry receives the largest portrait in the manuscript, ten lines high and extending across a full column.

[1] Dioclician is portrayed with his thirty-three daughters; Cordeill, Lear's daughter, is the sole woman ruler; Morwith's portrait includes the "grete beste that was blak & horrible & hidous" that devoured him; Hesidur is crowned by a cleric; multiple kings (Athelbright and Edelf, Cadwallader and Elfrid; seven kings for the heptarchy) are so portrayed, except for chapter 33, in which the reigns of thirty-three kings are listed but where the portrait of one stands for all; the baptism of Athelbright by St. Austin is included. A number of leaves are missing, presumably removed for their illustrations.

59. BL MS. HARLEY 1568

Heading: Here may a man here how Engelande was first callide Albion and thorow wham it had the name.

Begins: In the noble londe of Syrrie

Omits: Cad, QIL, "5w" heading (see below)

Changeover, 1333 to 1377: withoute any chalangynge of any man. Deo gracias. And so after this gracius victori þe kyng turnede ageyne vnto þe same sege of Barwyke

Changeover, 1377 to 1419: he diede at Shene & is enterede worschipfully at Westmynstre one whos saule God haue mercy. Amen.

And after the kyng Edwarde þe thyrde þat was borne at Wyndesore regnede Richard of Burdeux

Ends: And thene þe kynge enturede into the toun and restede him in the castell till þe towne was sett in rewle & gud gouernaunce.

Remarks: The manuscript, which is written in a single hand, is an inferior copy of the Heyneman MS. (see above), made before the latter lost its final leaves to 1419(r&g), or a poor copy from a common model. It is illustrated with rather crude imitations of the portraits in the Heyneman MS. (though that of Henry V is only of regular size) and includes occasional Latin sidenotes found therein.

Where the Heyneman MS. leaves almost two blank lines instead of a "5w" heading, a substitute heading occurs: "How the felde of Barwyke was discomfetede & þe toun delyuerd."

The adapted headings for the reigns of Henry IV and Henry V occur in corrupt form; that for the former reads: "Her endith þe lif of kyng Richarde with þe moriallite [*sic*] noticione of his deposicione. And now begynneth the lif of kyng Henry þe iiij^t & þe actes of his reigne þat folows in these wise."

60. FOLGER SHAKESPEARE LIBRARY MS. V.B.106 (725.2)
Heading: Here may a man heren how Englonde was ffyrst callid Albyon and thurgh whom it hadde the name.
Begins: [I]n the noble lande of Surre ther was a noble kyng and a myghty and a man of grete renowne that menne callid Dyoclysian
Omits: Cad, "5w" heading
Contains: QIL (see below)
Changeover, 1333 to 1377: withoute eny chalange of eny man. Deo gracias. And so aftre this gracyous victorye the kyng turned hym ayen onto the same sege of Berewike
Ends: tylle the towne was sette in rewle and good governaunce. Deo gracias.
Colophon: Quod Cogman. Si mea penna valet melior mea litera fiet. [*Repeated in a later hand*]

Remarks: Queen Isabella's letter is found in the chapter following that into which it is usually inserted:

> Howe Maystyr Walter of Stapulton bisshop of Excestre was byheued at London atte Standard in Chepe. Capitulo CC viij°.
>
> [A]nd in the same tyme kyng Edwarde was sore adredde leste menne of London wolde yelde hem vnto the qwene Issabelle and of the lettre that the qwene Issabelle sente to the mayre and to the aldremen of London which l[ett]re here foloweth in this manere: Issabelle by the grace of God qwene of Englonde...
> ...that alle menne passyng in the waie myghte se and redyn. And that same tyme kyng Edwarde sente Maystyr Walter Stapulton [cf. Brie 237/27-28]

It seems likely that the basic exemplar that the scribe was following was one that ended in 1377 and did not include this section of text. The supplementary text, however, that the scribe ("Cogman") used for the continuation to 1419 did include it (he must have had both exemplars open before him), though he noticed it a fraction too late to include in its normal CV position—and so he improvised by including it in the next chapter.

In the Halidon Hill passage only four wards of the Scottish army are given, which is usually an indication that a text is early in the CV tradition.

There is a list of chapter headings at the end of the text, added in 1604.

Subgroup (c)
61. HUNTINGTON MS. HM 136(1)[1]

Heading: Here may a man here that England was furst called Albion and thurgh whom it had the name.
First scribe begins: In the noble lande of Sirrie
Contains: Cad, QIL, Description of Edward III
Omits: "5w" heading
End of text to 1377 and beginning of "The Description of Edward III": the xj kalend of Iuyn he deid at Shene and is buried wurshipfully at Westmynster on whos soule God haue mercy. Amen.
This kyng Edwa[r]d was for sothe of a passyng goodnesse
First scribe ends on fol. 156v: in rewle and in gouernaunce.

Remarks: The text seems to be a combination of a CV–1377 f.c. Stage 3 text of the type found in BL Harley 266(1) with the continuation to 1419(r&g). They possess the same combination of features in the earlier part of the text, and, like BL Harley 266(1) (and NLS 6128), Huntington HM 136 accords a chapter number to the subheading on the array of the Scottish army at Halidon Hill:[2]

> This was the array of the Scottes howe þat þey comen in batailles ayens the ij kynges of Englond and Scotland. In the vauntward of Scotland were thees lordes. Capitulo CC xxiiij^{to}.

Like BL Harley 266(1), the text contains "The Description of Edward III," which follows immediately, with no heading (as in Harley 266 and Lambeth 738), after the death of that king.[3]

The *Brut* text is preceded by some Latin verses on historical subjects on the front flyleaves, and between fols. 83v–130 occurs a copy of the "Bridlington Prophecy," written in a fifteenth-century hand chiefly in the lower margins and starting at the beginning of the reign of Edward II.

Late-fifteenth- or early-sixteenth-century owners of the manuscript were John Leche of Nantwich, Cheshire, and Dorothy Helbarton, whose name appears throughout the volume in a series of marginal notes.[4]

---

[1] For (2), see item 92. See Dutschke, *Guide*, 1: 181–83; Ralph Hanna III, *The Index of Middle English Prose, Handlist I: A Handlist of Manuscripts Containing Middle English Prose in the Henry E. Huntington Library* (Cambridge, 1984), p. 15.
[2] See pp. 95–96.

³ See items 22 and 23.
⁴ See Dutschke, *Guide*, 1: 183, and Josephine Koster Tarvers, "English Women as Readers and Writers," in *The Uses of Manuscripts in Literary Studies: Essays in Memory of Judson Boyce Allen*, ed. Charlotte Cook Morse, Penelope Reed Doob, and Marjorie Curry Woods, Studies in Medieval Culture 31 (Kalamazoo, 1992), pp. 319–20.

Doubtful Manuscripts
MSS. Bodl. Rawlinson B.205, CUL Ee.4.32, TCC R.5.43, Leicester 47, and Sydney Nicholson 13 do not contain the Cadwallader episode, Queen Isabella's letter, or the "5w" heading (though the relevant leaf is missing in TCC R.5.43). They all present some or most of the standard 1419 continuation but are imperfect at the end; they could therefore belong to the CV–1419(r&g):B, although it is also possible, but less likely, that they ended in 1419(men). Like several manuscripts of the CV–1419(r&g):B, these may represent independent combinations of texts from different groups.

Although Huntington MS. HM 113 contains the Cadwallader episode and Queen Isabella's letter, it does not contain the "5w" heading; since the text is imperfect at the end it is included here.

62. BODLEIAN MS. RAWLINSON B.205

Heading: Here men may hiren how Engelond first was called Albioun and thurgh whome it hadde the name.
Begins: In the noble land of Sirrie
Omits: Cad (see below), QIL (see below), "5w" heading
Text to 1333 ends: Deo gracias dicamus omnes.
Ends imperfectly: and sir John [Cheyny knyght weren brou3t *catchwords*] [Brie 354/25–26]

Remarks: The text of the Cadwallader episode is not present, and the folios that might have contained Queen Isabella's letter are missing. Assuming that the latter was not present, then the first part of the text appears to be a copy of a CV–1377 f.c. Stage 1 text (cf. the ending words of the text to 1333 in Rylands Eng. 102 [item 12]: "Deo gracias dicamus omnes. Amen."; cf. also the following manuscript). To this, the scribe has added a continuation from a text ending in 1419.

Although the Cadwallader episode is not present, the manuscript contains the heading of the first chapter of the episode, written in the same hand as the main text: "How king Cadwaladre that was Cadwaleynes sone regned after his fader and was the laste kynge of the Britouns." The scribe then stroked this out and wrote the heading of the first chapter after the episode: "How kyng Offa was soueraigne aboue all the kynges of Engelond & how euery kyng werred vpon oþer. Capitulum Centesimum ij^m" [the ... ij^m *written in margin*].

It is probable that this curious situation arose because the scribe originally left blank lines for the chapter headings. At the conclusion of writing the main narrative, including the continuation to 1419 from a second exemplar, he inserted the chapter headings, taken, however, from his second exemplar, which contained the Cadwallader episode. Only after he had mechanically written the heading did he realize that his text did not in fact include the episode, and so he cancelled the heading and wrote the correct one, though he had to use the margin to get it all in.

63. CAMBRIDGE UNIVERSITY LIBRARY MS. EE.4.32[1]
Heading on fol. 24: Here may a man hure how Engelonde was ferst callede Albyon & þorwe wham hit hadde þe name.
Begins: In the noble land of Surrie
Omits: Cad, QIL, "5w" heading
Changeover, 1333 to 1377: withoutyn any chalengyng of any maner man. Deo gracias dicamus omnes. Amen. And so aftir this gracious victorie the kyng turned aȝen to the sege of Berwyk. And whan they of the towne saugh and herd how kyng Edward had sped they ȝolde to hym the town with the castell on the morne after the batayle
Ends imperfectly: And on the xij^e evyn come the duke of Almayn vnto þe [Brie 360/28–29]

Remarks: The combination of features and the ending of the narrative to 1333 suggest that the text to 1377 is based on a CV–1377 f.c. Stage 1 text (cf. the preceding manuscript). The continuation to 1419 is occasionally abbreviated and altered, as seen, for example, in the passage on the death of John of Gaunt:

> And in this same yere dyed syr Iohn of Gaunte the kynges vncle and duke of Lancastyr. And he lyth att Seynt Powlys in London besydes dame Blaunch hys wyfe.

> How þe erle of Derby and the duke of Norffolk were exiled and how the erle of Derby putt down kyng Richard. [*subheading in red*]

And in that same yere ther felle a discencioun betwyn the duke of Hertford [*sic*] and the duke of Norfolk [cf. Brie 355/15–22]

---

[1] The *Brut* is preceded in the manuscript by the prose *Three Kings of Cologne* (fols. 1–23v). A note at the top of fol. 23v records "Leaf 24 cancelled," and the foliation starts afresh with "Leaf 1" at the beginning of the *Brut* up to 184 (corrected from 180), that is, fol. 207 of the complete volume.

64. TRINITY COLLEGE, CAMBRIDGE, MS. R.5.43, PART II[1]
Begins imperfectly on fol. 39: bygan Leyr ayen wepe & made mych sorowe [Brie 19/1–2]
Omits: Cad, QIL, "5w" heading (see below)
Ends: Salyn Cheyne Mongomery & [Brie 384 n. 17]

Remarks: Leaves at the end of the 1333 narrative are missing, including any "5w" heading; if absent, then the text could have been based on the CV–1333 or CV–1377 f.c. Stage 1.

There are embellishments in the text, such as the changes from indirect to direct speech in the account of Edmund of Woodstock's trial, which heighten the dramatic quality of the normal CV–1333 narrative at various points:

> Tho answerid the goodman and seide, "forsoth ser vndirstondeth wele that I was neuer traytour to my king ne to the reme and that I do me on God and on all the world. And ferthermore by my kynges leve I shall it preve and defende as a man ought to do." Tho seide the Mortymere, "ser Edmonde, hit is so ferforth I knowe that it may nat wele be ageynseide. And in presence of all that here bene it shall well be iprovid." Nowe had this false Mortymere the same lettre that ser Edmond had take to ser Iohn Deuerell in the castell of Corff forto take vnto kyng Edward his brothir that ser Edmond wist not of ne supposid no thing that ser Iohn Daverell had be so false to deliuere his lettre in suche a wise to the Mortymere and þoght no manere thing of þat lettre [fol. 132v; and þoght ... lettre *catchwords; following leaves lost*] [cf. Brie 266/21–30]

---

[1] See Mooney, *Handlist*, p. 29. The *Brut* is preceded by the prose *Three Kings of Cologne*

(fols. 1–38). The ascription "Johan Hilles boke" appears on fol. 1.

65. UNIVERSITY OF LEICESTER MS. 47[1]

Heading: Here may a man here how England was first called Albyon and thorow whome it had his name.

Begins: In the noble londe of Surrye ther was a worthi kynge and a myghty man of grete renoune that men called Dioclocian

Omits: Cad, QIL, "5w" heading

Changeover, 1333 to 1377: withouten eny chalenge of eny man. Deo gracias. And after this graciouse victory the kynge turned hym agayne into the seide sege of Berwik

Fol. 106v ends: And ser Henry duke of Lancastre vndir pese & treuse went to the [Brie 310/10–11]

Ends imperfectly on fragmentary fol. 105v (bound in before fol. 106): ix[th] [. . .]minster [. . .] þat [. . .]le [. . .]cle [Brie 340/30–341/3]

Remarks: Many leaves are lost between fol. 106, which breaks off during 35 Edward III, and the scrap that now forms fol. 105, which ends during 9 Richard II.

The early (possibly fifteenth-century) ownership signatures of William and Edmund Chadertun (Chaderton) appear on fols. 54v and 77.

---

[1] See Ker, *MMBL III*, p. 99.

66. UNIVERSITY OF SYDNEY, MS. NICHOLSON 13[1]

Heading: Here may a man here howe Englond was ffyrst callyd Albyoun and afterward whanne hit that name hadde.

Begins: In the nobylle londe of Surre there was a nobyll kyng a stronge man and a myghty of body and of grete name that men called Dioclesioun

Omits: Cad, QIL, "5w" heading

Changeover, 1333 to 1377: withoute eny chalenge of eny man. Deo gracias. And so aftur this gracious victorye the kynge turned hym ayen to the same sege of Berwik

Ends imperfectly: And the baroun of Carewe with his retenewe was loigged on the watre syde and [Brie 388/9–10]

Remarks: The text to 1333 is changed verbally from that of the CV–1333, and in the thirty-three kings passage, after one instance of the 'after him" phrase, the text simply lists the king's name and gives the length of his reign.

The "5w" heading does not occur but a space sufficient for a chapter heading is left.

The text is clearly a copy, as errors show, and although it was written by two scribes, there is no significance to the point of changeover.

---

[1] See Margaret H. Engel, "An Edition of MS. Nicholson 13: f. 161r–f. 177v," M.A. thesis, University of Sydney, 1981, for a description of the manuscript and an edition of the text from 1377 to its end; I am grateful to Ms. Engel for a copy of her thesis. See also Keith V. Sinclair, *Descriptive Catalogue of Medieval and Renaissance Western Manuscripts in Australia* (Sydney, 1969), pp. 193–95.

67. HUNTINGTON MS. HM 113[1]

Begins imperfectly: þat þey wold al make amendis [Brie 3/10–11]
Contains: Cad, QIL
Omits: "5w" heading
Ends imperfectly: & wan him there grete worship & gre of þe feld. [And in þe next *catchwords*] [Brie 369/17–18]

Remarks: The unusual combination of features is similar to that in NLS 6128 of the CV–1377 f.c. Stage 3, Huntington HM 136 (which includes "The Description of Edward III"), and the texts of the CV–1419(men): A(b), but since no substitute "5w" heading appears in Huntington HM 113, it cannot be directly related to these texts.

---

[1] See Dutschke, *Guide*, 1: 149–50; Hanna, *Handlist*, p. 10.

The Common Version to 1419, with "Leyle" for Lear (CV–1419 [Leyle])

Verbal differences from the main tradition of CV texts are the major distinguishing feature of the group. They are most marked in the early chapters of the 1333 text and consist mainly of the substitution of one word by a synonymous word or phrase. Alterations (generally simplifications) of the grammatical structure of some sentences also occur. A further distinguishing feature is that King Lear is called "Leyle." The group consists of MSS. Glasgow Hunterian 74(1), Bodl. Rawlinson B.196, Lambeth 259, and BL Harley 4930.

68. University of Glasgow, MS. Hunterian 74(1)[1]

Heading: Here may a man here how Engelond was first called Albyon and afterwarde whan it hadde first þe name.
First scribe begins: In the noble londe of Sirrye
Omits: Cad, "5w" heading
Contains: QIL
Third scribe ends on fol. 113v: & manfully counterd with owre Englishe men.

Remarks: The first three scribes are contemporary and prepared the original text. Their dialects are, respectively, those of Northwest Essex, Central South Essex, and Southeast Suffolk (Ipswich area).[2]

The arms incorporated into the decoration of the first page—a shield (argent), a chevron (sable), and an annulet (sable) in chief, dexter canton—show that the manuscript belonged to a member of the Wauton family of Great Staughton, Huntingdonshire, which also had Bedfordshire connections.[3]

---

[1] For (2), see item 87. The full text is edited in vols. 2 and 3 of Lister M. Matheson, "The Prose *Brut*: A Parallel Edition of Glasgow Hunterian MSS. T.3.12 and V.5.13, with Introduction and Notes," 3 vols., Ph.D. diss., University of Glasgow, 1977.
[2] See Matheson, "The Prose *Brut*," 1: 227–40; cf. *LALME*, 1: 88, 3: 131–32.
[3] See Matheson, "The Prose *Brut*," 1: 323–29.

69. Bodleian MS. Rawlinson B.196

Heading: Here may a man here how Engelonde was first called Albyoun and afftterward whanne hit had first name.
Begins: In the noble londe of Surrie
Omits: Cad, "5w" heading (see below)
Contains: QIL
Ends on fol. 109v: yn rewle & in gouernaunce.

Remarks: The leaf is missing that contained the Halidon Hill narrative, including the array of the Scottish army.

70. LAMBETH PALACE LIBRARY MS. 259[1]

Heading: Here may a man here how Engelond was first called Albyon and aftirward whanne hit hadde fyrst name. Incipit prologus.
Begins illegibly on fol. 1.
Omits: Cad, "5w" heading
Contains: QIL
Ends imperfectly: And so whan all þinge was redy þe kynge hastyd hym to þe sege ward &c. [Brie 306/28–29]

Remarks: The text is probably as complete in its current state as when originally written, ending as it does at the end of the chapter on the battle of Wynchilsea part-way down the last leaf.

The *Brut* text is preceded by a calendar of Sarum use and a table of eclipses from 1384 to 1462. Front and end flyleaves contain copies of documents and many scribbles, including shields with a merchant's mark.[2] An early owner was William Bentelee (Bentele, Bentylee), whose rhymed curse on thieves appears several times.

---

[1] See James, *Descriptive Catalogue... Lambeth Palace*, pp. 404–406.
[2] For details of these documents (one of which is addressed to the prior of Newnham in Bedfordshire) and names, see James's *Catalogue*; the name of "William Mondeffeld de Charre" should be added.

71. BL MS. HARLEY 4930

Heading: Here may a man here howe that England was ffirst named Albyon and thenne afterward whenne that it hadde first name. Hic incipit prologus vt patet in sequentis.
Begins: In the noble lond of Surrey
Omits: Cad, "5w" heading
Contains: QIL
Ends imperfectly: Vpon which spech & conauntes it was sent to the court of Rome on boþe sydes [Brie 304/31–32]

Remarks on the CV–1419 (Leyle)
Glasgow Hunterian 74 probably preserves the original ending of the group,

which appears to have developed from some form of the CV–1419(men):B, although from a better text than that found in the extant manuscripts of that group, one that did not possess the "5w" heading. The extra lines to the 1419(r&g) ending in Bodl. Rawlinson B.196 are possibly a secondary addition made by the scribe in that manuscript itself or were present in a previous exemplar. The incomplete BL Harley 4930 and Lambeth 259 could have ended originally at either point, although it is possible that the Lambeth manuscript was not written beyond its present ending.

The Common Version to 1419, ending in "men" or (?) "in rule and governance" (CV–1419[men/?r&g])

The text to 1419 found in Chicago MS. 254 is best considered separately. Although written in the same hand as the succeeding continuation to 1445, which contains part of John Page's poem on the siege of Rouen, the continuation beyond 1419 is found appended to texts of very different groups.[1]

---

[1] See pp. 150–56.

72. UNIVERSITY OF CHICAGO MS. 254(1)[1]
Heading: In nomine Ihesu. Here may a man heren how Englonde was ffirste callyd Albyon and thurghe whom hit hadde þe name.
Begins: In þe nobyl lande off Syrrye
Omits: Cad
Contains: QIL, "5w" heading
Text to 1419(men) ends on fol. 124: and manfully countryd with oure Englyssch men.

Remarks: The text has none of the distinguishing verbal features of the CV–1419 (Leyle); it may well derive from a CV–1419(men):B text to which the few lines to the 1419(r&g) conclusion ("in rewle and in gouernaunce") have been added as part of the succeeding continuation, which was copied from a new exemplar of the type of TCC O.9.1.[2] A large "X," of indeterminate age, however, has been inserted in the text after the word "men" and also appears in the margin.

The manuscript was owned by John Nuton, who became prior of Battle

Abbey in 1463, as a note on a front flyleaf attests. A marginal note by the scribe (who makes many *notae* throughout) on fol. 49 suggests that the manuscript may well have been written at Battle Abbey:

> They þat desyre to here all þe lyfe of kyng William Conquerour lete þem turne ayen to þe begynnyng of þys boke & þer he may se both þe lyfe of hym & of hys auncetyrys.

The manuscript is still bound in its original wooden boards and sheepskin. Unless this is an imprecise reference to the preceding *Brut* account of William the Conqueror, there may have been some abandoned intention to include a work on the founder of Battle Abbey.

---

[1] For (2), see item 84.
[2] See items 117 and 83.

Continuation to a CV–1377 f.c. Stage 3 text from a Common Version text ending in 1419(r&g)

Princeton Taylor MS. 3 contains a continuation from a CV–1419(r&g) text that has been appended by a second scribe to a text of the CV–1377 f.c. Stage 3. As noted above (p. 50, and cf. item 14), such a procedure underlies the original accretion of continuations to the basic CV–1333 text—a continuation would be appended to an originally complete text and the whole would subsequently be recopied. Those manuscripts that contain composite texts ending in 1419(r&g) that were (or may have been) deliberately planned as unified combinations have been classified above as the CV–1419(r&g):B (with three subgroups), and the following item should be considered in that general context. However, since Princeton Taylor 3 was written by two scribes and shows no evidence of a unified program of copying, it has been treated as two separable items.

73. PRINCETON UNIVERSITY LIBRARY, TAYLOR MEDIEVAL MS. 3(2)[1]
Second scribe begins with heading on fol. 118v: And after kyng Edward the thrid that was borne at Wyndesore regned Richard of Burdeaux.
Second scribe ends on fol. 131v: in rule and governawnce.

[1] For (1), see item 20.

The Common Version beyond 1419, including John Page's poem "The Siege of Rouen" (CV–JP)[1]

Those manuscripts that carry the narrative beyond 1419 and also contain a substantial extract from John Page's poem "The Siege of Rouen" can be subdivided into three groups (the CV–1430 JP:A, the CV–1430 JP:B, and the JP:C), partly according to quite different textual antecedents up to the continuation containing the poem and partly according to the continuation itself. Groups A and B, to which most of the manuscripts belong, end in 1430 and contain Page's poem from line 637 of the full text. Group C consists of a continuation containing the poem from line 1157 appended to *Brut* texts of differing groups.

The CV–1430 JP:A contains the Cadwallader episode, Queen Isabella's letter, and a substitute heading for the "5w" heading, suggesting that it is probably based on the CV–1419(men):A. It also shows signs of some verbal expansion, for example, in chapter headings and in the addition of subheadings to the prophecies of Merlin. From the beginning of the reign of Henry V, the compiler began more and more to revise the text of his exemplar, adding details from what was apparently a London chronicle source. In some earlier form this chronicle had also been used by the compilers of the standard continuation to 1419(men) and the extra few lines to the (r&g) ending. This source contained at least part of John Page's poem on the siege of Rouen, which is reproduced in its verse form in the CV–1430 JP:A.

Distinctive features of the CV–1430 JP:B include its heading and the first words ("Some time") of the text, both of which are reminiscent of the Extended Version of the *Brut*. The first part of the narrative contains the Cadwallader episode and "The Description of Edward III" but omits Queen Isabella's letter and the "5w" heading. It is probably based on a CV–1377 s.c. text similar to that found in Lambeth MS. 491 into which the Cadwallader episode has been interpolated. To this has been added most of a standard continuation to 1419, which then switches in the second chapter of Henry V's reign to the continuation found in the CV–1430 JP:A.

The JP:C stands apart from the two previous groups. Although the three manuscripts in which it occurs are all written in single hands throughout, the narratives up to the continuation belong to very different groups and have been treated as separate items. The JP:C continuation begins with a shorter extract from Page's poem than that found in the A and B groups, followed by material in London chronicle format to either 1434 or 1445.

Although these texts containing Page's poem are not part of the main tradition of the Common Version, they are interesting as examples of complex aspects of *Brut* production (similar to what occurs even more often in the Peculiar Versions) and as illustrations of the close interrelationship between the *Brut* and the chronicles of London.

---

[1] See Rossell Hope Robbins, "Poems Dealing with Contemporary Conditions," *A Manual of the Writings in Middle English 1050–1500*, ed. Albert E. Hartung, vol. 5 (Hamden, 1975) pp. 1427–28, 1665–66. Page's poem is edited in John J. Conybeare, "On a Poem, Entitled the 'Siege of Rouen'," *Archaeologia* 21 (1827): 48–78; Frederic Madden, "Old English Poem on the Siege of Rouen," *Archaeologia* 22 (1829): 361–84; James Gairdner, ed., *Historical Collections of a Citizen of London in the Fifteenth Century*, Camden Society n.s. 17 (1876), pp. 1–46; John W. Hales and Frederick J. Furnivall, eds., *Bishop Percy's Folio Manuscript. Ballads and Romances*, 3 vols. (London, 1867–1868), 3: 533–41; Herbert Huscher, ed., *John Page's 'Siege of Rouen'*, Kölner Anglistische Arbeiten 1 (Leipzig, 1927); and (as part of the *Brut*) in Brie 404–22. The author's name is not given in any of the *Brut* texts but is found in BL Egerton 1995, which has the full text of the poem (see p. 144 below).

The Common Version to 1430, including John Page's poem "The Siege of Rouen": Group A (CV–1430 JP:A)

This group contains MSS. BL Cotton Galba E.viii, BL Harley 2256, Holkham 670, and CUL Ee.4.31 (though the poem is missing in the last). The second part of the composite text found in BL MS. Harley 266 can also be included here.

74. BL MS. COTTON GALBA E.VIII[1]

Heading on fol. 29: Here may a man here and knowe how Englonde was furst callud Albion and whom thorough [*marked for reversal*] hyt hadde hys furst name as ye shull fynde yn thys boke wyth many othyr thynges.
Begins: In the nobull londe of Surre
Contains: Cad, QIL, John Page's poem
Omits: "5w" heading (see below)

Page's poem (set out as verse) begins: and ofte we clepid and longe there stode and so we come doune to the duke of Exeture and there we gate non ansuere.

    And at Warwike that erle so fre
    We callid ofte it wold not be.

Page's poem ends:
    And alle that haue herd this redynge
    To his blisse Criste you brynge
    That for vs deied vpon a tree
    Amen sey we alle pur charite.
And in this yere was quene Iohna that was kynge Henryis the iiij^e arestid be Iohn duke of Bedfford

Text ends: and yet God sent hem good hele and welfare and scomfiture of all her enemyes blessid be God.

Remarks: A substitute heading appears for the "5w" heading: "How kynge Edward reskewyd the toune of Berewyke and how the kynge of Scotlond did hys homage to the kynge of Engelond."

    The carefully written manuscript also contains Lydgate's "Kings of England sithen William Conqueror" (fol. 2r–v)[2] and, in the same hand as the *Brut*, the Latin *Three Kings of Cologne* (fols. 3–28v).

    The name "Rycharde Rendale" (late fifteenth or early sixteenth century) occurs on an end flyleaf.

---

[1] Extracts from the first chapter and the whole second chapter that deal with the reign of Henry V are printed in Kingsford, *English Historical Literature*, pp. 299–309; the third chapter, including the poem, and the succeeding chapters to the end of the text are printed in Brie 394–439.
[2] See Mooney, "Lydgate's 'Kings of England'," pp. 256–63, 277.

75. BL MS. Harley 2256

Heading: Here may a man here and knowe how England was furste callud Albyon and thorugh whom hit hadde his firste name as 3e schull fynde in this boke with many othir thyngis.

Begins: In the nobul lond of Surre

Contains: Cad, QIL, John Page's poem

Omits: "5w" heading (see below)

Page's poem (set out as verse) begins: and ofte we clepud and long þere stode

and so we come doun to þe duke of Exeter & þere we gate noon answere.
 And at Warwik þat erle so fre
 We callid ofte it wold not be.
Page's poem ends:
 & all þat haue hirde þis redynge
 To his blisse Criste ȝou brynge
 Þat for vs deide vpon a tre
 Amen sey we alle pur charite.
And in this ȝere was quene Iohna þat was kyng Henreis wiff þe iiij⁣ᵉ arestid by Iohn duke of Bedfford
Text ends: and ȝit God sente hym good hele & welfare & scomfiture of all her enemyes blessid be God.

Remarks: The substitute "5w" heading found in the previous text occurs: "How kyng Edward reskewid þe toun of Berwik & how þe kyng of Scotlond dide his homage to þe kyng of Englond."
The name "Rouland Lathum" (fifteenth century?) appears on a front flyleaf. A deleted memo on a back flyleaf, retrospective in nature, reads: "Be hit knowen to all Crystyn men þat y Rychard Deuenysshe become d[. . .] ser(?) [. . .] the y[. . .] the viij day of Nouembre þe yere of kyng Herry vj⁣ᵗᵉ þe fyrst yere."

76. HOLKHAM HALL MS. 670
Table of contents begins imperfectly: How after the deth of Cassibelan Androgen the erle of Cornewaill reigned. Capitulum xxxviij⁣ᵐ.
Table of contents ends imperfectly: Capitulum C lxxxvj⁣ᵐ. How þe gode kyng Edward hilde his parlement and how þerto cam diuers lordes of Scotlond and how þey were accorded and swore to kyng Edward.
Text begins imperfectly: And whan this myschefe was bifall the peple of the lond tho made grete sorowe [cf. Brie 6/13–14]
Contains: Cad, QIL, John Page's poem
Omits: "5w" heading (see below)
Page's poem (written in prose lines) begins: And at Warwyk þe erle so fre we called ofte it wolde nat be
Text ends imperfectly during Page's poem: For a worde wronge out of warde myght make you to fare full harde. Therfore of wordes loke yᵉ be wise and sey no thing [without gode avise *catchwords*] [Brie 408/18–19]

Remarks: Folios are missing that would have contained the end of the table of contents and the beginning of the text, the prophecies of Merlin, and the substitute "5w" heading.

77. CAMBRIDGE UNIVERSITY LIBRARY MS. EE.4.31
Begins on fol. 203: How after kyng Henre regnyd hys sone Edward the worthiest knyght of alle the worlde and of kyng Alisaundyr of Scotlond. [Brie 179/1–2]
Contains: QIL
Omits: "5w" heading (see below), John Page's poem (but see below)
Text ends imperfectly: Mouns in Henaude þe whiche was sworn to hym to ben gode & trewe & to kepe þe lady in sauffe wafis [*read* ward] tille he come [aȝen *catchword*] [Brie 432/4–6]

Remarks: The *Brut* text from Edward I is used as a continuation of the longer version of Robert of Gloucester's *Metrical Chronicle* (fols. 53–200v), which probably was the original item in the manuscript.[1] (The Cadwallader episode is accordingly absent.)

The leaves are missing that would have contained the text of John Page's poem. The remaining text, however, agrees with that of the preceding manuscripts. It contains, for example, the substitute "5w" heading: "How kyng Edward reskewyd the toun of Berwyk & how the kyng of Scotlond dide hys homage to þe kyng of Englond."

---

[1] See Kennedy, *Manual*, pp. 2617–21, 2798. The original beginning of the manuscript was probably fol. 51. "Hughe Cooke" (sixteenth century) is noted as its owner on fol. 52. The manuscript now also contains a fragmentary *Wise Book of Philosophy and Astronomy* (fols. 1–6v; see Peter Brown, "The Seven Planets," in *Popular and Practical Science of Medieval England*, ed. Matheson, p. 9 and n. 16), Benedict Burgh's *Parvus Cato* (fols. 7–24), and the *Chronicle of Popes and Emperors* (fols. 25–50; see Dan Embree, ed., *The Chronicles of Rome* [forthcoming]).

78. BL MS. HARLEY 266(2)[1]
Continuation begins on fol. 93: And after kynge Edeward the iij^e that was borne att Wyndesore regned Richarde of Burdeux [Brie 335/5–6]
Contains: John Page's poem
Page's poem (written in prose lines with, sporadically, colons to indicate verse

endings) begins: & oft we clepyd & long there there [*sic*] stode and so we cam dovne to þe duke off Excestre & thare we gate non answere. And at Warwyk that erlle so ffre we callyd ofte hit wold not be

Page's poem ends: And þis cytee ffaste encresyd off brede & wyne ffysch & fflesch & thus ovre kyng made an ende off hys sege. And in thys ȝere was quene Iane þat was kyng Henre wyfe þe fferthe arestyd by Iohn duke off Bedeford

Text ends: and yet God sent hym gode hele & welfare and scomfyture of all here enemyes blessyd be God.

Remarks: Although the same scribe continues, a change of exemplar to a CV–1430 JP:A text takes place at fol. 93. A second scribe then takes over on fol. 128 in the course of the first chapter on the reign of Henry V (with the words "And anon the captayne come fforthe in the kyngges presens" [Kingsford, *English Historical Literature*, pp. 304–305]).

Page's poem breaks off sooner than in other texts of the CV–1430 JP:A, the deficiency being supplied by a prose paraphrase. Nevertheless, and despite the late fifteenth-century date of the manuscript, there is evidence to suggest that the basis of the text to 1430 was a textually early version of the CV–1430 JP:A, for a number of its readings are superior to those preserved in the other extant texts of group A.[2] Some additional material found in the other texts of the group is absent, such as the account of the duke of Bedford's naval victory off Harfleur at the end of the first chapter on Henry V and the accounts of the earl of Huntingdon's naval victory and the conclusion of the Council of Constance in the second chapter on Henry V.

---

[1] For (1), see item 22.

[2] See Kingsford, *English Historical Literature*, p. 302; Huscher, ed., *Siege of Rouen*, pp. 34–35, 37.

Remarks on the CV–1430 JP:A

The texts of the group show stylistic differences from the earliest CV wording, mainly in the addition of superfluous words and phrases. The wording of chapter headings is more discursive and additional headings have been inserted, for example, for the individual sections of the prophecies of Merlin to Arthur (in those manuscripts that possess this section of narrative).

There is no precise onset of the 1430 JP continuation, which is preserved in its fullest form in the JP:A; rather there is a gradual changeover from the usual 1419 continuation to the present continuation in the chapters that begin the reign of Henry V. In the first chapter on the reign of Henry V the stylistic additions become more significant and some extra material details begin to be incorporated.[1] The second chapter (printed by Kingsford) and the third chapter (printed by Brie, who does not notice any previous differences[2]) give progressively more information and differ in wording to some extent from the 1419 continuation.

It is likely that the 1419 continuation known to the compiler of the archetype of the 1430 continuation belonged to the CV–1419(men):A rather than the CV–1419(r&g):A; the evidence of the substitute heading for the "5w" heading supports this view on the grounds that the CV–1419(men):A would be more likely to possess a text that omitted this heading. In addition, a number of readings in Glasgow Hunterian 74 agree with the CV–1430 JP:A, and, as argued earlier, this text was based on a continuation ending "and manfully countered with our English men."[3] Kingsford seems to have been familiar with only the CV–1419(r&g), and his argument cannot be accepted that there were versions of the *Brut* ending earlier than 1419. He assumes "one perhaps ending in November 1415 or in October 1416, and others more certainly in July 1417 and November 1417," to which the continuation to 1430 was added (*English Historical Literature*, p. 133).

Unlike previous developments, where a new continuation is simply appended to an existing text, the compiler of the archetype of the 1430 JP text has reworked his original and has grafted on his continuation, blending it into the existing text of his exemplar before finally forsaking his exemplar to strike out on his own. The verbal similarities between the 1419 continuation and the 1430 continuation make it clear that the same sources were used for both, although the compiler of the 1430 version probably had additional sources of information.

The following passages, taken from Kingsford (1430 version), Brie (1419 [r&g] version), and Glasgow Hunterian 74 (as a reflex of the 1419[men] text), illustrate the development of the 1430 continuation.

In the first chapter on the reign of Henry V, the 1430 compiler follows a 1419 text, and the two versions are very similar. Although the "tennis-ball" story is related more briefly, as Kingsford remarks, the 1430 version has some fuller readings and some extra material details, as the following selected extracts show:

(1) þis worthi Prynce & King toke his leve, & went hym to Caleys warde by londe. And þe Frensch men herde of his komyng [Brie 377/11–13]

And the kynge the worthi prynce that God saue and kepe wold fro thens to Caleis so stronge thorough the londe and the Frensshe men herd of his comynge [Cotton Galba E.viii, fol. 133v; cf. Kingsford, *English Historical Literature*, p. 299]

Since the 1430 version was written after the death of Henry V, the phrase "that God saue and kepe" suggests that the 1430 compiler was using a source written while Henry was still living.

(2) & þere þay welcomyd hym, and brouȝt hym to London with moche honour and grete reuerence. And atte Seint Thomas watryng þere mette with hym the King and alle his lordeȝ yn gode aray. And þere was a worthi metyng betwene þe Emperour and þe King; & þere thay kussid togadreȝ, & braced ech othir. [Brie 380/31–381/4]

And there thei welcomyd hym with alle honoure and reu[er]ence and so the meyre and the aldremen with the cominnalte brought hym to Seint Thomas Waterynge withoute Southewerke and there the kynge met with hym with alle his lordis in a good and riall araye and there was a worthi and a solempne metynge betwix the emperoure and oure kynge and there kyssid togederis and myche obeysaunce yche shewid to othir and thankynge. [Cotton Galba E.viii, fol. 134; cf. Kingsford, *English Historical Literature*, pp. 299–300]

There is little new material here, but the effect is more graphic and immediate, and the use of "oure kynge" in the 1430 version suggests that Kingsford's opinion is correct, "that we have here a record drawn up at the time,"[4] that is, a return to the common original source. This is borne out further by the insertion of two passages which are not found in the 1419 continuation.[5]

In the second chapter the same processes are at work; the 1430 compiler has longer readings and is historically fuller in some respects. He is still using the *Brut* framework for chapter headings and for the general ordering of his material:

How kinge Henry the .vᵉ. purposyd and ordeynyd him ouere the see in to Fraunce and Normandie by the counceyle of all his lordis and comons of the reame of Englond.

And in þe .iiijᵉ. ȝere of kyng Henries regne þe .v. he helde his parlement at Westmynster in þe begynnyng of þe monthe of Octobur & lasted vnto þe purificacioun of oure lady þan nexte folowynge & þere was graunted vnto þe king to mayntene his werres bothe of spiretualte & temparalte a hole taxte & a dyme in sustenynge of hys werres & þan anone þe kyng prayed al hys lordis to make hem redy to strengthe hym in hys ryȝth & anone he lete make a newe retenew & charged all men to be redy at Hampton in Whitsonweke þan nexte folowing withouten any delay. [Glasgow Hunterian 74, fols. 110v–111]

How kynge Henry the v purposid and ordeynyd hym ouyr the see ayen into Fraunce and Normandye by counseill of hys lordis and cominnes off the Rewme.

And in the iiijᵉ yere of kynge Henryis regne the v the kynge haldynge his parlement at Westeminster in the bygynnynge of the monythe of Octobre the whiche parle[ment] endid aboute the puryfication of oure lady thanne nexte by comen assent of alle the clergye and temperalte ther was grauntid to the kynge bothe dymes and tallagis to fulfille the kyngis purpos in holdynge and susteynynge of chalenge and right that he had to Normandye and Guyane his trewe titull and right heritage. Wherefore the kynge chargid dukis erlis baronys knyghtis and squyeris to make hem redy in the best and moste worthy aray that thei coude or myght with all the strengthe of men of armys and archeris to helpe and strengthe hym yn his werris for the right of Engelond and that thei alle be redy to moustur at Hampton in the Witsonwoke thanne nexte comynge in all her aray as they ought to werre. [Cotton Galba E.viii, fol. 135; cf. Kingsford, *English Historical Literature*, p. 302]

The chapter heading, not found in the early CV texts, suggests again that a 1419(men) continuation was used by the 1430 compiler. The continual use of the phrase "oure kynge" is noticeable in the 1430 version in this chapter. Many details and distinct additional passages are incorporated that can be paralleled in other works, such as the account of the earl of Huntingdon's naval battle in 1417 and the murder of John, duke of Burgundy, in some London chronicles,[6] showing that the 1430 compiler is using the common source more and more.

In the third chapter (printed in Brie), both the 1419 and 1430 versions are based on John Page's poem *The Siege of Rouen*, and the 1430 JP:A version includes the second half of the poem in verse from line 637. However, it is clear that the 1430 compiler used the poem as reference from the beginning of the chapter, as the following passage shows:

How king Henre þe ffythe leyde a sege vnto þe cete of Rone. And how he gat þe cetee with strenthe & manhode.	How kynge Henry þe v leide sege to the cite of Rone and how he gate the cite with strengthe and manhode well and worthily.
And in þe vj^e ȝere of kyng Henries regne þe v^e he sente his vncle sere Thomas Beauford duke of Excestre with a fayre meyne of men of armys & archers tofore þe cetee of Rone and þere displayed here baneres & sente herodes vnto þe towne and bad hem ȝeld þat cetee vnto here king & here lege lord & þey sayde he toke hem non to kepe ne none he shoulde haue þere but ȝif hit were ryȝt dere ibouȝth & meved with here handis for oþere answere wolde þey none ȝeve but out go gonnes & þere þe duke toke good avysement of þe grounde all a-bowte. [Glasgow Hunterian 74, fol. 112]	And in the vj yere of kynge Henryis regne [*MS.* Regnyd] the v the kynge sent his vncle sir Thomas Beauford duke of Exetir with othir lordis and knyghtis men of armys and archeris to the cite of Rone and there displayid her baneris opynly byfore the cite of Rone and sent herodis to hem that were withynne the cite and bade hem yolde vp the cite in alle haste that was the kyngis righte or ellis thei shuld deie an harde and sharpe dethe and withoute eny mercy or grace and there he behild the g[r]ounde about the cite how thei myght best sette her sege to get that cite. And answere wold thei none yeue but meuyd with her hondis ouyr the wallis as

> who seyth "voydith the grounte and the place that ye ben on" and shotte tho many gunnys to hem. [Cotton Galba E.viii, fol. 137; cf. Brie 394/1–16]

The extra details of the 1430 version are paralleled in the full text of Page's *Siege of Rouen*, showing that the 1430 compiler had resorted to it even before he decided to give the unparaphrased poem in verse:[7]

> Howe the V. Harry our lege,
> With hys ryalte he sette a sege
> By for Rone, that ryche cytte,
> And endyd hyt at hys owne volunte.
> [Gairdner, ed., *Hist. Collections*, p. 1; lines 11–14]

> Whenne Pountlarge with sege was wonne,
> And ovyr Sayne then enter was be gunne,
> The Duke of Exceter that [lord so] hende,
> To Rone, yn sothe, oure kynge hym sende.
> Herrowdys with hym unto that cytte,
> To loke yf that they yoldyn wolde be,
> And alle soo for to se that grounde
> That was a boute the cytte rounde;
> Howe our kyng myght lay þer at a sege,
> If they wolde not obey to oure lege.
> When þe Duke of Exceter with grete re-
>   nowne
> Was come by fore the ryalle towne,
> He splayyd his baners on a bent,
> And herrowdys unto þe cytte were sent,
> To meke hem to oure kyngys merthe,
> Chargyd them uppon payne of dethe,
> Not withstondyng hym of hys ryght,
> But delyvyr the cytte to hys syght.
> For he dyd them to wytte with owtyn bade,
> He wolde not goo er he hyt hadde,
> But or he paste farre in space,

Wynne hys ryght thoroughe Goddys grace.
To that the cytte gaf non answere,
But prayde oure herrowdys furthe to fare.
They made a maner skorne with hyr honde
That they there shulde not longer stonde.
Gonnys they schott with grete envye,
And many were smytte pyttyfully.
[Gairdner, ed., *Hist. Collections*, pp. 2–3; lines 25–52]

The poem has been used by both the 1419 and 1430 versions, but the latter gives a much fuller paraphrase that follows very closely until the poem itself is reproduced in verse. It is a more polished version than John Page's rough original in BL Egerton 1995; presumably Page lived long enough to fulfill the promise made at the end of the original poem (in lines skipped in the *Brut* version):

With owten fabylle or fage
Thys procesce made John Page
Alle in raffe and not in ryme,
By cause of space he hadde no tyme.
But whenne thys werre ys at a nende
And he have lyffe and space he wylle hit amende.
[Gairdner, ed., *Hist. Collections*, pp. 45–46; lines 1305–10]

The 1430 compiler brings the narrative finally to the year 1430, using material which was probably not available to the compiler of the 1419 continuations.

Why the 1419(men) compiler did not proceed further with his loose paraphrase of the poem is uncertain, unless he did not have the full text of the poem to work with. The unsatisfactory conclusion, ending in the middle of the siege, is rectified in the 1419(r&g) continuation by the addition of a few lines of prose to bring the siege to an end. Brie believed that these lines were not connected with the poem.[8] The phraseology of the last lines, however, can be paralleled in the poem, which must surely have been known to their writer. For example:

(a) Both govnnys and quarellys went so thrylle,   & moche pople slayne dyuers tyme3 with Gune3, quarell, &

Trypget and spryggalde and grete ingyne,
They wrought oure men fulle moche pyne.
[Gairdner, ed., *Hist. Collections*, p. 16; lines 408–10]

oþer ordynaunce3. [Brie 390/29–30]

(b) They etete doggys, they ete cattys;
They ete mysse, horse and rattys.
[Gairdner, ed., *Hist. Collections*, p. 18; lines 471–72]

for þay hade ete al her hors, doggis and catte3. [Brie 390/34–391/1]

(c) And the chyldryn sokyng in ther pappe
With yn a dede woman lappe.
[Gairdner, ed., *Hist. Collections*, p. 35; lines 1003–1004]

and also saue yonge childryn lye & sowke her modir pappis þat weryn ded. [Brie 391/7–8]

---

[1] See Kingsford, *English Historical Literature*, pp. 299–300.

[2] See Brie, *Geschichte und Quellen*, p. 87: "Er beginnt abzuweichen an dem Punkte, wo Heinrich V. seinen Onkel Thomas Beauford gegen Rouen schickt."

[3] See pp. 104, 130–31. Thus the 1430 JP contains some of the more accurate details concerning Owen Glendower's rebellion.

[4] Kingsford, *English Historical Literature*, p. 299; a further, similar example is given by Kingsford on p. 300.

[5] Quoted in Kingsford, *English Historical Literature*, p. 300.

[6] See Kingsford, *English Historical Literature*, p. 301.

[7] Quoted from Gairdner's edition of BL Egerton 1995 in *Hist. Collections*; the line numbering is that of Huscher's critical edition. The dialect of BL Egerton 1995 is that of Surrey; see *LALME*, 1: 109, 3: 493.

[8] *Geschichte und Quellen*, p. 72.

The Common Version to 1430, including John Page's poem "The Siege of Rouen": Group B (CV–1430 JP:B)

The group contains MSS. BL Harley 753, Lambeth 331, and Illinois 116(2).

79. BL MS. Harley 753

Heading: Here begynneth the prologe of Brut.
Begins: Svm tyme in þe noble land of Surre ther was a noble kyng and a myghty and a man of grete power þat clepid was Dioclisian
Contains: Cad, Description of Edward III, John Page's poem
Omits: QIL, "5w" heading
Changeover, 1333 to 1377: without eny calenge of eny man. After which victory þe kyng turned ayene into Englond and ordeyned ser Robert Baillol with oþer wordes [*sic*] to kepe Scotland.

How kyng Edward went ayene into Scot[...] þe batayle of Scluys and Seint Omers and of þe tur[..]ment of Dunstaple and of Seint Georgis feste at Wyndesore. Capitulo [*repeated*] CC xxiiij°.

The vij yere of kyng Edward in þe wynter tyme he went into Scotlond
End of text to 1377 and heading of "The Description of Edward III": þe kyng Edward after tyme þat he had regned l wynter dyed at hys manere of Shene þe xj kalend of Iuyn and is buryed at Westminster.

Of þe distruccioun of kyng Edward. Capitulo CC xxix°.
Changeover, "The Description of Edward III" to 1419 continuation: and þe more harme is conteyned longe tyme after.

And after kyng Edward þe þirde þat was borne at Wyndesore regned Richard of Burdeux þat was prince Edwardes sone of Walys which prince Edward was sone of þe kyng Edward. Capitulo CC xl°.
Changeover, 1419 to 1430 continuations: And so þe lord Powes meyne brought hym out of Walys to London in a whirlecole and so in þe same whirlecole brought to Westminster halle byfore þe kynges iustice. And þere he was examyned and arayned of þo poyntes þat were put vpon hym [cf. Brie 386/19–22 and Kingsford, *English Historical Literature*, p. 308; see below]
Page's poem (set out as prose, with occasional colons to indicate line breaks) begins: and ofte we cleped and longe þere stode and so we come downe to þe duke of Excestre and þere we gate none answere.
Atte Warwyk þe erle so fre we cleped ofte it wold not be
Page's poem ends: And all haue herd þise tydyng to blysse Crist yow brynge þat for vs dyed on a tre. Amen seyde all for charitee.
And þis yere was quene Iohanne þat was kyng Henryes wyfe þe iiijth

arested by Iohn duke of Bedford
Ends imperfectly on rubbed last leaf: victorie and scomf[..]ure [Brie 439/27–28]

Remarks: The text probably ended originally at the same point as the CV–1430 JP:A.

The names of several sixteenth-century owners appear: "Thys ys Henry Brayne hys boke bey the leyff off Robartt Herdes and Ellen hys wyffes wryttyn the iiij day beffore he whas maryed" (fol. 165v; "Henry Brayne" also on fol. 125); "Rowland Shakerley" (13 Elizabeth [1571–72], fol. 127v; named also on fol. 134).

80. LAMBETH PALACE LIBRARY MS. 331[1]
Heading: Her begynned þe prologe of Brute.
Begins: Sum tyme in the noble land of Sirrye þer was a noble kyng and a myȝthy & a man of gret power þat clepyd was Dyoclician
Contains: Cad, Description of Edward III, John Page's poem
Omits: QIL, "5w" heading
Changeover, 1333 to 1377: without eny chalange of eny man. After whych victory þe kyng turned ayen into Englond & ordeyned ser Edward Bayllol with oþer wordy lordes to kepe Scotlond.

How þat þe kyng Edward went ayene into Scotlond & of þe batayle of Cluys & Seynt Omers & of þe turnament of Dunstable & of Seynt Georges fest at Wyndesore. Capitulo CC xxiiij.

The vij yere of kyng Edward in þe wynter tyme he went into Scotlond & reparayled þe castell of Kylbrigge ayenst þe Scottes
End of text to 1377 and heading of "The Description of Edward III": þe kynge Edward after tyme þat he had regned l wynter dyed at his maner of Shene þe xl kalendes of Iuyn & is buryed at Westmynster.

The distruxcyoun of kyng Edward. Capitulo CC xxix°.
Changeover, "The Description of Edward III" to 1419 continuation: & þe more harme is conteyned longe tyme after.

And after kyng Edward þe þirde þat was borne at Wyndesore regned Richard of Burdeux þat was prince Edwardes sone of Wales. Capitulo CC xl.

Changeover, 1419 to 1430 continuations: & so þe lord Poweys meyne brought hym out of Wales to London in a whircole & so in þe same whircole brought to Westmynster halle byfore þe kynges iustice & þer he was examyned & arayned of þo poyntes þat were put vpon hym

Page's poem (set out as prose, with stops and double virgules to indicate line breaks) begins: & so we come down to þe duke of Excestre & þere we gate non aunswere.

Atte Warwik þe erle so fre we called oft it wold nat be

Page's poem ends: & all have herd þis tidynges to blisse Criste you bringes þat for vs dide on a tree. Amen seid alle for charitee.

And þys yere was quene Iohanna þat was kyng Henryes wiff þe iiij[th] arested by Iohn duk of Bedford

Ends imperfectly on fol. 117v: by ordinaunce & commaundement of þe kyng & of his counsell þe bastard of Clarance & ser Iohn Kyghle [Brie 437/9–11]

---

[1] See James, *Descriptive Catalogue ... Lambeth Palace*, pp. 436–37.

81. UNIVERSITY OF ILLINOIS MS. 116(2)[1]

Third hand begins on fol. 185: [cap]tayne boþe of þe citee and off þe castel

Contains: John Page's poem

Page's poem (set out as prose, with occasional stops to indicate line breaks) begins:
And ofte we clepyd and longe þere stode. And so we come downe to þe duke of Excetre. And þere we gate none answere.

Atte Warwyk the erle so ffre we callid ofte it wolde nat be

Page's poem ends: And alle haue herde þis tydynges to blysse Cryst you brynge þat for vs deyde on a tre. Amen seyde alle ffor charyte.

And thys yeer was quene Iohanna that was kyng Henryes wyfe þe iiijthe arestyd by Iohn duke of Bedford

Ends: and yit God sent hem boþe hele and wellfare and scomfyture of alle here enmyes blessid be God.

Remarks: The third hand[2] in the manuscript begins fol. 185 in the middle of a word and completes the text from a new, CV–1430 JP:B exemplar, as textual comparison with BL Harley 753 and Lambeth 331 shows. The change in exemplar occurs as follows:

Mounser Guy Botteler was chieff cap[fol. 185; new hand and

exemplar]tayne boþe of þe citee and off þe castel and Mounsere Termegan and he was captayne off þe porte Caux. Mounsere le Roche was captayne off Devisyn. Mounsere Antony he was levetenaunt to Mounsere le Guy de Boteler. Harry Chamfewe was capteyne of þe port de Pount. Iohn Matrivers was captayne off porte de la castell. Mounsere Peneux was þo captayne off port de Seynt Hillarie. The bastard of Teyne was þo capteyne off port Martevile. And Graunt Iakes a worthy werriour was capteyne of alle þe ordenauncis outward on hors bak and on fote of men of armys þat isswid out of þe citee at alle þe portis to done þeir ffetis in poyntis of werre ayenst here enemyes. [cf. Brie 390/9–21, 398/11–24]

---

[1] For (1), see item 120.
[2] The change from the first to second hands occurs at a point of no textual significance. The leaves on which the third hand writes are more heavily lined than those before.

Remarks on the CV–1430 JP:B
As noted above, the group is composite, formed from several other groups. The heading and the first words ("Some time") of the two full texts resemble the Extended Version, but the other distinctive features of the EV are lacking.[1]

To 1377 the text is based on the CV–1377 s.c. of the type of Lambeth 491, which also includes "The Description of Edward III," but which did not, apparently, include the Cadwallader episode.[2] However, the text that the compiler used for the 1430 continuation would have certainly included this popular story, and the text that served for the 1419 continuation may also have included it.

After the 1377 text and "The Description of Edward III," the narrative continues with a normal 1419 continuation to almost the end of the second chapter on the reign of Henry V, where, in the middle of the account of Sir John Oldcastle, the text changes to that of the 1430 JP:A:

> and so þe Lorde Powys meyne brouȝt hym out of Walis to London yn a whirlecole; and so he was brouȝt to Westmynstre [1419 continuation: Brie 386/19–21]

> and so he was take there and arestid by the lord Powis and his meyne and brought oute of Walis into Engelond and so to London in a

whirlecole and so in the same whirlicole brought to Westeminstre hall to the parlement and byforn the kyngis iusticis [1430 JP:A continuation: Cotton Galba E.viii, fol. 137; cf. Kingsford, *English Historical Literature*, p. 308]

---

[1] See p. 173.
[2] See item 18.

Manuscripts containing John Page's poem
"The Siege of Rouen": Group C (JP:C)

In MSS. CUL Hh.6.9(2), TCC O.9.1(2), and Chicago 254(2) a continuation is found beyond 1419 that begins with a shorter extract from John Page's poem (corresponding to line 1157 in the full poem) and ends in 1434 or 1445. Although in all three manuscripts the continuation is written in the same hand as the preceding texts, these preceding texts are of such different groups as to justify treating the continuation separately.

82. CAMBRIDGE UNIVERSITY LIBRARY MS. HH.6.9(2)[1]
Page's poem (set out as verse) begins on fol. 158v:
    And more they shulde vndertake
    A castell for our kyng doo make [Brie 418/32–33]
Page's poem ends on fol. 161:
    And all that harde of þis talkyng
    To his blisse Criste theme brynge
    That for vs died vpon a tre
    Amen sey we all for charitee.

Off the tretis made bytwne the kyng off Yngland and off Fraunce. Capitulo ij^C xlviij°.

And in this same yere att þe feste of Witsonday the kyng lay at Maunt with all his lordes

Ends: which was grete hevynesse to all people. [Capitulo ij^C iiij^{xx} xviij° *del.*; Brie 467/18–19]

Remarks: The continuation follows without break immediately after the

1419(r&g) conclusion of the first part of the text.

---

[1] For (1), see item 145. An extract from 1420 to 1428 is printed in Brie 440–43.

83. TRINITY COLLEGE, CAMBRIDGE MS. O.9.1(2)[1]
Page's poem (set out as verse) begins on fol. 195v:
    And more thei shall vndertake
    A castell for oure kyng to make [Brie 418/32–33]
Page's poem ends:
    And all þat haue herd this talkyng
    To his blisse Crist theim bryng
    Þat for vs deied vpon a tree
    Amen say we alle for charite.
And in the same yere at the fest of Whitsontide the kyng lay at Maunt with alle his lordes and there held a roiall fest at that tyme among all his peple
Ends on fol. 225v (the names set out as in the London chronicles): Simon Eyre Maior. Johannes Derby Galfrid Feldyng vicecomites. Anno xxiiij^{to}.

Remarks: Although the original text is written in a single hand, a change of exemplar is indicated when the text to 1419 ends on fol. 195r, about one-third of which is left blank, and Page's poem begins the continuation on the verso of the leaf. The text, however, was conceived of as a whole, for the program of illumination continues. Thus the leaf on which the mayor and the sheriffs are recorded for the first year of Henry VI receives an illuminated border in the same manner as the beginnings of previous reigns were distinguished.

    At the conclusion of the original continuation, a later, fifteenth-century hand continues the text for one year from a London chronicle, on fol. 226v, beginning "Johannes Olney Maior. Robertus Horne Galfridus Boleyne vicecomites. Anno xxv^{to}." and ending "And they rode thoroughe London in theire passage outeward with a roiall meyny."

    On fols. 230–231 occurs a copy of an indenture, dated 26 December, 17 Edward IV (1478), between Walter Lokington and John Cokerych, wardens of the Fraternity of the Assumption of Our Lady in St. Margaret's Church in the close of St. Peter of Westminster, and James Fytt, citizen and tailor of London.

¹ For (1), see item 117. See Mooney, *Handlist*, pp. 136–38. The continuation from 1430–31 to the original end in 1445–46 is printed in Brie 456–90.

84. UNIVERSITY OF CHICAGO MS. 254(2)¹
Page's poem (set out as verse) begins on fol. 124:
    And more þey schulde vndyrtake
    A castel for oure kynge to make [Brie 418/32–33]
Page's poem ends:
    And all þat harde off þis talkyng
    To blysse Cryste hem brynge
    That ffor vs dyyde oon a tre
    Amen say we all ffor charyte.

Of a ffeste þat þe kyng made at Maunte at þe whych ffeste he made ij erlys & of embassatourys.

And in þis same yere at þe ffeste off Whitsontyd the kyng lay at Maunte with all his lordys
Ends imperfectly on torn fol. 149v: vnto þe feste off Saynt George [. . . (*torn off*) And þan þe *catchwords*] [Brie 488/4–5]

Remarks: The continuation follows without break immediately after the 1419(r&g) conclusion of the first part of the text and may have ended at the same point as that found in the preceding manuscript.

¹ For (1), see item 72. The manuscript belonged to John Nuton, prior of Battle Abbey.

Remarks on the JP:C
The relationships among the texts of the three manuscripts of the JP:C, and between them and the 1419(men) and the 1430 continuations, are complex.

The first part of each manuscript belongs to different textual groups that are not directly related. Textual comparisons show that none of the JP:C continuations were copied directly from any of the others and that each of the three texts has agreements with the other two members of the group.¹

TCC O.9.1 preserves most closely the annalistic format of the London chronicle source. On the other hand, Chicago 254 (which probably ended at the same point as the preceding text) and CUL Hh.6.9 (which ends some eleven years earlier) make some accommodation to the narrative structure of the *Brut* by introducing subheadings that approximate to chapter headings. This is particularly true of the text in the former manuscript, whereas the latter also inserts chapter numbers. Although it ends at an earlier point, CUL Hh.6.9 omits much material related to the French wars. Clearly, earlier texts must have existed from which the surviving texts of the JP:C were derived and then appended to texts of various groups.

The original text of the JP:C continuation was close in form to the source material and preserved the annalistic structure of the London civic chronicles, which also provided the raw material for the 1419 and 1430 JP continuations. Yet the surviving texts of the JP:C continue the narrative further (1434, 1445) than the more literary *Brut* continuations (1419, 1430), and it is reasonable to suppose that had this extra information been available to the compilers of the 1419 and 1430 continuations, they would have used it. Like the 1419 and the 1430 continuations, the JP:C texts, although based on common sources, were largely—though probably not entirely—independent adaptations of the source material.

The common sources for the various groups are clearly to be sought in the London City Chronicles. Although a single original source does not seem to have survived, there are sufficient agreements and disagreements in the extant civic chronicles to show that there once existed chronicles that provided the raw material for the *Brut* continuations.[2] The developing relationship may have occurred as follows.

The 1419(men) continuation was principally taken from a London civic chronicle[3] and from John Page's poem (adapted into prose).[4] To the primary civic chronicle source a continuation to 1430 was added,[5] and the compiler of the CV–1430 JP:A continuation reverted to it for his material, which he converted into a form analogous to the customary *Brut* text. Thus he omitted the names of mayors and sheriffs and presented his continuation in chapters, with headings taken from existing 1419 continuations as far as possible.[6]

A further addition to the primary source London civic chronicle, in one copy or another, appears to have brought it to 1434, and this stage is now represented by the text in CUL Hh.6.9. This continuation is less an adaptation to *Brut* form than a mere transcription of selected passages inserted primarily to bring the narrative up to date without any artistic or literary pretensions. There are some attempts to accommodate the form to that of the *Brut* by introducing some chapter headings and numbers, but the civic provenance is betrayed by the names of the mayors and sheriffs and by the typical civic chronicle opening-phrase "And in this same yere," which opens a great number of notices of individual events.[7]

The closeness, if not identity, of the chronicle sources of the 1430 continuation and of the continuation in the JP:C (here quoted from CUL Hh.6.9) can be seen in the following extracts (quoted from Brie):

(a) And also in the same yere, betwene Cristemesse and Candilmasse, the toune of Milon was yolden to the Kynge; and all the cheueteynys, with the soudiourys, were taken, and led to the Cite of Paris in the croke of the mone, they myght sey; for of hem ther scapid thens but a fewe on lyue. [1430 JP:A cont.: Brie 427/24–28]

And in this same yere, And in þe yere of grace a M^l IIII^c XX^{ti}, bytwene Cristemesse and Candilmasse, the Towne of Milloyne was yolden vp to the Kynge; And all þe Chiftains, with þe Souldeours, were take and ledde to þe Cite of Parys, "in þe Croke of þe mone," þei may say for theme; ffor þer escapede fro thens of þeme but a fewe on lyue, for þei of Paris did theme to dethe. [CUL Hh.6.9: Brie 440/10–15]

(b)

How that there ffill grete habundaunce off Rayn; And how dyuers sowdiourz went ouer the see.

And also in this same yere fro the begynnynge of the monythe of Appryell into the feste of All-Haloue, was so grete haboundance of Reyne, where-thorough not only heigh was distroyid, but also all maner of cornys, for it reynyd almoste euyry othir day, more or lesse, durynge the tyme aforeseid. [1430 JP:A cont.: Brie 435/6–10]

And in this same yere, & in þe yere of grace M^l IIII^c XXVII, from þe begynnyng of þe moneth of Aprile vnto the feste of All Halowen, was so abundaunce of Rayn that, not only hay was distroied, but Also all maner of Cornes; for it Raynede all-moste euery day, more or lesse, duryng this terme a-for-said. [CUL Hh. 6.9: Brie 442/8–14]

Since he believed that the common source of CUL Hh.6.9 and of TCC

O.9.1 was a London chronicle ending in 1445, Brie was unable to explain why the latter text should end eleven years later than the former.[8] Various explanations are possible.

It is, for example, possible that all three extant texts of the JP:C were copied from a text ending in 1445, through at least one intermediate stage (to account for agreements that each text has with each of the other members of the group), but that CUL Hh.6.9 was not completed.

Assuming, however, that this manuscript is in fact complete, then a plausible genesis may be that it was copied from an earlier stage of the text that ended in 1434 but which later received a continuation to 1445. Again, at least one intermediate text must have intervened between the original compilation and the existing witnesses, as textual agreements show, exemplified in the following notice for 1432–33 from the three texts:

> Off a gen[er]all counsell hold by3ond the see ffor to destroie eretikes & lollardes. Capitulo ij^c iiij^{xx} xiij^o.

> And in þis same yer anone aftir Cristemesse þe grete convocation & consaill of all þe landes of Cristeiance of all þe spiritualte & temporallte and of all seculer lordes and clerkis þat is to say bisshoppis & other was holden & begonne in þe citie of Basile in Ducheland for to make peace & vnite betwix all Cristen peple & for to destroie heretikes & heresie þat now reigneth amonge the peple. [CUL Hh.6.9: cf. Brie 466 n. 2]

> Of a grete conuocacion holde at Basyle yn Duchelande of alle Crystyn landys.

> And in þis same yere anone after Crystemas þe gret conuocacion and counceyle off all þe lande off Crystyanyte and also of oþer seculer lordes and clerkes þat is to say bysschops and othre was holdyn and bygunne in þe cyte off Basyle in Duchelande ffor to make vnyte and pees amonge all Crystyn pepyl and for to distroye heretykes and heresy þat now regnyth amonge þe pepyl. [Chicago 254, fol. 138v]

> And in this same yere, anon after Cristmasse, the grete conuocacion and consayle of all the landes in Cristendom, and also of all oþer seculer lordes, and Clerkes,—þat is to say, Bisshoppis and other [other which *MS.*] consayle began in the Cite of Basile in Duchelande, for to make vnite and peas emong all Cristen peple, and for to

destroye heretikes and erresye þat then reigned emong the peple. [TCC O.9.1: Brie 466/3–8]

Individual readings show the closeness of the three texts but also illustrate that none seem to be derived directly from any other.

Two points in the passage last quoted deserve separate comment. First, the headings in CUL Hh.6.9 and Chicago 254 indicate a primitive attempt at assimilation to the normal *Brut* format. Second, the use of "now" in CUL Hh.6.9 suggests that the original JP:C text may have been written around that date, that is, in 1434–35 (the reading being simply retained in a text continued to 1445 and thus occurring in Chicago 254), whereas the use of "then" in TCC O.9.1 is consonant with a suggested date of writing some eleven years later, that is, in 1445–46.

---

[1] Huscher, who did not have access to Chicago 254 (olim Quaritsch), concludes that neither CUL Hh.6.9 nor TCC O.9.1 is a copy of the other (*Siege of Rouen*, p. 36).

[2] The relationship among the extant texts of the London chronicles is highly complex, more so than Kingsford concluded (*English Historical Literature*, pp. 75–107); see McLaren, "Textual Transmission," pp. 38–72 (for the texts of the present *Brut* group, see pp. 41, 70–71 n. 25). Thomas and Thornley, eds., *Great Chronicle*, pp. xviii ff., see each text as more or less an independent production, drawing selectively upon common sources and upon one another. Many such texts have clearly been lost.

[3] Kingsford, *English Historical Literature*, pp. 76 and 292, argues that some texts ended at 1417 and 1419.

[4] It is possible that John Page's poem, in its revised form, was included in some lost London City Chronicle source, since three *Brut* continuations that used that common source include the poem in some form, whether in prose adaptation or in verse. However, Kingsford points out the paucity of poems in the extant texts of London chronicles (*Chrons. London*, pp. xxv–xxvi). The inclusion of Page's poem in the CV–1430 JP:A may have influenced the compilers of the JP:C.

[5] There is some evidence that one version of a London chronicle ended in 1430; see Kingsford, *English Historical Literature*, pp. 77, 80, 82–86.

[6] See pp. 138–42.

[7] The phrase is found, though more sparingly, in the more literary continuations based on London chronicles.

[8] Brie, *Geschichte und Quellen*, pp. 90–91 (read "1445" for "1345" on p. 90). Brie had not seen the Chicago text. The extant London chronicle text to which the *Brut* continuations are most closely related is found in BL Harley 540, transcribed by John Stow, which begins imperfectly in 1421 and ends in 1447; see McLaren, "Textual Transmission," p. 66, and the short extract in Kingsford, *English Historical Literature*, pp. 295–96.

The Common Version to 1461 (CV-1461)

The final group of texts in the Common Version contains the Cadwallader episode, Queen Isabella's letter, "The Description of Edward III," and a continuation that takes the narrative from the end of the siege of Rouen in 1419 to the year 1461 but omits the "5w" heading. The CV-1461 can be considered the culmination of the main tradition of the Common Version in that it presents the fullest form of the text taken to the latest date. However, it should be remembered that the CV-1461 developed from a subgroup of those texts that ended in 1419(r&g)—the CV-1419(r&g):B, subgroup (c), represented by Huntington MS. HM 136(1) (which, coincidentally, received in its turn an incomplete addition from the continuation to 1461).

The continuation from 1419 to 1461 appears in William Caxton's *editio princeps* of the *Brut*, under the title of *The Chronicles of England* (1480), and was probably compiled by him (see Remarks on the CV-1461 below). The only complete manuscript written in a single hand that contains the 1461 continuation is BL MS. Addit. 10099. Incomplete texts of the 1461 continuation are appended to texts of various groups in MSS. Glasgow Hunterian 74, Glasgow Hunterian 228, Bodl. Rawlinson poet. 32, Lambeth 264, Huntington HM 136, and Harvard 530. BL Cotton Claudius A.viii contains an extract covering the reign of Henry V. (A section of the 1461 continuation also appears in the Poly. 1461 W.C.; see the following group.)

85. "The Cronicles of Englond" (Caxton, 1480)[1]

Preface: In the yere of th'yncarnacion of our lord Ihesu Crist M CCCC lxxx and in the xx yere of the regne of kyng Edward the fourthe atte requeste of dyuerce gentilmen I haue endeuourd me to enprinte the cronicles of Englond as in this booke shall by the suffraunce of God folowe. And to th'ende that euery man may see and shortly fynde suche mater as it shall plese hym to see or rede I haue ordeyned a table of the maters shortly compiled & chapitred as here shall folowe which booke begynneth at Albyne how she with her susters fonde this land first & named it Albion & endeth at the beginnyng of the regne of our said souerain lord kyng Edward the iiij.

Table of contents begins: First in the prologue is conteyned how Albyne with hir sustres entred into this ile and named it Albyon.

Table of contents ends: Of the deposicion of kyng Harry the sixthe and how kyng Edward the fourth toke possession of the reame and of the bataille on Palme Sonday and how he was crouned. Capitulo cc lxiij & vltimo.

Heading: How the lande of Englonde was fyrst namd Albyon and by what encheson it was so namd.

Begins: [I]n the noble lande of Sirrie ther was a noble kyng and myhty & a man of grete renome that me called Dioclisian that well and worthely hym gouerned and ruled thurgh hys noble chiualrie so that he conquered all the landes about hym so that almost al the kynges of the world to hym were entendant.

Contains: Cad, QIL, Description of Edward III

Omits: "5w" heading

Changeover, 1419 to 1461: And than the kyng entred into the toune and rested hym in the castell till the toune was sette in rewle and in gouernaunce.

How the kyng of Englond was made heritier & regent of Fraunce and how he wedded quene Katherine. Capitulo CC xlv.

And anone after that Rone was goten Depe & many othir tounes in baas Normandie yaf them ouer withoute strok or siege [cf. Brie 391/14–16, 491/1–5]

Ends: And aboute midsomer after the yere of our lord M cccc lx and the first yere of his regne he was crouned at Westmynstre & enoynted kyng of Englond hauyng the hole possession of all the hole reame whom I pray God saue & kepe & sende hym the accomplisshement of the remenaunt of his rightfull enheritaunce beyonde the see & that he may regne in them to the playsir of Almyghty God helthe of his soule honour & wurship in this present lyfe & well & proufytt of alle his subgettis & that ther may be a verray finall pees in all Cristen reames that the infidelis & mysscreauntes may be withstanden & destroied & our faith enhannced which in thise dayes is sore mynusshed by the puissaunce of the Turkes & hethen men and that after this present & short lyfe we may come to the euerlasting lyfe in the blisse of heuen. Amen.

Colophon: Thus endeth this present booke of the cronicles of Englond enprinted by me William Caxton in th'abbey of Westmynstre by London. Fynysshid and accomplisshid the x day of Iuyn the yere of th'incarnacion of our lord God M CCCC lxxx and in the xx yere of the regne of kyng Edward the fourth.

Remarks: To the 1419(r&g) ending, the text is of the type of Huntington HM 136(1), which contains a similar combination of features.[2] As in that manuscript, a separate chapter heading and number (also listed in the table of contents) occur for the array of the Scottish army at Halidon Hill: "This was the aray of the Scottes how that they comen in batailles ayens the ij kynges of Englond and Scotland. In the vauntward of Scotland were these lordes. Capitulo ducendesimo xxiiij."

This edition of 1480 formed the basis for all subsequent printed editions (see pp. 339–48 below).

---

[1] For a typographical description, see William Blades, *The Life and Typography of William Caxton*, 2 vols. (1863; rpt. New York, n.d.), 2: 109–11. The *Chronicles of England* are often found bound with *The Description of England* (finished August 18, 1480), an extract from John Trevisa's translation of the *Polychronicon*, in the preface to which Caxton notes: "Hit is so that in many and dyuerse places the comyn Cronycles of Englonde ben hadde and also now late enprynted at Westmynstre."

[2] See item 61.

86. BL MS. ADDITIONAL 10099[1]

Table of contents begins on fol. 1: 31 sustres [*marg.*] Fyrst in þe prologue is conteyned how Albyne with h[.]r sustres entred into þis land & named it Albyon.

Table of contents ends on fol. 8: Ed. iiij^{tus} [*marg.*] Of þe deposicion of king Henry þe sixt. And how king Edward þe fourt toke possession of þe realm & of þe batail of Palme Sonday & of his coronacion.

Heading on fol. 11: How þe land of England was first named Albion and by what encheson it was so named.

Begins: In the noble land of Surry þer was a noble kyng and a man of gret renown that men callid Dioclician that wel & worthely gouerned him & keped him thorow his noble chivalry so þat he conquered al þe landes about him so þat almoste al þe kynges of þe world to him wer entendant.

Contains: Cad, QIL, Description of Edward III

Omits: "5w" heading

Changeover, 1419 to 1461: And þan þe king entred into þe town & rested him in þe castell til þe town was sett in rewl & gouernance.

How þe kyng of Englond Henry þe v^{te} was made heritier & regent of Fraunce & how he weddid quene Katerine. Capitulo CCxlv.

[A]none after þat Rone was goten Depe & many other townes in baas

Normandie yafe þame ouer without stroke or siege when þei vnderstode þat þe kyng had goten Rone.

Ends on fol. 203: which in thise dayes is sore mynushed by þe puissaunce of þe Turkes & hethen men and þat after þis present & short life we may come to þe euerlastyng life. Amen. Explicit.

Remarks: Fol. 9v contains historical notes in Latin. Fol. 10v contains a set of Latin verses and a mnemonic verse on the kings of England up to Henry VII.

After the *Brut* text occur a number of short items: (1) fols. 203v–204 were originally blank; fol. 204 contains Elizabethan notes on the accessions of the monarchs from Edward IV to Elizabeth, "whome God longe preserue"; (2) fol. 204v: Latin notes on the kings and their coronations from William the Conqueror to Henry III and on the election of Thomas Warthel to the abbacy of Westminster; (3) fols. 205–210v: a tripartite, English treatise (also found in BL Harley 2252, fol. 51v) on Edward IV's claim to the crowns of England, France, "castel legiounes," and Normandy, from A.D. 876 to Edward III; the text refers to Edward IV as the current king and ends with the initials "T. B." (see below); (4) fol. 210v also contains several of the provisions of the Treaty of Picquigny (August 29, 1475), including the proposed marriage of Edward IV's daughter Elizabeth to the Dauphin and an annual jointure of £60,000[2]; (5) fols. 211–212v: thirteen disarranged stanzas of Lydgate's "Dietary," here entitled "Doctrina sana," ending with the reversed name Thomas Burton; (6) fols. 213–226v: extracts from various chapters of the Latin *Polychronicon*, beginning in book 1, chapter 36 ("Giraldus refert..."); (7) fols. 227–233v: a Latin charter, dated at Roxburgh, January 25, 1355, from Edward Balliol, King of Scots, to Edward III of England, granting Edward III's overlordship; (8) fols. 234v–235v: a letter, dated at Ramsey, March 7, 1301, from Edward I to Pope Boniface VIII, concerning Edward's right to the kingdom of Scotland; and (9) fols. 236–246v: an alphabetical index to the *Polychronicon*, headed "Tabula super Policronicon."

The manuscript is on paper to fol. 204 and on vellum thereafter. It is written in an unprofessional hand, which may also be responsible for the historical notes (except for the Elizabethan notes on fol. 204).

Item (3) was probably composed before Edward IV's French expedition of 1475 and item (4) deals with the resulting treaty toward the end of that year. This need not imply, however, that the manuscript was written before 1480 (the date of Caxton's edition), though, given the inclusion of these items, it was probably written before Edward's death on April 9, 1483. First, the terms of the treaty were not made widely public in 1475.[3] Second, the proposed marriage became a central issue in diplomatic negotiations between 1479 and 1481 between England, France, and Burgundy, though any possibility of it taking place was destroyed by the Treaty of Arras (December 23, 1482) between France and Burgundy, which included an agreement that the Dauphin should marry Margaret of Austria.[4]

The manuscript belonged to Leonard Beckwith in 1634.

---

[1] See Peter Brown and Elton D. Higgs, *The Index of Middle English Prose. Handlist V: A Handlist of Manuscripts Containing Middle English Prose in the Additional Collection (10001–14000), British Library, London* (Cambridge, 1988), pp. 10–12. The 1419–1461 continuation is printed in Brie 491–533.
[2] See Charles Ross, *Edward IV* (Berkeley and Los Angeles, 1974), p. 233.
[3] See Ross, *Edward IV*, p. 236 and n. 1.
[4] See Ross, *Edward IV*, pp. 253–55, 284, 292.

87. UNIVERSITY OF GLASGOW, MS. HUNTERIAN 74(2)[1]

Fourth scribe begins on fol. 113: And moche people slayne dyuerse tymes wyth gonnes quarelles and other ordynaunce [Brie 390/29–30]

Changeover, 1419 to 1461: tyll the towne was sett in rulle & in gouernaunce.

And anone after þat Roone was gotten Depe & many other townes in the Basse Normandy gaue them ouer wythowt stroke or seyge

Ends imperfectly: he shulde not seke none occasiouns for to entre into such matters & þen [Brie 495/11–12]

Remarks: The fourth scribe, who belongs to the late fifteenth or early sixteenth century, continues immediately after the 1419(men) ending. Spaces are left for the chapter headings.

---

[1] For (1), see item 68.

88. BL MS. COTTON CLAUDIUS A.VIII[1]

Heading on fol. 2: The cronycle of kyng Henry the v that was kyng Henries sone.

Begins: And after the deth of kyng Henry the iiij[th] [Brie 373/3]

Changeover, 1419 to 1461: tyll the toune was sett in rewle and in gouernaunce.

How the kyng of England was made hertier and regent of Fraunce and howe he wedded quene Katerine. Capitulo CC xlv.

And anone after that Rone was goten Depe and many othir tounes in Baas Normandye yaf hem ouer withoute stroke or seige
Ends on fol. 12: on whos soule God haue mercy. Amen. [Brie 496/32–33]

Remarks: That this extract, which covers the reign of Henry V, is taken from a complete text is shown by the chapter number in the heading of the first chapter of the 1461 continuation, quoted above (cf. Brie 491/1–3 and n. 1).

---

[1] See Kennedy, *Manual*, pp. 2633–34, for this and other biographies of Henry V.

89. UNIVERSITY OF GLASGOW, MS. HUNTERIAN 228(2)[1]
Second scribe begins on fol. 149v: How the kyng of Englond was made heritor [*changed from* herityer] and regent of Fraunce and how he wedded quene Kateryne. Capitulo CC xlv°.

[A]nd anone after that Rone was gotyn Depe and many other tounes in Baas Normandye yaf them ouer withoute stroke or siege
Ends imperfectly: Vltima conseptam denunciat esse Mariam [Brie 495/32]

Remarks: The unprofessional hand is of the late fifteenth century. The text agrees with that of Caxton's 1482 edition of the *Chronicles of England*.

---

[1] For (1), see item 45.

90. BODLEIAN MS. RAWLINSON POET. 32(3)[1]
1461 continuation begins on fol. 151: How kyng Henry the vj regned beyng a childe not one yere of age and of the bataill of Vernoill in Perche.

Affter kyng Henry the v regned Henry his sone but a childe and not fully a yere old [Brie 497/1–5]
Ends on fol. 168: And that after this present & short lyfe we may come to the euerlastyng lyfe in the blisse of heuen. Amen. [Brie 533/30–31 and n. 10]

THE COMMON VERSION 163

Remarks: The continuation to 1461 begins with its third chapter, recounting the accession of Henry VI. It follows immediately upon the conclusion of a continuation copied from the PV–1422:A, which ends with the death of Henry V.[2] The same hand that finished the PV–1422:A text (the last of several hands that wrote the composite *Brut* text), beginning at the top of fol. 151, was also responsible for the 1461 section.

---

[1] For (1), see item 115; for (2), see item 160.
[2] See pp. 271–77.

91. LAMBETH PALACE LIBRARY MS. 264(2)[1]
New scribe begins on fol. 143: How kyng Henry the vjth regned beyng a childe not on yere of age and of þe bataille of Vernoill in Perche. Capitulum CC xlvij.

After kyng Henre þe v regned Henry his sone but a childe & not fully a yere olde [Brie 497/1–5]
Ends: And that after þis present & short lyf he may come to þe euerlastyng lyf in þe blisse of heuen. Amen.
Colophon: Thus endeth þis present booke of cronicles of Englond wryten by me Thomas Rydyng þe iiij day of Novembre þe yere of our lord M CCCCC X.

Remarks: Several leaves have been torn out between the end of the 1419(men) continuation and the beginning of the 1461 continuation, which begins with the third chapter. The sixteenth-century writer, Thomas Rydyng, was probably also the owner. His colophon is modeled on Caxton's.

---

[1] For (1), see item 28.

92. HUNTINGTON MS. HM 136(2)[1]
Second scribe begins on fol. 156v: [A]nd anone after that Rone was goten Depe and many other tounes in Baase Normandie yaf them over withowte stroke or siege [Brie 491/4–5]
Ends imperfectly on fol. 158: [A]fter kynge Henry the v regned Henry his

sone but a childe and not fully a yere olde whos regne begane the first day of Septembre [Brie 497/4–6]

Remarks: That the continuation, which is written in a neat fifteenth-century hand, ends at the foot of the recto of a leaf shows that it was not completed. Spaces are left blank for chapter headings.

---

[1] For (1), including early owners of the manuscript, see item 61. See Dutschke, *Guide*, 2: 181–83.

93. HARVARD UNIVERSITY MS. ENG. 530(2)[1]

Heading on fol. 204: Howe the kyng of Englond was made heriter & regent of Fraunce & howe he weddid qwene Kateryn.

Begins: and anone after that Rone was goten Depe & many other townes in Baas Normandy yaf them over withowte stroke [Brie 491/1–5]

Ends imperfectly on fol. 211v: certeyn shyppes la[. . .] with rye which eaysyd & dyd moch gode to the peple ffor corne was so skarse yn Englond that [Brie 507/24–26]

Remarks: The 1419 to 1461 continuation, which includes chapter headings but not numbers, is added in a late-fifteenth-century hand that does not appear elsewhere in the manuscript. This hand cannot, of course, be that of John Shirley, who is associated with the manuscript, since Shirley died in 1456.[2] The text agrees well with that of Caxton's edition.

---

[1] For (1), see item 146. See Voigts, "Handlist," pp. 20–22.
[2] See A. I. Doyle, "More Light on John Shirley," *Medium Ævum* 30 (1961): 93.

Remarks on the CV–1461

There is strong codicological and internal evidence, which I have adduced in detail elsewhere, to suggest that William Caxton was the compiler of the continuation from 1419 to 1461 and that the manuscript witnesses are copied either from his printed editions or, in the case of BL Addit. 10099, perhaps from the manuscript exemplar that Caxton had prepared for his compositor.[1]

There is no evidence that a manuscript tradition lies behind the continuation from 1419 to 1461. In Huntington HM 136, Glasgow Hunterian 74, Lambeth 264, Glasgow Hunterian 228, and Harvard Eng. 530, the continuation is appended by later scribes to texts belonging to various groups. The short additions in Glasgow Hunterian 74, Huntington HM 136, and Glasgow Hunterian 228 were possibly never finished; the text of the last agrees with that found in Caxton's second edition of the *Chronicles of England* (1482). The late copy in Lambeth 264, incomplete at the beginning, is clearly taken from Caxton.

BL Cotton Claudius A.viii presents itself as a biography of Henry V. It is not, however, an independent work but a close copy of Caxton's printed text covering the reign of that king.

The continuation in Bodl. Rawlinson poet. 32 follows upon a continuation that ends with the death of Henry V in 1422 and, like Lambeth 264, begins with the third chapter. The text corresponds almost exactly to Caxton's, and it ends with the prayer for Edward IV.

The *Brut* text in BL Addit. 10099 is written in a single hand and is the only manuscript that contains the full continuation. Both content and wording correspond almost exactly to those found in Caxton's *Chronicles of England*. It also contains a table of contents similar to that in the print where Caxton seems to claim this feature as his own contribution.

A verbal comparison with the London civic chronicle sources for the 1419 to 1461 continuation shows that BL Addit. 10099 could not be the exemplar for Caxton's *Chronicles of England*. It also shows that BL Addit. 10099 cannot simply be a copy from the print. There is evidence that some copies of texts printed by Caxton were made from the manuscript exemplars prepared for the press rather than from the printed books themselves. The more handsome of these were probably intended as presentation copies for royal or noble patrons, but more ordinary-looking manuscripts of this type presumably had less lofty purposes or recipients, perhaps of the merchant class. It is likely that BL Addit. 10099 falls into the latter category.[2]

The major source of the continuation was a civic chronicle of London, supplemented by material from the *Fasciculus temporum* of Werner Rolewinck, first officially published in Cologne in 1474 and in Louvain in 1475 by Johan Veldener, who had been Caxton's printing master and business associate. An addition to the notice of the invention of printing around 1456 suggests that printed books were easily available and cheap in England. This notice, reminiscent in phrasing of Caxton's *Advertisement* of ca. 1477, probably refers to the situation after Caxton's introduction of printing to England in the 1470s. The concluding prayer for Edward IV contains topical allusions appropriate to the year 1480, and many of the phrases used therein are paralleled or echoed in other such prayers or dedicatory epilogues by Caxton.

---

[1] See Matheson, "Printer and Scribe," pp. 594–601, 610–13, on which the present Remarks on the CV–1461 are based. The addition of Harvard Eng. 530, which agrees with Caxton's printed text, does not alter the arguments presented therein.

[2] In addition to the examples and references given in Matheson, "Printer and Scribe," p. 598 n. 21, see also N. F. Blake, "Manuscript to Print," in N. F. Blake, *William Caxton and English Literary Culture* (London and Rio Grande, 1991), pp. 287–90, 294–303.

Manuscripts containing the *Polychronicon* 1461 continuation and associated with "Warkworth's" *Chronicle* (Poly. 1461 W.C.)

Three manuscripts, Peterhouse 190, Glasgow Hunterian 83, and BL Harley 3730, form a closely linked group that illustrates in a striking way the methods open to a medieval scribe who wished to assemble a composite text. These manuscripts contain a continuation from 1419 to 1461 (Poly. 1461) formed by combining sections of text copied first from Caxton's printed *Chronicles of England* and then from the *Liber ultimus*, which was compiled by Caxton to complete his 1482 edition of the *Polychronicon*. In the two complete manuscripts, this composite continuation is followed by a short chronicle once attributed to John Warkworth (W.C.).[1]

The first section of Caxton's *Liber ultimus*, from 1358 to the end of the siege of Rouen in 1419, is itself partly based on a *Brut* text ending in 1419, quite possibly the 1480 edition of the *Chronicles of England*, supplemented from a copy of a London civic chronicle and from other sources.[2] In general, the *Brut* text is followed more closely in the earlier parts of this section, perhaps because the civic chronicle and the other sources were not as full for this period. As the supplementary sources became fuller, Caxton relied on them more and he made a number of compensatory abbreviations in the *Brut* text. Thus, for example, the whole story of the siege of Rouen is summarized as follows before the text begins to correspond to that of the continuation to 1461 found in the *Chronicles of England*:

> In the syxthe yere the kyng besyeged the cyte of Roan whiche endured half yere and more. And atte laste the cyte beyng in grete famyne putte oute moche peple as women and children whiche deyde

for honger moo than thyrtty thousand & also seyng that noo rescowse cam appoynted with the kyng & gaf ouer the toun vnto hym which he receyued. And anone after that Roan was goten Deepe and many other tounes in Baas Normandye gaf them ouer withoute strook or syege whanne they vnderstode that the kynge had goten Roan.

Capitulum xv

Also this same yere hadde ben a pees made and sworne bytwene the duc of Burgoyne and the dolphyn

The second section of the *Liber ultimus,* from 1419 to 1461, is essentially the same as the corresponding section in the earlier volume, with spelling changes and minor verbal alterations made by the compositor. Some short passages are deleted and some minor additions and corrections are made that are occasionally paralleled in the surviving London chronicles, and this part of the *Liber ultimus* could well have been set up from a marked-up copy of the *Chronicles of England.* The text ends with the prayer for Edward IV.

The chapters of the *Liber ultimus* are numbered from 1 ("Capitulum Primum") to 33 ("Capitulum Trisesimum Tercium"). Apart from the natural chapters provided by the beginnings of the reigns of Richard II, Henry IV, and Henry V, the divisions in the text to 1419 do not correspond to those in the *Chronicles of England.* After 1419, however, except for the redivision for chapter 15 quoted above (cf. Brie 491/1–8), the chapter divisions correspond, though no narrative chapter headings are used throughout the *Liber ultimus.*

---

[1] See Matheson, "Printer and Scribe," pp. 601–610; fuller descriptions of the manuscripts of this group and their relationships appear in my new edition of "Warkworth's" *Chronicle* in Lister M. Matheson, ed., *Death and Dissent: Two Fifteenth-Century Chronicles* (Cambridge, 1998).

[2] For a full account of Caxton's sources, see Matheson, "Printer and Scribe," pp. 603–607.

94. UNIVERSITY OF GLASGOW, MS. HUNTERIAN 83(2)[1]
Second scribe begins on fol. 128: withoute þe gates ffor spendyng off þer vitale. And anone our Englisch men droff them into the tovn agayn [cf. Brie 391/2–3]

Changeover, 1419 to Poly. 1461: And then þe kynge entred þe town & rested hym in the castell tyll þe tovn was set in rewell and gouernaunce.

How the kyng off Englond was made heritier and regent off Fraunce & how he wedded quene Katerine. Ca.

And anone after þat Roone was goten Depe & many oþer tovnes in Baas Normandy yaf them ouer without strok or siege

Poly. 1461 continuation ends imperfectly on fol. 140v: Ageynste whoos comynge the duke off Northffolke the [cf. Brie 531/18]

"Warkworth's" Chronicle begins imperfectly on fol. 141: the erle off Warwyke com home and herd her-off then was he gretely displeysed

"Warkworth's" Chronicle ends: and all was done by there oune foly &c.

Remarks: To the original *Brut* text the second scribe has prefixed a prologue taken from the Saint Albans edition of the *Chronicles of England* (?1483; see item 205). He also made a number of notes on the text, in Latin and English, throughout the manuscript, and he may also have inserted chapter headings throughout the text.

The scribe may have paused between completing the narrative to 1419(r&g) and adding the Poly. 1461 W.C. texts; beginning with the chapter heading "How the kyng of England..." (see above), the ink appears different and the writing is heavier and less neat on fol. 128r.

Starting with fol. 132, many of the pages of the Poly. 1461 continuation have Caxton's heading "Liber Vltimus (*or* ultimus)," and a number also include the corresponding folio number from the printed edition.

The leaf is missing that would have contained the end of the Poly. 1461 text and the beginning of "Warkworth's" *Chronicle*; it is simply a chance correspondence that the next words of the former would have been "erle of Warwycke" (Caxton, *Liber ultimus*) whereas the first words of the latter in the manuscript are "the erle off Warwyke."[2]

---

[1] For (1), see item 123.

[2] See the collation in J. Young and P. Henderson Aitken, *A Catalogue of the Manuscripts in the Library of the Hunterian Museum in the University of Glasgow* (Glasgow, 1908), p. 88.

95. PETERHOUSE, CAMBRIDGE, MS. 190(2)[1]
Second scribe begins on fol. 196v: and quyte hem lyke good men and þei slewh myche peple of owrys with gonnes and quarelles and this sege enduryd xx wekys and moor [cf. Brie 390/29–30]
Changeover, 1419 to Poly. 1461: and than the kynge enteryd the towne and restyd hym in the castell tyll þe towne was sette in reule and gouernawnce.

How the kynge of Englond was made herytier and regent of Fraunce and he wedde quene Kateryne.

[A]nd anone after that Rone was geten Deepe and many other townes and Baas Normandy yaf them ouyr withowte stroke or sege
Poly. 1461 continuation ends on fol. 214v: And the fyrste yer of his regne aboute mydsomer after þe yer of our lorde M^l CCCC lxj he was crowned at Westmynster and enyoynted kyng of Englond havyng the hole possessyoun of alle the hool reame whom I pray God saue and kepe and sende hym the complyshment of the remanent of ryghtfull enherytaunce wher so euer it be and he to lyff in God and he in hym. Amen.
Colophon: And her I make an ende of this lytell werke as myche as I can fynde after the forme of the werke byfore made by Ranulpd monke of Chester. And where ther is ony faught I beseche them that schal rede it to correcte it ffor yf I cowed haue founde moo storyes I wold haue sett in itt moo but the substaunce that I can fynde and knowe I haue shortely seett them in this boke to the entent that suche thynges as haue be don sith deyth or ende of the same booke of Polycronycoun be hade in rememberaunce and not putt in oblyuioun ne forgetynge. Prayenge alle them that schall see this simple werke to pardoun my symple and rude wrytynge. Ended the secunde day of Julij the xxij yer of the regne of kynge Edward the fourt and of the incarnacyoun of our lorde M^l CCCC iiij score and tweyne. Finysched and ended after the copey of Caxton then in [*ins. above*] Westmynster.
"Warkworth's" Chronicle begins on fol. 214v: [A]s for alle thynges that folowe referre them to my copey in whyche is wretyn a remanente lyke to this forseyd werke. That is to wytt that at the coronacyon of the forseyde Edward he create and made dukes his two brythir
"Warkworth's" Chronicle ends: and alle was doune by ther owne foly &c.
Remarks: The second scribe takes the narrative from the original ending in

1419(men) to 1419(r&g) and then writes the Poly. 1461 continuation and "Warkworth's" *Chronicle*.

As in Glasgow Hunterian 83, the Poly. 1461 section retains the chapter numbers of the *Liber ultimus*. The prayer for Edward IV that concludes this section (missing in the Hunterian manuscript) is abbreviated compared to Caxton's original text, but, apart from the last sentence, the colophon is that of the printed text.

The manuscript was presented to Peterhouse in 1481 by John Warkworth, master of the college, whose note of presentation and anathema appears on the verso of the front flyleaf.

---

[1] For (1), see item 24. The text of "Warkworth's" *Chronicle* is printed in James Orchard Halliwell, ed., *A Chronicle of the First Thirteen Years of the Reign of King Edward the Fourth, by John Warkworth, D.D.*, Camden Society o.s. 1 (1839).

96. BL MS. HARLEY 3730(2)[1]

Poly. 1461 continuation begins on fol. 106: How the kyng of Englond was made heritier and regent of France & how he wedde quene Katerine.

[A]nd anon after þat Roone was getyn Deepe and many oþer townes in Baas Normandy yaf them ouer without stroke or sege

Ends imperfectly: þe erle of March hys sone was comyng with [Brie 520/29–30]

Remarks: The manuscript is written by one scribe throughout and was copied from Glasgow Hunterian 83 (see Remarks on the Poly. 1461 W.C. below); nevertheless, it is convenient to consider it under the same group headings as its exemplar.

The continuation to 1461 was used by Brie to collate the CV continuation from 1419 to 1461 in his edition, where the manuscript is designated H.[2] A textual comparison, however, shows that the text is the same as that contained in the continuations of the two preceding manuscripts, that is, for the first chapters beyond 1419 it is based on a CV–1461 continuation, followed by the *Liber ultimus* version of the 1461 continuation. Again, the chapter numeration of the latter work is employed. The following are examples of additions found in the *Liber ultimus* and in BL Harley 3730 (H) but not in Caxton's *Chronicles of England* or BL Addit. 10099:[3]

THE COMMON VERSION 171

1. þe world [worde H] was nat worthy to haue his presence. [In þis yer was þe kynge of Scottes murthered in his chambour by nyght pytously which kyng hade ben presoner xv yere in Englond. And thei þat slew hym wer takyn efterward and hade cruell iustice. *add.* H] [BL Addit. 10099, collated with Caxton's *Chronicles* and BL Harley 3730 (H); cf. Brie 506/27 and n.]

the worlde was not worthy to haue hys presence. Jn this yere was the kynge of Scottys murthred in his chambre by nyght pytously whiche kynge had be prysoner xv yere in Englonde. And they that slewe hym were taken afterward & had cruel iustyce. [Caxton, *Liber ultimus* (1482)]

2. Also þis yere [the lorde Talbott leyd sege to Depe (y *del. between* e *and* p). But þe Dolphyn rescowed it and wan þe bastell þat Englischmen hade made. Also þis yere *add.* H] was A gret Affray in Flet Strete [BL Addit. 10099, collated with Caxton's *Chronicles* and BL Harley 3730 (H): Brie 509/16 and n.]

Also this yere the lord Talbotte had leyde syege to Dyepe but the dolphyn rescowed it and wan the bastyle that Englysshmen had made. Also this yere was a greete effraye in Fletestrete [Caxton, *Liber ultimus* (1482)]

Corresponding omissions of details also occur in BL Harley 3730 and in Caxton's *Liber ultimus*.

The text breaks off before the end of the 1461 continuation, but it is unlikely that "Warkworth's" *Chronicle* formed part of the manuscript (see Remarks on the Poly. 1461 W.C.).

---

[1] For (1), see item 124 and below.
[2] See Brie 2: viii, 491–520/30.
[3] These additions are, of course, also found in the other two texts in this group.

Remarks on the Poly. 1461 W.C.[1]
Glasgow Hunterian 83 is the original compilation consisting of a *Brut* text

to which the Saint Albans preface and the Poly. 1461 continuation and "Warkworth's" *Chronicle* were added. The last of these was probably added later than the other items, and it is possible that the first item was also added at the same time.

BL Harley 3730 was copied entirely from the Hunterian manuscript and probably ended with the note that now prefaces "Warkworth's" *Chronicle* in the Peterhouse manuscript, referring the reader to the text of this in the Hunterian manuscript. A short extract from the B-version of John Hardyng's *Chronicle* was added as preface to the Harley manuscript.

The text beyond 1419(men) in Peterhouse 190, also originally a discrete *Brut*, was copied from Harley 3730, the scribe including by mistake the note of reference to the Hunterian manuscript, to which he then turned to copy "Warkworth's" *Chronicle*.

The additions to all three manuscripts were probably made about 1483 or 1484 for fellows of Peterhouse, Cambridge, possibly in the college library.

The Poly. 1461 continuation follows the text of Caxton's *Chronicles of England* for its first four chapters, but in the course of the fifth chapter it changes to the text of the *Liber ultimus*.

---

[1] For a full account of the development of the group, on which the present remarks are based, and for speculations on the author of "Warkworth's" *Chronicle*, see Matheson, ed., *Death and Dissent*.

II. The Extended Version

The Extended and Abbreviated Versions

The primary distinguishing features of all groups of manuscripts of the Extended Version (EV) and of the related groups that constitute the Abbreviated Version (AV) are a short exordium not found in the Common Version, the words "Some time..." at the beginning of the Albina prologue, and the addition of selected details from the anonymous *Short English Metrical Chronicle* to the Albina prologue and the earlier part of the narrative.[1] A complex set of variations in the different versions of the exordium allows distinctions to be made among individual groups of texts. Other features, such as textual variations and differences of content in the later narrative, can be used to classify Extended and Abbreviated texts when the exordium or prologue is missing. These features include such details as the "first giants passage," the passage on Lud's naming of London, the Latin tag associated with King Blegabred, and other items in the list of test factors for the Extended and Abbreviated Versions (pp. 53–54; items 4 through 14).

As noted earlier in this study, the Extended Version can be divided into three groups (A, B, and C), characterized by three distinct recensions of the exordium. The Abbreviated Version has four groups (A, B, C, and D), again based on their recensions of the exordium; the exordia for EV groups A, B, and C correspond to those found in AV groups A, B, and C respectively, while AV group D offers an independent recension that is not paralleled in the EV. The Abbreviated Version differs from the Extended Version primarily in its abridgments of the narrative at various points (depending on the particular group or subgroup), including material after the death of Arthur and material surrounding the battle of Halidon Hill. The Cadwallader episode and Queen Isabella's letter are generally found in surviving EV and AV texts that are not physically defective at either point of the narrative; "The Description of Edward III" does not occur in any EV or AV texts.

Although individual groups within the Extended and Abbreviated Versions can be differentiated fairly easily, they are less internally coherent than those of the Common Version, and the precise relationships between the individual groups are not always clear. As will be seen, much scribal crossing has occurred (apparently among texts from a variety of groups), with a resulting array of correspondences and divergences among groups. Accordingly, the following layout has been adopted for sections II and III of the Classification of Texts:

1. description of the individual manuscripts and groups, first of the Extended Version (section II) and then of the Abbreviated Version (section III), with short accounts and preliminary discussions of the internal correspondences, divergences, and, where these can be ascertained, relationships among particular manuscripts of the individual groups.
2. at the end of section III, a full discussion of the interrelationships among all the groups and subgroups belonging to both the Extended and the Abbreviated Versions.

---

[1] For a representative example of the exordium text (from the EV–1419:B), see Introduction, Appendix 3. Brie treats texts of the Abbreviated Version under the Extended Version ("die erweiterte Fassung"), calling them "eine umfangreiche Klasse von MSS . . . , die nichts als verkürzte Wiedergaben jener sind" ("a large class of manuscripts . . . that are nothing but abbreviated renderings of [the Extended Version]"; *Geschichte und Quellen*, p. 84). This is an oversimplification, and the type of conscious change found in the Abbreviated Version texts makes it preferable to consider them as constituting an independent version.

The Extended Version to 1377 (EV–1377)

From remarks found in the exordia of most texts of the Extended and Abbreviated Versions, one can assume a now lost manuscript or group of manuscripts, based on a Common Version text, in which an exordium was first used and which ended with the death of Edward III in 1377:

> And þis booke made & compiled men of religioun & oþer good clerkes þat wreten þat bifell in her tymes and made þerof grete bokes and remembraunce to men þat comen aftir hem to heere and to see what bifell in þe londe afore tyme and callid hem cronycles. And in þis londe haue been from Brute to kynge Edward þe thridde aftir þe conquest C xxxij kynges whos lyues and actes ben compiled shortly in

þis boke þe whiche conteyneth CC xxxviij chapiters wiþoute þe prothogoll or prolog. [BL Harley 4827]

Both the finishing point of the text, that is, the death of King Edward III, and the number of chapters stated to have comprised the work point to an original text ending in 1377. It seems likely that this 1377 group was an embryonic EV rather than an AV for the following reasons:

1. It is unlikely that an exordium would be added to a projected abbreviation of the text, especially in view of the truncated state of the extant AV texts.
2. The use of literary sources found in the prologues and elsewhere in the extant EV and AV texts suggests a conscious attempt to produce a "show" text. It is even possible that the Cadwallader episode and Queen Isabella's letter were first introduced into the *Brut* canon in this group.
3. The relationships between the groups of the EV and AV, although unclear, suggest a prototype EV.

The remarks in the exordia of the surviving EV texts point to a text of the CV–1377 f.c. as having been the basis for the original form of the EV. There are, however, three stages of the CV–1377 f.c. (see pp. 88–90, 92–97): the first does not contain the Cadwallader episode nor Queen Isabella's letter; the second includes the Cadwallader episode; and the third includes both the Cadwallader episode and Queen Isabella's letter. There are, therefore, at least three possible explanations for the constitution and early history of the EV–1377:

(i) The EV–1377 was based on the CV–1377 f.c. Stage 1 and contained neither the Cadwallader episode nor Queen Isabella's letter.
(ii) The EV–1377 was based on the CV–1377 f.c. Stage 1 and first introduced the Cadwallader episode. This was then borrowed during the compilation of the CV–1377 f.c. Stage 2 and thus introduced into the development of the Common Version.
(iii) The EV–1377 was based on the CV–1377 f.c. Stage 3, which was first to include both the Cadwallader episode and Queen Isabella's letter.

Little weight can be put on the evidence that the EV–1377 contained *exactly* 238 chapters, for in manuscripts of the *Brut* chapter numbering—where found at all—tends to vary. However, possibility (i) can probably be discounted, for all *complete* texts of the extant EV and AV groups contain the Cadwallader episode and Queen Isabella's letter, which suggests that these were found in the early stages of the EV/AV development.

The Cadwallader episode in the *Brut* is taken from Book XII of Geoffrey of Monmouth's *Historia Regum Britannie*, and incorporates, in Latin, Geoffrey's biblical quotation: "Dedisti nos domine tanquam oues escarum et in gentibus dispersisti nos." Geoffrey's *Historia* reads: "Dedisti nos deus tanquam oues escarum & in gentibus dispersisti nos" (Ps. 43:12).[1]

In the chapter listing thirty-three kings of Britain, most texts of the EV–1419:A, EV–1419:B, and AV–1419:B contain a Latin tag that occurs after the name of Blegabred: "Qui quidem omnes regni cantares in modulis & musicis instrumentis superabant" (Harvard Richardson 35; BL Harley 4827 reads "... cantores ... supera"). This quotation is also based on some text of Geoffrey's *Historia*, and the corresponding phrase in Bürgerbibliothek Bern MS. 568 is "Hic omnes cantores quos retro etas habuerat et in modulis et in omnibus musicis instrumentis superabat."[2] Since the Latin tag is not found in CV texts, this indicates that a compiler involved in the EV knew Geoffrey's *Historia*, but whether it was the compiler of the EV–1377 is not definite, for the distribution of the tag is not universal. Either it was an independent addition made at some stage of the EV/AV development after the EV–1377, or it dropped out of certain EV/AV groups in the course of scribal transmission or by deliberate omission.

Possibilities (ii) and (iii) remain open. In view of the general character of the extant EV texts, which use details from literary sources, possibility (ii) allows a possible hypothesis concerning the genesis and early development of the EV–1377. We can suppose that the compiler was faced by a text of the CV–1377 f.c. Stage 1, containing neither the Cadwallader episode nor the Queen Isabella letter. His intention was to improve upon the text of his exemplar, and to this end he added an exordium and some details from the *Short English Metrical Chronicle* to the prologue and early parts of the narrative. For purposes of collation, the compiler was using a text of the *Historia Regum Britannie* (upon which the earlier parts of the *Brut* are ultimately based), and from this he may have inserted the Latin tag into the catalogue of British kings and a translation of the Cadwallader episode (perhaps on account of its connection with the Havelok tale). In the subsequent CV–1377 f.c. Stage 2 recension, the Cadwallader episode was introduced into the main development of the Common Version. Queen Isabella's letter was then added separately to the CV–1377 f.c. Stage 3 and thus appears in subsequent CV texts ending in 1419, from which source it was introduced into the EV–1419.

No manuscript of the EV–1377 appears to have survived. Extant EV and AV manuscripts carry the text to 1419, using the CV–1419(r&g) continuation, or, where incomplete, can be assumed to have once carried the text at least beyond 1377 and most likely to 1419. Some EV texts modify the "in rule and governance" ending by inserting "good" before one of the nouns— "in rule and (in) good governance" or "in good rule and governance"—but the formulaic nature of the phrase and the number of texts that end imperfectly weaken the taxonomic usefulness of this feature.

---

[1] Acton Griscom, ed., *The Historia Regum Britanniæ of Geoffrey of Monmouth* (London, 1929), p. 531. See also Neil Wright, ed., *The Historia Regum Britannie of Geoffrey of Monmouth, I: Bern, Burgerbibliothek, MS. 568* (Cambridge, 1984), p. 145.
[2] Wright, ed., *Historia*, p. 34; cf. Griscom, ed., *Historia*, p. 300.

The Extended Version to 1419, Group A (EV–1419:A)

Group A consists of MSS. Rylands Eng. 105, Harvard Richardson 35, BL Harley 24, BL Addit. 12030, Bodl. Rawlinson B.187, Takamiya 12, and Bodl. Tanner 188.

97. RYLANDS MS. ENG. 105[1]
Exordium begins: Here begynneth a boke in Englysshe tunge called Brute whiche entreteth of the first begynnyng of the lond
Exordium ends: And in this lond have ben with Brute vnto kyng Edward the thridde C xxxij kynges whos lyves actes and dedes ben compiled in this boke here folowyng the whiche conteyneth CC xxxviij chapiters withoute the prolog or protogoll.
Prologue heading begins: The prolog of this booke declareth how this lond was first called Albyon after the eldest doughter
Text begins: Some tyme in the noble lond of Surry
Contains: Cad, QIL
Omits: extra giants (see below), Latin tag, "5w" heading (see below)
Ends imperfectly: Of kinge Henri the vth borne at Monmouth in Wales son to king He[nri] the iiijth. [cf. Brie 373/1–2]

Remarks: The folio that would have contained the extra giant details in the prologue is missing.

In the chapter on the battle of Halidon Hill a redistribution of the numbering of the wards of the Scottish army has occurred, presenting only four and not five wards, and the "5w" heading is altered accordingly: "In the fourth warde of the Scottes were theis lordes."

A late marginal note on fol. 46v can be discounted: "This chronicle was mayde the xth yere of the reynge of kynge Henry the viiith by the right renouned and myghty" [breaks off]; the hand of the manuscript belongs to the second half of the fifteenth century.

Sixteenth- and early-seventeenth-century owners are "Thomas Hought'," "Ricardus Hobbes," "Hugo Wynnard," "Thomas Pawlyn, surgion in civitate London'."

---

[1] See Lester, *Handlist*, pp. 39–40; Tyson, "Hand-List," p. 172.

98. HARVARD UNIVERSITY MS. RICHARDSON 35

Exordium begins: [H]ere bygynneþ a boke in Englysche tonge þat ys called Brute of Ynglond wyche declareþe spekeþ and treteth of þe frust bygynnyng of þe londe of Ynglond

Exordium ends: And for to sey soþe in þis londe haue ben with þis Brute vnto kynge Harry þe v aftur þe conquest C xxxv kynges wos lyues actes & dedes ben all compiled schortely in þis booke here folowyng þe wyche conteyneþ CC xlj chapitures withoute þe protegoll oþer prologe.

Prologue heading begins: The prologe of þis booke declareþ how þis londe was frust called Albyon after þe eldest suster douȝter of þe ryal kynge Dyoclycian of Surre

Text begins: Svm tyme in þe noble londe of Surrey

Contains: extra giants, Latin tag, Cad, QIL

Omits: "5w" heading (see below)

Ends imperfectly: And so furth to Westmynstre and þer she was crowned quene of Englond. And þan was she broght ayen into þe kynges place. And þer was [Brie 351/8–10]

Remarks: The scribe has altered the name of the latest king in the exordium from Edward III to Henry V, though he has not altered the number of chapters to correspond to this change (chapter 238 ends with the death of Edward III, but the last chapter in the incomplete text is numbered 244; cf. a similar change in item 118). The folio is lost that would have contained the "5w" heading.

After the imperfect conclusion of the *Brut* text occur 22 pages of shields of arms, with the names of the bearers and the blazons. That the earl of Wiltshire is also called of "Vrmont" (that is, Ormond) gives a *terminus a quo* of 1452 for this section.[1]

The earliest (possibly fifteenth-century) name in the manuscript is that of "Rycharte Thomas of Nethe" (Glamorgan) and later marginal names also suggest a Welsh connection. The manuscript is decorated throughout with grotesque figures and fanciful creatures in the margins.

---

[1] See E. B. Fryde, D. E. Greenway, S. Porter, and I. Roy, eds., *Handbook of British Chronology*, 3rd ed. (London, 1986), pp. 487, 496; James Butler, earl of Wiltshire and Ormond, was executed in 1461. The manuscript is dated 1430–1500 in Kennedy, *Manual*, p. 2820.

99. BL MS. HARLEY 24[1]
Heading: Here begynnyth the kalendare of Brute in Englyssh tunge.
Exordium begins: Her begynnyth a booke in Englyssh tung that is called Brute of Englande which declarith and tretith of the furste beginnyng of the lande of Englande
Exordium ends: and [f..t.(?) *del.*] seye the sothe in this lande haue bene with this Brute vnto kyng Edw[a]rde the thirde after the conqueste C xxxij kynges whos lyues actes and dedes bene alle compilede shortly in this booke here [-re *ins. above*] folowyng the which conteyneth CC xxxviij chapitours withoute the protegoll othir prologe.
Prologue heading begins: The prologe of this booke declareth howe this lande was furste callede Albyon after þe eldest doughter
Text begins: Sume tyme in the noble lande of Surrey
Contains: extra giants, Latin tag, Cad, QIL, "5w" heading
Ends: in ruele and good gouernaunce. Deo gracias.

---

[1] The Arthurian narrative in this manuscript is printed in Karl Böddeker, "Die Geschichte des Königs Arthur," *Archiv* 52 (1874): 10–29.

100. BL MS. ADDITIONAL 12030[1]
Heading: Here begynnyth the kalendare of Brute in Englyssh as here after ye shall here.

Exordium begins: Here begynnyth a book in Englyssh tunge that ys called Brute of England which declareth speketh and tretethe of the furst bygynnyng of the lande of Englande

Exordium ends: and forto seye the sothe in this lande haue ben with this Brute vnto kyng Edwarde the thirde after the conqueste C xxxij kynges whos lyves actes and dedes ben alle compylede shortely in this book here folowyng the which conteyneth CC xliiij chapitours withoute the protegoll other prologe.

Prologue heading begins: The prologe of this book declareth howe this lande was furste called Albyon after the furste eldeste sustre doughter to the ryall kyng Dioclician of Surre

Text begins: Summe tyme in the noble lande of Surre

Contains: extra giants, Latin tag, Cad, QIL, "5w" heading

Ends imperfectly: afterwarde the kyng passing furthe by the cuntre aboute the brede of xx myles he wastede alle [Brie 298/8–9]

---

[1] See Brown and Higgs, *Handlist*, p. 42.

101. BODLEIAN MS. RAWLINSON B.187

Begins on fragmentary fol. 1: wyldyrnesse & no thyng [...] And thys booke ys calledde Brute aftyr [...] the lond whos name was Brute the [...] opynly ys declared yn dyuers chapyty[rs...] good clerkys and namely men of

Contains: Latin tag, Cad, QIL

Omits: extra giants (see below), "5w" heading (see below)

Ends imperfectly: the Scottes vnderstoode þan þat the [Brie 280/5]

Remarks: The folio that would have contained the extra giants in the prologue is lost and the text ends before the enumeration of the Scottish army at Halidon Hill.

The evidence for including the text here is, therefore, a combination of the features noted above and of textual comparisons with other texts of the group:

(a) the phrases given above from the fragmentary fol. 1.
(b) *second giants passage*:
 also the geawntys lyven be dyuers frwtys growyng ther and be fowlys vyld and tame and othyr grett bestys and yn specyalle be flesche of

schepe grett as hors the whyche weryn wolle as the her of a goote therof they makyn hem slawyns; and that lond to yow ys ordeynyd be des-
tanye and to yowr pepyll. [cf. Remarks on the EV–1419:A below]
(c) *Lud passage*:
this kyng Lud loved more to dwell at Newe Troye þen in any oþer
place of þe lond wherfor he commaundid that þat cite shuld not no
lenger be called Newe Troy but Ludentoun or Ludestoun as sum bokes
seyen after his name Lud for in þat cite he mad most cost of byldyng.
And ther he mad a gate al oute of þe ground and lat hit to be called
Ludgate after his name. And he lat walle þe toune and dike hit also
but afterwardis þe name of þis cite was chaunged with Saxons tonge
and by variaunce of lettres and was called London. And Normandis
and Frenchemen and oþer alyauntes call it Loundris. And these clerkes
call it in Latyn Ciuitas Londinarum. [see pp. 238–39 below]
(d) there are no AV features; for example, Constantine reigns after Arthur
and the Engist's heptarchy passage agrees with the other members of
the group.

The form of Coryn's paramour's name is paralleled in Harvard Richardson 35 (and in the AV–1419:A[b]): "yef Erneborowe þi paramour my3th
wete that on man only ferde thus with þe sche wold neuer love þe."

The hand of the manuscript is similar to the first hand of Glasgow Hunterian 83, a text of the AV–1419:A(a).

102. TAKAMIYA MS. 12
Begins imperfectly: hem home into hir owne cuntre and their hem q[...].
And it byfell thus aftrewarde that this dame Albyne b[.]come so stoute
and so stately [Brie 2/5–7]
Contains: extra giants, Latin tag, Cad, QIL, "5w" heading
Ends imperfectly: And so king Henry the v^{te} gate and conquerid all the
tovnes and the castelles pyles strengþes abbeis vnto Pountelarge and frome
thens vnto the citee of Roon. [Brie 386/10–12]

Remarks: The evidence for including the text here is a combination of the
features noted above supported by textual comparisons with other EV–
1419:A texts, as follows:

(a) *first giants passage*:
and thei conceyvid and brough furth geantz of the whiche men callid

one Gogmagog chief king of hem all and he was xl fote in length and xij in breede. One othre hight king Wydy and duellid vppon one highe hill within Shropshire that is callid the Wreken. One othre Onewen [-ne- *ins.*] the forte. Ane othre Bonde at the brugge ende brothre to Onewen; one othre Laugherygo Bondes sonne whome Onewenz eme slough aftre in [*ins.*] a bataille assignid bytwix hem two vnwitting to hem both; and grete multitude moo of giauntz that were callid many diuers names. And in this manere thei come furth and weren borne horrible giauntz in Albion and thei duellid in cavis and in hilles at heir luste and had the londe of Albion as hem liked vnto the tyme that Brute come and arryvid at Tottenesse that was in the Ile of Albion and their this Brute conquerid and scomfite the giauntz abouesaide and slough the moste parte of hem as othre bookes openly declareth.

(b) *second giants passage*:
Also the gyauntz lyven by diuers fruites growing their and by foulez wilde and tame and othre grete bestes and in especiall by flesshe of shepe grete as hors the whiche were woll as here of geyte wherof thei maken hem slavens and þat londe to you is ordeynid by destenie and to your poeple.

(c) *Coryn's paramour passage*:
Than saide Brute to Corin "yef Erneborowe thi paramour might wit that one mane onely ferde thus foule with the she wolde neuir love the."

(d) *Lud passage*:
he commaundid that that citee no lenger shulde be callid Newe Troie bot Ludentoune or Ludestoune as sum bookes sein aftir his name Lud for in that citee he made most coste of belding and ther he made a gate all out of the grounde and callid hit Ludgate aftir his name and he made wall the toune and diche it also bot aftirwarde the name of this cite was chaungid by Saxons tonge and variaunce of lettres and was callid London and yete is bot Normandez and othre aliens call it Loundres and clerkes callez it Ciuitas London.

(e) *Engist's heptarchy passage*:
The furst kingdome was Kent their that Engest himself reignid and was lorde and maistir of all that othre. And one othre king had Sussexe where nowe is Chicestre; the iij had Wessex; the iiij had Essex; the v hadde Estangle that nowe is callid Northfolke and Southfolk Marcheneriche that nowe is to saie the erledome of Nichole; the sixte had Leycestre; the vij Oxenford Gloucestre Winchestre Warewik and Derbyeshire.

(f)   there are no AV features; for example, Constantine reigns after Arthur.

Sixteenth-century notes of ownership name Thomas Mettham of Brayton in Yorkshire (who has made many notes and drafts of letters), John Baxter, Robert Red, and Richard Wattsoun (Watson). The names of John Frobyser and Richard Walsby also occur.

103. BODLEIAN MS. TANNER 188
Begins imperfectly: with here strength yche one of hem toke a certayne con-
   trey and euery man in his lande lete calle hym kynge [cf. Brie 22/30–32]
Contains: Latin tag, Cad, QIL, "5w" heading
Omits: extra giants (see below)
Ends imperfectly: And at his furst commyng [to her iustes xxiiij *catchwords*]
   [Brie 343/14–15]

Remarks: The text begins after the point at which the giants' passages would have occurred.

The text is included here on the evidence of the combination of features noted above and of textual comparisons with other texts of the group:

(a)   *Lud passage*:
   This Lud loved more to dwell atte Troy than in any other place of the londe wherfore he commaunded that cite no lengur be called Newe Troy but Londestoun as bokes seyne aftur his name Lud for in that cite he made moste cost of byldyng. And there he made a gate alle oute of the grounde and called hit Ludgate aftur his name. And he made the walles of the towne and dichid hit. But afturward the name of the cite was changed by Saxons tonge and variaunce of letteres and was called London and yit is. But Normandes and other aliens calle hit Loundours. [Cf. the two preceding texts.]

(b)   *Engist's heptarchy passage*:
   And Engist wente through the londe and sesud all the londe with all the ffrauncheys into his hande. And in euery place þat he come he lete caste doun chirches and houses of religioun and destroied Cristondome through all the lande. And made change the name of the londe and lete calle hit Engislonde and nowe by corrupcioun of tong is called Englond. And he departed the lande to his men and made therin vij kynges ffor to streynth the londe. The furst kyngedom was Kente there that Engist hymself reigned and was lorde of. And that other kynge

had Sussex. And the thirde had Westsex. The fourth had Essex. The v had Eastangle and nowe is called Norffolk and Suffolke and the erledom. The vj had Leycestre Northamptounshire Hertfordshire [*in bottom marg.*] and Huntyngdoun. The vij had Oxonfordshire Gloucestre Wynchestre Warwike and Derbyshire.

(c) Constantine follows Arthur.

Remarks: The spaces for chapter headings have been left blank.

Remarks on the EV–1419:A
Among the four manuscripts that are complete at the beginning, Rylands Eng. 105, Harvard Richardson 35, BL Harley 24, and BL Addit. 12030, there are a number of details that suggest that the Rylands text reflects in the main an earlier stage of the development of this group than the Harvard and BL manuscripts do, although the redivision of the Scottish army at Halidon Hill and some verbal abbreviation must be secondary developments in the Rylands text. In turn, Harvard Richardson 35 seems to represent an earlier stage than the BL texts, the heading and title of which must be a secondary development since they occur in no other EV group. The Latin tag associated with Blegabred found in the Harvard and BL texts but not in Rylands Eng. 105 is, however, paralleled elsewhere in the EV and AV manuscripts.

In the prologue and opening chapters, additional details, taken from the *Short English Metrical Chronicle*, are found in the EV. In this work, a description of Gogmagog and of the giants' mode of existence is found after Brutus's arrival in England and just prior to the giants' attack:

> He was of swyþe gret strengþe
> Fourty fot he was in lenþe
> & xij. fro his elbow to his hond
> & xx. in brede men hym fond
> In gret hulles þei woned here
> & lyued by erbis [and] wilde dere
> Melc & water þei dronke noȝt ellis
> As þe Brut hit seis & tellis[1]
> Schep þei hadde as hors gret
> Þerof [þei] maden hom sclaueyns
> So palmers weryn & painim(s).
> [Zettl, ed., *Metrical Chron.*, p. 2, lines 25–36]

Details from this passage are added at two points in the EV texts:

(a) At the end of the prologue relating the Albina story, which is given thus in the CV:

> & they conceiued, and after þei broughten forth Geauntes, of þe which on me called Gogmagog, and anoþer Laugherigan, & so þei were nompned by diuers names; & in þis manere they comen forth, and weren boren horrible Geauntes in Albion; & þey dwellyd in Cauys & in hulles at here will, & had þ{e} lond of Albyon as hem liked, vn-to þ{e} tyme þat Brut Arryved & come to Tottenesse, þat was in þ{e} Ile of Albyon. and þere þis Brut conqueryd & scomfyted these geaunt3 aboueseyd. [Brie 4/26-34]

The corresponding passage in Harvard Richardson 35, collated with BL Harley 24 (H) and Addit. 12030 (Add), reads:

> And þey conceyued & brou3th forþe gyountes of þe wyche men called one Gogmagog chefe kynge [*repeated* Add] of þem all [*repeated* Add]. And he was xl foote of [in H, Add] length & xij in brede. Anoþer hy3th kynge Wydy & dwellyd vpon an hye hylle withinne Shorpshire [*sic*] þat was [ys H, Add] called þe Wreken; one oþer Onewen le fort; anoþer Bonde at þe brygge ende broþer to Onewen [le forte *add.* H]; one oþer Laugherygo Bondes sone whom Onewens [Qnewens H] eme slowe aftur in a [*om.* Add] batayle assygned bytwyxte þem to [*om.* H] vnwytyng to þem boþe; & grete multitude mo of gyantes þat weren called mony diuerse names. And in þis [same *add.* H] maner þer come fourthe & weren borne horryble gyantes in Albyoun & þer dwelled in caues and in hylles at þer lust and hadde þe londe of Albyoun as þem lyked vnto þe [*om.* Add] tyme that Brute came and aryved atte Totenesse þat was in þe Ile of Albyon and þer þis Brute conquered and sconfited þe gyantes aboue-sayde and slou3th þe most partye of þem as oþer bokes openly declareth &c. [Harvard Richardson 35]

Unfortunately, as noted above, the relevant leaf in Rylands Eng. 105 is missing, but from a comparison with the corresponding passage in other EV and AV groups, the extra giants and folklorish details of the Harvard and BL texts can be seen as secondary additions, possibly not having occurred in the Rylands text or not in such extended form.

(b) The remainder of the lines from the *Short English Metrical Chronicle* quoted above are incorporated into Diana's prophecy to Brutus. Harvard Richardson 35, again collated with BL Harley 24 and Addit. 12030, reads:

> Also þe gyantes leuen by diuerse frutes growyng þer and by foules wylde & tame & oþer grete bestys & inspecyally [enspeciall H, in especiall Add] by [*om.* H] flesche of schepe grete as horses [hors H, horse Add] þe wych weren wolle as here of gote wherof þey make [made H] þem sclauyns [slauyns H, Add]. And þat londe to ȝow ys ordeyned by destenye & to ȝoure peple.

The corresponding section in Rylands Eng. 105 is:

> And thies giauntz live by diuers frutes and rootes of the erth and foules wilde and tame and other grete bestes and in especiall bi grete shepe as grete as hors which weren wolle as herre wherof thei make hem slavyns. And that lond to you is ordeyned by destany and to your peuple.

The "erbis" of the *Short English Metrical Chronicle* appear to have become "rootes of the erth" in the Rylands text, which omits the *Chronicle*'s qualifying phrase "of get," which appears in the Harvard and BL texts—that is, each text preserves details from the source, although each is close to the other. Minor errors in BL Harley 24 suggest that it is secondary to BL Addit. 12030.

A further detail that helps to distinguish the EV–1419:A from other groups is the name of Coryn's paramour in chapter 4, which is not given in the CV:

> Then seyde Brute to Coryn "ȝyf Erneborowe [Erneburgh H, Add] þy paramoure myȝt wyte þat one man onely ferde þys [thus H] foule with þe sche wolde neuer loue þe." [Harvard Richardson 35]

This detail is also taken from the *Short English Metrical Chronicle*, where the relevant lines read:

> & if þe worde of þe spronge
> þat o man þe stod so longe
> Geant or champion
> Al þi honour were ileide adon
> & nameliche to þi lemman
> þat is so fair a womman
> Whenne Coryneus hurde þat

> þat Brut of his lemman spak
> Of Erneborw [*vrr.* ernebourwe, Erneburh,
>   erneburgh]
> þat maide hende
> To Gogmagog he gan wende...

[Zettl, ed., *Metrical Chron.*, p. 4, lines 71–80; variant readings from Marion C. Carroll and Rosemond Tuve, "Two Manuscripts of the Middle English 'Anonymous Riming Chronicle'," *PMLA* 46 (1931): 122; Joseph Ritson, ed., *Ancient Engleish Metrical Romancees*, 3 vols. (London, 1802), 2:273; CUL Dd.14.2, fol. 261v; see also Zettl, ed., *Metrical Chron.*, pp. l–li]

In the listing of the kingdoms of Engist's heptarchy, the Rylands and Harvard texts (especially the former) preserve a reading that is closer to that of the CV and the other EV/AV texts than that of BL Harley 24 and Addit. 12030:

> The vij hade Oxenford, Gloucestr', Wynchestre, Warwik, and Darbyshire. [CV, Bodl. Rawlinson B.171: Brie 55/13–14]

> the vijth had Oxfordshire Gloucestreshire Winchestre Wari[k] and Derbyshire. [Rylands Eng. 105]

> And þe vij hadde Oxenfordschyre Gloucestreschyre Wynchestreschyre Warwykeschyre & Darbyschire. [Harvard Richardson 35]

> and the vij had Oxenfordeshire Gloucestershire Worcester Warwyke and Derbyshire. [BL Harley 24]

Thus a number of details suggest that BL Harley 24 and Addit. 12030 can be considered as slightly apart from Rylands Eng. 105 and Harvard Richardson 35, which appear to be closer to the ultimate source in the CV and to have points of agreement with other EV and AV groups that the BL texts do not have. Textual details associate the imperfect texts in Bodl. Rawlinson B.187, Bodl. Tanner 188, and Takamiya 12 with Harvard Richardson 35 rather than with Rylands Eng. 105.

---

[1] Probably an Anglo-Norman chronicle, possibly *Le Brut DEngletere abrege* (or some source common to both the *Short English Metrical Chronicle* and the Anglo-Norman work), which is printed in Zettl, ed., *Metrical Chron.*, pp. 92–107. But cf. M. Dominica Legge, "The Brut Abridged, A Query," *Medium Ævum* 16 (1947): 32–33.

The Extended Version to 1419, Group B (EV–1419:B)

Group B contains MSS. BL Harley 4827; BL Harley 2182; Edinburgh 185; Glasgow Hunterian 230; CUL Addit. 2775; CUL Ff.2.26; Trinity Coll., Oxford, 5; BL Addit. 24859; Virginia 38–173; Lincoln Cathedral 98; NLW Addit. 442D; and Bodl. Rawlinson poet. 32(1). With the exception of the last two manuscripts, the texts of this group are generally consistent with one another. A text of the exordium from this group is printed in the Introduction, Appendix 3; it differs from that of the EV–1419:A in ways discussed more fully below, along with further lexical differences between the EV–1419:B and the CV and other EV groups (pp. 237–40).

104. BL MS. HARLEY 4827[1]

Heading: Here bigynneth a booke whiche is callid Brute the Cronicles of Englond. Capitulo primo.
Exordium begins: This boke treteth and telleþ of þe kynges & principal lordes
Prologue heading begins: The prolog of þis book declareth hou this lande was callid Albioun aftre þe eldest doughtre of þe riall kyng Dioclisian of Surry
Text begins: Somtyme in þe noble land of Surry
Contains: Latin tag, Cad, QIL, "5w" heading
Ends: in reule & in gouernaunce.

Remarks: A slip of vellum interleaved between fols. 56 and 58 contains a copy in a Chancery hand of a bill, apparently dated 36 Henry VI (1457), requesting letters of safeconduct for John Ponce and four of his servants.

---

[1] Kennedy, *Manual*, p. 2819, erroneously dates the manuscript to the sixteenth century.

105. BL MS. HARLEY 2182

Heading: Here begynneþ a boke which is callid Brute þe cronycles of Englonde. Capitulo j°.
Exordium begins: This booke treteþ techeþ and telliþ of kingis and of principalle lordis þat euere were in þis londe
Prologue heading begins: The prolog of þis boke declareþ how þis londe was callid Albyon after þe eldist douȝter
Text begins: Somtyme in þe noble londe of Surreye

Contains: Latin tag, Cad, QIL, "5w" heading
Ends: in reule and in gode gouernaunce.

Remarks: At the end of the text, on fol. 185, occurs a short note by a sixteenth- or seventeenth-century annotator: "printinge was firste invented in Germanie at Magance in the yere of our redempcion anno 1458 & was brougt into England in the yere of our lord 1471." The wording is reminiscent of the *Great Chronicle of London* and of Caxton's comments in the *Liber ultimus* of his printed *Polychronicon*.[1]

On the front flyleaf occur the early modern name of George This(?), an owner of the manuscript, and the later name of William Jones.

---

[1] See Matheson, "Printer and Scribe," pp. 599–600 and n. 30.

106. EDINBURGH UNIVERSITY LIBRARY MS. 185
Heading: Here begynneth a boke which is called Brute the cronyculis of England. Capitulo primo.
Exordium begins: This book tretiþ & telliþ of þe kingis and princepall lordis
Prologue heading begins: The prolog of þis book declariþ how þis land was callid Albyoun aftir þe oldest doughtir of þe ryall kyng Dioclysyan of Surry
Text begins: Svmtyme in þe noble lond of Surry
Contains: Latin tag, Cad, QIL, "5w" heading
Ends: in good rule and gouernaunce. Deo gracias.

107. UNIVERSITY OF GLASGOW, MS. HUNTERIAN 230
Original text begins imperfectly: his lettris patent vnto these xxxiij^{ti} kingis [cf. Brie 2/32]
Contains: Latin tag, Cad, QIL, "5w" heading
Ends: in good rule & gouernaunce. Deo gracias.

Remarks: The text up to the imperfect beginning has been supplied in a modern copy taken from Glasgow Hunterian 74(1) (item 68).

The text is included here on the evidence of the giants' passages and the enumeration of the thirty-three kings (see pp. 190–91, 193–94 below).

Some aphorisms written by a "Rychard Wylloughbe" occur on the last folio. The manuscript seems to have been owned by the Willoughby and Zouche families of Nottinghamshire and Derbyshire.[1]

[1] See Boffey, *Manuscripts of English Courtly Love Lyrics*, p. 124 and n. 33.

108. CAMBRIDGE UNIVERSITY LIBRARY MS. ADDITIONAL 2775
Begins imperfectly: his letters patent vnto these xxxiij^{ti} kingis [cf. Brie 2/32]
Contains: Latin tag, Cad, QIL, "5w" heading
Ends: in good rule & gouernaunce. Deo gracias.

Remarks: The first folio is now fragmentary; it is possible that Glasgow Hunterian 230 (see the preceding manuscript), which begins at the same point, was copied from the Cambridge manuscript at some time after this folio was damaged.

109. CAMBRIDGE UNIVERSITY LIBRARY MS. FF.2.26
Begins imperfectly during exordium on fragmentary fol. 1: þe þridde aftir þe [. . .] kingis whos lyues & actis ben [. . .] in þis book þe which conteyneth CC xx[. . .]tris wiþoute þe protholog or prolog.
Prologue heading: [T]he prolog of þis book declarith how þis lond was callid Albioun aftir þe eldist doughtir of þe rial king Dioclisian of Surry þe which douȝter was callid Albyne and sche wiþ hir xxxij sisters were exilid out of her owne lond for grete trespaces þat þey hadde doon and arryued in this lond casuely wheryn was no lyuyng creature but wilde berstis [*sic*] and how vnclene spiritis lay by hem and þey broughten forth horrible gyauntis and Brute killide hem. [cf. p. 65 above]
Contains: Cad, QIL
Omits: Latin tag (see below), "5w" heading (see below)
Ends imperfectly: almyȝti God hadde many tymes done for Thomas loue of Lancastre many grete myracles to many men & women that [Brie 263/6-8]

Remarks: The text ends before the battle of Halidon Hill. Many folios are missing throughout the manuscript, including those that contained the chapter on the thirty-three kings, but the internal details, insofar as they remain, agree with those of other EV–1419:B texts, as follows:

(a) *first giants passage*:
& so conceyuede and brouȝte forþ grete gyantis of þe whiche oon was

callid Gogmagog and he was xl feet of lengþe & xij feet [*repeated*] of brede

(b) *second giants passage*:
and in þat lond was wont to be manye giauntis and now ther ben but fewe and þat lond is al wildirnes in the which gyauntis lyuen þere bi herbis & bi rootis and þere ben scheep as grete as hors and þat lond is ordeyned for 3ou & for 3oure peple and þere schule we [*corr. to* 3e *in marg.*] dwelle.

(c) *Coryn's paramour passage*:
Þanne seide Brute vnto Coryn "If Eneburgh þi paramour my3te wite þat oo man ferde so foule with þee sche wolde neuer loue þee."

In 1856, Frederic Madden implied that the text ended in 1377, and since the manuscript was imperfect when Brie examined it, Brie relied on Madden's description to assume that it was a text of the CV–1377.[1] The prologue heading and internal details are, however, those of an EV text, and Madden was mistaken in believing that it ended in 1377.[2]

The appropriate volume of the catalogue of Cambridge University manuscripts, published in 1857, describes the manuscript as being then in the same imperfect state as it is now.[3] It cannot, therefore, be supposed that the text represents the posited EV–1377, for the EV–1419:B shows many secondary features unique to the group (see below), and these features are found in CUL Ff.2.26.

The dialect of the text is that of the Central Midland literary standard.[4]

---

[1] Frederic Madden, "Prose Chronicles of England Called the Brute," *Notes and Queries* 2nd ser., 1 (1856): 2–3; Brie, *Geschichte und Quellen*, p. 56.

[2] It seems likely that Madden did not examine the manuscript personally, for he remarks elsewhere in his article that "None of the copies I have examined are older, however, than the fifteenth century; and it would be desirable to know if those referred to at Cambridge are coeval with the period at which they conclude" (3).

[3] *A Catalogue of the Manuscripts Preserved in the Library of the University of Cambridge* (Cambridge, 1857), pp. 346–47, where the manuscript is described as possessing 104 leaves and breaking off at "cap. ccxvi" of Caxton's *Chronicles of England* (1480).

[4] Samuels, "Some Applications of Middle English Dialectology," pp. 84–85 and n. 5.

110. TRINITY COLLEGE, OXFORD, MS. 51

Heading: Here begynneth a boke the whiche is callyd Brute the Cronycler [*sic*] of Inglond. Capitulo primo.

Exordium begins: This book tretyth & tellyth of the kynges & the pryncipal lordys

Prologue heading begins: The prologe of this boke declaryth how this lond was callyd Albyon after the eldest dovter of the royall kyng Dyoclycyan

Text begins: Some tyme in the noble lond of Surre

Contains: Latin tag, Cad, QIL, "5w" heading

Ends imperfectly on fol. 216v: & the dolfyn & the duke of Burgoyne [Brie 389/29]

---

[1] See S. J. Ogilvie-Thomson, *The Index of Middle English Prose, Handlist VIII: Manuscripts Containing Middle English Prose in Oxford College Libraries* (Cambridge, 1991), p. 93.

111. BL MS. ADDITIONAL 24859

Begins imperfectly: and so withinne a litil while he bicame of so greet power that men wiste not whiche were the kyngis men ne whiche were Engistis men [Brie 52/31–53/1]

Contains: Latin tag, Cad, QIL, "5w" heading

Ends: in reule and gouernaunce.

Remarks: Additional evidence for including the text here can be found in the Engist's heptarchy passage:

> The first kyng was of Kent and there Engist himsilf regnyd and he was lord and maistir of the oþere kyngis; þe secund was kyng of Southsexe; þe iij^e was kyng of Westsexe; þe iiij^e was kyng of Essexe; þe v^e was kyng of Estangle that is callid Northfolk and Southfolk; and the vj^e was kyng of Leicestre-schire Northampton Hertford and Huntyngdoun; þe vij^e was kyng of Oxenford Gloucestre Wynchestre Warwik and Derbischire. [cf. pp. 193, 196 below]

Brie, however, thought that this text belonged to the CV–1419 and used it for collation purposes for his texts for 1333 to 1377 and 1377 to 1419, describing it in his edition as: "*T* = MS. Br. Mus. Add. 24,859, a late but accurate transcript from a MS. of the second half of the 15th century which closes with the capture of Rouen in 1419."[1]

---

[1] Brie, *Geschichte und Quellen*, p. 63; Brie 2: vi.

112. UNIVERSITY OF VIRGINIA MS. 38–173[1]

First complete lines of fragmentary fol. 1v (fol. 1r illegible): assent wroot [. . .]el tacches of her wyues vnto here fad[. . .] Dioclisian biseking him to sette a remedie [cf. Brie 2/24–27]

Contains: Latin tag, Cad, QIL, "5w" heading

Ends imperfectly: þe king prayede alle his lordis to make hem [. . .]o strengthe him his riȝt and þanne anone he [lete *catchword*] [Brie 382/2–3]

Remarks: Additional evidence for including the text here consists of:

(a) *second giants passage*:
and in þat londe was wonte to ben many geauntes but now þer been but fewe & þat londe is al wildernesse in þe whiche geauntes lyuen þere by herbis and by rootis and þere ben scheepe as greet as an hors & þat londe is ordeyned for ȝou and for ȝoure peple and þere schulle ȝe dwelle.

(b) *Coryn's paramour passage*:
Thanne seide Brute vnto Coryn "if Eneburgh þi paramour myȝt wyte þat oo man ferde so foule with þee sche wolde neuer loue þee."

(c) *33 kings passage*:
The j^e kinge of þese xxxiij^ti kingis was callid Gorbodia and he regnyd xij ȝere. The ij^e kynge was callid Morgan and he regnyd ij ȝere. The iij^e kynge was callid Githnaus [*sic*] and he regned vj ȝere. [*etc.*]

(d) *Engist's heptarchy passage*:
The j^e kyng was of Kent þer Engist himsilf regnyd and was lorde & maister of alle þe oþer kyngis. The ij^e was kynge of Souþsex; þe iij^e was kynge of Westsex; þe iiij^e was kynge of Essex; þe v^e was kynge of Estangle þat is now Northfolke and Souþfolke; and þe vj^e was kynge of Leicestre-schire Northamton Hertforde & Hontyngdon. The vij^e was kynge of Oxenforde Gloucestre Wynchestre Warwike and Derbyschere.

---

[1] See George H. Reese, "The Alderman *Brut*: A Diplomatic Transcript, Edited with a Study of the Text," Ph.D. diss., University of Virginia, 1947, esp. pp. 14–21 for a description of the manuscript and its history.

113. LINCOLN CATHEDRAL MS. 98[1]

Heading on damaged fol. 174: Hire bigynneth a bok wiche is callid Brut the

Cronyclis of Engelonde. Capitulo primo.
Exordium begins: This boke tretith & tellith of the kingis & principal lordis
Prologue heading begins: The prolog of this book declareth how this londe was callid Albioun
Text begins: Sumtyme in the noble londe of Surry
Ends imperfectly on fol. 181v: ffor he was duk of Burgoyn þorugh Fowyn þat he had spousid wiche was douȝtir & heir [vnto the duke of *catchwords*] [cf. Brie 26/18–19]

Remarks: Only one quire of the *Brut* text survives; with other items, it has been appended to form this composite manuscript.

The text is included here on the strength of the exordium and prologue, supported by the following passages:

(a) *first giants passage*:
& so þey conceyvid & brouȝt forth gret gyauntis of the wiche oon was called Gogmagog & he was xl feet of lengthe & xij feet of brede. And thes giauntis dwelleden in diuers placis in this londe Albioun in cavis & in mounteyns into the tyme þat Brute come into this lond & arryvid at Toteneys in Devenshire & þanne this Brute scomfitid & conqueryd alle these giauntis & slowȝ hem all.

(b) *second giants passage*:
& in þat londe þere was wonte to ben many geauntis but now þere ben but fewe & þat londe is al wildernes in þe wiche geauntis lyven þere by herbis & by rootis & þere ben shepe as grete as hors & þat londe is ordeyned for ȝow & for ȝour puple & ther shulde ȝe dwelle.

(c) *Coryn's paramour passage*:
Thanne seid Brute vnto Coryn "ȝif Eneborugh thi paramour myght wet þat oo man ferde so foule wiþ the she wolde neuere loue the."

---

[1] See Rodney M. Thompson, *Catalogue of the Manuscripts of Lincoln Cathedral Chapter Library* (Cambridge, 1989), pp. 73–75; Julia C. Crick, *The 'Historia Regum Britannie' of Geoffrey of Monmouth, III: A Summary Catalogue of the Manuscripts* (Cambridge, 1989), pp. 130–33.

114. NATIONAL LIBRARY OF WALES MS. ADDITIONAL 442D[1]

Heading: Here begynneth a booke whiche is called Brute the Cronycles of Englonde. Capitulo primo.

Exordium begins: This booke treteth and telleth of þe kynges and principal lordes
Prologue heading begins: The prolog of þis booke declareth hou þis was callyd Albyon aftre þe eldest doughtre
Text begins: Somtyme in þe noble londe of Surry
Contains: Latin tag, Cad, QIL, "5w" heading
Ends: in reule and in gouernaunce.

Remarks: The internal features are those of the preceding texts until the end of the chapter on the battle of Halidon Hill, that is, the point where the CV text to 1333 continues with the 1377 continuation. The concluding section of the Halidon Hill chapter and the first section of the chapter "How King Edward made a duchy of the earldom of Cornwall..." are omitted, and the text reads:

> And þis victorie bifelle to þe Englissh men in Sent Margaretes euen in þe yere of oure lorde Ihesu Crist M^l CCC xxxij And while þis doyng last þe Englissh knaues nomen þe pilfre of þe Scottes þat were queld euery man þat he my3t of þe kynges frendes of Englond wiþ tovnes & castelles & meny oþere of her lordships and meny harmes shames and despites dede vnto þe queen. Wherfore þe kyng whanne he herde of þese tidynges he was strongliche moued and þerwiþ anangred and sent dyuers lettres ouere see to þe queen and to oþere þat were his frendes gladyng hem and certefiyng þat he wolde be þere himself in alle þe haste þat he might. [cf. Brie 286/4–8, 294/4–10]

Thereafter the text becomes normal again until it ends in 1419(r&g). The omission of material does not make sense as it stands and has probably occurred through scribal error; it is of interest, however, since the AV–1419:B also exhibits the omission of material around this point (see pp. 226–27).

---

[1] See Marx, "Middle English Manuscripts," pp. 371–73, for a description and an analysis of the contents (Marx mistakenly assigns the text to my "Common Version" [373]).

115. BODLEIAN MS. RAWLINSON POET. 32(1)[1]
Heading on fol. 57: Here begynneth a boke which is called Brute the Cronacle of England. Capitulo &c.
Exordium begins: This boke treteth techeth and telleth of kyngis and of pryncipall lordis

Prologue heading begins: The prologg of this boke declareth how this lande was called Albioun after the eldest doughter
Text begins: Sum tyme in the noble lande of Surrey
Omits: Latin tag
Contains: Cad
EV–1419 text ends on fol. 115v: and this batail was ended at Tunbrigg in the ij^{de} yer of his raigne vppon Saint Calixtis day and he lyeth att Walteham.
Colophon: Here endeth the Cronacles from Brute vntill William Conquerour.

Remarks: The extra details in the prologue and opening chapters are similar to those in the other EV–1419:B texts (although minor verbal differences suggest that the text stands at one further remove), but in the chapter listing the kings of Britain, although the kings are enumerated (the last being numbered twenty-nine), the Latin tag on Blegabred does not appear. Constantine reigns after Arthur's death.

The naming of Engist's heptarchy is slightly shorter than in either the CV or the EV, but the introductory wording is closer to the CV or EV–1419:A than to the other EV–1419:B texts, whereas the remainder corresponds in general to that of the EV–1419:B:

> And then thai changed the name of this land. And callid hit [*ins. above*] after the name off Engeist and that no man yn no wyse wer so hardy to call hitt Bretaigne. And then Engeist departyd the lond betwene hym and his men and made vij kynges for the mor strengþe of hymself so that the Bretons shuld cum no mor among ham. The first kyng was of Kent ther that Engeist hymself raigned above all the oþer kynges. The ij^d was of Sowþesex; the iij^d of Westsex; the iiij^{be} of Estsex. The vth of Esthangele which ys now Northfolke and Sowthfolke. The vj was of Laicesttre Northampton Hertefford and Huntyngdon. The vij^{be} kyng was off Oxfford Glowcettre Wynchester Warwyke and Derbysher. [cf. pp. 192, 193, and Brie 55/2–14]

The *Brut* text is written in a number of hands, who were clearly supervised carefully in the production of the composite text. Medieval foliation by one of the scribes in the top right corner of the rectos of the leaves shows that the *Brut* text was originally written as a separate text and that it was originally conceived of as a whole to the end of the continuation to 1422.

The beginning of the EV text occurs on medieval fol. "j" (modern fol. 57). The last medieval folio, numbered "iiij^{xx} xiijj" (modern fol. 150), contains on its verso text from near the end of the 1422 continuation, which is finished by a new hand on fol. 151. The new hand then proceeds with a CV–1461 continuation that was probably not part of the original plan.

The composite *Brut* text became the eighth part of a larger compendium manuscript in the late fifteenth century. In the general table of contents the *Brut* text is called "The olde Cornecles and the newe" (fol. 2). A "tabyll off all the kynges that euer raignyd yn Englond" and the lengths of their reigns (fols. 55v–56v) precedes the *Brut* text, on which it is clearly based; the table begins with Brutus and ends "Henre the vj raygnyd xxxix yere."

---

[1] For (2), see item 160; for (3), see item 90. Part of fol. 65v is reproduced in M. B. Parkes, *English Cursive Book Hands 1250–1500* (1969; rpt. Berkeley and Los Angeles, 1980), plate 12(ii).

The Extended Version to 1419, Group C (EV–1419:C)

Group C contains MSS. CCCC 182, TCC O.9.1(1), Bodl. Laud Misc. 571, Princeton Garrett 150, Illinois 116(1), Soc. of Antiquaries 223, and Huntington HM 133. For discussion of its recension of the exordium and further changes compared to the CV and other EV groups, see pages 237–40 below.

116. CORPUS CHRISTI COLLEGE, CAMBRIDGE, MS. 182
Exordium begins: Here begynneth a booke in Englissh tonge called Brute of Englonde or the Cronicles of Englonde compilinge and treatynge of the saide lande
Prologue heading begins: The prloge [*sic*] of this booke declareth and tellith
Text begins: Sum tyme in the noble londe of Surre
Omits: Latin tag
Contains: Cad, QIL, "5w" heading
Ends: in rule and goueranase [*sic*].

Remarks: A sixteenth-century hand has added a colophon: "Explicit usque ad annum 7ᵐ Henrici quinti."

117. TRINITY COLLEGE, CAMBRIDGE, MS. O.9.1(1)[1]
Exordium begins on fol. 49: Here begynneth a booke in Englissh tonge called

Brute of Englond or the Cronicles of Englond compilyng and tretyng of the seid lande
Prologue heading begins: The prologe of this booke declareth and telleth how this lande was first called Albioun after the eldest doughter of the roiall kyng Dioclician of Surre called Albyne
Heading to text: Here begynneth the ffirst chapter.
Text begins: Somtyme in the noble lande of Surre ther was a noble and a worthy man called Dioclician a grete conquerour and a myghty man
Omits: Latin tag, "5w" heading (see below)
Contains: Cad, QIL
EV–1419:C ends on fol. 195: in rewle and in gouernaunce.

Remarks:[2] The name of Coryn's "lemman" is not given and the names of Ebrak's children are omitted.

The manuscript is illustrated throughout with well executed borders and initials, though the rubrication of chapter headings was not completed. Headings are thus omitted in the chapter containing the battle of Halidon Hill and a space is left where the "5w" heading would appear.

A break occurs in the manuscript between fol. 100r (the death of "Alrude" and the flight of Godwin [Brie 128/10]) and fol. 103r (the arrival in England of Edward the Confessor [Brie 128/11]). Much of fol. 100r is left blank; fols. 100v–101 contain notes on Ireland, the number of bishoprics, shires, towns, etc.; fols. 101v and 102r are left blank (except for the later name "William Barret" on the latter; the beginning of a late deed of Will. Barret of Sholton in Staffordshire appears on fol. 231v); on fol. 102 appears a fine set of illustrations to the life of Edward the Confessor, consisting of seven scenes in six compartments. The break seems to have been deliberately left for the paintings, and there does not appear to have been a change of exemplar at this point.

---

[1] For (2), see item 83. See Mooney, *Handlist*, pp. 136–38. Earlier items in the manuscript are "Heruest hath iij monethis" and prose lives of St. Katherine, St. James, and the Virgin; for these and other minor items, see also James, *Western Manuscripts . . . Trinity College, Cambridge*, 3: 439–41.
[2] See also p. 151 for a London connection.

118. BODLEIAN MS. LAUD MISC. 571
Exordium begins on fol. 6: Here begynneth a boke yn Englyssh tonge called

Brute of Engelond or the Cronycler of Engelond compyled and tretyng of the sayd londe

Prologue heading begins: The prologge of thys booke declareth & telleth how thys lande was ffirste called after the eldest doughter of þe ryall kyng Deoclisyan off Surre

Heading to text (damaged): Here bigynneth the cronycle of a wo[...] called Dyoclisian which was a grete conquerour & conquered many [...]

Text begins: Some tyme in the nobbe [*sic*] lande of Surrey

Omits: Latin tag

Contains: Cad, QIL, "5w" heading

Ends imperfectly (see below): And yn þe firste yere of his reigne for grete [Brie 373/5–6]

Remarks: The text is prefaced by an early modern table of kings and chapters to Henry V.

The exordium, which omits some phrases found in other manuscripts of the group, is subdivided into sections, some parts of the text being laid out as headings in red. The number of kings who have reigned in England is computed up to Henry VI, instead of up to Edward III (cf. item 98); the number of kings has been changed, but the number of chapters said to be in the book seems to have been left alone (the edge of the leaf is damaged, but "CC xxx[...]" is visible).

Coryn's "lemman" is not named, and the names of Ebrak's children are omitted.

The text ends in the midst of a line, partway down fol. 142v (four lines into chapter 244), and is presumably as complete as it ever was.

After the imperfect ending occurs an early note of ownership (part of the leaf has been cut away): "This boke is gevyn to Esabell Alen of the bequest of her hunkull ser William Trouthe vicary in the close of Salisbury to the entent that sche schuld pray for hym of whom God of his [*ins.*] sawle haue mercy. Delyueryd by the handes of hir ffader and moder William Alen [...] Elenor his wiff which Elenor [which Elenor *ins.*] desessyd vpon ser [*del.*] Mary Mawdlen eve the [...] of kyng H. vij^{ti} of whom God of her saule haue mercy. Amen. Quod Esabel(?)."

119. PRINCETON UNIVERSITY LIBRARY, GARRETT MS. 150[1]

Begins imperfectly during exordium on fragmentary fol. 1: pi[...] lond [...] was fyrst a wyldreness[...]nd forlete and no thyng theerin [...]ut wylde bestis and fowlis

Prologue heading begins: The proloog of this book declarith and tellyth
Omits: Latin tag, "5w" heading (see below)
Contains: Cad, QIL
Ends: in rewle and in governaunce. Explicit.

Remarks: The names of Ebrak's numerous sons and daughters are omitted (Brie 15/15–24).

An addition is made to the chapter heading that begins the reign of William the Conqueror: "Here endith the cronicles of alle the kynges before the conquest and next folowith William Bastard duke of Normandie that conquerid alle Englond. Off William Bastarde and howe he gouerned hym wel and wysely & of the warre that was betwene hym & the kyng of Fraunce."

The chapters between the death of Mortimer and the establishment of the duchy of Cornwall are omitted (Brie 272/6–292/26), a gap that includes the Halidon Hill chapter. This gap is very suggestive of the omission of material around the same point that occurs in the AV–1419:B (see pp. 226–27). Taken with the evidence of the "double heading" to the reign of William the Conqueror, it might seem possible that these reflect a change to an exemplar that also underlies the AV–1419:B. The evidence of the following text, however, suggests that this is not the case and that the gap in Princeton Garrett 150 is the result of scribal error.

Early owners of the manuscript include Sir John Sulyard (died 1488), justice of the King's Bench, and "Syr Thomas Bourgyer knight" (also "T. Bourgchier"), the constable of Leeds Castle, who married Sulyard's widow, Anne, and who died in 1492.[2]

---

[1] See Bennett, Preston, and Stoneman, *Summary Guide*, p. 45.

[2] And *not* Thomas Bourghier, archbishop of Canterbury (d. 1486), as mistakenly noted by me in *Analytical and Enumerative Bibliography* 3 (1979): 265. See Boffey, *Manuscripts of English Courtly Love Lyrics*, pp. 122–23 and nn. 29 and 30 (where other books associated with the influential Bourchier family are also noted); Meale, "Patrons, Buyers and Owners," pp. 216 and 233 n. 87, where the signature of "John Sulyerd" is noted; Carol M. Meale, "'. . . alle the bokes that I haue of latyn, englisch, and frensch': Laywomen and Their Books in Late Medieval England," in *Women and Literature in Britain 1150–1500*, ed. Carol M. Meale, 2nd ed. (Cambridge, 1996), pp. 142–43.

120. UNIVERSITY OF ILLINOIS MS. 116(1)[1]

Exordium begins: Here begynneth a boke in Englysshe tonge called Brute of

Ingelond or the Cronycles of Ingelond compylynge and tretynge of þe seyd londe
Prologue heading begins: The prologe of þis boke declareþ & telleþ
Text begins: Some tyme in þe noble londe of Surry
Omits: Latin tag
Contains: Cad, QIL, "5w" heading
Second hand ends on fol. 184v: Nowe wille I tel ȝou whiche were þe chieff capteyns & governoures of þis cite of Rone. Mounser Guy Botteler was chieff cap [Brie 390/8–10]

Remarks: As in the preceding text, the names of Ebrak's children are omitted and the addition to the heading to the reign of William the Conqueror appears. Unlike the previous text, however, there is no loss of material around the Halidon Hill chapter.

A change of exemplar is indicated where the third hand of the manuscript continues in mid-word on fol. 185 with a CV–1430 JP:B continuation.

---

[1] For (2), see item 81.

121. SOCIETY OF ANTIQUARIES MS. 223

Text begins: Som tyme in the noble lande of Surry
Omits: Latin tag
Ends imperfectly: And whenne she came vnto age she [Brie 67/23–24]

Remarks: The hand of this paper manuscript, which belongs to the late fifteenth century, becomes progressively more of a hurried scribble.[1] The text is probably complete as the scribe left it, for it ends about two-thirds down fol. 45v.

The text is included in this group on the evidence of:

(a) *first giants passage*:
grete gyauntes of the whiche men callyd one of hem Gogemagoge chefe of hem all xl ffoote longe & xij foote of breede & an othir was called Wydy & he dwellyd in Shropeshyre vppon an hyghe hyll callyd the Wrekyn and an other Onowen and an othir Bounde and many othir there weren & called dyuerse names & dwelled in depe caues & on hyghe hyllys and mountetaynes whiche gyantes gate vppon her moders more gyantes [vppon her moders *del.*] to multeplye there people

at theyre owne luste & wyll vnto the tyme that Brute come and sloughe many of them and conquered the londe &c.

(b) *second giants passage*:
& that ile is compassed all with the see and no man may come ther but all shyppes and in that londe were wonte to be many gyauntes but now þer be but few and so that is but wyldyrnes ne no erthe tylled ne none sede isow of no maner graynes; also the gyauntes lyue be dyuers frutes growyng there and be fowles wylde and tame and othir grete bestes and in especyall by fleshe off sheepe grete as horses whyche beryn woll as it were here of gotes where-of they maken hem slavens and that londe is to you ordeyned by desteny and to yowre people.

(c) *Coryn's paramour passage*:
and than seyde [seyde *repeated*] Brute vnto Coryn "yefe thy lemman wyste þat one farde so fowle the she wolde neuyr loue the after."

(d) As in the other texts of the group, the names of Ebrak's children are omitted.

---

[1] Three examples of the development of the hand are given in Parkes, *English Cursive Book Hands*, plate 21 and p. 21.

122. HUNTINGTON MS. HM 133[1]

Begins imperfectly: Fraunce. And whanne he come aӡene intoo þis londe he belded [*first* e *over* y] a fayre tone and now es a cytee [cf. Brie 15/10–11]

Omits: Latin tag, QIL (see below)

Contains: Cad

Ends imperfectly: nay he shulde notte be transled the same erle Thomas of Lancaster vntoo the tyme that he was [Brie 263/12–13]

Remarks: The folios are missing that might have contained QIL.

An examination of the first chapters of the text shows it to agree well with the other EV–1419:C texts. As in these, the names of Ebrak's numerous children are omitted.

In the chapter relating the construction by Bladud of the hot baths at Bath, there is a verse addition (written as prose), apparently unique among extant EV and AV manuscripts, taken from the *Short English Metrical Chronicle*.[2] The verses occur at a point where the CV–1333 remarks "as þe gest telleþ" (Brie 16/16), a phrase that is omitted in the other EV–1419:C texts. The Huntington manuscript is at times carelessly written, presenting readings at a further remove from the ultimate CV sources than the corresponding readings in the other texts of the group; it cannot, therefore, represent the original of the group in its present form. It is striking, however, that the verses on the hot baths should come from the *Short English Metrical Chronicle*, from which source other details were added to the EV; possibly the Huntington text reflects an earlier stage of the EV that contained those verses.

---

[1] See Dutschke, *Guide*, 1: 177–78; Hanna, *Handlist*, pp. 13–14.
[2] Zettl, ed., *Metrical Chron.*, pp. 7–8, lines 156–84.

III. The Abbreviated Version

The Abbreviated Version contains four primary groups: the AV–1419:A (with three subgroups), B, C, and D. Important features that help distinguish these groups and subgroups are the form of the exordium, specific details of content, and the kinds of abridgment found in the individual texts. As we have seen, the exordia in groups A, B, and C agree well with the corresponding exordia in groups A, B, and C of the Extended Version, while that of group D has no EV counterpart. As in the EV, the wording of details ultimately derived from the *Short English Metrical Chronicle*, such as the name and designation ("paramour" or "leman") given to Coryn's mistress, is a very useful taxonomic tool.

Abridgments occur throughout the AV narratives, but those that have proved most significant for this classification include the chapter on thirty-three kings of Britain, the handling of material after Arthur's death, and the treatment of chapters around the battle of Halidon Hill, as well as other passages and details that will be encountered in the descriptions and discussions below. Thus, for example, the AV–1419:A(a) and the AV–1419:A(b) drastically abbreviate the chapter on the thirty-three kings by simply omitting the names and lengths of reign of all but the last. The AV–1419:A(a), the AV–1419:A(b), the AV–1419:B, and the AV–1419:C omit four chapters after the death of Arthur, whereas the AV–1419:A(c) and the AV–1419:D apparently repair this omission with a single, substitute chapter on Arthur's successor Constantine that is drawn from Geoffrey of Monmouth. Except for one atypical (but explainable) member of the group, the AV–1419:B is marked by the wholesale omission of material around the battle of Halidon Hill.

The Abbreviated Version to 1419, Group A (AV–1419:A)

Group A consists of three subgroups, the AV–1419:A(a), the AV–1419:A(b), and the AV–1419:A(c), which share the same exordium (with verbal variations) found in the EV–1419:A but are otherwise not derivable one from the other.

The Abbreviated Version to 1419:
Group A, Subgroup (a) (AV–1419:A[a])
This subgroup contains MSS. Glasgow Hunterian 83(1), BL Harley 3730(1), and Bodl. Digby 185.

123. UNIVERSITY OF GLASGOW, MS. HUNTERIAN 83(1)[1]
Exordium begins on fol. 15: Here begynnythe a boke in Engleshe tonge callyd Brute of Englond qwyche declarethe and tretethe of the ferst begynnyng of England
Prologue heading begins: The prologe of þis boke tellethe how þis land was first callid Albioun efter þe [qwiche *del.*] eldest doochter
Text begins: Svm tyme in the noble land of Surre
Omits: Latin tag, four chapters after Arthur, "5w" heading (see Remarks on the AV–1419:A[a] below)
Contains: Cad, QIL
AV text ends imperfectly on fol. 127v: the armed men drew owte þe beggers & þe povyr peple [cf. Brie 391/1–2]

Remarks: The AV–1419:A(a) text is the original text of the manuscript, to which the second scribe later added prefatory material and a Poly. 1461 continuation, together with a text of "Warkworth's" *Chronicle*.

The first hand is a secretary book hand similar to one of the hands in Bodleian Arch. Selden B.24, which has been described as "a typical Scottish hand of the end of the fifteenth century."[2] The language is northern.

---

[1] For (2), see item 94. For a fuller account of the manuscript, its texts, and its history, see Matheson, ed., *Death and Dissent*.
[2] Parkes, *English Cursive Book Hands*, p. 13 and plate 13(ii).

124. BL MS. HARLEY 3730(1)[1]
Exordium begins on fol. 2: Here begynnythe a boke in Englysch tonge called Brute of Englond which declareth and treyateth of þe fyrst begynnyng of Englond

Prologue heading begins: The prolog of þis boke telleth how þis land was first callid Albioun efter þe eldest doughtur
Text begins: Sum tyme in the noble land of Surrye
Omits: Latin tag, four chapters after Arthur, "5w" heading
Contains: Cad, QIL
AV text ends on fol. 105: in reule and gouernaunce.

Remarks: The *Brut* text, including the continuation to 1461 (now incomplete), was copied by two scribes from the preceding manuscript and thus shares the same internal features.

The second scribe has prefixed on fol. 1r–v an extract from the epilogue of the later version of John Hardyng's *Chronicle*.[2]

---

[1] For (2), see item 96. For a fuller account of the manuscript, its texts, and its relationship to the preceding manuscript, see Matheson, ed., *Death and Dissent*.
[2] See Kennedy, *Manual*, pp. 2644–47, 2836.

125. BODLEIAN MS. DIGBY 185

Exordium begins: Her begynnyth a booke in Englisch tong called Brute of Englond which declareth and treteth of the first begynnyng of Englond
Prologue heading begins: The prolog of this boke tellith how this lond was furst called Albion after the eldist doghter
Text begins: Svm tyme in the noble lond of Surrey
Omits: Latin tag, four chapters after Arthur, "5w" heading
Contains: Cad, QIL
Ends on fol. 79: in revoll and governaunce. Explicit.

Remarks: The *Brut* is the first item in the manuscript and is followed by Hoccleve's *Regiment of Princes*, Hoccleve's stories of Gerelaus and his wife and of Jonathas and his paramour, and the unique text of *King Ponthus and the Fair Sidone*.[1]

The manuscript belonged to, and was possibly commissioned by, the Hopton family of Swillington (near Leeds) in Yorkshire, whose arms are incorporated in the decoration of the initials of the first words of the major works. Mather (followed in *LALME*) suggests that it might have been written for Sir William Hopton.[2]

The language is of the West Riding of Yorkshire, "somewhat northernized, but of late type."[3]

[1] See M. C. Seymour, "The Manuscripts of Hoccleve's *Regiment of Princes*," *Edinburgh Bibliographical Society Transactions* 4 (1974): 276–77; Frank J. Mather, Jr., "King Ponthus and the Fair Sidone," *PMLA* 12 (1897): xxiii–xxiv.

[2] See Mather, "King Ponthus," pp. xxiv–xxv and facsimile. Mather claims that Hopton was the treasurer of Edward IV ca. 1465, but he is not listed as such in Fryde, Greenway, Porter, and Roy, eds., *Handbook of British Chronology*, p. 107. Carol Meale suggests that this manuscript may have been the "booke of Englisshe callid Occlif" that Thomasin Hopton bequeathed to her son in 1498; see Meale, "'... alle the bokes that I haue of latyn, englisch, and frensch'," p. 141.

[3] *LALME*, 1: 147.

Remarks on the AV–1419:A(a)
The exordium agrees well with that found in the EV–1419:A. The first passage on the giants, however, does not include the extra giants found in the EV–1419:A:

> & thei conceved & brogth for [furth G, H] giantes of the which men called on Gogmagog chef of theym all & he was fifty fote in lenght & xij in bred and all [*om.* G, H] the other were called dyuers names & dwellyd in hie hylles & montayns and in this maner thei came forth and were borne horrible giantes in Albioun & dwellid sum of theym in caves [coves G, H] & in hilles at [and G, H] their lyst & had the land of Albioun vnto the tyme that Brute come & arrived at Tottnesse in the Ile of Albioun & ther thys Brute conquered and scomfytt theis giantes aboueseyd & slogh the most parte of theym as bokes openly declareth. [Bodl. Digby 185, collated with Glasgow Hunterian 83 (G) and BL Harley 3730 (H)]

The second giants passage reads as follows:

> Also the giantes lyven by dyuers frutes grovyng ther & by fowles wyld & tame & other bestes & in esspeciall by flesch of schep gret as horsses wich weren wolle as her of gete wherof thei mak theym slavyns. And that land is to you ordenyd by destyne & to your people. [Bodl. Digby 185]

The name of Coryn's paramour is omitted and she is called his "leman":

> And than said Brute vnto Coryn "And yff thy leman wist þat oon

man farde so fowle with þe scho wald neuer love the efter this."
[Glasgow Hunterian 83]

In the chapter listing the thirty-three kings of Britain in the CV and EV, the text is drastically shortened and the chapter reads:

How xxxiij kinges regnede in peass.

And efter the deith of Esidure xxxiij kinges regnede in this land euerichon efter othere. And þe last of þaim at regned was callid Ely and he had iij sones Lude Cassibalane and Enemyen. [Glasgow Hunterian 83]

The names of Ebrak's many children (Brie 15/15–23) are omitted.

After the death of Arthur four chapters, recounting the reign of Constantine and his war with Mordred's sons, the reigns of Adelbright and Edelf, the story of Conan and Argentil, and the reign of Curan (see Brie 90/28–92/30), are omitted, and Arthur's successor is thus Conan. (This omission is, of course, a distinguishing feature of four of the six AV groups and subgroups.)

The text is abbreviated in many places, such as the chapters on and around the reign of King John (see Remarks on the Extended and Abbreviated Versions, below).

In the chapter on the battle of Halidon Hill the parts of the Scottish army are enumerated in the text without any rubricated subheadings, the text is abbreviated, and only three wards of the Scottish army are given:

And in þe thyrd ward was theis lordes: Iames Steward of Colden Aleyn Steward William Habraham William Morne [Morice B] and many oþer with vij^C men of armes and xvijM^l of commons so þat þer was iij batailles wele arrayed in armes to mete oure kyng conteynyng in þe nowmbre lxiijM^l & lv grete lordes lede þer [this B] men so arrayed in thre [iiij B] batailles. [Glasgow Hunterian 83, collated with Bodl. Digby 185 (B)]

The Abbreviated Version to 1419:
Group A, Subgroup (b) (AV–1419:A[b])

Subgroup (b) designates the text of BL MS. Royal 18.B.iv.

126. BL MS. ROYAL 18.B.IV

Begins imperfectly: of him had skorne and dispite and wolle not doo his wille [Brie 2/7–8]

Omits: Latin tag, four chapters after Arthur

Contains: Cad, QIL, "5w" heading

Ends imperfectly: And than the cite of Roan was byseged bothe be land and be water and whenn all this was done the shipes come vp than come the erle of Warwik [Brie 389/4–6]

Remarks on the AV–1419:A(b)

The single text of this subgroup stands apart from the texts of the preceding subgroup of the AV–1419:A in several respects and it may reflect an earlier stage of the AV–1419:A(a). However, the texts of that subgroup cannot be directly derived from it, for they often preserve details that are closer to the ultimate CV source (see, for example, the passage on Engist's heptarchy). The evidence for including it as a subgroup of the AV–1419:A consists of:

(a) *first giants passage*:

of the whiche men called one Gogmagog chief king of hem all and he was xl foote in lenghe and xij in breede and all that othre was called diuers names and duelled in high hilles & montains. And in this manere thei come furthe and were borne horrible giaunts in Albion and duelled some of hem in caves and in hilles at there luste and had the lande of Albion vnto the tyme that Brute come and arryved at Totnes in the Ile of Albion. And there this Brute conquered and scomfit thes giants abouesaide and slogh the moste parte of hem as bookes openly declareth.

(b) *second giants passage*:

Also the giauntes lyven be diuers frutes grewing there and by wilde foule & tame and othre grete bestes and in especiall by flesshe of shepe grete as hors whiche weren wolle as heire of gotes wherof thei maken hem slavyns. And that lande to you is ordeyned by desteyne and to your peple.

(c) *Lud passage*:

This Lud loved more to duell at Troie than at eny othre place of the lande. Wherefore he commaunded that citee no lenger be called the Newe Troie bot Ludentoun or Luddestoune as sume bokes sayn aftre his name Lud for in that citee he made moste coste of byggyng. And there he made a gate all oute of the grounde and called it Ludgate aftre his owne name. And he made walle the toune and diche it also bot aftrewarde the name of cite was chaunged by Saxuns tonge and variance of lettres and was called Londoun. And yete is bot Normans and othre aliens callen it Loundres and clerkes callen it Ciuitas Londoun.

(d) *33 kings passage*:
Aftre the dethe of Esydoure reigned xxxiij kynges in Britaine ichon aftre othre in peace. And the laste of hem was called Ely and he reigned bot vij monethes and had iij sonz Lud Cassibilan and Enemioun.

(e) *Engist's heptarchy passage*:
And Engeste seised all the lande into his hande. And in euery place where he come he lete caste doune churches and houses of religioun. And distroied Cristendome thrughoute the lande and made chaunge the name [the name *repeated*] of the lande that noman of his were so herdy aftre that tyme to calle this lande Britoun bot calle it Englyslonde. And nowe by corrupcioun of tong it is called Englonde. And he departed all his lande to his men. And made therin vij kynges for to strength the lande that the Britonis therafter shulde neuir come therin: the furste kyngdome was Kent ther that Engest hymself reigned and was lorde and maister of all that other. And one othre kyng had Sussex where nowe is Chichestre; the iij had Westsex; the iiij had Essex; the v kyng had Estangle nowe called Norffolk and Suffolk; the vj had Leycestre-shir Northampton-shir Hertfordshir and Huntyndoun; the vij had Oxenford Gloucestre Wynchestre Warwyk and Davenshir.

In the 33 kings passage the AV–1419:A(b) retains the length of Ely's reign, whereas in the Lud passage the AV–1419:A(a) preserves details that are closer to the ultimate CV source.

As in the AV–1419:A(a), the names of Ebrak's children are omitted.

In some important features, however, the text does not agree with the texts of other AV–1419:A subgroups:

(a) *Coryn's paramour passage*:
Than saide Brute to Coryn "yf Erneburgh thin paramoure might wit that one man onely ferde thus foull with the she wolde neuir love the."

(b) *Halidon Hill passage*:
the full array of the Scottish army, that is, all five wards, including the "5w" heading, is given.[1]

[1] The leaves have been bound out of order around this part of the text.

The Abbreviated Version to 1419,
Group A, Subgroup (c) (AV–1419:A[c])
This subgroup consists of two manuscripts, BL Royal 18.A.ix and Huntington HM 131. Although their texts are not very close, they have been grouped together because they both contain resemblances to the EV–1419:A and include the names of Ebrak's children. It is possible, however, that the two texts are independently derived from a form of text that underlies both them and the AV–1419:D; if so, then they should be assigned to separate groups.

The two texts share a common chapter, based on Geoffrey of Monmouth's *Historia*, on Arthur's successor Constantine (similar to that found in the AV–1419:D). This chapter occurs at a point where four chapters appear in the CV and EV. Significantly, these chapters are omitted in the AV–1419:A(a), the AV–1419:A(b), the AV–1419:B, and the AV–1419:C, suggesting that an acute scribe recognized the lacuna and turned to Geoffrey to supply the omission.

127. BL MS. ROYAL 18.A.IX
Heading on fol. 8: Here begynneth the kalendre of Brute in Englesshe.
Exordium begins: Here begynneth a booke in Englesshe tung called Brute of Englonde the whiche declareth of the furste begynnyng of the lande
Prologue heading begins: The prolog of this boke declareth howe the lande was called Albion after the eldest suster [*sic*] of the roiall king Dioclician of Surre
Text begins: Svme tyme in the noble lande of Surre
Omits: Latin tag, "5w" heading (see below)
Contains: substitute chapter after Arthur, Cad, QIL
Ends imperfectly: ther was noumbre in the citte by haraldes [Brie 390/22–23]

Remarks: The names of Ebrak's children are given.
The four chapters after the death of Arthur are replaced by a single chapter on Constantine, after whom reigns Conan (see the following text).
The text is not directly related to the other AV–1419:A subgroups; in general, it seems to be most closely related to the EV–1419:A, although (as

in the preceding group) the Latin tag on Blegabred is not found in the thirty-three kings passage.

The heading is paralleled in BL Harley 24 and Addit. 12030 and the extra giants of the EV–1419:A appear (see below).

The Engist passage, although extensively abbreviated, has similarities to that found in the EV–1419:A; the confusion of Worcester with Winchester found in BL Harley 24 and Addit. 12030 (but not in Rylands Eng. 105, Harvard Richardson 35, and the other texts of the EV–1419:A) is not made, that is, the text reads "Wynchestre Warwyk and Darbyshire."

In the Halidon Hill passage there is a partial agreement with Rylands Eng. 105 rather than BL Harley 24 in that the Scottish army is divided into four divisions: "and in the laste parte of the bataill of Scotlande wer thes lordes: the erle of Dunbar keper of the castel of Berwyk...."

Selected textual features that agree with the EV–1419:A are:

(a) *first giants passage*:
grete gyauntes wherof one was called Gogmagog the king of theym all the whiche was xl fote of lenght xij of breed; and one was called Wydy the whiche duelled vpon an highe hille in Shropshire called the Wreken; one othre was called Oneweine le fort; one othre Bounde; and othre ther weren called diuers names. And thus was the gyauntes brought forthe in thys lande and duelled in caues and hylles and montanes and inhabitte the lande vnto Brute come and conquered theym and sloughe of theym and drove many of theym owte of the lande.

(b) *second giants passage*:
And the giauntes that been ther lyve with rotes and grete bestes and ffowles and myghti shepe wherof they maken theym slavyns and clothes.

(c) *Coryn's paramour passage*:
Thanne saide Brute in scorne vnto Coryne "yf Erneborowe thine paramour knewe that one man fared thus by þe she wolde neuer loue the after this."

The *Brut* text is prefaced by a geographical survey abstracted into English from Higden's *Polychronicon*, beginning on fol. 2, "Primus Liber Cronicorum. Ivlius Cesar a wyse manne," and ending incompletely on fol. 7v, "in the whiche regioune was furste the people of Gotelande whos...."[1]

---

[1] The abstract corresponds to Churchill Babington, ed., *Polychronicon Ranulphi Higden*

Monachi Cestrensis, vol. 1, Rolls Series 41 (London, 1865), pp. 41–151.

128. HUNTINGTON MS. HM 131[1]
Exordium begins: Here begynneth Brute in Englysshe the whiche declareth and treteth of all the kinges and of all the notable actes and dedes the whiche hathe bene done in this lande sithe the furste begynnyng of this lande

Prologue heading begins: The prolog of this boke declareth howe this lande was furste called Albioun after the eldest doughter

Text begins: Some tyme in the noble lande & roialme of Surre

Omits: Latin tag, "5w" heading (see below)

Contains: substitute chapter after Arthur, Cad, QIL

Ends: in gouernaunce and rule.

Remarks: The names of Ebrak's children are given.

As noted above, this text has been grouped with that found in BL Royal 18.A.ix since they share (though with a number of verbal differences) a common chapter on the reign of Constantine. This chapter parallels closely the corresponding account in Geoffrey of Monmouth's *Historia*,[2] suggesting that there may have been some gap in the text (reflected in the omission of four chapters in several other AV groups). The substitute text is here printed from Huntington HM 131, with selected substantive variant readings from BL Royal 18.A.ix (R):

> Howe Constantyne cosyn to Arthure reigned and was werred opon by Mordrede two sones. Capitulo lxxix° [lxxxix R].
>
> Aftir Arthur reigned hys cosynne Constantine. Thanne come Mordred two sonnes wyth a grete multitude of Saxouns and werred agains this Constantine and oftetymes dide him meche herme and hurte. But he prevayled vpon theym & drove þat one vnto London and þat othir vnto Winchestir; and in this same tyme deide Daniell the bysshop of Bangoure an religious manne; and in this same tyme was the bysshop of London [Gloucestre R] made erchebysshop of Caunterbury. And thys Constantine pursewed thes two brethre and come vnto Wynchestre & besegid it and Mordred sonne that was þer fledde into þe churche of Seint Amphibale and atte the high altier he was take and slaine; and that othir fledde into an hous of ffreres atte London and was take and slaine also; & thanne this Constantine

reigned iiij yere and was slaine of Conan and hys felyship and buried atte Stonehenge besyde Vter Pendragoune.

Of king Conan howe he reigned wele and worthely and welbeloued. Capitulo lxxx° [lxxxx° R].

In the Halidon Hill chapter, the Scottish army is divided into three "battles," the last of which is subdivided into two wings; the "5w" heading is replaced by the words "and in þat oþre wyng was þe erle of Dunbar." The subsequent text on the battle is abbreviated:

> and þis was done vpon Seint Margarettes even the yere of our lorde M^l CCC xxxij. And thanne þes two kinges torned vnto the sege of Barwyk and þei yelde vp þe toune and þe castell

As in the previous text, the Huntington text must be derived from an earlier stage of the EV-1419:A than is represented by the extant manuscripts of that group, for it shows a number of similarities to other EV and AV groups.

Selected textual features are:

(a) *first giants passage*:
by straunge meanes spirites of þe ayer diuersely hadde forto done with theym and procreate vpon theim grete giauntes the whiche inhabetted the lande after theim wherof one was called Gogmagog king of þem all the whiche was xl fott of lengthe and xij in brede and one oþer was called Wydy the whiche duelled vpon an highe hylle in Shropshire called the Wreken and one othir Onewenne le Fort and one oþer Bounde and thus þei were called diuers names and they duelled in caues and mountains and inhabited þe lande vnto þe tyme that Brute come and sloughe many of þem the whiche arryved atte Totenesse.

(b) *second giants passage*:
and þat lande ys wyldiernesse and þer be inne grete gyauntes and many wylde bestes and thes gyauntes maken theym slavyns of þer skynnes and lyven with ther fflesshe.

(c) *Coryn's paramour passage*:
and thanne said Brute vnto Corynne in skorne "and Erneborough thy paramour knewe that one manne dide so to the she woulde neuer love þe after þis."

(d) *Lud passage*:
And after þe dethe of þis Ely reigned Ludde hys sonne and well gou-

erned þe roialme and welbeloued of hys people and this Ludde loued well to abyde atte New Troie & he commaunded it shulde nomor be called Newe Troie bot Luddentoune or Luddestoun and þer he made grete coste for he made Ludgate and lete call it after hys ovne name Ludde and he made the toune to be diched and afterwarde was the name of London changed and called Londoun and after Normans it ys called Loundres and in Latynne Londonie.

(e) *Engist's heptarchy passage*:
and than Engest seised all the lande into hys hande and caste dovne churches and houses of religioune and distroied Cristendome and chaunged the name of þe lande and called it Engestlond or Engyslonde and charged þat noman shulde calle it Britaine and after þat by correpcion and brieve tonge it is called Englonde. And thanne he made therin vij kinges: the furste was Kent þer himself was king; the secounde Sussex; the thyrde Westsex; the iiij Essex; the v Northfolk & Suffolke Marcheneryche nowe Lyncoln; the vj Leycestre Northamphire Hertefordshire Huntyngdon; the vij Oxefordshire Gloucestre Wynchestre Warwyk and Derbyshire.

---

[1] See Dutschke, *Guide*, 1: 174–75; Hanna, *Handlist*, p. 13.
[2] See Wright, ed., *'Historia Regum Britannie,'* p. 132.

The Abbreviated Version to 1419, Group B (AV–1419:B)

This large group consists of MSS. Glasgow Hunterian 443; BL Harley 1337; Bodl. Hatton 50; BL Harley 6251; BL Stowe 71; Jesus Coll., Oxford, 5; Bodl. Tanner 11; Michigan 225; Alnwick 457A; NLW Peniarth 396D(2); Bodl. Rawlinson C.901; and Bodl. Rawlinson B.190. The second section of the PV–1419(r&g):D (MSS. TCD 5895 and BL Harley 7333) is also taken from a text of this group (see pp. 268–71).

Although this group possesses a number of distinctive features, the most obvious are the B-recension of the exordium, shared with the EV–1419:B (see Introduction, Appendix 3), and a major loss of narrative material around the battle of Halidon Hill in all but one text, which has probably switched to a second exemplar by that point.

129. UNIVERSITY OF GLASGOW, MS. HUNTERIAN 443

Heading: Her begynnyth a boke wyche that ys callyd Brute of the Croneclis of Engelonde.

Exordium begins: [T]þe wych booke tretyth & lellyth [*sic*] of þe kyngys and princypall lordys

Prologue heading begins: Here begynnyth a prolog. [Here ... prolog *in red*] [T]the prolog of þis boke declaryth how þis lond was callyd Albione aftyr þe heldest douȝter

Text begins: Some tyme in þe nobyll lond of Surre

Omits: Latin tag, four chapters after Arthur, Halidon Hill material

Contains: Cad, QIL

Ends imperfectly: the capetayn come out and delyueryd þe kayis and the castell to our kyng & Bawayis & þe othyr [Brie 384/21–22; the rest of the line and a partially decipherable catchword have been erased]

Remarks: As in the other texts of this group, the names of Ebrak's children are given.

Several kings are omitted in the thirty-three kings passage, and the omission of the Latin tag on Blegabred in this text is probably not significant.

The chapters around the reign of King John are heavily abbreviated (see pp. 241–42 below).

The omission of the Halidon Hill chapter is part of a longer omission. The text breaks off in mid-sentence near the foot of fol. 133 in the chapter recounting the downfall and execution of Roger Mortimer. Fol. 133v was left blank and the text resumes at the top of fol. 134 with the chapter on the naval battle at Winchelsea (Brie 303/25). Such a physical break in the manuscript raises the possibility that a change of exemplar occurred at this point.[1]

The dialect is that of Central Surrey and there are orthographic similarities to manuscripts written in religious houses south of London.[2]

---

[1] A second physical and textual lacuna occurs between fols. 165v (Brie 368/14) and 168 (Brie 373/1: the beginning of Henry V's reign).

[2] *LALME*, 1: 89, 3: 495–96. See M. L. Samuels, "Kent and the Low Countries," in *Edinburgh Studies in English and Scots*, ed. A. J. Aitken, Angus McIntosh, and Hermann Pálsson (London, 1971), p. 13.

130. BL MS. HARLEY 1337
Heading: Here begynnyth a book callyd the Croniculis of Englond.
Exordium begins: This book tretith & tellith of all þe kyngis & principall lordis
Prologue heading begins: The prologg of this booke [*written as a heading*] conteynethe [C *decorated initial*] xxxv chaptirs; þe first declarithe howe þis londe was callyd Albioun aftir the eldest douȝter
Text begins: Som tyme in the nobill londe of Surre
Omits: four chapters after Arthur, Halidon Hill material
Contains: Latin tag, Cad, QIL
Ends: in rewle and governaunce.
Colophon: Here endith a book callyd the Croniclis of Englonde made & compilid by notabil clerkis of aventuris of kyngis þat were in þis londe and howe þey died.

131. BODLEIAN MS. HATTON 50
Heading: Here begynnyth a book callyd Brute of þe Croniculys of Englonde.
Exordium begins: This book tretith & tellith of all þe kyngis & principall lordis
Prologue heading begins: The prologg. The prologg of this book declarith how þis londe was callid Albyon aftir the eldest douȝter
Text heading: Here begynnyth the first chaptir of this book of Croniculis.
Text begins: Som tyme in the nobill londe of Surre
Omits: four chapters after Arthur, Halidon Hill material
Contains: Latin tag, Cad, QIL
Ends: in rewle and governaunce.
Colophon: Here endith a book callyd Brute of the Croniculis of Englonde made & compiled by notabill clerkis of all the actis & dedis of kyngis þat evir wer in this londe to take exsaumpill what fil tofore our dayes.

132. BL MS. HARLEY 6251
Heading on damaged fol. 1: Here begynnyth a book call[.]d Brute [. . .]
Exordium begins illegibly.
Prologue heading begins: The prologg. The prologg of þis book declarithe howe þis londe was callid Albion aftir þe eldist douȝtir of þe riall kynge Dyoclysiane

Text heading: Here begynnyth the first chaptir of this booke.
Text begins: Som tyme in the nobill lond of Surre
Omits: four chapters after Arthur, Halidon Hill material
Contains: Latin tag, Cad, QIL
Ends on damaged and stained folio: castell tyll [...]ernaunce.
Colophon: Here endithe the Croniculis of Englonde made and compilid be notabill clerkis to men to rede & to see what fill tofore in hire dayes.

Remarks: The signature of Bartholomew Towers, dated 1614, appears on fol. 57.

133. BL MS. Stowe 71

Heading on fol. 3: Assit principio sancta Maria meo. Here bigynneth the Boke of the Cronyculez of the kinges of Englond.
Exordium begins: [T]his boke tretith and telleth of all kynges and principall lordis
Prologue heading (within exordium) begins: The prologge of this boke declareth how this londe was called Albyon after the eldest dowter of the riaall emperour Dioclisian of Surre the whiche dowter called Albyon
Text heading: The furst chapeter of maide Albyon and of hir xxxij^{ti} susters.
Text begins: [S]vmtyme in the nobyll londe of Surre
Omits: four chapters after Arthur, Halidon Hill material
Contains: Latin tag, Cad, QIL
Ends imperfectly: north side of the host whiche was byfore the forest of Leonez [cf. Brie 390/2–3]

Remarks: The text offers some secondary readings, as in the text heading above and in the following selected passages:

(a) *first giants passage*:
And they conseyved and brought furth horribyll geauntes off the whiche one was called Gogmagog and he was xl fote of length and xij fote in brede. And theise geauntez dwelled in diuerse placez in this londe and in othir londys in cavys and in mounteynez vnto the tyme that Brute come and arryved at Tottenesse that was in the Ile of Albyon. And this Brute slowe hem icheone.

(b) *second giants passage*:
And in that londe was wonte to be many geauntez but nowe þer be but fewe and þat londe is but wyldernesse and the geauntez leven by herbys

and by rotys and with flessh as of shepe als moche as an hors. And þat londe is ordeyned for yow & your pepyll.

(c) *Coryn's paramour passage*:
And thanne seid Brute to Coryn "if Embron thi paramour wist þat one man had done the suche a velanye she wolde neuer loue the."

(d) *Lud passage*:
[A]fftyr the deth of Ely reigned Ludde his sone and gouerned the londe well and worthely and honoured his God and hated his wickid puple.... And than was the name of the cite chaunged bi writinge of clerkes and called it Villa Londonias and so the name was called London and Frengshmen calle it Londris. And this king lete walle and diche the toun abowte.

(e) *Engist's heptarchy passage*:
And Engeste went throwe the londe & sesed all the lond into his honde. And in euery place þer he come he threwe doun chirchez and howses of religioun and distroyed Cristendome throwe-oute the lond and chaunged the name of this londe that noman of his were so hardy to calle it Breteyn but called it Engestes londe and departed all this lond to his men and made þerinne vij kynges forto strength the londe that the Bretonys þerafter shuld neuer come therinne. The ffirst kyngdome þerof was Kent ther as Engest hymselff reigned & was lorde and maister of all that othir. Anothir king hadde Sussex where now is Chester. The third had Westsex; the iiij hadde Essex. The v hadde Estangyll that now is called Northfolk and Suthfolk Marche that now is to say the erledom of Nicholl; the sixt had Leycetershier Northhampton Hertford and Huntingdonshir. And the vij hadde Oxinford Glowcester Wynchester Warwik & Derbyshir.

Remarks: The name of Thomas Bromley(e), dated 1576, occurs on the front flyleaves.

134. JESUS COLLEGE, OXFORD, MS. 5[1]
Heading: Here begynneth the boke called Brute of the Cronicle of Englond.
Exordium begins: The whiche boke tretith and tellith of all the kynges & principall lordis
Prologue heading begins: The Prologe. The prologe of this booke declarith howe this londe was called Albioun aftir the eldest doughter of this riall king Dioclisiane of Surre the whiche doughter was called Albyne

Text heading: Here begynnith the first chapiter of this boke called the Cro-
niclis of England.
Text begins: Svm tyme in the nobill londe of Surre
Omits: four chapters after Arthur, Halidon Hill material
Contains: Latin tag, Cad (see below), QIL
Ends: in reule and gouernaunce.

Remarks: The number of chapters contained in the text is mentioned neither in the exordium nor at the end of the text, where no colophon occurs.

The Cadwallader episode is included, but the king is mistakenly called Cadwalyn, son of Oswyn, and the real Cadwalyn is omitted.

---

[1] See Ogilvie-Thomson, *Handlist*, p. 38. The story of Vortiger and Merlin is printed in E. O. Powell, "From The Brute of the Chronicle of England," *Folklore* 48 (1937): 91–93.

135. BODLEIAN MS. TANNER 11
Heading: Here begynnyth a book callyd the Croniclis of Englond.
Exordium begins: Thes book tretithe of all þe kyngis & pryncypall lordis þat evir weer in this lond & of aventurs & wondirfull thyngis & batayllis & oþir notabill actis werris conquests
Prologue heading (within exordium) begins: And this book declarith howe this londe was callid Albioune aftir the eldest douȝter of þe riall kynge Dyoclysiane of Surre þe wich douȝter was callid Albeyn
Text heading: Here begynnyth þe first chaptir.
Text begins: Som [. . .] þe nobill londe of Surre þer was a man of grete renown callid Dyoclisiane
Omits: four chapters after Arthur, Halidon Hill material
Contains: Latin tag, Cad, QIL
Ends: in rewle & gouernaunce.
Colophon: Explicit Cronicucle [*sic*] Anglie.

Remarks: The text, although clearly an AV–1419:B, appears to combine features reflecting both an earlier and a later stage of the group than the other manuscripts present. The wording of the exordium is textually later than that of the EV–1419:B or of Glasgow Hunterian 443, and the prologue heading is absorbed into the text. The number of chapters in the work is mentioned neither in the exordium nor in the brief colophon.

Further passages also show that the text contains wording later than that of other AV–1419:B texts, for example:

(a) *first giants passage*:
And they conseyvid horribill geauntis of þe wich oon of hem was callid Gogmagog and he was xl foot of lengith & xij foot of brede. And these geauntis dwellid in diuers placis in this londe & in othir londis in cavis and in mownteynys onto þe tyme þat Brute come & aryvid at Tottenes þat was in the Ile of Albioun and ther þis Brute scomfitid these geauntis echon & sclouȝe hem all.

(b) *second giants passage*:
And in þat londe was wont to be meny geauntis but nowe ther been but fewe & þat londe is all wildirnes. And þe geauntis lyvyn with herbis and with rotis & with flessh of shepe as grete as an hors and þat londe is ordeyned for yeur pepill.

(d) *Coryn's paramour passage*:
Than seyd Brute to Coryn "yf Emberoun þy paramoure wist herof she wold nevir love the þat o man had the so defoulid."

(e) *Lud passage*:
This kyng Lud lovid more to dwell at Troy þan in eny oþere plase of the londe. Wherfore he comaundit þat þe cete shuld no lenger be callid Newe Troy but Ludstoun and ther he made a feir gate callid Ludgate. And after þe name of þis town was chaungit by variaunce of lettris & callid London.

As in the other texts of the group, considerable material is lost around the battle of Halidon Hill. Unlike the other texts, however, a short bridging passage appears, possibly supplied to ameliorate the narrative dislocation in the text:

And þan kynge Edward of Scotlond toke his leve of kynge Edward and went to his own londe.

Howe kynge Edward was crowned kyng of Scotlonde.

Aftir it fill þat þis Edward Bailloll governed hym so evill among his lordis þat had doon for hym that they set no price by hym. Wherfor atte laste he was feyn to flee þe londe. And þan kynge Edward sawe þe grete stryfe þat was in Scotlonde & come to þe castell of Berewik. And þan ser Iohn Bailloll þat was þat tyme kyng of Scotlond considerynge howe þat God did meny myraclis for kynge Edward of Englonde [*etc.*] [cf. Brie 280/27–28, 306/30, 307/4–6]

The fifteenth-century name "William Cardynall" on p. 212 may be that of the scribe.

136. UNIVERSITY OF MICHIGAN MS. 225[1]

Begins imperfectly: And that same nyghte they cut hir husbondis throtis [cf. Brie 3/27–30]

Omits: four chapters after Arthur, Halidon Hill material

Contains: Latin tag, Cad, QIL

Ends: in rewle & governaunce.

Colophon: Here endithe a boke callid Brute of the Croniculis of Englond made & compilid by notabill clerkis of al the actis of all þe kyngis that evir was in this londe sithens Brute first conquerid it.

---

[1] See Lister M. Matheson, "A Fragment of *Sir Eglamour of Artois*," *English Language Notes* 17 (1980): 165–68.

137. ALNWICK CASTLE MS. 457A

Begins imperfectly on fol. 48 (see below): calle them kyngis and oon of them men called [...]land and a nothir men called Davyller [cf. Brie 22/32–23/1–2]

Omits: Cad (see below), four chapters after Arthur, Halidon Hill material

Contains: Latin tag, QIL

Ends imperfectly on fol. 47v (see below): sir Aliaundir Nevelle archibisshop of York and sir Roberte Vere marquys of Develyn and the [erle of Oxinford catchwords] [Brie 342/13–14]

Remarks: The manuscript consists of two long sections of text (fols. 1–47v, 48–69) written by a single scribe. As presently bound, these sections have been reversed in order, the later section of text appearing before the earlier section.

As it stands, the manuscript begins with a fragment on the murder of Alured by Earl Godwin, and the present fol. 1 begins during the reign of King Harold, "of Englond and falslie brake his couenaunt þat he hadde made afor vnto duke William" (Brie 135/23–24). This section continues to the now imperfect end of the text given above (fol. 47v).

The second section begins on fol. 48 as above, and ends imperfectly on fol. 69v, "þaie were discomfited and slayn and while thaie faught and þe bataille endured þe kyng went prevely vnto Walis" (cf. Brie 94/29–31). The intervening material originally between the second and first sections, including the Cadwallader episode, is now lost, apart from the fragment on Alured.

Other than the combination of features noted above, additional evidence for placing the text in the AV–1419:B includes the passage recounting Lud's renaming of New Troy:

> This Ludde loued more to dwell at Troy thanne in any othir place of þe lond wherfor he comaunded the citee to be called no lenger New Troy but Ludstrun [sic] and withinne that citee he made muche bildyng and ther he made a gatte and lette call it Ludgatte after his name and he made wall the toun and diche it. And after þe name of the towne was chaunged by Saxons tonge and varyeng of letters and called Londoun and alions and Normans callith it Loundris and clerkes callith it Ciuitas Londoun and he regned xj yere and died and lith at Londoun withinne þe same gatte that he lette make.

Early names that appear in the manuscript include "Wyllyam Shelley" (fol. 63v), "Thomas Denny" (fol. 59v), "John Dennye of Burnewoode" (fol. 62v).

138. NLW MS. PENIARTH 396D(2)[1]
Begins imperfectly on fol. 3: And Brute and his men hem manly defendid [Brie 7/15–16]
Omits: (see below)
Contains: Latin tag, Cad, QIL
Ends imperfectly: þe erle of Marche þat þe kynge sent to skeme þe se costes þer rose soche [cf. Brie 385/11–12]

Remarks: The folio is missing that would tell who reigned after Arthur; the folios containing the Halidon Hill material are also lost. The evidence for including the text here is:

(a) *Coryn's paramour passage*:
   Than seid Brute to Coryn "if Emboron þi paramour my3t wete þat o man ferd so foule with the she wold neuer love þe."
(b) *33 kings passage*: "after him" linkage and Latin tag on Blegabred.
(c) *Lud passage*:

This Lud loved more to dwell at Troye þan at any oþer place of þe londe ffor he commaundid þat cyte no lenger be called Newe Troye but London Ludston as som bookes seye after his name Lud for in þat cyte he made most byldynge. And þer he made a gate owt of þe grounde and callid it Ludgate after his owne name. And he made wall þe towne and diche it also but afterward þe name of þe towne was chaungid be Saxonye tonge and varyaunce of letters and callid London and 3it is but Normans and oþer alyons call it Londris and clerkes call it Civitas London.

(d) *Engist's heptarchy passage*:
And þe fyrst kyngdom þerof was Kent þer Engest hymself regned and he was kynge and lord of all þe tother. Anoþer kynge had Sussex where now is Chester. And þe thyrd had Westsexe [*etc.*]

---

[1] For (1), see item 199. See Marx, "Middle English Manuscripts," pp. 362–64, for a description and an analysis of the contents (Marx mistakenly assigns the text to my "Peculiar Texts and Versions").

139. BODLEIAN MS. RAWLINSON C.901

Begins imperfectly: powere and first conquered all the londe of Lygers. And after he wold have conqueryd all Scotlonde and Wales. But Scatere came with his mene and gafe hym grete bataill. [Brie 23/19–21]
Omits: four chapters after Arthur, Halidon Hill material
Contains: Latin tag, Cad, QIL
Ends: in reule and governaunce.

Remarks: In typical AV–1419:B fashion, material is omitted around the battle of Halidon Hill (Brie 271/23–303/24). The highly cursive hand is also similar to that found in many of the other texts of this group.

140. BODLEIAN MS. RAWLINSON B.190

Begins imperfectly: shamyd and abassyd and sayde al theis conducyons should be amendid in all thyng to ther fader [cf. Brie 3/10–11]
Omits: four chapters after Arthur
Contains: Latin tag, Cad, QIL
Changeover, 1333 to 1377: and whilis this doyng enduryd the Englisshmen

knavis token ther palfreys and went ther way whedir they wolde. And
after this victory the kyng turnyd hym agayne to the sege of Berwik [cf.
Brie 286/6–9, 291/1–2]

Ends: And than the kyng enterid into the towne and restid hym in the castel
into the tyme that he hade see the towne in rewle and gouernauns.

Remarks: Exceptionally for this group, there is no omission of material
around the battle of Halidon Hill. The text must, however, be included in
the AV–1419:B on the evidence of:

(a) *first giants passage*:
and they conseywide and browt forth orrybill giauntis of the whiche on
was callid Gogmagog and he was xl fote of lengith and xij fote of brede
and theis geauntis dwellid in diuerys placys in this londe & in odyr
londys in cauys in mountaynys oonto the tyme that Brwte com arywyd
at Tottenes that was in the Ile of Albyon and this Brut slouȝe hem
echon.

(b) *second giants passage*:
and in þat londe was wont to be many gyaunttes but now ther be but
fewe & that londe ys but wildernes and the gyauntis lewyn by erbis &
be rotes and with flesshe as of shepe as moche as an hors and that
londe ys ordaynid for ȝowe & ȝowre pepill.

(c) *Coryn's paramour passage*:
And then seide Brute to Coryn "yf Embron thi paramowr wist that
oon man had do the soche a welony she wolde neuer loue the."

(d) *33 kings passage*: "after him" linkage and Latin tag on Blegabred.

(e) *Lud passage*:
And this kyng Ludd lowyd more to dwell at London then in any oder
place in the londe and therfore he wolde that cete shulde no more be
callid Newe Troy but Ludston and then he mad most byldyng in that
towne. And ther he let make a gate owte of the grounde and let cal hit
Ludgate after his name and then was the name of the cete changid be
writyng of clerkys and cald it Villa Londoniarum and so þe name was
callid London and Frenchemen call it Loundrys and this kyng Ludd let
wall and deche the towne all abowth.

The incomplete beginning has been supplied by a modern transcript from
a manuscript in the Cambridge University Library; other missing material
has been supplied by Thomas Hearne from Bodl. Ashmole 793. The
original hand is very similar to that of Glasgow Hunterian 443.

It is possible that this text represents a blend of an AV–1419:B text with a CV text (see Remarks on the AV–1419:B below) and that it should be considered under the texts of the Peculiar Versions.

Remarks on the AV–1419:B
With the exception of Bodl. Rawlinson B.190, the manuscripts of the AV–1419:B form a relatively homogeneous group. Although they appear closely connected, textual comparison shows that a number of intervening texts have been lost. Certain conclusions can, however, be drawn about the likely development of the text.

Since the other EV and AV groups state in the exordium the number of chapters contained, we can infer that Glasgow Hunterian 443, which does likewise, represents a more original state of the text at this point than the remaining (complete) manuscripts do, for they either extract this small piece of information and use it as a colophon or they omit it entirely.

The omissions around the battle of Halidon Hill are suggestive of the development of the group, and are presented below:

MS.	breaks off	restarts
Hunterian 443	Brie 271/30	Brie 303/25
Hatton 50	Brie 280/26	Brie 304/13
Harley 1337	Brie 280/31	Brie 304/22
Harley 6251	Brie 280/13	Brie 304/22
Stowe 71	Brie 280/26	Brie 304/7
Jesus Coll. 5	Brie 280/26	Brie 304/7
Tanner 11	Brie 280/28	Brie 306/30 (plus a short bridging passage, then Brie 307/4)
Michigan 225	Brie 280/26	Brie 306/30
Alnwick 457A	Brie 280/26	Brie 306/30
Peniarth 396D(2)	[fols. missing]	
Rawlinson C.901	Brie 271/23	Brie 303/25
[Harley 7333, TCD 5895	Brie 280/26	Brie 305/11]

Bodl. Rawlinson B.190, of course, omits no material at this point and could therefore represent the earliest stage of the internal development of the AV–1419:B group. In textual details, however, this text is further removed from the CV or the EV–1419:B than is, for example, Glasgow Hunterian 443. Accordingly, it cannot be the precursor of the group, from which the other texts have derived.

It is possible that Bodl. Rawlinson B.190 is a witness of an early exemplar closer to the original CV and EV wording, but it is equally possible, if the medial omission is an original feature of the AV–1419:B, that the scribe of Bodl. Rawlinson B.190, finding a gap in his AV–1419:B exemplar, changed to a CV exemplar for the remainder of his text. It may be significant that chapter headings are not inserted for several chapters from the start of the reign of Edward II, though the hand of the text remains the same.

The extent of the omissions suggests that BL Stowe 71 and Jesus Coll., Oxford, 5 represent an earlier stage in the group than the other texts since they omit the least amount of material, and the omissions found in the other manuscripts (with the exceptions of Glasgow Hunterian 443 and Bodl. Rawlinson C.901) can be contained within the scope of their omissions. However, as suggested above, Glasgow Hunterian 443 may be based on exemplars from two groups, and since it contains the phrase noting the number of chapters contained in the work, it can therefore be considered as indicative of (though not identical with) the earliest development of the group.

Except for Glasgow Hunterian 443, none of the other extant manuscripts tells in the exordium how many chapters were in the original text, but BL Harley 1337 and Bodl. Hatton 50 append a short colophon based on phrases taken from the exordium. This seems to represent a stage following on that represented by Glasgow Hunterian 443. The lack of colophon in Jesus Coll., Oxford, 5 may be an individual peculiarity, since in respect of the medial omission the text appears earlier than that of Bodl. Hatton 50. In this regard, BL Harley 1337 must represent an earlier stage insofar as it continues the text farther than the other manuscripts at the onset of the omission, but at the same time it does not restart the text until a later point than the other manuscripts.

One possibility is to suppose an original text that broke off at the same point as BL Harley 1337 and Harley 6251 (Brie 280/31), recommenced at the same point as BL Stowe 71 and Jesus Coll., Oxford, 5 (Brie 304/7), and contained the full exordium of Glasgow Hunterian 443, that is, that did not append the colophon.

The extant manuscripts divide into the following subgroups:

a. Glasgow Hunterian 443;

b. Bodl. Rawlinson C.901 (restarts at same point as a);
c. BL Harley 1337 and Harley 6251 (break off before Halidon Hill at the same point as e and f; restart at the same point);
d. Stowe 71; Jesus Coll., Oxford, 5; and Michigan 225 (break off at the same point as e, f, and g; restart at the same point);
e. Bodl. Hatton 50 (breaks off at the same point as d, f, and g);
f. the AV–1419:B text that underlies TCD 5895 and BL Harley 7333 of the PV–1419(r&g):D (breaks off at the same point as d, e, and g);
g. Alnwick 457A (breaks off at the same point as d, e, and f);
h. Bodl. Tanner 11.

There are similarities among the hands in which a number of the manuscripts of this group are written. Glasgow Hunterian 443, BL Harley 1337, BL Harley 6251, and NLW Peniarth 396D are all written in extremely similar cursive hands with similar chapter rubrication and decoration and coloring of chapter initials. Jesus Coll., Oxford, 5 is written in a hand similar to those of the corrector and rubricator in Glasgow Hunterian 443. Bodl. Hatton 50 and Rawlinson B.190 are written in similar hands which have some likeness in style to the hands of the other manuscripts of the group.

It is possible that these manuscripts are the product of one scriptorium or "school" of writing, perhaps in the London area, and are in fact representatives of a primitive type of "mass-production" of cheap, quickly executed texts to meet public demand for what was an extremely popular work. That a number of *Brut* manuscripts were produced in such a manner could account in part for composite texts or texts that appear to have anomalous features within a particular group.

The Abbreviated Version to 1419, Group C (AV–1419:C)

Group C, which begins similarly to the EV–1419:C, consists of MSS. Bodl. Ashmole 793 and Illinois 82(1).

141. BODLEIAN MS. ASHMOLE 793
Exordium begins: Here begynneth a booke in Englishe tong callid Brute of Englond or the Cronycles of Englond compilyng and tretyng of the said land
Prologue heading begins: The prologge of this booke declareth and telleth

howe this land was furste called Albioun aftre the eldeste doughtir of the roiall kyng Dioclician of Surre called Albyne
Text begins: Some tyme in the noble lande of Surre
Omits: Latin tag, four chapters after Arthur, "5w" heading
Contains: Cad, QIL
Ends: and manfully countred with our Englisshe men.
Colophon: Heere endeth the Booke of Cronycules.

142. UNIVERSITY OF ILLINOIS MS. 82(1)[1]

Exordium begins in first hand on fol. 8: [H]ere begynneth a boke of Englisch tong callid Brute of Englond or the Croniclez of Englond compilyng & tretyng of the seid lond

Prologue heading begins: [T]he prolog of þis boke declareth & telleth how þis land was first called Albyoun after þe eldest doughter of þe roial kyng Dioclician of Surre called Albyne

Text begins: [S]ome tyme in the noble land of Surre ther was a noble & a worthi man callid Dioclician a grete conquerour & a myghty man

Omits: Latin tag, four chapters after Arthur

Contains: Cad, QIL

First hand ends on fol. 164: & grete luffe betwene þe kyng & his lordes [Brie 248/12–13]

Remarks: A second (and then a third) hand takes up the narrative at the end of the AV–1419:C text just before the battle of Halidon Hill, copying from a new exemplar, a text of the PV–1437. There is a narrative dislocation in the text at the point of change to the new exemplar.

Fols. 1–7 contain various historical memoranda in at least two hands, including lists based on the *Brut* text of significant dates and events from 1042 to 1461. The hand that adds the Latin headings at the beginnings of the reigns of Henry IV, Henry V, and Henry VI writes a similar note on the coronation of Edward IV and a short account (fols. 6–7) of Edward's victories in 1471.[2]

---

[1] For (2), see item 166. The manuscript is misbound throughout; a typewritten chart gives the correspondences between the (correct) medieval foliation and the (incorrect) modern foliation of the volume as now bound.

[2] See p. 285.

Remarks on the AV–1419:C
The names of the extra giants found in the EV–1419:A and the EV–1419:C occur.

Unlike the EV–1419:C, the name of Coryn's paramour is given, as in other EV and AV groups. She is called his "leman," as in the EV–1419:C; both name and designation are paralleled in the AV–1419:A(a) and the AV–1419:D: "Than said Brute 'if Erneborowe thi lemman wiste that one man had putte the to such a rebuke she wolde neuer love the'" (Bodl. Ashmole 793).

Unlike the EV–1419:C, the names of Ebrak's children are listed.

The 1419(men) conclusion to Bodl. Ashmole 793 is unparalleled among other complete EV and AV texts and may indicate that an AV was originally made from the hypothetical EV–1377, to which the continuation to 1419(men) was first added. (However, it is possible that the scribe's exemplar was incomplete and that he changed at some point to another text containing the 1419[men] continuation.)

The Abbreviated Version to 1419, Group D (AV–1419:D)

This group, which contains a new exordium that is not paralleled in a corresponding EV group, consists of MSS. BL Stowe 70, University Coll., Oxford, 154, and CUL Hh.6.9(1).

143. BL MS. STOWE 70
Exordium begins: [T]he first inhabityng of þis lande hou women first inhabit it and aftir þat Brute inhabit it & conquered þe gyauntes
Prologue heading begins: [T]he prologe of þis boke declareth hou this lande was callid Albyon aftir þe eldest douȝtre of þe roiall kyng Dioclician whiche was callid Albyne
Text begins: [S]ome tyme in þe lande of Surre
Omits: Latin tag, "5w" heading (see Remarks on the AV–1419:D below)
Contains: substitute chapter after Arthur, Cad, QIL
Ends: in gouernaunce and reule and cried his peace amonges the citezeins &c.

144. UNIVERSITY COLLEGE, OXFORD, MS. 154[1]
Exordium begins: The furste inhabityng of this lande howe women furste in-

habit it and after that Brute inhabit it and conquerid the gyauntes
Prologue heading begins: The prologge of this boke declareth howe this lande was called Albioun aftir the eldest doughter of the royall king Dioclician the whiche was called Albine
Text begins: Some tyme in the lande of Surre
Omits: Latin tag, QIL (but see below), "5w" heading (see Remarks on the AV–1419:D below)
Contains: substitute chapter after Arthur, Cad
Ends: in gouernaunce and rule and cried hys peace amonges þe citezeins &c. Explicit.

Remarks: The folios are missing that would have contained Queen Isabella's letter.

---

[1] See Ogilvie-Thomson, *Handlist*, p. 121.

145. CAMBRIDGE UNIVERSITY LIBRARY MS. HH.6.9(1)[1]
Exordium begins: The first inhabytynge of þis lande how women first inhabit it and after that Brute inhabit it and conquered the geauntes
Prologue heading begins: The prologe of this booke declareth hou þis lande was callid Albion after the eldest doughter of the royall kyng Dioclician the which was callid Albyn
Text begins: Some tyme in the lande of Surre þer was a myghty & a roial kyng callid Dioclisian
Omits: Latin tag, "5w" heading (see Remarks on the AV–1419:D below)
Contains: substitute chapter after Arthur, Cad, QIL
Ends on fol. 158: in gouernaunce and reule and cried his peace amonges the citezeins &c.

Remarks: The AV–1419:D text is followed by a JP:C continuation, written in the same hand (item 82).

---

[1] For (2), see item 82.

Remarks on the AV–1419:D
Details of the AV–1419:D are as follows:

(a) *first giants passage*:
Of þe which oon was callid Gogmagog þe which was maister of theme all. And he was fourty foote of lengh & xij of brede. And an other was callid Widy & thes geauntes duelleden in diuers contreis & montayns & hilles & lyued of rutes and with herbes & wilde bestys & wild foules. And thei regned in þis lande vnto þe tyme þat Brute come and conquered them & inhabit it and made townes & cites. [CUL Hh.6.9]

(b) *second giants passage*:
þou shalt fynd an ile callid Albion compassid with þe see so þat no maner thyng may com vnto it bot foules þe which is wildirnes & inhabited with grete geauntes the which lyven dyuersly with herbis & rutes & flesh of grete shepe & þis land is ordenyd for the & thi mene. [CUL Hh.6.9]

(c) *Coryn's paramour passage*:
and þo saide Brute in skorne of him "if Erneburgh thy lemman wiste þat oon man dide so vnto thee Coryne she wolde neuere loue þee." [BL Stowe 70]

The names of Ebrak's children are given.

As in the AV–1419:A(b), though in slightly more confused form, the four chapters after Arthur are replaced by one chapter on Constantine, after whom reigns Conan:

Howe kyng Arthur delyuerde the roialme vnto Constantyne his cosynne þat was Cadors sonne.

And after this Arthur reigned his cosyn Constantyne. Than come Mordredis two sonnes with a grete multitude of people of Saxouns ageyns Constantyne & faught with hym bot Constantyne ouercome theme & drove theme vnto London. And þat one flede þer and þat other vnto Wynchestre. And in this same tyme died þe bishoppe of Baungor & that tyme þe bishoppe of Baungour was made bishoppe of London. And than this Constantyne pursued Mordrede sonnes & found theme þat [*read* at] Wynchestre & besegid it. And oon of theme fled into a chirch & þer he was taken in the chirche of Seinct Amphybale at high awter & slayn & þat other fled into [a chirch *del.*] an house of religione of freres & their he was take & slayne. And this Constantyne was aftirward slayn at Conan Meredok & his felishippe & buryed at Stonheng beside Vter Pendragoune.

How kyng Constantyne was werred vpon by Mordredis two sonnes.

And than reigned [*repeated*] Conan a wondre proude manne & a wickid [CUL Hh.6.9]

In the Halidon Hill chapter, much of the text is abbreviated. The battle itself is highly abbreviated and the nobles comprising the wards of the Scottish army are not named, the relevant sections being totally omitted:

And than vpon Seint Margaretes even þe yere of our lorde M¹ iij^C xxxij the Scottes come fersely in thre batailles welle arraied in here wynges at evensongtyme and at þat tyme was floode at Berewike þat no man myght wende ouer neither on hors ne vpon foote. And þe water was betwixe þe two kynges & Englande so þat they must nedes fight or be drownede. And than kyng Edwarde of Englande & kyng Edwarde of Scotlande maid þere batailles redy & þer wynges of þe prisest & þe best archers that þei myght fynd in all þe hooste. And þe Scottes were nombrede vij^xx thousandes and whanne the Englishmen met þe Scottes our archers shot sharply & sore vnto þe Scottes and ouerthrewe thousandes of theme & shote so faste that the Scottes myght nott helpe themeself so þat many of theme were killid & slayn there. And oure Englishmen pages toke þe Scottes mennes hors whan their maisteres weren dede. And þan kyng Edwarde of Englande & kyng Edwarde of Scotlande þankede allmyghty God of þat glorious victorie ffor þe Scottes hadden no more strength agains þe Englishmen than fyue shepe agains a woulfe. And þis bataill was doon vpon Hollydoune Hille wher were slayn xxxvM¹ v^C & xx Scottes and of Englishmen but vij. [CUL Hh.6.9; cf. Brie 283/14–286/4; 286/4–9 are omitted]

The three texts correspond well in content, but cannot be directly derived one from another, as, on a simple level, the respective headings of the chapter following that on the battle of Halidon Hill show:

Hou kinge Edwarde made a duchie of þe erledome of Cornewaill. [BL Stowe 70]
How that kyng Edward made meny lordis and how he was mevid off the title off Fraunce. [CUL Hh.6.9]
Howe king Edwarde made one erle duchie of þe erledome of Cornewayll and of þe furste chalange of Fraunce. [University Coll., Oxford, 154]

Each preserves something of the wording of the original CV heading:

Hov King Edwarde made a Duchye of þe Erldom of Cor[n]waile; &
also of vj. oþere erles þat were newe made; & of þe ferste Chalangyng
of þe reaume of Fraunce. [CCCC 174: Brie 292/26–28]

The three texts are very close, however, and could easily have derived from a common original.

Remarks on the Extended and Abbreviated Versions

Brie assumed a simple relationship between the groups of the EV: that the EV–1419:A as typified by BL Harley 24 was the earliest stage after the EV–1377, the probable erstwhile existence of which Brie recognized; that the EV–1419:B was derived directly from the EV–1419:A; and that the EV–1419:C was very close to the EV–1419:A. He further assumed a simple one-to-one relationship between the EV and AV texts: that the AV–1419:A was derived from the EV–1419:A; the AV–1419:B from the EV–1419:B; the AV–1419:C from the EV–1419:C; and the AV–1419:D from a supposedly lost group, the EV–1419:D.[1]

However, a comparison of texts from different groups shows that the relationships are far more complex on account of discrepancies between the "corresponding" EV and AV groups and similarities between supposedly unrelated groups. As a standard of comparison we can use the CV–1333 and other CV texts containing later continuations. The relationships between the groups are difficult, and the evidence is often capable of more than one interpretation, but the following discussion represents the development that seems most plausible.

The Exordia of the Extended Version and the Abbreviated Version

The exordium of the hypothetical EV–1377 was partly based on the expansion of two short passages in the body of the CV text that describe chronicles written in English during the reign of King Ossa (i.e., Offa) and a chronicle made by (or at the instigation of) King Alfred. The details from the CV and the corresponding passages in the EV and AV exordia are laid out in Tables 1 and 2, which appear on pages 235 and 236.

Comparison of the passages in Tables 1 and 2 suggests that there is a highly complex textual history underlying the extant manuscripts and groups. The erstwhile existence of a number of lost groups or complicated crossing between groups must be posited to account for the readings of the extant groups.

Table 1. Chronicles Made in Ossa's Time

CV–1333: & on boke he made of Englisshe, of Auentures of kynges and of bataies þat hade bene done in þe lande. [Brie 102/14–15]

EV–1419:A
And it telleth of alle the kynges and principall lordes that euer were in this lond and what aventures thinges as batailles conquestes and other thinges fell in this lond and by whome and by what manere. [Rylands Eng. 105]

EV–1419:A
And also hit tellith of the kyngus and principall thingus and also of lordis that euir were and reyghnede in the seyde lande frome the furste vnto þe laste and what aventurs and wonderfull thingus as batailles warres conquestus and othir meruelous myracles and thingus notables þat befelle in the same lande and by whome and by what maner. [BL Harley 24]

EV–1419:B
This boke treteth and telleþ of þe kynges & principall lordes þat euer were in þis londe & of auentures & wondreful þinges and batailles & oþer notable actes werres conquestes þat bifelle in þis same londe. [BL Harley 4827]

EV–1419:C
... and then of alle the kynges and grete lordes and principall actes þat haue been doon in the same lande as of batellys werres and other aventures and conquestes of the seid lande. [TCC O.9.1]

AV–1419:A(a)
And also it tellethe of all the kinges & principall lordes þat euer werr in þe same lord fro the first vnto þe laste & qwat aventurs and wonderfull thinges werres batails & conquestes & other thinges notable that fell in þe londe. [Glasgow Hunterian 83]

AV–1419:A(b)
[missing in BL Royal 18.B.iv]

AV–1419:B
þe wych booke tretyth & lellyth [sic] of þe kyngys and princypall lordys þat euyr was in þis londe and of aventur and wonderdyrfull [sic] thyngis and batayll and oþir notabyll actys warres conquestys þat befyll in þis same lande. [Glasgow Hunterian 443]

AV–1419:C
And than of all the kynges and grete lordes and principall actes that hath be done in the said lande as of batailles werres & other aventures & conquestes of the said land [Bodl. Ashmole 793]

AV–1419:A(c)
and also of all the kinges & princi-pall lordes that hath reigned in this lande from the furste vnto the laste and what aventures actes & mer-vailles hathe happed and fall in the same lande. [BL Royal 18.A.ix]

AV–1419:A(c)
the whiche declareth and treteth of all the kinges and of all the notable actes and dedes the whyche hathe bene done in this lande sithe the furste begynnyng of this lande [Huntington HM 131]

AV–1419:D
And þis chapitour maketh men-cioun of alle the kynges þat haue regned in this lande and of the principall actes & dedes þat were doon wiþin þe lande and hou longe þei regned. [BL Stowe 70]

Table 2. Chronicles made in Alfred's Time

CV-1333

But Abbottes, prioures, & men of religioun, writen þe lifes and dedes of kynges, & in what contre; & in what maner eueryche kyng deide, and of bisshoppis also, and þerof made grete bokes, & lete calle ham þe Cronicles. [Brie 102/32–103/3]

EV-1419:A

And after this hit declareth of diuers thinges compiled and drawen by dyvers holy men and namely by men of religioun as in abbeis and priories of Englond þe whiche wrote and cronicled as it fell and happed in the londe and made grete bokes and remembraunces of suche as bifell in theire tyme and lete calle hem the Cronicles. [Rylands Eng. 105]

EV-1419:A

...the wiche gestis and romayns as it folowith here after mani dyuers goode men and grete clerkes and namely men of relygion as in abbais prioures of Englande haue compilede and wretone that befelle in here tyme and made therof grete bookes and remembraunces of alle men that come after hem to hire and to see what byfelle afor and was doone in this lande and lete calle hem Cronicles and seye the sothe in this lande. [BL Harley 24]

EV-1419:B

And þis boke made & compiled men of religioun & oþer good clerkes þat wreten þat bifell in her tymes and made þerof grete bokes and remembraunce to men þat comen aftir hem to heere and to see what bifell in þe londe afore tyme and callid hem Cronycles. [BL Harley 4827]

EV-1419:C

the which booke many good men as abbottes priours and many other men compiled and written alle maner of aventures þat bifell in there tyme and made therof grete bokes and remembraunces and let calle theym Cronicles. [TCC O.9.1]

AV-1419:A(a)

...þis boke þe qwiche many diuerse good men and grete clerkes & namely men of religeoun as in abbais and priores of Englande hathe compilid & writen qwat befall in þaire tyme and made þerof grete bokes & remembrance till all men that come after them to here and to see qwat befell afore & was done in this lond & lete call þaim Cronycles. [Glasgow Hunterian 83]

AV-1419:A(b)

[missing in BL Royal 18.B.iv]

AV-1419:B

And þis boke made and compilid men of religione and oþir good clerkys þat wryttyne what be fyll in thre [sic] tyme and mad þerof grett bokys and remembrance to men þat comen aftyr hyme to her and see watt befyll in þe lond afor tyme and callyd heme cronycle. [Glasgow Hunterian 443]

AV-1419:C

The which booke many goodemen as abbottes priours and many other men compiled & writen all maner of aventures that bifell in there tyme and made therof grete bokes & remembraunces and lete calle hem Cronicles. [Bodl. Ashmole 793]

AV-1419:A(c)

...this book the whiche wyse menne as abbottes and priours and menne of religioune compiled what befell in ther tyme makyng of suche dedes and actes grete reremembraunces & called them þe Cronicles. [BL Royal

AV-1419:A(c)

and this boke made abbottes priours and othre goode clerkes and yn especiall king Eldrede a wyse king some time of Britaine that who that come affir shulde haue knoweleche howe the lande was ruled and gouerned

AV-1419:D

And þis boke compyled grete clerkes as abbottes prioures and men of religioun þe which writen and engroced þe lyues and þe actes of euery kynge as þey regned and made [þerof add. CUL Hh.6.9] grete bookes and called hem þe Cornicles [BL Sloane 70]

Thus in the first detail the EV–1419:A and the EV–1419:B keep the words "adventures, things [surely a corruption of "kings" in the CV], battles" in the same order as the CV, but the EV–1419:C has the phrase "þat haue been doon in the same lande," which is found in the CV. There is a cross-group correspondence between the EV–1419:B and the AV–1419:B on one hand and the AV–1419:A(a) on the other in the use of the words "wonderful" and "notable." The AV–1419:D retains the phrase "þat were doon wiþ in þe lande," as does also the AV–1419:C, and the former group also adds a phrase taken from the second detail in the CV, "hou longe þei regned."

Indeed, in the second detail the AV–1419:D preserves best the wording of the original CV source, which must indicate the one-time existence of earlier groups since the AV–1419:D cannot underlie the EV texts. Yet—admittedly a minor and perhaps coincidental point—the EV–1419:A text of Rylands Eng. 105 retains the definite article in the last phrase, "and lete calle hem the Cronicles."

The Extended Version Groups

Brie does not explicitly state that the EV–1419:C is based on the EV–1419:A, but he implies this when he says of the former that "Diese Gruppe steht A sehr nahe. Der Hauptunterschied besteht in einer grossen Reihe abweichender Lesarten, die sich durch den ganzen Text verstreut finden. Ausserdem sind die lateinischen Worte in Kap. 34 fortgefallen" ("This group stands very close to A. The main difference consists of a great series of variant readings that are found scattered throughout the whole text. Moreover, the Latin phrase in chapter 34 has been omitted.")[2] It is, however, clear that the A and C groups must have developed separately out of the EV–1377 and that they cannot be directly connected, as the following comparisons suggest.

Of the three extant EV groups, only the A group contains the original CV giants, although it is possible that lost texts of A (and possibly Rylands Eng. 105) contained a list of giants more like that surviving in the C group and that the extra details of BL Harley 24 and Addit. 12030 are secondary and peculiar additions:

CV Gogmagog ... Laugherigan ... & so þei were nompned by diuers names [Brie 4/27–29]

EV–1419:A
Gogmagog chef kyng of þem alle... Wydy... Onewen le fort... Bonde at the brugge ende... Laugherygo... grete multitude moo of giauntes that weren callede many dyuers names [BL Harley 24]

EV–1419:B
Gogmagog [BL Harley 4827]

EV–1419:C
Gogmagog chief of hem all... Wydy... Oneven... Bounde... And many other ther were and called dyuers names [TCC O.9.1]

Similarly, in the addition of details from the *Short English Metrical Chronicle*, the A texts have clearly preserved the wording of the original verse text in the *Chronicle* more closely.

On the other hand, the C group preserves more closely the wording of the CV in a number of instances, for example, the account of the eponymous naming of London by Lud. The CV–1333 text reads:

> This Lud louede more to duelle at Troye þan at eny oþere place of þe lande; Wherfore þe name of Troye was lafte, and þo was callede þe citee of Ludstan; but now þat name is chaungede þrouȝ variance of lettres, and now is callede London. and þis kyng made in the citee a faire gate, and callede it Ludgate, after his name; and þe folc of þe citee lete hight Loundres. [Brie 31/18–24]

The C group, although it presents some changes, mainly of a minor nature, is close to this and is certainly much closer to it than the corresponding section in the A group. The reading of the C group is given first:

> This Lud loued more to dwell at Troye then in any other place of the lande. Wherfore the name of Newe Troye was loste and then was the cite called Luscan [*sic*]. And that name is chaunged thurgh variance of letter and now is callid London. And this kyng made in the cite a feyre gate and called it Ludgate after his name. And folk of the cite let calle hit Loundrys. [TCC O.9.1]

> This kyng Lud loved more to dwell at Newe Troye þen in any oþer place of þe land; wherfor he commaundid that þat cite shuld not no lenger be called Newe Troy but Ludentoun or Ludestoun as sum bokes seyen after his name Lud for in þat cite he mad most cost of byldyng. And ther he mad a gate al oute of þe ground and lat hit to be called Ludgate after his name and he lat walle þe toune and dike hit also but afterwardis þe name of þis cite was chaunged with Saxons

tonge and by variaunce of lettres and was called London and Normandis and Frenchemen and oþer alyauntes call it Loundris and these clerkes call it in Latyn Ciuitas Londinarum. [Bodl. Rawlinson B.187; in Bodl. Tanner 188 the last words (*these clerkes ... Londinarum*) are omitted]

Also, the Latin tag associated with King Blegabred is not found in the C group, as it is not found in Rylands Eng. 105, which may represent an earlier form of the A group than BL Harley 24 and Addit. 12030, and this correspondence may suggest that the tag was not found in the EV-1377. Similarly, the name of Coryn's paramour is omitted in both Rylands Eng. 105 and in the C group.

The EV-1419:B, however, does appear to have been based on some early form of the A text rather than on some form of the C text, although it cannot be directly derived from any of the extant A manuscripts. In general, as illustrated in Tables 1 and 2 above, the exordium of the B group is closer to that of the A group than to that of the C group. However, the additional details given below show, first, a parallel (perhaps fortuitous) between B and C rather than between B and A; second, an instance of independent omission in B; and third, a further instance in which B is closer to A than it is to C:

(a) *A*: Here begynneth a boke in Englysshe tunge called Brute [Rylands Eng. 105]

    B: Here bigynneth a book whiche is callid Brute the Cronicles of Englond [BL Harley 4827]

    C: Here begynneth a booke in Englissh tonge called Brute of Englond or the Cronicles of Englond [TCC O.9.1]

(b) *A*: howe it was first wildernesse [Rylands Eng. 105]
    B: [omitted]
    C: how it was first a wilderness and forletten [TCC O.9.1]

(c) *A*: And this boke is called Brute after hym that made the boke and inhabite this lond whos name was Brute the which lete calle the lond Bretayne after his owne name [Rylands Eng. 105]

    B: And this lande is callid Bretaigne aftir him þat first enhabited it whos name was callid Brute [BL Harley 4827]

    C: This booke is called Brute after Brute þat first conquered this lande and let calle this lande Bretayn after his name [TCC O.9.1]

The Lud passage again shows that the B group is closer to the A text than to the C text (see the parallel A and C passages quoted above):

> this king Lud lovede more forto dwelle at Newe Troye þane at any oþer place of þe londe wherfore he commaundid þat the cite of Newe Troye be callid noo more þat name but calle it Ludston & somme bookes sey aftir his name Lud for in þat cite he made most byeldynge & þere he made a gate out of þe grounde & callid it Luddis gate aftir his owne name & he dede doo make cite wallid & dyke it al aboute. But aftirwarde the name of this cite was chaungid by sownyng of tungis & by varyaunce of lettris and callid it London & ȝit oþir naciouns callith it ȝit into this day London & clerkes callith it Ciuitas London. [Glasgow Hunterian 230]

Further points supporting a close connection between the A and B groups are:

1. Except for Bodl. Rawlinson poet. 32, the B group texts give the name of Coryn's paramour, as do the majority of the A texts.
2. Similarly, the B texts contain the Latin tag on Blegabred, as do the majority of the A texts.
3. Like BL Harley 24, an A text, most (though not all) of the B texts insert *good* into the phrase ending the text to 1419, and sometimes add *Deo gracias*, for example:
   > in ruele and good gouernaunce. Deo gracias. [BL Harley 24]
   > in good rule & gouernaunce. Deo gracias. [Glasgow Hunterian 230]
   > in reule and in gode gouernaunce. [BL Harley 2182]

The B group contains a number of details that show that it is derivative and not the direct line from the EV–1377 through which the other EV groups are connected to the original EV group. The enumerations of the British kings and of the kingdoms of Engist's heptarchy are both further from the original CV text than the corresponding A and C texts. In addition, there are numerous verbal differences and alterations, some of which are illustrated below in the discussion of the relationship of the EV–1419:B and the AV–1419:B (see pp. 243–46).

The Abbreviated Version Groups

The single text of the AV–1419:A(b), that of BL Royal 18.A.ix, can be derived from a text of the EV–1419:A, although once more we must assume one or more lost texts that united features now found only in separate texts of the A group. Thus we note the following correspondences between BL Royal 18.A.ix and features contained in the A-group texts:

1. The heading of the text is paralleled in BL Harley 24 and Addit. 12030, the only EV texts to have this heading.
2. The exordium is that of the A group.
3. The extra giants resemble those in the EV–1419:C and to some extent those in BL Harley 24 and Addit. 12030, and possibly approximate more closely to those that were once contained in Rylands Eng. 105, although "Laugherigan," one of the original CV giants, is not found.
4. The name of Coryn's paramour is paralleled exactly in Bodl. Rawlinson B.187 (although it is also paralleled in the EV–1419:B).
5. The lack of the Latin tag on Blegabred is paralleled in Rylands Eng. 105.
6. The chapter on the kings of Britain is not abbreviated as it is in the AV–1419:A(a) and therefore corresponds to the normal text found in the EV–1419:A.

This group has been treated first among the AV groups because it does not partake of the striking agreements between the rest of the AV groups that lead to the conclusion that there is a far more complex relationship between them than a simple one-to-one relationship with the EV groups.

The formal textual feature that is most immediately striking is the omission of four chapters after the death of King Arthur so that Conan succeeds to the throne instead of Constantine (see further below). This feature occurs in the AV–1419:A(a), the AV–1419:B, and the AV–1419:C, but is not paralleled in the EV. It is not found in the AV–1419:A(c) and the AV–1419:D, which resemble one another at this point.

Equally significant is the close verbal agreement between the AV–1419:A(a) and the AV–1419:B in those chapters that occur after the opening sections of the text. This agreement is well illustrated in the narrative recounting the reign of King John, where the texts of both AV groups agree against the texts of the EV and CV and must therefore be related. The following extract from Glasgow Hunterian 83, a text of the AV–1419:A(a), is collated with Michigan 225 (M), a text of the AV–1419:B, and should be compared with the CV as printed by Brie (155/9–156/22):

How king Iohn was rebell agans þe pope.

[A]nd att þe [atte M] last þe pope sentt by hys autorite & enioyned two bischops of England þat yff king Iohn wold nott cesse of his [the M] persecucioun þat he did to [vnto M] holy chirch ne vnderfong maister Steven Langtoun ne the prioure & his monkes þat thei suld do þe generale enterdyting yff it wer nede [om. M] and enionede iiij bischopes to fulfill itt. Þe first was þe bischop of London; þe [and the M] ij^e þe bischop of Ely; þe iij^e [the add. M] bischop [of add. M] Wauter; and þe iiij^e bischop Giles. And þes foure come to þe king knelyng vpon there kneys full sore wepyng besechyng þe king to doon þe popes commandementes [commaundement M] and schewed him þe bulles of þe enterdyting bott for no prayer þe king wald nott [om. M] consent þerto. And than thes iiij bischopes seyng this on þe morow [on...morow om. M] after þe annunciacioun of oure lady pronounsed þe enterdyting throughoute England so þat all [the M] chirch dores wer schut & closid through [thurughoute M] England. And king Iohn seyng this toke [he toke M] into his handes [honde M] all þe possessiouns of holy chirche throute þe realm and ordenyd men for to kepe hem. And than þe bischopes accursed [cursid M] all hem þat medeled with holy chirch goodes ayenst þe will of hem. And when þe [om. M] king wold nott cess of his malace þe iiij bischopes went hem oure þe see to þe archebischop of Canterbury and take [tolde M] hym all þe doing. And þe archebischop heryng hereof bad tham goo agayn to Canterbury and he wold come theder to þam [thider hemselfe M] or send suche as suld do as [so M] muche as himself there. And thei come agayn to Canterbury. And than come thithinges to þe king that þe [om. M] iiij bischopes wer comen agayn and for-as-mich as he micht nott come himself he sentt theder lordes both temperell and spirituell [spirituell and temporall M]. And so the king was entrered [sic; entretid with M] to vnderfong the archebischop [bisshoppe M] and þe prioure also and his monkes and that he suld neuer after that tyme tak [do M] no thing of [ayenst M] holy chirch ayenst the will of hem þat awed þe [om. M] goodes. And also that þe king suld mak full amendes to hem of whom he had take any goodes. And þat holy chirch suld have all ffraunches [hir ffraunchisis M] in likewis as itt was [he had M] in king Edwardes tyme þe confessour. [Glasgow Hunterian 83]

Despite this correspondence, however, one cannot simply assume that the AV–1419:A(a) and the AV–1419:B are the same text to which the exordia of different EV groups have been added. The earlier portions of the AV–1419:B are inextricably linked to the EV–1419:B, not only on account of the exordium but also on the verbal level. The composition of the opening chapters of the AV–1419:B is demonstrated by the following analysis of the text in which the EV–1419:B group is represented by BL Harley 4827 and the AV group by Glasgow Hunterian 443. References are given to the corresponding text in the CV printed by Brie. The evidence for connecting the EV–1419:B and the AV–1419:B consists of:

1. Similar omissions in the EV–1419:B and the AV–1419:B of CV–1333 phrases or sentences, such as the following examples quoted from Brie:
(i) so þat he conquered alle þe landes abowte hym [Brie 1/8–9]
(ii) & þere þey lyved in ioy and merthe y-now, that it was wonder to wete [Brie 1/21–22]
(iii) þat it was wonder to wete [Brie 2/10–11]
(iv) & byhestes, & also for ʒiftes, and warnyd hem in fayr maner vpon all loue and frenschipe þat þei scholde Amende hir lithir condicions [Brie 2/13–16]
(v) wherfore þo xxxiij kynges, vpon A tyme, and often-tymes, beten here wyfes, for þey wende that þei wolde haue Amended here tacches and here wykkyd thewes; but of such condicions þei were þat, for fayr speche & warnyng, þei deden the wors, & for betynges eft-sone mych wors. [Brie 2/17–22]
(vi) & þo made voide al þat were þerin, so þat no lyf was among hem but sche & here sustres y-fere [Brie 3/13–14]
(vii) seth þat I am come of a more hyere kynges blod þan my housband is [Brie 3/18–19]
(viii) ful wel y wot, fayr sustres, þat oure housbandes haue playned vnto owre fadir vpon vs, wherfore he hath þus vs foul reproued & dispised [Brie 3/20–23]
(ix) þat was here fadir [Brie 3/36–4/1]
(x) & be-toke alle her frendes to Appolyn, þat was her god [Brie 4/3–4]
(xi) with al his mayn [Brie 5/8]
(xii) and hym withhelde [Brie 5/14]
(xiii) & a worthy of body and of his dedes [Brie 5/15–16]
(xiv) in his werre; & schortly for-to telle, so weel & worthyly he ded, þat he [Brie 5/17–18; both groups replace this by the one word *and*]
(xv) all here lyvys tyme [Brie 5/22]

(xvi) as God wolde [Brie 5/23]
(xvii) vnwetyng his fadir, & aȝens his wyl [Brie 5/28]
(xviii) whan god wolde [Brie 6/4–5]
(xix) þat was Sylveynes sone [Brie 6/7]
(xx) & [so] schul men of þat Cuntre be called for euermore [Brie 11/20]

2. Similar readings in the EV–1419:B and the AV–1419:B that disagree with the CV–1333 reading (the last three examples are taken from a later point in the texts):

CV–1333	EV–1419:B	AV–1419:B
A noble kyng and myghty, & a man of grete renoun, þat me called Dyoclician [Brie 1/5–7]	a man of grete renoun callid Dioclisian	a mane of gret renoun callyd Diocliciane
almoste all þe kynges of þe world to hym were entendaunt [Brie 1/9–10]	almooste all þe kynges not Cristen to him weren contributours and obedient	all most all þe kyngys Crystyne wher to hyme contributours and to hym obbedyente
at A certayn day, as in his lettres was conteyned, to make A ryal feste [Brie 1/17–18]	at a certeyn day at which day he wolde make a riall ffeste	att a sertyn day at wyche day he wyll make a ryall fest
And hit byfelle þus aftyrward þat [Brie 2/5–6]	And aftirward	And aftyrward
Wherefore þe kyng þat hadde wedded Albyne, wrote þe tacches & þe condicions of his wyf Albyne, & þe lettre	wherfore þese xxxiij kynges bi her comon assent wrote þe euel tacches of her wyues vnto her fadre Dioclisian bi-	wherfor þes xxxij [sic] kyngis by her comen asente vrote the evyll techys of her viuis vnto her fader Dyoclisian

sent to Dioclician, her fader. And whenne þe other kynges herde that Albynes lord had sent lettre to Dioclician, anon þey sente lettres enseled with here seeles [of] þe condicions and þe tacches of here wyfes. [Brie 2/22–27]	sekyng hym to sett a remedye in þis matere	beseken so [sic] sett remedy in thes maters
he was sore a-schamed, & bycome wonder Angry & wroth toward his doughters [Brie 2/29–30]	he was wondre wroth toward his douʒtres	he was wondyr wrote toward hys douʒtors
þer was a noble knyght & a myghty, & a man of gret power, þat me callyd Eneas [Brie 5/5–6]	þer was a miʒti & a manly knyʒt y-callid Eneas	was a myʒty and a manly knyʒthe called Eneas
lost & dystroyed [Brie 5/7]	destroied	dystroid
he had herd of hym, and wyst wel þat he was a noble knyght [Brie 5/14–15]	he herde muche worship of him and þat he was a noble knyʒt	he herd muche worscip of hyme and þat he was a nobyll knyʒth
in beryng of hym [Brie 5/35–6/1]	in childyng of hym	in chyldyng of hym

his Arwe mys-happed & glacede; And so there Brut quelled his fader. [Brie 6/9–10]	his arowe glaunsid aside and killid his fadre þer forþ-riȝt	his harrow clenchyd and kyllyd his fadyr þer forth-rythe
an hauene of Totnesse [Brie 10/29–30]	an hauen þat is now callid Totenesse	ane hawyne þat ys now callyd Totennas
þe sawte of Gogmagog [Brie 11/17]	þe mounte of Gogmagog or elles it is callid Gogmagoges lepe	the monte of Gogmagog or ells Gogmagoges lepe
and clymede vnto þe mount; but when þai saw [Brie 61/31–32]	a-whanne þey came vp to þe toppe of þe mounte þei seigh	And when þay com vppon þe topp of þe monte þay sey
and come aȝeyn into þis lande [Brie 62/3]	and so þei brouȝt hem into þis londe	and so þey brouth heme into this lond
for euermore [Brie 62/8]	and so it is callid ȝitte into þis day	and so yt ys into þis day

These selected examples show that the EV–1419:B and the AV–1419:B are closely connected, for they agree in making the same omissions from the CV–1333 text, and they further agree in possessing similar readings which disagree with the CV–1333 text. However, a further set of readings, taken from the same early and later extracts as the above examples, show that the two groups cannot be directly related, that is, the AV–1419:B cannot be derived simply from the EV–1419:B because the readings of the AV–1419:B correspond to or are closer to the readings of the CV–1333.

3. Dissimilar readings in the EV–1419:B and the AV–1419:B, where the AV–1419:B reading corresponds to or is closer to the CV–1333 reading in some respects (in a number of instances the AV–1419:B presents a blend of CV and EV–1419:B readings):

THE ABBREVIATED VERSION 247

CV–1333	*EV–1419:B*	*AV–1419:B*
At which day, þedir þey comyn, & brought with hem Amyralles, Prynces & Dukes, & noble Chiualrye [Brie 1/19–20]	and þei came at his comaundement and also dukes & erles and oþer peple wiþoute nombre	At wyche day þey comen bothe kyngis dukys and erllys and much oþyr pepyll out of nombyr
among all þo knyghtys [*vr.* kynges] þat tho were at that solempnite [Brie 1/24]	vnto all þese kynges assembled at þis grete solempnite	amongis all þes kyngis assembeledd at þis solemnite
And all her other sustres, eche on bere hem so euel ayens here lordes [Brie 2/9–10]	& alle her oþer sustres deden in þe same manere	and all þe oþir sustyrs bare heme in þe same maner
And for-as-mych as hem thought þat here housebondes were not of so hye parage comen as here fadyr [Brie 2/11–12]	and for-also-muche as her lordes weren of lower degree þan þei were þei were þe more stoute	and for theyr lordys wer of lowere parage þane þey wer þey wer þe stouter
& whan sche had so seyd, all here sustres seyd þe same [Brie 3/19–20]	and þanne all þe sustres promysed þe same	And all her sustyrs sayd þe same
so þat þei neuere schulde come aȝen; & so he dede [Brie 3/35–36]	and so he exilid hem oute of his lande	And so he dede

þei fedde hem with erbes & frutes in seson of þe ȝeer [Brie 4/17]	þei fedden hem all wiþ herbes & fruytes þat þei founden many daies	þey feddyne hym opon herbys & frutys in þe seson of þe ȝer
and bycomen wondir fatte [Brie 4/19]	and so þei wexid wondre fatte & rank	and wondyr fat wexen [*ins. above*]
Whanne þe Deuyll that perceyued [Brie 4/24]	And whanne þe feend conceyued þe corragiouste of þese wymmen	And when þe [*ins. above*] develis þis consayuyd
kyng Latyme ȝaf al þat land þat was Turocelyns, & ȝaf it to Eneas in mariage with Lamane, his doughter, the moost fayr creature þat eny manne wiste [Brie 5/19–21]	kyng Latym gaf all þat londe to Eneas and maried his douȝter Lema vnto him whiche was a faire creature	kyng Latyme gaff al þe lond to Eneas in maryage with Leman hys douȝtyr a fayr creaturr
in ioy & myrthe [Brie 5/22]	in ioie & blisse	in ioy and myrth
And whan Asquanius his fader yt wyste [*vr.* wist þerof], anon he lete enquere [Brie 5/31–32]	And his fadir Asquanius herde hereof and leete enquere	And when hys fadyr Asquanius wyst þerof he lett enquer
he went vpon A day with his fadir to pley & solace [Brie 6/7–8]	he went vpon a day wiþ his fadre to wodde forto hunte and disporte him	he wente oppon a day with hys fadyr to wood forto play and solas

& therfore he nome all his men, & went vnto þe See, & hadde wynd & wedir at wille [Brie 10/27–29]	wherfore anoon he ordeyned all his men to þe shippes and sailed forþe in þe see and þei had wynde and wedre at her wille	and þerfor he toke all his men and went into þe see and had wynd and weddyr at wyll
& þer þey founde neiþer man ne woman [Brie 10/30–31]	and þei founden neiþer man woman nor childe	and þer þey fonden neþyr man ne vommane
þo was Brut wonder glad [Brie 10/34]	þanne was Brute wondre gladde & ioyful of hert	Thane was he [*ins. above*] wondyr glad
When þe Britons hade herde of þis þing, þai went and sworen ifere amonges ham, þat þai wolde gone to seche þe stones [Brie 61/23–25]	And whanne þe Bretons herden telle of þese merveilous stones þei saiden amonges hem þat þei wolde goo in to Yrlonde & sechen þese stones	When the Brutons herd of this tydynges þei went and swore amonges hem þat þey wold see and serch the stonys
and toke wiþ ham Vter, þe kynges broþer, to bene here cheueteyne, & xv M^l men; and Merlyn conseilede ham forto gone into Irlande and so þai deden. [Brie 61/25–27]	and toke wiþ hem Vter þe kynges broþer & Merlyn to ben her chieften and her counseilour and toke also wiþ hem xv M^l of men and wenten þidre.	& toke with hym Vter þe kynges brother to be her cheveten and xv M^l men with hem and Merlyn conceilyd hym to gone to Irlond and so þay did
þai saw þe stones,	þei seigh þe stones	þay sey þe stonys

and þe maner how þai stoden, þai hadden grete mervail [Brie 61/32–33]	stonde merveillously	and þe maner how þat [*sic*] stonden and merweyll grettly therof
and saide bituene ham þat noman shulde ham remeve, for no strenghe ne engyne, so huge þai weren, and so long [Brie 61/33–62/2]	and saide amonges hem þat no man shulde remeve hem þei were & huge and so longe	and sayd bytwene heme þat noman shull remeve hym of þe place neythyr be strynth eiethir be engyne so hug and so long
and when þe kyng saw þat it was made, he þankede Merlyn [Brie 62/5–6]	and whanne þe kyng saugh þat it was doo aftir his entent he þanked Merlyne	and whene þe kyng saw þat yt was mad he thankyd Merlyne hugely

Although in the examples cited the AV–1419:B has details that are closer to the CV, there are also many cases where the AV–1419:B reading appears to partake of both the CV and EV–1419:B readings. That it agrees with the CV indicates that the AV–1419:B cannot simply have passed through the EV–1419:B stage. It could quite easily, however, be a compilation made from both the CV and the EV–1419:B texts. We have already seen the agreement between the AV–1419:B and the AV–1419:A(a) in the King John chapters, but in many of the examples in (3) above the AV–1419:A(a) has readings which are dissimilar from those of the AV–1419:B and are also further from the CV readings. Accordingly, it cannot be assumed that the AV–1419:B is a compilation formed from the EV–1419:B and the AV–1419:A(a). The same can be said of the AV–1419:C, in which verbal differences from the above AV–1419:B readings are again found.

The AV–1419:A(a) cannot be derived purely from the text of BL Harley 24 and Addit. 12030, primarily because it does not show any traces of any of the peculiar features associated with these texts. Whether it was taken from one of the other EV–1419:A texts is more difficult to decide as these texts are incomplete, and in any case it has already been suggested that some texts of this EV group have been lost, texts that once exhibited a slightly different form of certain features from that contained in the extant manuscripts. Verbally, the AV–1419:A(a) would seem within the limits of textual variance for the EV–1419:A, but there has clearly been contact with some other AV group, as the common omission of chapters after Arthur and the verbal agreements with the AV–1419:B described above attest. The question is, in which direction were the AV texts influenced, and which group first made these omissions and verbal changes? Further questions occur, whether there was an AV made from the EV–1377, and whether the common features of the AV groups should be attributed to this.

The unusual point at which the AV–1419:C ends (see p. 230) might suggest that this text was derived from an original AV ending in 1377 to which a 1419(men) continuation was added. If this is so, however, then the AV ending in 1377 must have differed considerably from the AV–1419:C, for in its present state it could not have been the basis of the AV–1419:A(a) or AV–1419:B, both of which have readings that are closer to the CV source. Once more, the AV group cannot be simply an abbreviation of the EV group, as there are a number of correspondences with other AV and EV texts in features that are not contained in the EV–1419:C, for example:

1. Lud's naming of London has affinities with the EV–1419:A (see pp. 238–39) and the AV–1419:B (see p. 240):

    This Lud loued to abide atte Troie more than at any othre place of the land. Wherfore he commaunded it shulde no lengir be called Newe Troie but Lodentoun or Ludestoun as some bokes sayn aftre his name Lud for in that cite he made moste costes. And ther he made a gate oute of the grounde and called it Ludgate. And he made walle the town and dich it. And aftre this the name of the cite was chaunged by Saxons tong and variaunce of lettres and was called London and yit is but Normandes callen it Loundres and Frenshmen and clerkes Ciuitas London. [Bodl. Ashmole 793]

2. Coryn's paramour's name is given.
3. Conan reigns after King Arthur.

On the other hand, the King John chapters do not correspond to the AV–1419:A(a) and the AV–1419:B, which suggests that if these groups are to be closely connected, then the AV–1419:C would have to precede the others, for in these chapters it corresponds closely to the CV text. In its present form the AV–1419:C text cannot underlie the other AV groups, as a number of its readings are at a further remove from the ultimate CV source than those preserved in other AV groups, but this may point to an earlier stage of the EV or AV texts than those preserved in the extant manuscripts.

Further evidence for the existence of an EV or AV "Ur-text" is provided by the AV–1419:A(c) and the AV–1419:D. These groups are related through a common chapter on Constantine (based on Geoffrey of Monmouth's *Historia*), who is succeeded by Conan, thus omitting Adelbright, Edelf, and the Havelok story. That this occurs where other AV groups omit four chapters suggests that some ancestral text was defective around this point.

Brie assumed that the texts of the AV–1419:D were derived from a now lost group D of EV texts, that is, an EV group with the D exordium, but there is no evidence to support this, and the apparent symmetry between the EV and AV groups has been shown above to be false. Certainly the group appears to have been based on some lost form of EV or AV text, for unlike in the other AV groups—apart from the AV–1419:A(c)—Constantine follows Arthur and the King John chapters, although abbreviated and altered verbally, are not the same text as that of the AV–1419:A(a) or the AV–1419:B.

It seems most probable that the AV–1419:D is based on some precursory form of the EV, for it shows a number of features now found separately in other EV texts and in AV groups that are apparently related either to this lost group or to the extant AV–1419:D. The following similarities and points of contact occur:

1. The exact wording of the present form of the D exordium may be an original feature of the AV–1419:D, but it is clearly based on an early EV exordium and retains reminiscences and verbal variations of phrases in extant EV groups, in, for example, the details in Tables 1 and 2 above and the following additional details:

AV–1419:D	*EV–1419:A*	*EV–1419:B*
And þis Brute biganne first þe citee of London and callid hit Troye in remembraunce of grete Troye fro þe whiche he and his lynage come	And this Brute bigan first the cite of London the whiche he leete be called Newe Troye in remembraunce of grete Troy from whens he and alle	& þis same Brute biganne first þe citee of London þe whiche he lete calle þat tyme Newe Troye in þe remembraunce of þe olde Troye ffrom

	his lynage were comen	whens he & his lynage weren come
and arryued vp into þis lande and inhabited it and lyued straungely whereinne weren no creatures but wilde beestes and briddes and fowles a lande desolate. And aftirward it was inhabited with giauntes til þe tyme þat Brute come [BL Stowe 70]	And they arryved in this lond casuelly where none lyvyng creature was at that tyme but wilde bestes and alle wildernesse. And houghe thay lyved by herbes and rotes and other manere frutes. And houghe the spirites ley by hem in mannes liknesse and gate vppon hem horrible giauntes the whiche reigned here in this lond to Brute cam and drove hem owte and sloughe of hem many oon [Rylands Eng. 105]	and arrived in this londe casuelly where in was no lyuyng creature but wilde beestes. And hou vnclene spirites lay bi hem and þei brouȝt forth horrible geauntez and Brute killid hem [BL Harley 4827]

2. The phraseology used to describe and name Coryn's paramour—*Erneb(o)urgh thine/thy lemman*—resembles that employed in the AV-1419:C and parallels the *Short English Metrical Chronicle*.
3. As in some texts of the EV-1419:A and in the EV-1419:C, the Latin tag on Blegabred is not found.
4. There are suggestions of the EV-1419:A text in the passage describing the naming of London by King Lud:

> Aftir the dethe of Ely reigned hys sonne Ludde the whiche gouerned the lande wele and worthely and was welbeloued and he made in Newe Troie an gate called Ludgate and for he loued that cite of London so moche and abode ther he made it be called Luddentoune or Luddestoune aftir hys name Ludde and he made moche werke aboute London and diched it and dide called it London by Saxouns tung and Nor-

mandes calle it Loundres. [University Coll., Oxford, 154; cf. the A text given on pp. 238–39 above, especially that of Bodl. Tanner 188].

5. There is a slight hint of the EV–1419:B in the passage naming the kingdoms of Engist's heptarchy, where the AV–1419:D reads:

and this Engest made many kinges in the lande as was afore tyme: the furste was Kent there he reigned himself. The secounde was Chichestre; the threde Westsexe; the fourte Estsexe; the v Norffolk and Suffolk and Lyncolne; the vj Leycestir Northampshire Hertford and Huntingdounshire; the vij Oxenforde Gloucestir Wynchestir Warrewyk and Derbyshire. [University Coll., Oxford, 154]

The ellipsis of the subject after *the furste* is reminiscent of the EV–1419:A, for logically the subject must be "kingdom" and not "king," but the subsequent use of *was* and not *had* is closer to the type of construction used in the EV–1419:B (see the EV–1419:A and EV–1419:B texts on pp. 182, 183–84, 193 above).

6. There are similarities in the Halidon Hill chapter to texts of various groups. Like Bodl. Rawlinson poet. 32 and all but one of the AV–1419:B texts, material is omitted around the battle. However, like the AV–1419:A(a), only three wards of the Scottish army are listed, although the phraseology is different, and the AV–1419:D simply says that "the Scottes come fersely in thre batailles welle arraied in here wynges," whereas the AV–1419:A(a) lists the wards and the lords contained in each.

The verbal affiliations of the AV texts to the corresponding EV texts, that is, those that contain a similar exordium, show that the inception of the AV texts must have been a complex compilation system in many instances, crossing texts of different groups and using such texts for purposes of collation. The best example of this is the complexity of the relationships between the earlier parts of the AV–1419:B and the AV–1419:A(a) texts and their EV counterparts.

In view of the "poor" nature of the final texts in terms of fidelity to the basic CV text, it is perhaps surprising that such great effort has gone into the blending of different groups, for not only complete sections of text have been extracted and fitted together, but there also seems to have been an attempt to blend texts on the verbal level. Nevertheless, codices such as Bodl. Ashmole 793 and Digby 185 show that well-executed manuscripts were being prepared of AV texts.

The evidence presented above suggests strongly that a number of texts have been lost, and whether the exact interrelationships of the EV and AV groups can now be established is difficult to predict. It is quite possible that the skill shown in crossing and collating texts, together with the loss of manuscripts, has obscured the precise lines of relationship to such an extent that complete disentanglement is impossible. There is some evidence of centers of production for *Brut* manuscripts (for example, the manuscripts and texts of the AV–1419:B), and within these there was undoubtedly a circulation of both texts and ideas in an apparently professional setting which could produce, if required, high-quality manuscripts, probably in response to specific orders.

---

[1] See Brie, *Geschichte und Quellen*, pp. 82–85.
[2] Brie, *Geschichte und Quellen*, p. 84.

IV. Peculiar Texts and Versions

This general grouping covers manuscripts that contain individual or peculiar texts, including several groups that are related to the textually complicated nexus of Latin *Brut* texts.[1] Also included here within the extended family of Middle English *Brut* texts are several works that were translated back into English from the Latin *Brut*s and short works, often no more than king-lists, based on *Brut* texts. These texts can be roughly divided into the following categories:

1. Reworked texts and versions of all or part of a *Brut* text, sometimes abbreviated or expanded by interpolations from other works. Such texts often include added materials of historical or literary interest and occasionally include continuations beyond the 1419 ending that is common among CV texts.
2. Material of an individual nature forming a section of a longer *Brut* text that belongs to an otherwise distinct group. (Where such sections themselves belong to distinct groups, as, for example, when a recognizable change of exemplar has occurred, then they have been treated under the appropriate group.)
3. Appendages to some work other than the *Brut*.
4. Very brief works that have used the *Brut* as a primary source.
5. The second translation of the Anglo-Norman *Brut*, attributed to John Mandeville.

In the case of individually reworked texts, it is likely that there was only one copy of many of such versions, that is, the text we now possess. It is also quite likely that other similarly individual texts once existed but are now lost. Where related groups of texts occur, their textual affiliations often require the assumption of lost groups or texts that would explain the relationships of those that survive.

The texts are organized below according to the categories noted above. Identifiable groups and individual texts are distinguished as PV–[date], that is, Peculiar Version, ending in [a specified year]; texts to 1419 that reached the (men) or the (r&g) endings are so denoted when such can be determined. Unrelated groups or individual texts that end (or originally ended or may have ended) at the same point are further distinguished by the addition of A, B, C, etc. They are generally ordered here within the general categories outlined above by their actual or presumed ending date, unless they are closely associated with a distinct version that ends in an earlier year.

---

[1] Kennedy has treated some of these works under headings separate from the *Brut*; see *Manual*, pp. 2636–40.

Reworked Texts and Versions

*The Peculiar Version to 1377,
with a continuation to 1419 ending "in rule and governance"
(PV–1377/1419[r&g])*

146. HARVARD UNIVERSITY MS. ENG. 530(1)[1]

Heading on fol. 59: Loo heer my lordes maystres and felawes may yee see a truwe and brief abstracte of þe Cronycles of þis reaume of England frome þe tyme þat euer ma[n]kynde enhabited hit into þe tyme of þe laste Edwarde: reedeþe or heereþe þe soþe here filowing.

Text begins: [I]n þe noble land of Sirye þer was a worþy kyng and mighty and a man of huge renoumee þat men cleped Dyoclycyan

Omits: Cad, QIL, "5w" heading (see below)

Changeover, 1333 to 1377: Þis bataylle and descounfiture byfell vpon Saynt Magretes even in þe yeere of oure lorde M¹ CCC xxxij. Ne douteþe it not but amonges alle þoo men þat were lefft deed in þe feelde of þe Skottis þe pillours ande þe poure men of þ'Englishe partye gate gret goode. Whane þis descounfiture was þus doone and eonded þe kynge of Englande retourned ageyne vnto þe seegge of Berewyk [cf. Brie 286/4–9, 291/1–2]

Text to 1377 ends on fol. 180v: þe whiche kynge Edward whane he had þus nobuly regned and possessed þe coroune with muche knightly labour and lytell rest lyche as yee haue herde þis cronycle more pleynly declare and specefye oon and ffyffty yeeres and more þe xj kalendes of Iuyn he dyed in his manoyre at Sheene worshipfully entered and buryed in þ'abbay of Westmynstre vpon whos soule Ihesu lorde haue mercy for thyn greuous gret and pytous passyoun.

Subheading on fol. 180v: Nowe my gracyous lordes and feyre ladyes my maystres ande specyall ffreendes and goode ffelawes vouchesauf here now I beseche yowe to here þe cronycle of þis sayde Richarde þe Secounde sone and heyre to prynce Edward and heyre to þis same kynge Edward; þe whiche Richard of his nobley and prouidence had ferme pees ande loue with alle þe Crysten prynces; howe riche he was howe noble howe loued and howe dredde thoroughe alle þe reaumes & provynces and howe þat ffame & ffortune by þeyre cruwell werre subuerted al his estate royall into mysery to þe lamentacioun and pytous compleynt of euery gentill herte; þe whiche cronycle was lamentabuly compylled at Parys by hem of Fraunce in þeyre wolgare langage and nowe translated by daun Johan Lydegate þe munk of Bury.

Chapter heading: And aftir kynge Edwarde the iij^{de} that was borne at Wyndesore regned Richard of Burdeux that was prynce Edwardes sone of Wales whiche prynce Edward was sone and heyre of kynge Edward of Wyndsore.

Text to 1419 begins: [A]nd affter þis kynge Edward the iij^{de} þat was borne at Wyndsor regned Richard þe secunde þat was prince Edwardes sone of Walis

Text to 1419 ends on fol. 204: And thane the kynge entrid the towne & rested hym in the castell til the towne was sette in goode rule and goode gouernaunce. Deo gracias.

Remarks: The manuscript is associated with John Shirley (died 1456) and also contains *The Complaint of Christ*, Lydgate's *Guy of Warwick*, *The Three Kings of Cologne*, *The Governance of Princes*, and Lydgate's *Serpent of Division*.[2]

The first part of the *Brut* text has been copied from a CV text ending in 1377, supplemented by the 1377 to 1419 continuation from a text that ended in 1419(r&g), here attributed by Shirley, at least in part, to John Lydgate. The reference to "þe laste Edwarde" in the heading is to Edward III and not Edward IV.

At some point after 1480 material copied from Caxton's 1419 to 1461 continuation in his *Chronicles of England* (item 85) has also been added.

The wording of the *Brut* text has been altered throughout, usually slightly though sometimes more extensively, by the use of what Shirley must have thought more colorful language and by the addition of reflexive references to the work (as in the short prologue and the end of the 1377 text quoted above).

The battles and wards of the Scottish army at Halidon Hill are renamed; the fifth ward becomes "þe skurage" (fol. 165, margin) and the "5w" heading is replaced by the following: "Þis is þ'arraye of þe skuroures ande þe renners for þe sauegarde of þeos batayiles."

The 1377 to 1419 continuation is written in the same hand as the text preceding it; the form of that text and the added subheading, however, indicate that a change of exemplar has taken place. The attribution to John Lydgate may be Shirley's genuine error, but it could also be a deliberate promotional ploy.[3]

---

[1] For (2), see item 93.
[2] On Shirley, see Doyle, "More Light on John Shirley," pp. 93–101. For a fuller account of the contents, see Voigts, "Handlist," pp. 17–22.
[3] See Henry N. MacCracken, ed. *The Minor Poems of John Lydgate*, Part I, EETS e.s. 107 (1911), p. xii; Walter F. Schirmer, *John Lydgate: A Study in the Culture of the XVth Century*, trans. Ann E. Keep (London, 1961), p. 82 n. 1.

The Peculiar Version to 1419: Group A (PV–1419:A)
The Peculiar Version to 1451/1460 (PV–1451/1460)
Cleveland Public Library MS. White W q091.92–C468 and TCD MS. 489 contain the same PV text up to 1333, after which point the Cleveland text continues to 1419 while the Dublin text continues its narrative to 1451 and then adds a document of 1460.

147. CLEVELAND PUBLIC LIBRARY MS. JOHN G. WHITE COLLECTION W Q091.92–C468[1]
Heading by first scribe on fol. 13v (first of two fols. numbered 13): Here folowith the Cronicles of Englond shortly abreggid.
Text begins on fol. 13 (second of two fols. numbered 13): Dioclisian sumtime the mighti king of Surry
Contains: Cad
Omits: QIL (see below), "5w" heading (see below).
First scribe ends on fol. 75v: And eche of thees capteins had vM[l] men of armis which proued manfull men when thei issuid [u *by corr. above*] out of the cite both on hors bak and on fote. [cf. Brie 390/21–26]
Second scribe begins on fol. 75v: & at þe fyrste cominge of oure kinge ther wer nombred to be within þe citie of menn women & children by her-

audes CCC M¹. And this sege of Roone endurid xx^ti weekes. [cf. Brie 390/22–30]

Second scribe ends on fol. 75v: in goode rule & governance. Deo gratias.

Remarks: An introductory text begins on fol. 1, "Iosephus of Iewis the noble was the first auctour of the book of Policronica," and ends on fol. 13v (the first of two folios numbered 13) "whos names beth in the begynnyng of the first book of Policronicon more pleinly rehercid and the scriptur and chapiters accordyng to the same." This piece is "more shortly drawen out of Pollicronicon," and, after briefly indicating the contents of the seven books of Higden's *Polychronicon*, it gives a general geographical survey of the world, especially of the biblical lands, culled from that work.

---

[1] For a description, see Phyllis Moe, ed., *The ME Prose Translation of Roger d'Argenteuil's Bible en François*, Middle English Texts 6 (Heidelberg, 1977), pp. 9–13.

148. TRINITY COLLEGE, DUBLIN, MS. 489[1]

Brut *text begins imperfectly*: [...]euer. These women londid in Devenshyre. And [...] Englond þat tyme was wyldernes and woodes full [...] wylde bestis and venemous serpentes

Contains: Cad, QIL

Omits: "5w" heading (see below)

Changeover, 1419 to 1451: And with hem cam a kny3t of Fraunce. He brou3t þe keyes to þe kynge and 3ilde vp þe towne vn Seynt Wolstons day in Ienyver þe yere of owre lorde M¹ CCCC° xviij°. And þat seege endurid xxv weekes saf a day. And whan þe kynge leide fyrst seege to Rone þer was within CCC M¹ people of men women and chyldren but þer dyed for hunger þe iiij^th parte beside hem were slayne. Tho was þe cytezens raunsom at fyfty M¹ li. to pay at serteyn dayes. Þe duke of Excestyr was made capitayne of Rone. And so þe kynge restid hym þer awhile and all his oost. And whan he had conquerde all Normandye tho wente he vp in to Fraunce and conquerd grete parte of the londe for all þe townes and holde he cam by þe Frenshmen 3ilde it vp and Mewes Embry and Parise

Narrative text ends on p. 206: Anno M¹ CCCC lj^ti kynge Herry þe vj fel in mervellous infyrmyte whiche endurid xviij monythis in so mcch þat he my3t not helpe hymself ne know þe peple abowt hym. Anno M¹ CCCC lij^ti Edward þe son of Herry þe vj^th was born at Westmynster in þe ffeste of Seynt Edward þe Confessour. Anno M¹ CCCC liijᵗⁱ The batayle of Seynt Albones where þat a grete parte of þe kynges people were slayne þat is to sey Edmonde duke of Somerset Herry erle of Northhumberlonde lord Clifford &c. Anno domini Millo. CCCC° lv° At Bloreheth was slayn lord Audeley and xxiiijᵗⁱ kny3tis with hym.

Accord (1460) between Henry VI and Richard, duke of York, begins on p. 207: Blyssid be Ihesu in whos hande and bounte restith and is þe pees and vnyte betwix princes and þe wele in euery reame

Accord ends on fragmentary p. 213: And that no lettyrs patent riallex of record nor act iudiciall made or done afore this tyme not repellid nor reveocid ne oþer wise voyde by the lawe by þe preiudiciall or hurt by þe present act. [cf. *Rotuli Parliamentorum*, vol. 5, pp. 378–79]

Remarks: The *Brut* is prefaced by a copy, imperfect at both beginning and end, of the same introductory text found in the previous manuscript. It begins, "Exherses þe kynge made a bridge be crafte of þe devils to werre vpon Greece," and ends, "In Rome was [. . .]age syttynge vn an hors of iren þe ima[. . .]e hors weyed xv M¹ li. and be crafte wa[. . .]de."

---

[1] Kennedy, *Manual*, p. 2820, dates the manuscript to the sixteenth century; I date it to the late fifteenth century.

Remarks on the PV–1419:A and the PV–1451/1460
In both manuscripts, the *Brut* text is preceded by a short geographical text that was intended as a loosely connected introduction.

After the Albina story at the beginning of the *Brut* occurs a chapter, entitled "The genologie of Adam" in the Cleveland text, which traces the descendants of Adam through (amongst others) Noah, Saturn, Jove, Trogens, his son Ilus (founder of *Ilea*, later changed to *Trogea* "Troy"), Achilles, his son Eneas, his son Ascanius, his son Siluis, to his son Brutus.[1] This chapter may also be based on the *Polychronicon*, Book 2.[2]

The *Brut* text is almost entirely changed verbally and is often much abbreviated in favor of augmentations from other sources. In the early chapters proper names are given in Latinized forms and many legendary details are added to the already legendary narrative of early kings from another source that occasionally resembles material found in the PV–1422:A or the PV–1437:A. Several details apparently taken from romance sources appear in the

Dublin text's narrative of Arthur, and both texts contain a short version of the romance story of Havelok.

The verbal differences and textual alterations continue in the later parts of the text also, as seen in the articles of treason brought against Thomas of Lancaster, which are given point by point.

Queen Isabella's letter to the citizens of London occurs in the Dublin text but does not appear in the Cleveland text. However, the wording of the chapter in which it would have occurred in the latter suggests that it was present in the text that was the ultimate basis of this version; its omission is, therefore, a secondary development.

The texts of the two manuscripts correspond up to 1333 but diverge widely thereafter. The starting point of this divergence occurs just before the battle of Halidon Hill, and the relevant passages in the two texts are as follows:

> At midsomer then aftir Englishmen toke up alle the ffeyre of Hadington in Scotlond and toke and slou3 a [*ins. above*] grete nombre of Scottes. This werre was in Scotlond in the viij yere of [the *del.*] kyng Edward aftir the conquest of Englond þe þird. Then king Edward ordeyned a gret counseil at London and purueid him a gret host & com to Berwik upon Twede and leid his sege therto. And to him come sir Edward Bailol king of Scottis with anothir power of Scottes to strength the king and then shotte thei her gunnes and engines into the toun and destrued many housis and slue much peple which longtyme continued til at last com the Scottes out of Scotlond in iiij bateils wel arraied in armes. Then kyng Edward of Englond and Edward king of Scottes appareild her peple in oþir iiij bateils. And on Halidon Hille beside the toun of Berwik metten thees two hostis togider. King E. discumfitid the Scottes and slue of them xxxvM^l & vijC. This victorie done the king retourned to his sege of Berwik and thei yildid the toun and þe castell vnto the king. [Cleveland White W q091.92–C468]

> At the missomer than aftyr Englissh toke vp all the feyre of Hundyngton in Scotlonde and toke and slewh grete nombre of Scottes. This warre was in Scotlonde in þe xiij 3ere of kynge Edward þe iij^{de} after þe conquest of Englonde. And after in his tyme he had grete werre with Fraunce and Scotlonde. And ser Edward his fyrst begoten son toke þe kynge of Fraunce in batayle. And þis ser Edward dyed prince and lyeth at Caunterburye. He had a son callid Richard [TCD 489]

This and the succeeding narrative in the Cleveland text almost certainly represents the original reworking of the *Brut*, whereas the immense abbreviation of the rest of Edward III's long reign is secondary and possibly even unique to the Dublin manuscript, which also seems to change exemplar at this point.

The ending-point of the first scribe in the Cleveland text suggests strongly that the ultimate CV base was a text of the CV–1419(men):A; to this the second, later scribe added from a text ending in 1419(r&g), abbreviating slightly and omitting a sentence already covered in the first scribe's work, as can be seen from the changeover lines given above.

After the sudden abbreviation of the reign of Edward III, the account of Richard II in the Dublin manuscript is much closer to the CV text, though some abbreviation continues to occur. Details in the siege of Rouen narrative suggest that the basis for this section of the text was the CV–1430 containing John Page's poem. The material that follows the end of the siege, though heavily abridged, has verbal agreements with both the 1430 and 1461 continuations but agrees entirely with neither: it is based on a London civic chronicle similar to that found in BL Cotton Cleopatra C.iv, as a number of common entries with identical wording show, and the material was converted into narrative *Brut* format.[3] The documentary material from the Rolls of Parliament that concludes the manuscript was probably intended as a suitable ending to the increasingly sketchy notices of battles in the Wars of the Roses.

---

[1] Cf. a similar interpolated chapter in Lambeth 84 (item 178).
[2] See Churchill Babington, ed., *Polychronicon Ranulphi Higden Monachi Cestrensis*, vol. 2, Rolls Series 41 (London, 1866), pp. 219–445.
[3] Printed in Kingsford, ed., *Chrons. London*, pp. 117–52.

The Peculiar Version to 1419: Group B (PV–1419:B)

149. RYLANDS MS. ENG. 207[1]
First scribe begins imperfectly: heir vnto the roialme bot he was not of
    strengthe. Bot nevirthelesse this Donebande [cf. Brie 23/16–18]
Contains: Cad, QIL
Omits: "5w" heading (see below)
First scribe ends imperfectly on fol. 103v: lyke vnto tourmentours more thanne

vnto Crystenmen and heaven [cf. Brie 297/4–5]
Second scribe begins on fol. 105: Englond. The xx yer off kyng Edward he wente ouer in to Bretayn & in to Gascoyn [Brie 297/11–13]
Second scribe ends imperfectly: þer wer not dede not passed xxxvj bodies thonket be Ihesu. Anone þe kynge [cf. Brie 379/26–29]

Remarks: The change of scribes is marked by a change from vellum to paper, the intervening blank leaf being of the latter. As it stands, the manuscript was patched together some time before 1749 from two originally discrete, though perhaps both incomplete, manuscripts.

The first part of the text, written by the first scribe, is much changed verbally from the CV–1419 from which it is probably derived, and there are some similarities to EV texts, though the Latin tag associated with King Blegabred is not found.

In the chapter on the battle of Halidon Hill only four divisions of the Scottish army are found (see below), and a substitute for the "5w" heading occurs in the text: "And of þe iiij bataille was thes captains...."

Examples of verbal changes and abbreviation are:

(i) *33 kings passage*:
The furst was called Gorbodian and he reigned xij yere. Aftir him Morgan ij yere. Aftir him Eighnaus vj yere. Aftir him Idwalier viij yere. [*etc.*]

(ii) *Engist's heptarchy passage*:
The furste was Kent wher himself was king and maistir. The secounde was Sussexe and Chichestir. The thrid Westsex. The iiij Essex. [*etc.*]

(iii) *Halidon Hill passage, with the end of the 1333 text and the beginning of the 1377 continuation*:
And thanne king Edwarde of Englonde & king Edwarde of Scotlande apparayled ther people into four batailles and euery bataill of Englesshe hadde two wynges of price archiers the whiche provid themself goodemen that daye ffor thei shotte so that þe Scottes myght not helpe themself and ther was slaine of the Scottes partie xxxvM^l v^C & xij and of Englysshemenne bot vij and at this bataill the Englysshe pages pursewed the Scottes as they wolde haue fledde. And whenne thei of the toune of Berwyk sawe the scomfayture of the Scottes þei yelde vp þe tovne wyth the castell wherof the king ordeyned & made to be kepers the same sir Edwarde Ballol with othyr worshipfull menne ffor himself come into Englonde wyth a glorious victorie. And in the vj^{the} yere of hys reigne he wente into Scotland againe in the wynter tyme and the

Scottes come dovne and obeyed him in all thing. [cf. Brie 285/7–291/14]

---

[1] See Lester, *Handlist*, pp. 51–53; Tyson, "Hand-List," p. 186.

The Peculiar Version to 1419: Group C (PV–1419:C)

150. BL MS. ADDITIONAL 70514

Begins imperfectly: [A]nd in the reialme of Fraunce aftir the desese of Seint Lewes and Philipp le bele his sonne

Chapter ends and Brut *text begins*: One Philippe the sonne of Charles count of Waloys and the ȝonger broþer of kynge Philipp le bele by vsurpacon withoute title of right toke vppon hym the croune of Fraunce ffrome whome ben descendid all the Frenche kynges sen þat tyme.

Of kynge Edwarde the thride aftre the conqueste. Capitulo CC xij°.

And aftre this kynge Edwarde of Carnervan reigned ser Edwarde of Wyndesoure his sonne [cf. Brie 247/20–23]

Contains: "5w" heading

Changeover, 1333 to 1377: withoute eny chalange of eny man. Deo gracias. And so aftre þis gracious victorie the kyng turnede hym aȝane to the same sege of Berwike

Ends imperfectly with catchwords (last page extremely rubbed): cause [. . .] he shuld make [Brie 352/6]

Remarks: In this fragment of a longer compilation the *Brut* text is augmented from another source with material on French history at the imperfect beginning of the text (cited above).

Fourteen lines of additional material praising Edward III is appended after his death (after Brie 332/19), though the text is not that of the "Description of Edward III" (Brie 333–34).

From the foot of fol. 29v to fol. 32 appears a genealogical narrative with roundels of Edward III's descendants. The set of roundels that concludes the pedigree of Edmund, earl of March, was originally only partially filled in, ending with the children of Richard, duke of York (died 1460): King Edward, Edmund, and George, duke of Clarence (so created in 1461), but possibly not including Richard, created duke of Gloucester towards the end of

1461, who may have been added later along with Ann, Elizabeth, and Margaret.

After two and a half folios of pedigrees, the narrative returns to the *Brut* on fol. 32v with the accession of Richard II, numbered chapter 239 (Brie 335/1), finally ending incompletely during the reign of Richard II in chapter 241.

On fol. 32 occurs an obit for Sir Robert Hill: "Robertus Hill armiger pater subscripti Egidij Hill obijt in anno domini millesimo quadrugentesimo octuagesimo et tercio decimo. M° CCCC° lxxxxiij°." Further obits then appear for Egidius (died 1546) and his wife Agatha (died 1552), who were buried at Nettlecombe in Somersetshire.

The Peculiar Version to 1419, ending "in rule and governance":
Group A (PV–1419[r&g]:A)

151. BODLEIAN MS. LAUD MISC. 733
Begins on fol. 18: In the noble lande of Surrie ther was a noble king and also a myghty and of grete renoune that men called Dioclician
Contains: Cad, "5w" heading
Omits: QIL
Ends: in rule and gouernaunce.

Remarks: The text must be the result of the crossing of texts of at least two groups. The introductory chapters show the lexical alterations of the CV–1419 (Leyle), but since Lear is correctly named, the exemplar must have changed by that point. The combination of the inclusion of the Cadwallader episode and the omission of Queen Isabella's letter is unusual (though not completely unknown) and may indicate that a second change of exemplar has occurred, possibly after the 1333 ending "withoute ony chalenge of ony man. Deo gracias." The manuscript is well-written and handsomely illustrated with miniatures, and this may be indicative of a desire to produce a "presentation" copy with a carefully selected text.

The *Brut* text is preceded on fols. 1–17v by an illustrated treatise on arms written by the same scribe.[1]

The name "Elizabett Dawbne" (possibly fifteenth-century) occurs on the first flyleaf, that of "George lord Bergevenny" on the second. It is noted on fol. 17v that the volume belonged to W. Woods, clerk of the Privy Council, in 1586.

[1] This work also occurs in BL Addit. 34648, fols. 3v–8v, and BL Harley 6097, fols. 1–10 and 12–49v; all three texts are printed in Evan John Jones, ed., *Medieval Heraldry: Some Fourteenth-Century Heraldic Works* (Cardiff, 1943), pp. 213–20.

The Peculiar Version to 1419, ending "in rule and governance":
Group B (PV–1419[r&g]:B)

152. BODLEIAN MS. E MUSAEO 39
Heading: Here may men here and knowe how England ferst beegan and was klepid Albioun & by whom it resseyuede that name.
Begins: In thee noble land of Svrrye theer was a worthy kyng myghtty and ryght riche and of greet renown that heyghtte Diaclisian
Omits: Cad, "5w" heading (see below)
Contains: QIL
Ends: in rule and in governavnce.

Remarks: Although the combination of the omission of Cad and the inclusion of QIL can be paralleled in the CV–1419(men):B and the CV–1419 (Leyle), the text is much altered verbally and probably represents an individual reworking of a CV–1419 text. Thus, for example, the chapter on the thirty-three kings begins with the standard CV "after him" type of linkage (cf. Brie 30/23–27), but quickly shifts to a simpler listing:

> Thee ferste kyng of thee xxxiij his name was hoten Gorbodian and hee regnede xij yeer. And after hym regnede Morgan ij yeer. And thanne Eighnaus vj yeer. Idwalan viij yeer. Rohugo xj yeer. [*etc.*]

There are only four divisions of the Scottish army at Halidon Hill and a rubricated substitute heading appears: "And in thee fourthe batatayle [*sic*] of Scotlonde in that warde theeroffe weren thus manye of lordys ore more."

The Peculiar Version to 1419, ending "in rule and governance":
Group C (PV–1419[r&g]:C)

153. LINCOLN COLLEGE, OXFORD, MS. LAT. 151[1]
Heading: Here may a man here how Englond was first called Albioun and thurgh whom it had the name.

Begins: In the noble lond of Sirrie there was a noble kyng and a myghty and a man of grete renowne that men called Dioclisian
Contains: Cad, QIL
Omits: "5w" heading (see below)
Ends on rubbed leaf: and rested hym in the castell till þe [...] was sette in reste and in governaunce.

Remarks: The text is written in two hands. Although the point of change-over (on fol. 78; Brie 161/18, "And when") is of no textual significance, there may have been a change of exemplar to a text that contained a defective continuation from 1333 to 1377. Chapter headings and numbering are sporadic after the change of scribe.

There are considerable omissions of material, including complete chapters, from the narrative on the reign of Edward III, including the chapter on the battle of Halidon Hill. The omissions occur at the end of the text to 1333 and in the continuation from 1333 to 1377 (but they do not belong to the short continuation to 1377 [see pp. 90–92]).

---

[1] See Ogilvie-Thomson, *Handlist*, p. 42. The manuscript is also described, with an account of the omissions, in Ker, *MMBL III*, p. 642. Ker notes the presence of a possessive on fol. 175v in the description of the retinues camped before Rouen—"my mayster Nevell þe erlis sone of Westmerlonde" (cf. Brie 388/13–14)—but this reading occurs in other texts.

The Peculiar Version to 1419, ending "in rule and governance":
Group D (PV–1419[r&g]:D)

Two manuscripts, TCD 5895 and BL Harley 7333, contain a text that is a blend of a CV text with one of the AV–1419:B.

154. TRINITY COLLEGE, DUBLIN, MS. 5895
Begins imperfectly on fol. 3: him in his chambre. And whan thei were come he spak to hem of her wickidnes [Brie 3/5–6]
Omits: Latin tag, four chapters after Arthur, Halidon Hill material
Contains: Cad, QIL
Ends: And than the kyng entrid into the towne and restid him in the castell til the towne was sette in rule and gouernaunce agayne.
Colophon: Expliciunt Cronicul.

155. BL MS. HARLEY 7333[1]

Begins imperfectly: him prevelyche vnto Southamptoun to mete þere þe too bretherin [Brie 126/26–27]
Omits: Halidon Hill material
Contains: QIL
Ends imperfectly on fol. 24v: in þe yer of the incarnacioun of oure lorde Ihesus Criste a M¹ iijC iiij^{xx} xj wherof þe peple wer sor agaste [& dred þat wengeans shold com sone *catchwords*] [cf. Brie 338/8–10]

Remarks: The scribe who wrote the *Brut* was one of (at least) six scribes responsible for writing the manuscript, which is an anthology of verse and prose works compiled over some period of time. His work accounts for over half the surviving text. A number of the works have textual or spelling similarities to texts associated with John Shirley, and the manuscript may have been owned by the Augustinian abbey of St. Mary de Pratis in Leicester.[2] The dialect of the scribe who wrote the *Brut* (and also fols. 94–97, analysed by the editors of *LALME*) is that of the northern part of Hampshire.[3]

---

[1] See Seymour, "The Manuscripts of Hoccleve's *Regiment of Princes*," pp. 269–71, and John M. Manly and Edith Rickert, eds., *The Text of the Canterbury Tales*, 8 vols. (Chicago, 1940), 1: 207–18, for descriptions, the Leicester associations, and detailed lists of the contents, which include works by Chaucer, Lydgate, Burgh, Hoccleve, and Gower and the *Gesta Romanorum*. Manly and Rickert call the manuscript "[a] library of secular literature, in 7 'books'" (p. 207). See also Boffey, *Manuscripts of English Courtly Love Lyrics*, p. 17, where it is suggested that this "enormous library of material ... probably served the needs of a religious community."

[2] See Manly and Rickert, *Canterbury Tales*, 1: 212–13; Seymour, "Manuscripts of Hoccleve's *Regiment of Princes*," p. 271.

[3] *LALME*, 1: 113 (first entry on BL Harley 7333), 3: 161. The dialects of other scribes are also assigned to northern Hampshire; see *LALME*, 1: 113 (second and third entries on BL Harley 7333), 3: 159–60.

Remarks on the PV–1419(r&g):D
Although the imperfect text of BL Harley 7333 begins past the point of changeover from a CV to an AV–1419:B text, it can be grouped with TCD 5895 on the basis of distinctive correspondences with the later text (see below). Textual comparisons show, in fact, that BL Harley 7333 preserves the wording of the group more accurately than TCD 5895.

The text of this group is an amalgamation of a CV text with a text of the

AV–1419:B, within which additional omissions of material have occurred.

The added details about the giants do not occur in TCD 5895, and the passage concerning Lud's naming of London corresponds to the text of the CV. In the chapter recounting Arthur's return to England to meet the threat of Mordred, however, the text begins to correspond to that of the AV–1419:B (around Brie 89/12). Arthur is succeeded by Conan, who is succeeded in turn by his son "Crofte" (CV and AV–1419:B "Certif," Conan's cousin).

A considerable omission, typical of the AV–1419:B, occurs in the texts of both manuscripts around the chapters that include the battle of Halidon Hill:

> And þat same tyme it fille þat þe kyng of Englond helde his parlement atte Castel vpon Tyne. And ser Edwarde kyng of Scotlond come þider and did to him feaute & homage for þe reame of Scotlond the which quene Isabel and Mortemer toke awey þorou3 her fals counsail.
>
> And in þe xxx^{ti} yere of his reigne about Witsontide he ordeyned a parlement at Westmynster. And þere it was certified þat Philip þe kyng of Fraunce was dede. [TCD 5895; cf. Brie 280/17–26, 305/11–13]

Following a process already begun in the AV–1419:B, there are further omissions of text, often of narrative that relates overseas events, as, for example, in the chapter that begins with the great windstorm of 1362:

> Off þe grete wynd.
>
> And aboute Seint Mawrus day aboute evynsong tyme þere rose suche a wynde oute of the south with sich a fersnes þat it blewe downe howsis & chirchis & towres to the grounde & stepelis & othir strong [þinges *add*. TCD]. And all oþere workes that stode still were soo i-shake þat ben yit sene that shall euermore be febeler and this wynde lastid vij dayes withoute sesynge. And aftir there folowed suche wateres in hey tyme in harveste þat all felde werkes were much lefte on-don. And than prince Edward toke the lordshipe of Guyen & did to his ffadir fealte & homage & went ouer the see into Gascoyn [wiþ *add*. CV] his wyf and his childerin [wyf... childerin *om*. TCD]. And anon aftir the kyng made his sone sir Leonell duke of Clarens & sir Edmond his othir sone erle of Cambrigge. And than come into Englonde iij kynges þat is to sey þe kyng of Fraunce the kyng of Cipris & the kyng of Scotlonde to speke with the kyng of Englonde and

thei had gret worshipe. And when þey had ben here longe tyme ij of hem went home ageyne. But the kyng of Fraunce thorow grete sekenesse was lefte in Englonde. And in the xxxix yere of his reigne was an huge froste and hit lasted from Seint Andrewis-tide till xiiij calendours of Aperill and þan they telled & sewe. & in the xl yere of kynge Edwarde was borne Edward prince Edwardes sone. And in the xlj yeere of kyng Edwarde was borne at Burdewx Richard the seconde son of prince Edward whiche Richarde was kynge of Englonde aftirwarde as ye shaull here.

Of the batell of Spayne betwene prince Edward & Harry the bastarde of Spayne. [BL Harley 7333; cf. Brie 314/32–320/2 (315/15–18, 315/31–316/8, 316/ 10–24, 316/29–319/34 are omitted)]

The Peculiar Version to 1422: Group A (PV–1422:A)
The Peculiar Version to 1437: Group A (PV–1437:A)
The Peculiar Version to 1437,
with a continuation to 1461 (PV–1437/1461)

These three groups are closely related one to another and to the Latin *Brut* texts. However, several texts present considerable difficulties of affiliation, both within the individual groups and in the relationships between the groups themselves and to other groups of texts. The degrees of their relatedness differ greatly, and there may well have occurred some collation and combining of texts. Alternatively, it is possible that fuller forms of the text, now lost, ended in 1422 and (as suggested by the Latin *Brut*) in 1437, and that the surviving texts are offshoots of these and of subsequent subgroups. Speaking of certain representatives from these groups, Kingsford rightly remarks that "[t]he overlapping and interlacing of these Chronicles makes the history of their development a difficult problem."[1] In this respect they are similar to the various chronicles of London.[2]

---

[1] Kingsford, *English Historical Literature*, p. 128.
[2] See Gransden, *Historical Writing II*, pp. 228–230; Thomas and Thornley, eds., *Great Chronicle*, pp. xxv–xxix; McLaren, "Textual Transmission," pp. 55–56.

The Peculiar Version to 1422: Group A (PV–1422:A)
The group contains MSS. Bodl. Laud Misc. 550, Coll. of Arms Arundel 8,

TCD 506, and BL Sloane 2027. The central section of the composite text in Bodl. MS. Rawlinson poet. 32 also belongs to this group.

156. BODLEIAN MS. LAUD MISC. 550

Heading: How this land was first callid Albion and of whom it had that name ye shal here as foloweth aftirward.

Begins: In the yeer fro þe begynnyng of þe worlde M^{l}M^{l}M^l lxxxix^C þer was in þe noble lond of Grece

Contains: Cad, heptarchy material after Cad (see Remarks on the PV–1422:A below), QIL

Omits: "5w" heading (see following)

Changeover, 1333 to 1377: Aftir this king Edward wente into Scotland and besegid þe toun of Berewic and hadde a gret bataille with þe Scottis on Halidoun Hil beside þe toun of Berewic at whiche bataille were slayn of þe Scottis xxxvM^l vij^C xij and this was on Saint Margaretis eve in the yeer of our lord M^l CCC xxxij and in þe morow aftir the bataille was don þe Scottis deliuerid þe toun of Berewic to king Edward. And þe xj yeer of his regne was seen and apperid in þe firmament a lemyng sterre that was callid Stella Comata [cf. Brie 272/3–286/9, 291/1–292/18]

Changeover, 1419 to 1422: Whanne the king hadde entrid þe toun and restid hym in þe castel til þe toun were set in rewle and gouernaunce thanne Cawdbeek and othir garisons þere nygh were yolden vnder the same appointement. Þanne þe dolfines ambassiatours as it was before accorded with ful power to do al thing as he were there himself cam to þe king to Roon [cf. *"Davies's" Chronicle*, p. 48]

Ends on damaged fol. 120v: and thanne a sore & [...]uent malady him assailid and fro day [...]y him vexid til he deide in þe castel of Boys Vincent þe laste day of August whanne he hadde regned ix yeer v monthes iij wokes and iij daies and is buried at Westmynstre. On whos soule Ihesus Cr[...] haue mercy. Amen. [cf. *"Davies's" Chronicle*, p. 52]

Remarks: From William Rous on, each succeeding reign generally begins on a new page.

In 1605 the manuscript belonged to Richard St. George, Norroy Herald, as a note of ownership attests.

157. COLLEGE OF ARMS MS. ARUNDEL 8

Heading: How thys londe was forste calde Albyon & of whom hit had that name ye shall here as hit ffollowyth afterward.

Begins: In the yere from the begynyng of the worde M¹M¹M¹ DCCCC there was yn the noble londe of Grece a worthi kyng & a myghty and a man of grete renowne that was calde Dyoclusyan

Contains: Cad, heptarchy material after Cad (see Remarks on the PV-1422:A below), QIL

Omits: "5w" heading (see following)

Changeover, 1333 to 1377: and for his treson he wasse drawen & honged and on Seint Andrwes day nexte after the kinge wente into Scottlonde & besegid the towne of Berwyke & had a grete batell with the Scottes at Halydoune Hyll besides the towne of Berwyke at þe whiche batell weren slayne of the Scottes xxxvM¹ DCCxij and this wasse on Seinte Margaretes even the yere of oure lorde Ihesu Criste M¹ CCCxxxij and on the morrowe aftre that the batell wasse don the Scottes delyuered the towne of Berwyke to kinge Edwarde. The xj yere of his regne wasse sene & appered in the firmament a lemyng sterre þat wasse calde Stella Comata [cf. Brie 272/3–286/9, 291/1–292/18]

Changeover, 1419 to 1422: & when þe kinge had entred the cite he rested hym in þe castell tyll hit wasse sette in rwle & gouernance. Then Cavdebecke & oder garnysons there ny3e weren yolden vndre þe same appointement. Then the dolfyns embassettours with full power as he wer himselfe presente comen to the kinge to Rouen [cf. *"Davies's" Chronicle*, p. 48]

Ends on fol. 68: but thenne a sore & a fferuent malladye hym assayled & dayle hym vexed till he deyd yn the castell of Boyse Vyncente the laste day of Auguste the ix yere v monythes iij wokes and iij dayes of his regne & ys buryed at Westmynstre. [cf. *"Davies's" Chronicle*, p. 52]

Remarks: The text is written by two scribes, but the point of changeover is of no textual significance.

The reigns of Henry IV and Henry V begin on new pages.

158. TRINITY COLLEGE, DUBLIN, MS. 506

Begins imperfectly: regned alone in Englond Walis and Scotland as right heir and he was the firste that euyr werid croune in this lond. He made also a statute and a lawe [cf. Brie 23/27–31]

Contains: Cad, heptarchy material after Cad (see Remarks on the PV-1422:A below), QIL

Omits: "5w" heading (see following)

Changeover, 1333 to 1377: and for his treson he was drawe and hangid on Saint Andrewes day. Aftir this king Edward wente in to Scotland and beside [*sic*] the toun of Berwic and hadde a greet bataille with þe Scottis on Halidoun Hil beside þe toune of Berwic. Atte whiche bataille were slayn of þe Scottis xxxvM^l vij^C xij and this was on Saint Margaretis eve in þe yeer of our lord M^l CCC xxxij. And in þe morow aftir þe bataille was don þe Scottes deliuered the toun of Berewic to king Edward. And þe xj yeer of his regne was seen and apperid in þe firmament a lemyng sterre that was callid Stella Comata

Ends imperfectly: And þe said ser Harri Percy leet crye openly and saide þat he was chief cause that king Richard was deposid and most helper to king Harry for to brynge him in wenyng þat he wolde haue amendid þe gouernaunce and þe rewle of the reme and now king Harri rewlith worse [cf. *"Davies's" Chronicle*, p. 28]

Remarks: Each section in the heptarchy material that follows the Cadwallader episode is given a separate chapter number.

The beginning of the reign of Richard II is accorded a new page, as is also true of the reigns of several kings after William the Conqueror.

The text ends in a passage based on the continuation to the *Eulogium Historiarum* that describes incidents preceding the battle of Shrewsbury.

159. BL MS. SLOANE 2027

Begins on fol. 96v: In the yer ffro the begynnyng off the world M^{l}M^{l}M^l ixC lxxx^e ther was yn the noble land of Grece a wurthy kyng and a myghty & a man of grete renoune

Prologue ends on fol. 97v, mid: and callid this land Bretayn as ytt shal be seide her afftirwarde.

Text resumes on fol. 170: Whan kyng Iohn had don hys curage the enterdytyng was relesyd thurgwh all Englond the vij^{te} day of Iull [cf. Brie 166/4, 16–18]

Ends imperfectly on fol. 188v: the erle of Dunbarre become ys man & the kyng yaff ym the [cf. *"Davies's" Chronicle*, p. 22]

Remarks: The *Brut* is used to frame the B version of Robert of Gloucester's rhymed *Chronicle*, which ends on fol. 169v with the ascent to the throne of Henry III.[1] The dialect of the Robert of Gloucester text is that of Warwickshire, while the language of the *Brut*, written by the same scribe, is "slightly more northerly."[2] On fol. 96 appears the early ownership signature of "Wylliam Braundon of Knoll [Knowle, south-east of Birmingham] in the counte of Waruyke" (repeated elsewhere).[3] The name and date "Iohn Osbvrn 1546" occur in the margin of fol. 97.

Other works in the manuscript are the 1408 English translation of Vegetius's *De Re Militari* (fols. 1–36v), John Russell's *Boke of Nurture* (fols. 37–52v), and Lydgate and Burgh's *Secrees of Old Philosoffres* (fols. 53–92v).[4]

---

[1] See Kennedy, *Manual*, pp. 2617–21, 2798.
[2] *LALME*, 1: 116, 3: 526–27.
[3] See Meale, "Patrons, Buyers and Owners," pp. 216, 233–34 n. 88.
[4] Listed in Charles R. Shrader, "A Handlist of Extant Manuscripts Containing the *De Re Militari* of Flavius Vegetius Renatus," *Scriptorium* 33 (1979): 303; described in Geoffrey A. Lester, ed., *The Earliest English Translation of Vegetius' 'De Re Militari'*, Middle English Texts 21 (Heidelberg, 1988), p. 19. See also Frederick J. Furnivall, ed., *Early English Meals and Manners*, EETS o.s. 32 (1868), pp. 117–99 (John Russell); Robert Steele, ed., *Lydgate and Burgh's 'Secrees of Old Philisoffres'*, EETS e.s. 66 (1894).

160. BODLEIAN MS. RAWLINSON POET. 32(2)[1]

PV–1422:A text begins on fol. 116:[2] How William Bastard duk of Normandy came into this land & slow king Harold.

Contains: QIL

Omits: "5w" heading (see following)

Changeover, 1333 to 1377: And for his tresoun he was drawe and honged. And on Seint Andrew dey after this kyng Edward went into Scotland and besegid þe toune of Berwik and had a gret batell with the Scottes on Halydom [*sic*] Hull besides þe toun of Berwik at wich batell were slayn of þe Scottes xxxvM^l vij^C xij and this was on Seint Mergeretes eve in the yer of our lord M^l CCC xxxiij. And in the morwe after the batell was don the Scottes deliuered the toune of Berwik to king Edward. And in the xj yer of his reign was sen & apered in the firmament a lemyng stere þat was called Stella Comata

Changeover, 1419 to 1422: When þe king had entred in þe town & rested him in þe castell til þe castell were sett in rewle and gouernance then Caudebek & oþer garisons þer negh were yelden vnder þe same apoyntment. Then þe dolffen inbasitours as it was afore acorded with full power as he wer þer himselff came to þe king to Roon

PV–1422:A text ends on fol. 151: and then a sore a feruient malady hym asoiled and from dey to dey hym vexed till he died in the castell of Boys Vincent the last dey of August when he had reyngned ix yere v monythes and iij wekes and iij deys and is buried at Westminster.

Remarks: The changeover from an EV–1419:B exemplar to one of the PV–1422:A has resulted in some small overlap of narrative material concerning the arrival of William the Conqueror and the death of Harold.

Almost all of the continuation to 1422 is the work of one scribe. A change of hand occurs at the top of fol. 151, and a new scribe completes the text to 1422 before proceeding with the CV–1461 continuation, copied from Caxton's *Chronicles of England*. At least this last section of the composite *Brut* text must, therefore, have been written after the publication of Caxton's edition in 1480.

---

[1] For (1), see item 115; for (3), see item 90.
[2] Fol. 116 also has the heading "Willielmus Conquestor Raigne."

Remarks on the PV–1422:A
The text of this group exhibits both abbreviation of the basic *Brut* text throughout and the addition of material from other sources. Examples of each kind that characterize the group are as follows:

(a) Dioclician is identified as king of Greece rather than of Syria, though the version of the Albina story is of the "Syrian" kind in which the sisters' plot succeeds.

(b) The thirty-three British kings are listed mainly by name and length of reign:

> The firste king of tho xxxiij kinges me callid Garbodia and he regned xij yeer. Morgan regned ij yeer. Eighanus vj yeer. Idwalan viij yeere. [*etc.*] [TCD 506]

(c) The short account of Engist's naming of the land and of his heptarchy is omitted in the abbreviated narrative of Vortiger (see Brie 55/6–14; see also [g] below).

(d) The dealings between Vortiger and Merlin are reduced to one chapter.

(e) Constantine reigns after Arthur, but the two CV chapters are reduced to one.

(f) Constantine is succeeded by "Aureli Conand," "Vortiperi," and

"Malgon" before returning to "Cortif"; the two CV chapters relating the reigns of Adelbright and Edelf are omitted.

(g) After Cadwallader occurs an expanded account, based on a short reference in the Cadwallader narrative, entitled "Of þe departing of the vij kyngdomes" (Bodl. Laud Misc. 550), which treats the lines of kings in each of the seven kingdoms of Engist's heptarchy. This account is followed by king "Alfray" (that is, Alfred); the five intervening CV chapters are omitted.

(h) A number of details and minor stories, often of a religious character, are added to the reigns of the Anglo-Saxon and Danish kings (for example, to Athelstan, Eldred, Edwin, Edgar, Edward the Confessor, Edmund Ironside, Harthaknut).[1] Unlike the CV, Athelstan, Edmund, Eldred, and Edwin receive separate chapters.

(i) The foundation of the New Forest is transferred from William Rous to his father, William the Conqueror, with an added comment: "Þe comyn English Cronicle saith that William Rows made this forest but it is vntrewe" (Bodl. Laud Misc. 550). Additional material after the death of William the Conqueror includes the story of his father's meeting with his mother and the latter's dream while pregnant.

(j) St. Anselm sees William Rous's death in a vision of all the English saints, including St. Alban, who flings an arrow of fire to earth.

(k) Henry II has a miraculous encounter at Cardiff with an old man who warns him to ban Sunday markets. Rosamond and the finding of the bones of Arthur and Guinevere at Glastonbury are also noted under Henry II.

(l) The reigns of Henry III, Edward I, Edward II, and, to a lesser extent, Edward III are abbreviated.

(m) The battle of Halidon Hill is abbreviated, as given above.

(n) Merlin's prophecies regarding Henry III, Edward I, and Edward II are omitted.

(o) Details from the continuation to the *Eulogium Historiarum* (such as a mention of the ampulla containing the coronation oil and Richard's resignation speech) occur in the reigns of Richard II and Henry IV. The cause of Richard's death is not given.

(p) For the majority of kings after William the Conqueror, detailed notes of their marriages and issue are made at the end of their reigns.

---

[1] See Brie, *Geschichte und Quellen*, pp. 93–94.

The Peculiar Version to 1437: Group A (PV–1437:A)
The Peculiar Version to 1437, with a continuation to 1461 (PV–1437/1461)
The PV–1437:A, which shows considerable internal crossing of texts, contains MSS. Nottingham County Council DDFS 3/1, TCC O.11.11, Takamiya 18, Harvard Eng. 750 (both texts), Illinois 82(2), and TCD 505. The texts of the PV–1437/1461 (Bodl. MS. Lyell 34 [known from its editor and former owner as *"Davies's" Chronicle*] and the composite NLW MS. 21608D) should also be considered here, since all of the former and part of the latter are based on a text ending in 1437 to which a continuation from 1440 to 1461 has been added.

In a number of instances, text from an exemplar ending in 1437 with the murder of James I of Scotland has been grafted on to or into a text copied from an exemplar that belongs to some other recognized group (see the remarks on individual manuscripts and on the PV–1437:A below). Material from the PV–1437:A is used in the final section of the PV–1436:A (see pp. 296–301).

161. NOTTINGHAM COUNTY COUNCIL MS. DDFS 3/1

Heading on fol. 4: Of the first enhabityng of the Ile o Albion and of whom hit had that name.

Begins: In the noble londe of Surre ther was a noble kynge and a myghti a man of grete renowyn called Diaclusian

Contains: Cad, heptarchy material after Cad, QIL

Omits: "5w" heading (see following)

Changeover, 1333 to 1377: And for his tresoun he was drawyn and honged and on Seint Andrews day aftir kynge Edward went ynto Scotlond and bisegid the towne of Barwik and had a grete bataille with the Scottes at Halydoune Hill besyde the towne of Barwyk at the whiche bataille weren slayn of the Scottes xxxvM^l DCCxij and this was yn Seint Margaretis day evyn the yere of oure lord M^l CCCxxxij. And yn the morowe aftir the batell was done the Scottes delyuerd the towne of Barwik to kynge Edward. And þe [*ins. above*] xxj yere of his reigne was sene and appered yn the firmament a lemynge sterre that was callid Stella Comata

Changeover, 1419 to 1422: Whan the kynge hadde entred the citee and rested him yn the castell tyll it were sette yn reulle and gouernaunce. Than Cawdebecke and oder garresons there nyghe were yolden vnder the same appoyntement. Than the dolfyns embassatoures with full power as he were there himselfe came to the kynge to Roone

Changeover, 1422 to 1437: And than a sore and a feruent maledy him assayled and dayly him vexsed till he deyd yn the castell of Boys Vyncent the last day of August the ix yere v monythes iij wekys and iij daies of his reigne and ys buryd at the chirch of Westmynster.

Of kynge Harry the sixt the son of kynge Harry [*ins. above*] the vth after the conquest.

After the noble and victorious prince kynge Harry the vth reigned his son kyng Harry the vj[th] [cf. *"Davies's" Chronicle*, pp. 52–53]

Ends: the seid James kynge of Scottis goynge toward his bedde havyng no more clothes on him but his shurte cruelly was slayn and as it was seid he hade xxx woundes of the which viij [*sic*] were dedely &c. And [cf. *"Davies's" Chronicle*, p. 56]

Remarks: Despite the concluding "And," the rest of the final folio is left blank and the text is complete as it stands.

In a number of important ways the Nottingham text stands apart. The beginning of the text is unique among PV–1422:A and PV–1437:A texts in the wording of its heading, the lack of an introductory date, and the designation of Dioclisian as king of Syria rather than of Greece.

Further differences from the PV–1422:A and other PV–1437:A texts, in which the Nottingham text agrees more closely with the ultimate CV source, are that the short account of Engist's heptarchy appears and that Constantine's reign is recounted in two chapters.

Given the generally derivative relationship among the other texts of the PV–1437:A and the PV–1422:A, these differences presumably mark a secondary development peculiar to the Nottingham text. It is possible that it represents a combination of texts in which the point of changeover occurs after Constantine, since the subsequent text agrees with that of the other members of the group.

The *Brut* is prefaced (fols. 1–4) by a brief Latin account of world history from the Creation to Brutus and subsequent English history to Henry II, followed by two short accounts, also in Latin, of the spread of Christianity and religious sites.

162. TRINITY COLLEGE, CAMBRIDGE, MS. O.11.11[1]
Heading: How this lond was first callid Albion and of whom it hadde that name ye shall here as foloweth aftirward.

Begins: In þe yeer fro þe begynnyng of þe worlde M^{l}M^{l}M^l ix^C lxxxx ther was in the noble lond of Grece a worthi kyng and a myghty & a man of greet renoun that was callid Dioclician

Contains: Cad, heptarchy material after Cad, QIL

Omits: "5w" heading (see following)

Changeover, 1333 to 1377: and for his fals treson he was drawe and honged on Saynt Andreux day. Anno vij. [*marg.*] Aftir this kyng Edward wente into Scotland and besegid þe toun of Berewic and hadde a greet bataille with the Scottis on Halidoun Hill beside þe toun of Berewic at whiche bataille were slayn of þe Scottis xxxvM^l vij^C xij. And this was on Saynt Margaretis eve in ye yeer of our lord M^l CCC xxxij. And on the morow aftir the bataille þe Scottis delyuerid the tovvn of Berewic to kyng Edward. Anno xj°. [*marg.*] The xj yeer of kyng Edward was seen and apperid in the firmament a lemyng sterre that was callid Stella Comata

Changeover, 1419 to 1422: Whanne þe kyng hadde entrid the toun and restid him in þe castell til þe toun were set in rewle and gouernaunce thanne Cawdebek and othir garisons there nygh were yolden vnder the same appoyntement. Thanne þe dolfinez ambassiatours as it was before accorded with full power to do all thyng as he were there himselff cam to þe kyng to Roon.

Changeover, 1422 to 1437: and thanne a soor and a feruent malady him assaillid and fro day to day him vexid til he deide in þe castel of Boys Vyncent þe laste day of August whanne he hadde regned ix yeer v monethis iij wokis and iij daiez and is buried at Westmynstre. [fol. 128v; fol. 129r *left blank*]

[A]ftir the noble and victorious prince kyng Harri þe v regned his sone kyng Harri þe vj that was bore at Wyndesore

Ends: þe said kyng of Scottis as he was goyng toward his bed hauyng no more on him but his shirte cruelly and vnmanly was slayn and as it was told he hadde on him xxx^{ti} woundis wherof vij were dedly &c.

Remarks: From the accession of William the Conqueror each reign begins on a new page, and after each of the reigns of Arthur and of Henry V a page is also left blank.

In the left margin at the end of the text occurs an addition in a different hand: "Y dar say no more."[2]

---

[1] See Ker, *MMBL II*, pp. 261–62; Mooney, *Handlist*, p. 150 (Mooney ascribes the final,

marginal addition to "the hand of the main scribe").
[2] A later, sixteenth-century addition is attributed to "John Ardyns sunns" writing; see Ker, *MMBL II*, p. 261.

163. TAKAMIYA MS. 18
Heading on fol. 2: Cronica Bruti in Anglicis D[. . .]cianus Rex. Prima. How this londe was first callyd Albyon and of whom hit hadde that name ye schal here as ffolwith aftyrwarde.
Begins: In the yere ffrom the bygynnynge off the worlde iijM^l ix^C iiij^x x there was in the noble lorde [*sic*] off Grece a worthy kynge and a myghty and a man of gret renoun þat was callyd Dioclisian
Contains: Cad, heptarchy material after Cad, QIL
Omits: "5w" heading (see following)
Changeover, 1333 to 1377: And for his false treson he was drawe and hangid on Seynt Andrewis day. Aftyr þis kynge Edwarde wente into Scotlonde and beseghid the towne of Berwic and hadde a gret bataile with þe Scottes on Halydounhill beside the towne of Berwic. Atte wiche bataile were slayne of þe Scottes xxxvM^l vij^C & xij. And þis was on Sent Margaretis eve in þe yere of oure lorde M^l iij^C xxxij. And on þe morwe after þe bataile þe Scottes delyueryd þe towne off Berwic to kynge Edwarde. The xij yere off kynge Edwarde was seen and apperid in þe firmament a lemynge sterre þat was callid Stella Comata
Changeover, 1419 to 1422: And whanne þe kynge hadde entryd the towne and restyd hym in þe castell tyll þe towne were set in rule and gouernaunce. Thanne Cawdebek a[nd] oþere garysons þere nygh were yoldyn vndir the same appoyntement. Thanne þe dolfynez enbassatours as hit was bifore acordid with ffull powere to do all thynge as he were there hymselffe cam to þe kynge to Roon
Changeover, 1422 to 1437: And þanne a sore and a fervent maladye hym assaylid and fro day to day hym vexid tyll he deyde in the castell off [By del.] Boys Vincent the laste day off August whanne he hadde regnyd ix yere v monthis iij wyks and iij dayez and is buryed at Westmynster.

Off kynge Harry þe sexte aftir the conquest.

Aftir the noble and victorious prynce kynge Harry þe v^{the} regnyd his sone kynge Harry the sexte þat was bore at Wyndssore
Ends: And aftirwarde abowte þe monthe off Marche be exitacion off þ'erle

off Athell and othir the seyde kynge of Scottes as he was goynge towarde his bed hauynge no more on hym but his scherte cruelly and or.manly was slayne; as hit was tolde he hadde on hym xxx woundis where-off vij were dedly. Y dar say [. . .]ore. [Y . . . ore *marg*.]

Remarks: The manuscript is written in a late, unprofessional hand. Fol. 1 contains an astrological item on the distance between the earth and the moon. The name of Francis Welles appears at the foot of fol. 3.

The final, marginal comment should be compared with the final, marginal comment added to the preceding manuscript.

164. HARVARD UNIVERSITY MS. ENG. 750 (FIRST TEXT)

Heading on fol. 8: How thys lond was first callyd Albion and of whome yt hadde yat name ye shall heare as folowyth afterward.

Begins: In the yere from the begynnyng of the world 3990 there was in the noble lond of Grece a worthy kyng and a myghty and a man cf great renoun that was called Dioclycian

Contains: Cad, heptarchy material after Cad, QIL

Omits: "5w" heading (see following)

Changeover, 1333 to 1377: for his treson he was drawne and hangyd on Saynt Andrewys day. After thys kyng Edward went ynto Scotland and besegyd the towne of Berewic and had a great bataylle with the Scottes on Halidoune Hyll bysyd[. .] the towne of Barwic [and had . . . Barwic *ins. in top marg.*] at which batuyille were slayne of the Scottes [of the Scottes *ins. in marg.*] xxxvM^l vijC xij and thys was on Saynt Margaret[. .] eve in the year of ower lorde M^l iij^C xxxij and on the mor[. .] after the batayll was done the Scottes deliueryd the towne of Berewic to the kyng Edward; and the xj year of kyng Edward was seyn and apieryd yn the firmament a lemyng sterre that was caullyd Stella Cometa

Changeover, 1419 to 1437: Whan the kyng had entryd the town and restyd hym yn the castell tyll the towne were set yn ordre and gouernaunce than Cawdebeec and other garisounes there nygh wer yeldyd vnder the same apoyntmen(?) [*badly written*]; thanne the dolfynes ambassiatours as yt was befor accordyd wyth full power to all thyng as he were thear hymself came to the kyng to Roone

Changeover, 1422 to 1437: and than a soore and a fervent maladie hym assailled and from daye to daye hym vexid tyll he died yn the castell of Bois Vincent the last daye of August whan he had reignyd ix yeares v moneths iij wekes and iij dayes and ys buried at Westmynster on whose soule Ihesu Crist haue mercy. Amen.

Of kyng Harry the vjth

After the noble and victorious prince kyng Harry the vth reigned his sonne kyng Harry the vjth that was borne at Wyndsore
Ends on fol. 69v: the sayd kyng of Scottes as he was goyng to hys bede havyng no more on hym but hys shirte cruelly and vnmanfully was slayne and so as yt was told he hadde on hym xxx woundes which vij were dedly.

Remarks: After the Cadwallader episode occurs the additional heptarchy material, here entitled "Of the departyng and boundyng of the vij kyngdomes," separated into sections on each kingdom. The other additional details found in Bodl. Lyell 34—for example, the remark on the New Forest and the story of William the Conqueror's conception—also occur. The reigns of Henry III, Edward I, and, to a lesser extent, Edward II and Edward III are abbreviated.

The hand of the text belongs to the very late fifteenth or, more probably, sixteenth century. The first folios of the manuscript contain various historical notations and chronologies; after this first *Brut* text occur further historical notes and extracts, a second *Brut* text (see below), Roger of Wendover's *Flores Historiarum*, a short account in English of the retinue of Edward III at the siege of Calais, and Nicholas Trevet's *Chronicle*.

165. HARVARD UNIVERSITY MS. ENG. 750 (SECOND TEXT)
Heading on fol. 82: How William Basterd duk off Normandy cam in to England and kylyd king Harold.
Begins: Whane duke Wylliam off Normandy herede yt Harold was crowned
Contains: QIL
Ends on fol. 101v: they were clepyed a people without a heade the which did muche harme in the parties of Fraunce [Brie 314/24–25]

Remarks: This second, excerpted *Brut* text is written in a hasty sixteenth-century hand and agrees textually with the first text in the manuscript, from which it was presumably copied.

166. UNIVERSITY OF ILLINOIS MS. 82(2)¹
Second hand begins on fol. 164v: And sone after was the olde kyng Edward his fader translated fro þe castel of Kyllyngworth into the castell of

Berkley & þer thoro treasoun of ser Roger Mortimer he was sleyn with a sprite of copir brenyng put in at his fondement

Changeover, 1333 to 1377: wherfor he was drawe & hangyd on Seynt Andrews day. Anno vij°. [*marg.*] After this kyng Edward went into Scotland & beseg[..] the toun of Berwic & had a grete batel with þe Scottes on Halidoun Hille beside þe toune of Berwic at which batell wer slayn of the Scottes xxxvM¹ vijC [...] & þis was on Seint Margaretes evyn in the yer of our lord M¹ CCC xxxij. And on the morowe after þe batell the Scottes delyuerd the toun of Berwic to kyng Edward. Anno xij°. [*marg.*] The xj 3er of kyng Edward was [...] & apperid in the firmament a lemyng sterre þat was callede Stella Comata

Changeover, 1419 to 1422: Whan þe kyng had entrid þe toun & restid hym in þe castill tyll the toun were sette in rewle & gouernaunz than Cawdbeke & oþer garisones þer negh aboute wer yolden vnder þe same composicioun. Than þe dolffyns ambassetores as it was befor accorded with full poar to do all thing as he wer ther himselff cam to þe kyng to Roon

Changeover, 1422 to 1437: And þan a sore & a feruent malady hym assaylid and ffrom day to day hym vexid tyl he deid in the castill off Bois Vincent the last day of August safe oon the ix^the yer v monethis iiij wekys & iij dayes of his rayn and is buried at Westmynster. On whos soule Ihesu Crist haue mercie. Amen.

Sequitur de Henrico sexto. Henricus sextus incipiebat regnare vltimo die Augusti anno domini millesimo quadrugentesimo vicesimo secunda & regnabat triginta & octo annis & dimidio anno & tribus diebus videlicet usque quartum diem Marcij anno domini millesimo quadrugentesimo sexagesimo.

[O]ff kyng Harry the vj^th the sone of kyng Harry the vth. Affter the nobil & victorios prynce kyng Harry the v^the reigned his sonne kyng Harry the vj^the þat was bore at Wyndesore

Third hand ends: the said kyng of Scottes as he was goyng to his bed hafyng no mor vpon hym but oonly his shyrt cruelly & vnmanly was slayn and as it was saide he had on hym xxx woundes wheroff vij wer dedely. I dar write no fferther. [I... fferther *marg.*]

Remarks: This section of text is written by two scribes, but the point of changeover has no significance and there has been no change of exemplar.

PECULIAR TEXTS AND VERSIONS   285

The PV–1437:A text has been added to a text of the AV–1419:C, with some narrative dislocation at the point where the change of exemplars occurred. The final comment of the text suggests that it is connected with that of TCC O.11.11 (see above).

The reigns of Henry IV and Henry V are prefaced by headings in Latin similar to that before Henry VI's (for which, see above); these headings are later additions in the same hand that writes several of the historical memoranda at the beginning of the manuscript.[2]

---

[1] For (1), see item 142.
[2] See p. 229.

167. TRINITY COLLEGE, DUBLIN, MS. 505[1]

Heading on p. 87: How thys lond was fyrst callyd Albyon and of whom hyt had that name he [*sic*] schal here as folowthe aftyrward.

Begins: In the here [*sic*] fro the begynnyng of the world M^{l}M^{l}M^l ix^C þer was in þe nobull lond of Grece a worthy kyng and a myghty and a man of grete renwne that was callyd Diclycyan

Contains: Cad, heptarchy material after Cad, QIL

Omits: "5w" heading (see Remarks below)

Changeover, 1333 to 1377: And euery man toke whatt he myght and withoute chalenge of ony man. With Deo gracias. [With...gracias *in red*] And also aftyr this gracious victorye the kyng turned hym ayein vnto the sege of Berewyk

Changeover, 1419 to 1437: And att euery gate iij or iiij M^l of gud mennes bodies well armyd and manfully countred with owre Englissmen. And in þe vij yere of this same kyng Herry he lay att the segge of Roan. And the xvij day of Ianue 1 [*sic*] hitt was yolden to owre kyng. And thys sege lasted xxj wekys. And then cam þe capitaines and browght þe keys to owre kyng and delyuered hym the toune. And all the Frensch sodyers where voyd owte of the toune with heyre horse and hernes. And the comynnes of the toune abode styll payng yerely vnto the kyng for all maner costommes fermes and quatrimes xxM^l marke. And when the kyng had enterid the toune and rested hym in the castell tyll the toune where sett in rewle and gouernaunce. And then [*ins. above*] tythingis cam to London the vj da [*sic*] of Feuer. And then the duke of Bedford with a fayre mayne of Englond

Text to 1422 breaks off imperfectly on p. 284 during "Coronation of Queen Katherine": The kyng of Scotlond in his astate on the liffte side of the quene wych att euery course was serued aftyr þat the quene and the

Text to 1437 begins on p. 285: Aftyr the nobull and victorious prince kyng Herry the v^{te} regned his sonne kyng Herry the vj^{te} that was borne att Wyndesore

Text to 1437 ends: The seid kyng of Scottis as he was goyng to his bede hauyng no more on hym bott his schert cruelly and vnmanly was slayne. And as hitt was tolde he had oon hym xxx wondes where-of vij where dedely.

Remarks: This text is a careful blend of texts from two groups, evidently in order to produce as full a version as possible. Up to the reign of Henry III, the text follows that of the usual PV–1437:A. Accordingly, the narrative contains the text on the heptarchy after the Cadwallader episode, followed by the chapter on King "Alfray" and other additional details found in, for example, Bodl. Laud Misc. 550.

However, since the reigns of Henry III, Edward I, Edward II, and Edward III are abbreviated in the PV–1437:A, at or about the accession of Henry III the scribe switched to a CV text similar to (but somewhat fuller than) that found in Pennsylvania State MS. PS. V–3A, including the continuation beyond 1419 found therein (items 32 and 181). Thus the abbreviation found in the later chapters of the PV–1437:A is not found and Merlin's prophecies regarding Henry III, Edward I, and Edward II appear. The full text of the reign of Edward III is given and the array of the Scottish battles at Halidon Hill is included. Instead of the normal "5w" heading occurs the heading "How the erle of Dumbar holped the Scottes at þis bataill," which is also found in the CV–1419(men):A(b).[2]

The scribe continued to use this second, CV text into the narrative of Richard II's reign but clearly had his PV–1437:A text available for consultation, for on p. 256 he adds a minor detail in the margin from the PV–1437:A, that Queen Anne knelt before the lords appellant in a vain effort to save the life of Sir Simon "Beuerle" (i.e., Burley). Pages 257–58 are a stub containing narrative from the PV–1437:A that is not present in the main text. Deficiencies in the CV exemplar must have become apparent, for the scribe continued with the PV–1437:A text for the end of Richard's reign (including the ampulla reference and a full account of Richard's resignation of the crown).

For the reigns of Henry IV and Henry V the scribe combined what he considered the fullest or most accurate material from his two exemplars. The account of the siege of Rouen is primarily from the CV exemplar, followed by an imperfect copy of the continuation to 1422 found in Pennsylvania State PS. V–3A. A page is missing after the beginning of the chapter on Queen Katherine's coronation, and the text resumes with the accession of Henry VI, taken from the PV–1437:A.

The manuscript also contains Latin genealogical chronicles from Noah to Edward IV (with drawings, roundels, and commentary to Edward I; pages 6–56), from Adam through Old Testament figures and Roman rulers (pages 59–62), emperors and popes (pages 63–78), and archbishops of Canterbury (with roundels and commentary; pages 79–83). The first of these genealogical works notes Edmund, son of Queen Elizabeth Woodville, as earl of Huntington, a title he held from 1471 to 1475. In the last work, the entry on Thomas Bourghier, archbishop of Canterbury from 1454 to 1486, has been erased.

The *Brut* is immediately prefaced by a full-page drawing, with informational roundels, of buildings and rural scenes representing England (page 86).

The manuscript has sixteenth-century Welsh associations: on page 1 occur Welsh verses on the zodiac, dated 1593, attributed to and in the hand of Lewys Dwnn, a deputy herald.[3] Page 2 contains early-seventeenth-century notes on the Chicester family.

---

[1] See Marvin L. Colker, *Trinity College Library Dublin: Descriptive Catalogue of the Mediaeval and Renaissance Latin Manuscripts*, 2 vols. (Aldershot and Brookfield, 1991), 2: 935–38.
[2] See pp. 100–104.
[3] See Colker, *Descriptive Catalogue*, 2: 938.

168. BODLEIAN MS. LYELL 34 (*"DAVIES'S" CHRONICLE*)[1]

Heading: How this land was first callid Albion and of whom it hadde þat name and how þe geauntez were ygote ye shul here as foloweth afterward. Capitulum primum.

Begins: In þe yeer fro þe begynnyng of þe worlde M^{l}M^{l}M^l ix^c þer was in þe noble lond of Grece a worthi kyng and a my3ti and a man of gret renoun þat was callid Dioclician

Contains: Cad, heptarchy material after Cad, QJL

Omits: "5w" heading (see following)

Changeover, 1333 to 1377: Thanne wente kyng Edward in to Scotland forto helpe þe said Edward and besegid þe toun of Berewic and þe Scottes cam doun and faught with þe kyng at a place callid Halidoun Hill beside Berewic and at þat bataille were slayn of þe Scottes vij erlis M^{l}ccc horsmen and of oþer peple xxxvM^l vij^C xij. And of Englishmen þat marvail is to wite were ded a kny3t a squyer and xij foot men and nomo and this was on Saint Margaretis eve in þe yeer of our lord M^l CCC xxxij and þus was þe toun of Berewic yolden to þe kyng and þe castel also. And aftirward þe said ser Edward Bayloll as right here of Scotland dede his homage too kyng Edward of Englond at New Castel vpon Tyne. And aftir þis þe Scottis rebellid ayens kyng Edward wherfore in þe hard frosty wynter he wente in to Galoway and wastid all þe cuntre vnto þe Scottissh Se and abood in þe castell of Rokesburgh all the wyntertyme. Þe xj yeer of kyng Edward in þe moneth of Iuyn was seen and apperid in þe firmament a lemyng sterre þe whiche clerckis callid Stella Comata and þat sterre was seen in dyuers partiez of þe firmament. [cf. Brie 281/21–286/9, 291/1–292/19]

Changeover, 1419 to 1422: Whanne the king hadde entrid the toune, and restid him in the castel til the toun were set in rewle and gouernaunce, thanne Cawdebeek and othir garisons there nyghe were yolden vndir the same appoyntement. Thanne the dolfynee3 ambassiatours, as it was before acordid, with ful power to do all thyng as he were there himself, cam to the king to Roon [*"Davies's" Chronicle*, p. 48]

Changeover, 1422 to 1437: and thanne a sore and a feruent maladie him assaillid, and fro day to day him greuousli vexid; til he deide in the castelle of Boys Vincent, the laste day of August, whanne he hadde regned ix yeer v monethis, iij wikis, and iij daie3, and is buried at Westminstre: on who3 soule Almyghti God haue mercy. Amen.

Of kyng Harry the vj^{te} aftir the conqueste, sone of kyng Harri the v^{the}, and of the bataille of Vernulle, &c.

Aftir the noble and victorious prince kyng Harri the V, regned his sone kyng Harri the vj^{te}, that was bore at Wyndesore [*"Davies's" Chronicle*, pp. 52–53]

Continuation to 1437 ends: the said kyng of Scottis, as he was goyng toward his bed, hauyng no more vn him but onli his shirte, cruelli and vnmanli was slayne; and as it was said he hadde on him xxx woundis, wherof vij were dedly. [*"Davies's" Chronicle*, p. 56]

Continuation from 1440 to 1461 begins: The xix yeer of kyng Harri, the Friday before midsomer, a prest callid ser Richard Wyche, that was a vicary in Estsexe, was brend on the Tourhille for heresie [*"Davies's" Chronicle*, p. 56]

Continuation to 1461 ends: and the Wennesday next after, vppon the morow, Edwarde the noble erle of Marche was chosen kyng in the cyte of Londoun, and began for to reygne, &c. [*"Davies's" Chronicle*, p. 110]

Remarks: The manuscript is written by two scribes, but the point of changeover, on fol. 189v, in the year 1450, does not seem to indicate a change of exemplar at that point. The death of James I of Scotland in 1437 does, however, mark a break in the text and probably a change of exemplar since the ensuing narrative continues with the year 1440.

The text to 1437 is closely related to those of the PV–1422:A and the PV–1437:A and contains many of the distinguishing features and details noted above under the PV–1422:A. Thus the extended heptarchy material occurs after the Cadwallader episode and the additional anecdotes appear under the reigns of Athelstan, Edmund, Eldred, and Edwin, who each receive a separate chapter.

Some differences in the arrangement of materials occur, for example, in the narrative on William the Conqueror. The foundation of New Forest is credited to William the Conqueror, but the comment concerning the "common English Chronicle" does not appear; William's conception and his mother's dream are present, though at a different point in the chapter than in the related texts.

The text cannot, however, be directly derived from the PV–1422:A or the PV–1437:A, for in a number of features it is closer to the original CV. Thus, the short account of the establishment of Engist's heptarchy appears; Merlin's dealings with Vortiger are recounted in several chapters (rather than one conflated chapter); the reign of Constantine is accorded two chapters; and Constantine is followed by the CV succession of Adelbright and Edelf.

Compared to texts of the PV–1422:A and PV–1437:A, the text of Bodl. Lyell 34 is consistently expanded throughout from sources such as the *Polychronicon* and saints' legends, as the following examples show.

The second chapter is headed "How þe iij sones of Noe departid al þe worlde betuene thaym and how Brut was gote and bore and how he slow his moder and aftirward his fader and how he cam in to this lond." The narrative begins "Hit is ywrite in þe croniclez of þe Grekis þat þe iij sones of Noe aftir Noez flood..." and ends "Anchisez gat Eneas þat was a worthy knyght and a man of greet power and duelde in þe cite of Troie."

Similar additions include an account of the visit to Britain of Joseph of Arimathea under the reign of Cymbeline, an account of the destruction of Jerusalem during the reign of Westmer (called "Marms" in this text), and an account of the death and assumption of the Virgin attributed to St. Elizabeth (that is, Elizabeth of Schönau).

Unlike the PV-1422:A, the text is not heavily abbreviated for the reigns of Henry III, Edward I, and Edward II. Similarly, the reign of Edward III is abbreviated but not as heavily as in the PV-1422:A, as is shown by the Halidon Hill passage cited above where several verbal details are closer to the CV.

Although a number of leaves are now missing, the reign of Richard II contains the added details from the continuation to the *Eulogium Historiarum* in addition to material that is unique.[2] The continuation from 1440 to 1461, found in full in this manuscript and in part in the next, has no direct relationship to the corresponding text in Caxton's *Chronicles of England*.

Like Bodl. Laud Misc. 550, Bodl. Lyell 34 allows a new leaf for the beginning of each king's reign after Richard II.

The dialect of the text is that of Surrey.[3]

---

[1] See de la Mare, *Catalogue*, pp. 85–87. The text from 1377 to 1461 (from the accession of Richard II to the accession of Edward IV) is printed in John Silvester Davies, ed., *An English Chronicle of the Reigns of Richard II, Henry IV, Henry V, and Henry VI Written Before the Year 1471*, Camden Society o.s. 64 (1856); quotations are, where possible, taken from this edition.

[2] See Kingsford, *English Historical Literature*, pp. 122–24, 127–29.

[3] *LALME*, 1: 150, 3: 499.

169. NATIONAL LIBRARY OF WALES MS. 21608D[1]

Table begins on fol. 1: Tabula huius libri &c. How this londe wasse firste called Albioun and after whan yt hadde that name and howe the gyaunte wasse geton ye shall here as folowethe after. Capitulum primum.

Table ends on damaged fol. 8: Off kynge Harry þe sexte [of dei.] after þe co[n]quest the sonne off kynge Harry the v^{te} and off þe bataille &c. and of many oþer thynges.

Heading on fragmentary fol. 11: Assit principio sancta Maria meo.

How this lond was first called Albio[...] had þat name and how the giau[...] here as folowthe after.

PECULIAR TEXTS AND VERSIONS   291

Text begins on fragmentary fol. 11: In the [...]
Contains: Cad, QIL, "5w" heading
Omits: heptarchy material after Cad
Changeover, 1333 to 1377: and this victory fell to the Englissh men opon
    Seynt Margretes eve in the yere off our lorde Ihesu Criste M° CCC xxxij
    and whilis this wasse doynge the Englissh knavez toke the pelage off the
    Scottes that were killed eueryman that he myght take withoute knawelage
    off eny men. Deo gracias. And so after this gracius victory the kynge
    retourned agayne vnto the same seege off Berwicke
Changeover, 1377 to 1419: And when this noble kynge Eduuarde hadde
    regned lj yere and more the xj kalend off Iuyn he died in his maner off
    Shene and ys worshupfully buried atte Westmynstre on whosse soulle all-
    myghty Godde haue mercye. Amen.

And after kyng Edward þe iij^{de} þat was born at Wyndesore rengned [*sic*]
Richard of Burdeux þat was prince Edwardes sonne and of the debate þat
was betwen ij esquierez and þe lord Latymer for þe erle of Dene the
bisshop of Northwiche wente vnto Flaundres and how kyng Richard was
wedded and how he wente vnto Scotlond and how he made nve dukes
and erles and of oþer thynges &c.

After kynge Eduuard the iij that wasse born atte Wyndesor regned Ri-
charde the secunde
Changeover, 1419 to 1422 continuation: Then the kynge entered the tovn and
    rested hym in the castell till the tovn were sette in rule and gouernaunce.
    And anon Cawdebec and oþer garisons ther nygh were yolden vndir the
    same appoyntemente. And then the dolfynes ambassitoures as yt wasse ac-
    corded befor with full power to do all thynge as he were hymselfe ther
    came vnto the kynge to Roon
Continuation to 1422 ends and "Coronation of Queen Katherine" begins: and
    þen a soore and a fervente malady hym assaylled and fro day to day grev-
    osly hym vexed till he died in the castell off Boys Vyncente the laste day
    of Auguste when he hadde regned ix yere v monethes iiij wekes and iij
    dayes and ys buried atte Westmynstre on whose soulle allmyghty Godde
    haue mercy. Amen.

Off þe coronacyoun of queyn Kateryn.

The vj^{te} day of Feueryere þat fell opon a Sonday in Lent dame Kateryn
wasse crovned quene atte Westmynster

"*Coronation of Queen Katherine*" *ends on fol. 181*: a tigre and Seynt George ledyng yt &c.

Continuation to 1437 begins on fol. 182: Of kyng Henry the vj^{te} after þe conqueste þe sonne of kyng Henry þe v^{te} and of the bataill of Vernull and of þe sege of Caleyse and of þe sege of Rokesburgh and of þe deth of þe kyng of Scottes and of Alynour Cobham & of maister Roger Bolyngbroke and of Iacke Cade of Kente and of the deth of the duke of Suthfolke and mony other thynges.

After the noble and victorius prince kynge Herry the v^{te} regned his sonne kynge Henry the vj^{te} þat wasse borne atte Wyndesore

Continuation to 1437 ends: þe forseide kynge as he wasse goynge towarde his bedde havynge nomore on hym but only his shirte cruelly and vnmanly [out(?) *del.*] by William Grame wasse slayn and as yt wasse seide & tolde he hadde on him xxx^{ti} wondes wherof vij were dedly. [*"Davies's" Chron.*, p. 56]

Continuation from 1440 to 1461 begins: Anno ix^{no} [*marg.*] The ix yere of þis kynge Herry the Sonday before mydsomer a preest called ser Richarde Wyche þat wasse vicar in Essex wasse brente opon the Toure Hyll for heresy [*"Davies's" Chron.*, p. 56]

Ends imperfectly: the duke off Southefolke William de la Poolle and oþer of his assente hadde made delyueraunce of Angeo and [cf. *"Davies's" Chronicle*, p. 68]

Remarks: Internal features in the earlier and later portions of the text generally agree with those of the preceding text in Bodl. Lyell 34. The central part of the text, however, does not agree with the Lyell text, since it omits the additional account of the heptarchy and also contains the "5w" heading. The wording of the changeover from 1333 to 1377 suggests that this central portion has been taken from a CV text ending in 1377, after which the compiler returned to a text of the type of Bodl. Lyell 34. The account of the coronation of Queen Katherine seems to be an independent interpolation (though cf. item 166). The text for the reign of Richard II is complete and can thus supply the defective text found in the preceding manuscript. In its complete state the text probably ended at the same point as Bodl. Lyell 34, in 1461.

Fol. 181v contains an epitaph on Matthew Gogh, whose death in 1450 is noted in the text on fol. 189.[2]

[1] See Marx, "Middle English Manuscripts," pp. 373–76, for a description and an analysis of the contents.
[2] See Marx, "Middle English Manuscripts," p. 382 n. 42.

Remarks on the PV–1437:A and the PV–1437/1461
As noted above, it is difficult to account for the text of Nottingham County Council DDFS 3/1, which may be the result of a combination of texts. The full texts of the PV–1437:A found in TCC O.11.11, Takamiya 18, and Harvard Eng. 750 could be derived from the PV–1422:A, with which they share a set of common features and additions (see pp. 276–77), to which has been added a continuation from the accession of Henry VI (1422) to the murder of James I of Scotland (1437).

An alternative possibility should, however, be noted: that the PV–1437:A might have been the source of the PV–1422:A, which deliberately omitted the narrative on Henry VI (perhaps because it was compiled at a politically uncertain time in the late 1450s or early 1460s). If this were the case, then the presumed precedence of the English PV–1437:A over the second version of the Latin *Brut* would need to be re-examined.

In addition to independently interpolated material, the PV–1437/1461, as represented by Bodl. MS. Lyell 34, shares a number of augmentations with the PV–1422:A and the PV–1437:A: for example, the extensive narrative on the kingdoms of the Anglo-Saxon heptarchy that occurs after the Cadwallader episode (with the omission of five chapters found in the CV); the anecdotes in the reigns of Athelstan, Edmund, Eldred, and Edwin, to each of whom is devoted a separate chapter; additional material on William the Conqueror (though reordered); Anselm's vision; and the Rosamond story.

Yet in other respects, the PV–1437/1461 is closer to the CV: for example, the inclusion of the short account of Engist's heptarchy; two chapters on Constantine and the normal CV succession thereafter; and additions in the reigns of Richard II and Henry IV. The text of the PV–1437/1461 is not heavily abbreviated for the reigns of Henry III, Edward I, and Edward II. Although the Halidon Hill narrative is considerably shortened, it is not as truncated as that found in the PV–1422:A and the PV–1437:A, and in a number of verbal details the passage is closer to the CV original.

The CV–1437/1461 in Bodl. Lyell 34 cannot, therefore, be directly derived from the PV–1422:A or the PV–1437:A. Its basis is either a combination of texts of the PV–1437:A and the CV, or (less probably) it reflects in its narrative to 1422 an earlier, more expanded version of the PV–1422:A than that contained in the surviving manuscripts of that group, to which the continuation to 1437 was appended. (Under the alternative possibility, that the PV–1437:A precedes the PV–1422:A, then one could perhaps view the PV–1437/1461 as an offshoot of an early stage of the PV–1437:A.) Whatever the immediate source or sources, the basic text was then augmented by some reordering in the narrative, by further interpolations, and by the continuation from 1440 to 1461.

The Peculiar Version to 1422: Group B (PV–1422:B)

This small group, which has no direct connection with the PV–1422:A, consists of MSS. NLW Peniarth 397C and Bodley 754.

170. NLW MS. Peniarth 397C[1]

Begins imperfectly: north countre and wolde ben avenge of his fadres deth Vortiger [Brie 62/15–16]

Contains: Cad, QIL, "5w" heading

Changeover, 1419 text to 1422 continuation: And there he made for hym a riall and a solempne ternement and beried hym by quene Anne his wyff as his owne desir was on the further side of Seynt Edwardes shrine in the abbey of Seynt Petris of Westmynster. In this same yere the lorde Cobham that is to saye sir Iohn Oldecastell was idampnyd for a loller [cf. Brie 373/13–16, Kingsford, ed., *Chrons. London*, p. 69]

Ends: Also the laste day of Auste in the x yere of his reigne the forsaide noble kyng Henrye the v endid his lyf at Boys Seint Vincent beside Paryse. Also in the vij day of Novembre he was nobly enterid at Westmynster on whos soule Ihesu haue mercy. [cf. Kingsford, ed., *Chrons. London*, p. 74]

---

[1] See Marx, "Middle English Manuscripts," pp. 364–69, for a description and an analysis of the contents.

171. Bodleian MS. Bodley 754

Begins imperfectly on fol. 2: And to her ffadir said thay wold make all amendis [Brie 3/10–11]

Contains: Cad, QIL, "5w" heading

Changeover, 1419 text to 1422 continuation: And there he made for him a solempne terment and byryed him by quene Anne hys wyfe as his own wyll was on the souþe syd of Seynt Edwardes shryne in the abbey of Seynt Petrus at Westminster. In þis same yere the lord Cobham that is to say ser Iohn Oldcastell was dampned for a loller [cf. Brie 373/13–16, Kingsford, ed., *Chrons. London*, p. 69]

Ends on damaged fol. 154: [..]rry the fyfte dyed [*ins. above*] at Boys Seint Vincent by side Pares als[...] Novembre he was noble entyred at Westminster on whose soule [...] Amen. Explicit. [cf. Kingsford, ed., *Chrons. London*, p. 74]

Remarks: The missing first folio and other missing text have been supplied at a later date.

Remarks on the PV–1422:B

The basis for the text to the beginning of the reign of Henry V is a CV–1419. The narrative for the reigns of the kings from Edward the Confessor to Henry III has been much expanded by the interpolation of secular and religious anecdotes, Latin verses, visions, physical descriptions of the kings, and so on, occasionally attributed to Marianus Scotus but in fact taken from the *Chronicon ex chronicis* attributed to Florence of Worcester and from Eadmer's *Historia Novorum in Anglia*.[1] The compiler may also have used the *Polychronicon*. A typical addition is that of the story of Rosamond, the mistress of Henry II:[2]

> Tho he grewe opon and boldely mysvsid a damysell called Rosamounde for whom he made a bovr at Wodstoke in the parke of a mervellous werkyng lyke to Dydalis bovr that the quene shulde not welle fynde hir but she dyed withinne a while and was buried in the nonery of Godstow. And hathe wreton vppon hir toumbe these verses—
> > Hic iacet in tumba Rosamundy non rosa munda
> > Ron redolet set olet quod redolere solet—
> That is as moche to say in Englisshe "here lythe in the tumbe nat the clene rose but Rosamunde; she stynkith and not smellith soote that somtyme smellid withovte goostly boote."

From the reign of King John to Richard II the normal CV–1419 text is followed; Henry IV's reign, however, is heavily abbreviated. The account of the final imprisonment and death of Richard II (Brie 360/8–26) is moved forward to the end of his reign, thus allowing the reign of Henry IV to begin neatly on a new leaf.

Soon after the beginning of the reign of Henry V, the compiler changed to a text based on a London chronicle very similar to that found in BL Cotton Julius B.ii (see changeover above), though not identical with it, as shown by minor additional entries in the continuation.[3]

---

[1] See Antonia Gransden, *Historical Writing in England c. 550–c. 1307* (Ithaca, 1974), p. 145; Marx, "Middle English Manuscripts," pp. 364–66. Marx suggests that the conflation of Florence and Eadmer may have taken place in the compilation of a Latin monastic chronicle, which was then used by the compiler of the CV–1422:B.

[2] The popularity of this and similar stories is evinced by its inclusion in several *Brut* texts, such as the PV–1422, PV–1437:A, and Bodl. Lyell 34 (where a truncated form of the story appears) and twice in Lambeth 84 (as a marginal addition to the reign of Henry II and, by error, as part of the account of Edward III, although the compiler has then stroked out the story). These texts vary in detail and in general moral viewpoint.

[3] Printed in Kingsford, ed., *Chrons. London*, pp. 1–116. With reference to NLW Peniarth 397C, Marx ("Middle English Manuscripts," pp. 366–68) argues that the later part of the text is derived from Caxton's printed edition of the *Polychronicon* (1482); however, the compiler of the PV–1422:B and Caxton have independently used a common London chronicle source.

The Peculiar Version to 1436: Group A (PV–1436:A)

MSS. BL Harley 53 and Lambeth 6 form a small group that has used either two *Brut* texts, probably an EV–1419 text and a PV–1437:A text, or an exemplar that already combined two such texts, as the basic framework into which many passages have been inserted from a number of sources.

172. BL MS. HARLEY 53[1]

Latin heading on fol. 14 (followed by 16 Latin verses): Liber de Cronicis Anglorum primo de Albina.

Heading (folio damaged): Here begynne the cronicles of kynges of Englo[...] tyme that it was first inhabit and of theire [...] be dyuers auctores is declaret & [...]

Begins: After the begynnyng of this worlde M^l [...] yere. In the noble

lande of Surry wa[...] and a strong man of body and of g[...] was clep-
it Dioclusian

Contains: Cad, QIL (underlined in red)

Omits: "5w" heading (see Remarks on the PV–1436:A below)

Changeover, 1419 to 1422: And then þe kyng entert into þe toune of Roane and hym restit in þe castell till þe toune was sette in ruyle and in gouernaunce. And aftur þat was Caudebek and oþer garisons þer negh yolden to þe kyng vnder the same appoyntement.

Of the trety of pees þat was betwene kyng Henry of Englond and kyng Charles of Fraunce and of þe mariage of kyng Henry þe v^{te} and dame Kateryn þe kynges doughter of Fraunce and so þe pees made and fynysshit.

When kyng Henry of Englond had goton Roane as before is said the dolfyns enbassatures as it was accordit before with full power to do al thynges as he were þere hymself present comen to þe kyng to þe said cite of Roane [Brie 559/16–27]

End of text to 1422, and narrative from 1437 continuation: And þen a sore and a fervent malady hym toke and fro day to day hym vexit til he deyed in þe castell of Bois de Vincent the last day of August when þat he had regnet ix yere v monithis iij wekes and iij days and aftirward he was brought into Englond riolly and enterid at Westemynster.

After the noble victoriose prynce kyng Henry the v^{te} regnet his sone Henry the vj^{te} that was bore at Wyndesore in the fest of Saint Nycolace the Confessoure and began to regne in þe age of ix monithes and xv dayes. [Brie 563/27–35; cf. *"Davies's" Chronicle*, pp. 52–53]

Continuation to 1436 begins: And to Richard erle of Warrewik was commyttit þe kepyng of hym [Brie 563/35–564/1]

Continuation to 1436 ends imperfectly: And when þis bullewerk was þus wonne vppon hem of Gaunt they of Brugges were glad and logh hem of Gaunt [Brie 580/30–31]

Remarks: A genealogy from Adam to Henry VI (fols. 2-11v) contains Richard of Gloucester (born October 1452) but not Edward, Prince of Wales (born October 1453), suggesting that the manuscript may have been written between those dates. A coat of arms and motto on fol. 13v has been ascribed to the Stokes family.[2]

[1] Extracts are printed in Brie 534–80, collated with Lambeth 6, to which references are here made.
[2] See Kingsford, *English Historical Literature*, p. 125 n. 4: "'Silver, a chevron azure with three trefoils silver, within a border gules bezanty'; and the motto, 'Laus Deo honor et gloria'." Kingsford does not, however, give a source for his ascription to the Stokes family.

173. LAMBETH PALACE LIBRARY MS. 6[1]

Heading: Here begynne the cronicles of kynges of Englond sith the tyme that it was first inhabit and of their actes as be dyuers auctores is declared and testyfyed.

Begins: After the begynnyng of this worlde iij^{Ml} CCC & lx yere. In the noble lande of Surry was a myghty kyng and a strong man of body and of gret fame which was clepid Dyoclesian

Contains: Cad, QIL

Omits: "5w" heading (see Remarks on the PV–1436:A below)

Changeover, 1419 to 1422: And þen the king entird into the toune of Roan & hym rested in the castel till the towne was sette in ruyle & in gouernaunce. And aftir þat was Caudebek & oþer garisons þere negh yolden to the kyng.

Of the trety of pees that was betwene kyng Henry of Englond and kyng Charles of Fraunce and of the mariage of kyng Henry the v^{te} and dame Katheryn the kyngis doughtir of Fraunce and so the pees was made & fynysshid.

When king Henry of Englond had geton Roan as before is said the dolfyns ambassatours as it was accorded before with full power to do al thingis as he were þer hymself present comen to the king to the said cite of Roane

End of text to 1422, and narrative from 1437 continuation: And þen a sore & a feruent malady hym toke & fro day to day hym vexid til he dyed in þe castel of Bois de Vycene þe last day of August when þat he had regned ix yere v moneth iiij wekes & iij dayes and aftirward he was brought into Englond ryally & enteryd at Westmynster.

Afftir þe noble & victoriose prynce king Henry the v^{te} regned his son Henry the vj^{te} and began to regne in þe age of ix monethes & xv dayes. [Brie 563/27–35; cf. *"Davies's" Chronicle*, pp. 52–53]

Continuation to 1436 begins: And to Richard erle of Warrewik was comittid þe kipyng of hym [Brie 563/35–564/1]
Continuation to 1436 ends: & to shippe at Sandwich wher-as lay redy in þe hauen iij^C sailes to abyde his comyng. [Brie 584/16–17]

Remarks: This text is often given the name the "St. Albans Chronicle" (the text is headed "The Cronicle of St Albans" in a sixteenth-century hand), but there is no apparent connection with either that abbey or the town.

The manuscript is illustrated throughout with magnificent paintings, probably by a Flemish artist (though James suspects two artists). A number of notes survive, written in English in the lower margins, that give directions to the illustrator concerning the subjects to be illustrated.

The arms in a shield incorporated into the bottom border on fol. 1 have been associated with those of the descendants of William Purchas, mercer, city chamberlain of London from 1484 to 1492, alderman from 1492 to 1502, sheriff in 1492–93, and mayor in 1497–98; he died in 1503.[2]

---

[1] See James, *Descriptive Catalogue . . . Lambeth Palace*, pp. 15–18; Eric G. Millar, "Les principaux manuscrits à peintures du Lambeth Palace à Londres," *Bulletin de la société française de réproductions des manuscrits à peintures* 9 (1925): 15–19 and plate 44. The end of the continuation to 1436, missing in the previous text, is printed in Brie 581–84.

[2] See Millar, "Les principaux manuscrits," p. 16 n. 1. See also John W. Papworth, *An Alphabetical Dictionary of Coats of Arms . . . Forming an Extensive Ordinary of British Armorials* (1874; rpt. London, 1961), p. 795 ("Arg. a lion ramp. sa. over all on a fess az. three bezants. PURCHAS, co. York."; and Meale, "Patrons, Buyers and Owners," pp. 206, 226–27 n. 38. On Purchas, see Alfred B. Beaven, *The Aldermen of the City of London Temp. Henry III–1908/1912*, 2 vols. (London, 1908, 1913), 1: 101, 138; 2: lxi, lxiv, 18. A selection of the illustrations has been made available separately as a slide set in the series "Masterpieces of Mediaeval Art" (London: World Microfilms).

Remarks on the PV–1436:A

The PV–1436:A is an elaborate, well-executed compilation that uses two types of *Brut* text derived from either independent manuscripts or a manuscript in which the two types were already combined, as well as a number of supplementary sources.[1] Almost uniquely among the English texts (cf. the PV–1437:B), it begins with the version of the Albina narrative found in the Anglo-Norman *Des Grantz Geanz* and the Latin *Brut*, although details and language from the Middle English *Brut* text are introduced. As in the latter,

Dioclisian is named king of Syria rather than Greece, and he is said to have thirty-three daughters. However, in accordance with the Anglo-Norman version, the youngest daughter reveals her sisters' murderous plot against their husbands, who thus survive. The thirty-two unrepentant sisters are exiled and arrive in Albion, where the details of their *modus vivendi* are described. The devil impregnates the women, whose children then lie with their mothers and beget sons and daughters of great stature. These and, in turn, their incestuous offspring constitute the race of giants whom Brutus will destroy.[2]

Details are also introduced from the *Short English Metrical Chronicle* that correspond to details in the EV groups borrowed from the same source, though the first of these occurs at a different point. The giants' mode of existence is described (after the account of their generation in the Albina story) as follows:

> This geauntes lyued on wilde dere and on herbes and rotes and drank watir and mylk of rugh shep and gete and of theire here they made hem sclaueyns as pelgrymes vsen. [Lambeth 6; cf. pp. 184–85 above]

A second detail occurs later, at the same point as in the EV, when Brutus mocks Coryn's initial lack of success in wrestling Gogmagog:

> Then Brut said to Corineus thes wordes: "Corineus and þe worde spryng of the how you ert thus put to the wurse al thy worship is lost for that day was neuer seyne that thou was thus put to þe wurse as thou ert now here and yf Heruburgh thy loue it wist she wolde neuer loue the aftir this tyme." [Lambeth 6; cf. Zettl, ed., *Metrical Chron.*, p. 3, line 65–p. 4, line 79 (see pp. 186–87 above), and the readings in the EV groups on pp. 186, 191, 193–94 above]

The blend of wording in this passage suggests that the compiler was using both an EV text and the *Short English Metrical Chronicle*.

The subsequent text continues to use the *Brut* as its primary framework, combined with material adapted from Langtoft's *Chronicle*, Geoffrey of Monmouth's *Historia Regum Britannie* (for example, Latin verses, the thirty-three kings chapter, Merlin's Latin prophecies to Vortiger), the *Short English Metrical Chronicle* (for example, the building of the hot baths at Bath), and other subsidiary sources.[3] A number of Latin verses occur in Harley 53 only (for example, at the start of the text, before the accession of Lucy, after Gurmond's expedition to France, and at the beginning of the section on Anglo-Saxon history).

At the end of the Cadwallader episode the compiler comments on sources, noting William of Malmesbury, Henry of Huntingdon, Peter Langtoft, and "the bok of Latyn" (Geoffrey's *Historia*).

The subsequent text to the death of Edward I in 1307 is a combination, to varying degrees in different sections, of the *Brut* and material adapted from some version of Langtoft's *Chronicle* (which ends in 1307), with the addition of numerous interpolations.[4] Henceforth the *Brut* forms the framework for the narrative, but with many interesting additions and alterations in every reign.

The text from 1419 to a point just after the beginning of the reign of Henry VI is based on the PV–1437:A, though the compiler may also have borrowed some details for the text before 1419.[5] However, after the first sentence of the continuation from 1422 to 1437 the compiler switches to a continuation that seems to be original, though its general shape may have been influenced by the 1422 to 1437 continuation. It concentrates heavily on events in Flanders and may, therefore, reflect personal involvement in those events. Lambeth 6, which carries the narrative beyond the imperfect conclusion of BL Harley 53, contains a long mocking song against the Flemings (Brie 582/18–584/10).

It is possible that Lambeth 6 was directly based on BL Harley 53 or that both manuscripts were derived from a common exemplar. A number of the Latin verses found in the latter are omitted from the Lambeth text; similarly some mocking lines of verse in the Halidon Hill chapter have been left out, though a space has been left for them for a later insertion, probably in red, that was not executed. In general, the text of Harley 53 preserves better the wording of the identifiable sources than does that of Lambeth 6.

---

[1] See Brie, *Geschichte und Quellen*, pp. 104–109, for an analysis based on BL Harley 53. Sections from the post-Conquest narrative, including several of the interpolations, are printed in Brie 534–84.
[2] Cf. the abbreviated Anglo-Norman text in Brereton, ed., *Des Grantz Geanz*, reproduced in Carley and Crick, "Constructing Albion's Past," pp. 92–112 (even pages).
[3] Cf. Kennedy, *Manual*, p. 2632.
[4] Some of the material for the extended account of Thomas Becket may have been based on "þe bok of his lyf which is not littill" (Lambeth 6) to which the reader is referred for further information.
[5] See Kingsford, *English Historical Literature*, pp. 123–24.

The Peculiar Version to 1437: Group B (PV–1437:B)
This group is most immediately associated with texts of the Latin *Brut* and is related to, though not directly associated with, the PV–1437:A. There has been some uncertainty whether this group should in fact be truly considered a *Brut*, since it is not directly derived from the other English texts, and it is included here under the "extended family" concept (see the remarks on the group below).[1] The group is formed of MSS. Columbia Plimpton 261, Holkham 669, and Bodl. Ashmole 791.

---

[1] Brie, *Geschichte und Quellen*, p. 100, describes Holkham 669 as a translation from a Latin chronicle, of which BL Lansdowne 212 is an example, that is not directly connected to the *Brut*. Later, discussing other Latin manuscripts similar in type to Lansdowne 212 (though he does not note the connection), Brie mistakenly asserts that their Albina text "has nothing to do with our *Brut*" (p. 128). Kennedy, *Manual*, pp. 2638–40, classifies the manuscripts of the English group as a separate chronicle from the main *Brut*, though he remarks, correctly, that "Matheson . . . would presumably classify these in his fourth category of miscellaneous versions of the *Brut*" (p. 2639).

174. COLUMBIA UNIVERSITY LIBRARY MS. PLIMPTON 261

Heading: Here begynnyth þe New Croniclis compendiusli ydrawe of þe gestis of kyngis of Ingelond wiþ oþir notable and meruelose þyngis þat happed & fortuned in ther tymes from þe firste kyng Brute þat cam in to þis land in þe yere from þe begynnyng of þe world ijM^l CCC lxxx to þe xiiij [x *rubbed or partially erased*] yere of kyng Harry þe sixte anno [domini 1426 *add. in marg. by another hand*]

Begins: The reme of Brytan þat now is ycallid Inglond at þe firste namynge þerof was ycalled Albion. But for what cause and whi hit was so ycalled almoost no cronicle maketh mencyoun. Neuer-þe-lasse hitt is founde in a certayn story þow hit be not of greet auctorite þat aboute þe yere from þe makyng of the worlde M^{l}M^l ix^C iiij^{xx} xviij in Greke-land þer was a my3ti kyng hauyng þe lordschipp aboue all oþir kyngis a man of greet stature hauyng a wiffe of þe same makyng of þe whiche he begate xxx dou3ters of þe same stature of þe whiche þe eldist was ycallid Albyna

Contains: Cad, heptarchy material after Cad

Omits: QIL, "5w" heading (see Remarks on the PV–1437:B below)

Changeover, 1419 to 1422: Then after long hongre þe cytezens dredyng to dye for hongre and hauyng noon hope of socour putt them in þe kyngys grace and yelded vp þe town; þis seege endured from þe begynnyng of August to þe begynnyng of Ianuar. And after þat þey had Roon þey had soon þe castell of Cawdebeke & as meny as were in Roon. Then Charlis and þe dolphyns messangers com to Roon to þe kyng

Changeover, 1422 to 1437: grete sikenes toke hym and euery day encresyd vnto þe tyme þat he was brouȝte to his deth. And so he yelded his sowle to God þe laste day of August in þe castell of Boys Vyncent besyde Paryse when he had regnyd ix yere v monthes iij wekys and iij days. And he is yberyed att Westmyster att whoos deth was kyng Charlys and þe ij quenys of Ingelond & o Fraunce.

Harry þe vj þe sone of þe noble kyng Harry þe v ybore att Wyndesore in þe feeste of Seynt Nycholas beyng of ix monthis and xv days of age on Seynt Leonarde-is day toke þe gouernaunce of þe reme.

Ends: as he splaide hymself to bedward and for noyse of traytors þat he herde talkyng in a corner fled in to an howse of esement hauyng on but oonly hys scherte and his breche he was yslayn of a Scotte ycalled Wylliam Grame. And as hitt was seide he had vnto xxx woundes in his body where-of vij were deth woundes. And for the playn euydence here-of a legate of þe popis beyng þat tyme in Scotlond as hit was seyde bare þe kyngis scherte wyth hym and schewed hitt to þe pope. &c.

Colophon: Explicit liber Cronicorum. Quod Ricardus Rede.

Remarks: The attribution in the colophon to "Ricardus Rede" corresponds to a similar attribution in Bodl. MS. Rawlinson C.398, a copy of the Latin *Brut* from which the PV–1437:B was translated (see p. 46).

175. HOLKHAM HALL MS. 669

Heading: Here begynnythe the Newe Cronuclys compendyusly idrawe of the gestys of kynges of Ynglond with meny other notable & meruelowse þyngys þat happyd and fortunyd in þer tymys from þe first kyng Brute þat cam ynto þis land þe yere from þe begynnynge of þe worlde ijM^l CCC iiij^{xx} x to þe xiiij yere of kyng Harry þe sexte.

Begins: The reme of Bretayne þat nowe ys callyd Ynglond at þe first namyng þerof was callyd Albyon

Contains: Cad, heptarchy material after Cad

Omits: QIL, "5w" heading (see Remarks on the PV–1437:B below)

Changeover, 1419 to 1422: Than after long hunger þe cytezens dredyng to dye for hunger & hauyng noon hope of socor put þem yn þe kyngys grace & yelded vpp þe town. Thys sege enduryd from þe begynnyng of Auguste [þey *del.*] to þe begynnyng of Ianuary & after þat þey had Roon þey had soon þe castell of Cawdebeke & as meny as wer ny Roon. Than Charlys & þe dolphyns massangers com to Roon to þe kyng

Changeover, 1422 to 1437: grete sykenesse toke hym and euery day encresyd vnto þe tyme þat he was y-[brw3 *del.*]brow3th to hys deth. And so he yeldyd hys sowle to God þe laste day of August yn þe castell of Boys Vyncent besyde Parys whan he had reynyd ix yer v monthys iij wekys iij dayes. And he ys yberyed att Westemester att whoys deþ was kyng Charlys þe ij quenys of Inglond & of Fraunce.

Herry þe vj þe son of þe nobyll kyng Herry þe v ybore att Wyndesore yn þe feste of Seynt Nycholas beyng of ix monthys & xv dayes of age on Seynt Leonardes day toke þe gouernaunce of þe reme.

Ends: as he splayed hymselfe to bedde-warde and for noyse of traytors þat he herd talkyng yn a corner fled ynto an howse of esement hauyng on but onely hys scherte and his breche he was yslayn of a Scotte ycalled Willyam Grame. And as hit was seyde he had onto a xxx woundys yn hys body where-of vij were deþ woundys. And for a playn euydence herof a legate of þe popys beyng þat tyme yn Scottelond as hit was seyde bare þe kyngys scherte wiþ hym and schewyd hyt to the pope.

176. BODLEIAN MS. ASHMOLE 791[1]

Begins imperfectly during genealogy of Brutus (see below): [Ju]piteres sone ybegetene of Electra þe whiche Dardanus by strengþe of armys gate þat regioun and reynyde fyrste þere-in.

Contains: Cad, heptarchy material after Cad

Omits: QIL, "5w" heading (see Remarks on the PV–1437:B below)

Changeover, 1419 to 1422: Then after longe hungure þe cytezens dredynge to dye for hungure & hauynge noo hope of socoure putt þem in þe kyngys grace and yeldyd vppe þe towne. Þys sege enduryd from þe begynnynge of Auguste to þe begynnynge of Ianuarye. And after þat þey had Roon þey had soone þe castelle of Cawdebeke & as mony as were ny3e Roon. Þan Charelys & þe dolphyns messangeres come to Roone to þe kynge

Changeover, 1422 to 1437: grete sykenes toke him & euery daye encresyd vnto þe tyme þat he was brou3te to his deþe. And so he yeldyd his soule to God þe last daye of Auguste in þe castelle of Boyes Vyncente besyde Paryse when he had reynyd ix yere v moneþys iiij wekys & iij dayes & he ys beryed atte Westemynster. Atte whose deþe was kynge Charelys and þe ij quenes of Inglond and of Fraunce.

Herry þe vj þe son of þe noble kynge Herry þe v bore atte Wyndesoure in þe feste of Seynte Nicholas beynge of ix moneþys & xv dayes of age and on Seynte Leonardys daye toke þe gouernaunce of þe reme.

Ends on fol. 59v: as he spayde hymselfe to bedde-warde and for þe noyse of traytoures þat he herde talkynge in a corner fledde into an house of esemente havyng on hym but onely hys scherte & hys breche he was sleyne of a Scotte callyd Wyllyam Grame. And as it was seyde he hadde vnto a xxx woundys in his body wherof vij were deþe woundes. And for þe pleyn euydence herof a legate of þe poopys beynge þat tyme in Scottelande as it was seyde bare þe kyngys scherte wyþ hym & schewyd it to þe poope.

Remarks: The *Brut* text is followed on fols. 60–84v by the English translation of Martinus Polonus's *Chronicle of Popes and Emperors*.[2]

---

[1] Brief extracts from this manuscript, transcribed in 1672, are found in Bodleian Ashmole 1139.iv.2, fol. 80r–80v.

[2] See Kennedy, *Manual*, pp. 2663–64, 2879–80; Embree, ed., *The Chronicles of Rome* (forthcoming). This work is also found in conjunction with a *Brut* text in CUL Ee.4.31 (see item 77).

Remarks on the PV–1437:B

The PV–1437:B, entitled the "New Croniclis," is a fairly close and accurate translation of a text of the longer class of the second version of the Latin *Brut*, some texts of which use the title "Nova Cronica," and thus shares the features found in the Latin compilation (see pp. 44–46). The basis for the English text must have resembled closely the texts in MSS. Corpus Christi College, Cambridge, 311; Bodleian Rawlinson B.169; and St. John's College, Oxford, 78.

Since the Latin text may have been partially modeled on the PV–1437:A in its narrative to 1377 and was based on that group for its narrative from 1377 to 1437, there are many points of similarity between the PV–1437:B and the PV–1437:A, although the two groups are not directly related.

As in the Latin text and the PV–1437:A, the narrative for the reign of

Edward III is abbreviated. The "5w" heading does not occur; the battle of Halidon Hill and the changeover from 1333 to 1377 appear as follows:

> The vij yere kyng Edward beseged and toke þe town of Berwyke a greet batayle furste ydon bytwyxte hym and þe Scottis on Halydon Hylle wher of þe Scottis were yslayn viij erls M¹ and CCC horsemen and of þe comynte xxxv M¹. And þat hitt is mervayle to sey on the Englisch party were slayn but oon kny3th oon squyer and xij fotemen. The xij yere kyng Edward went into Flaunders and associatyd to hym Bauarrus þe emperoure.

The Peculiar Version to 1437: Group C (PV–1437:C)

177. INNER TEMPLE LIBRARY, PETYT MS. 511, VOL. XI¹
Heading on fol. 66: Here men mowe knowe how Engelonde firste was callid Albion and thorowe whom it hadde the name of Albion.
Begins: In the noble londe lof [*sic*] Surrye
Omits: Cad, QIL, "5w" heading
Changeover, 1333 to 1377: without eny calangynge of any man. Deo Gracias.

> How kinge Edwarde chalangid firste þe kingdome of Fraunce and how he made vij duchies of vij erldomes.

> In the yere of our lord M¹ CCC xxxvij and þe xij yere of kinge Edwardes regne [cf. Brie 286/8–9 and 292/26–31]

Changeover, 1419 exemplar to Latin Brut *exemplar*: And whan this kinge Herry þe iiij^th had regned xiij yere and more he deied at Westmyster and is buried at Criste Churche in Caunturbury.

> How kinge Herry the v regned the whiche was a noble conquerour and a victorious knyght in bataile to whom ffortune was euer frendely and gate his righful enherytaunce in Fraunce with dynte of swerde þat alle his enmyes of him had drede and fere. Alas for his deth for he regned but ix yere and an halfe.

> And aftir the deth of kinge Herry the iiij^th regned his sone Herry the vth prince of Walis duke of Cornewale and erle of Chester þat was bore at Monmothe in Walys. And in the xx day of þe moneth of Marche he was

crowned at Westmyster. And in þe firste yere of his regne ther aros heretikes and lollardes purposynge to sle the kinge and to destroie the clergye of Engelonde. [cf. Brie 372/16–33, Kingsford, *English Historical Literature*, p. 315, and Brie 373/1–6, 18–21, Kingsford, *English Historical Literature*, p. 316]

Changeover, 1419 to 1437: And þere were nombred in þe cite at the firste comynge of þe sege of men women and children CCCCM^l of the whiche durynge the sege the[r] deied in þe same cite for hungur lM^l. And þe sege dured from the bigynnynge of Auguste til Ianuar next folowynge and tho it was yolde to the kynge. And aftir he gate Gisours with the castell and þe towne of Seynt Denyse

Changeover, 1422 to 1437: This gloriouse kinge and conquerour Herry the vth in alle batailles and iorneyes that he had to done God shewid hym gret grace for in alle he had the victory. And whanne he had regned ix yere v monthes iiij wekis and iij daies a gret infirmyte fille vpon him with whiche he deied at Boyez de Vyncent in Fraunce byside Paris þe last day saf oon of August and from thens he was caried and is wurshipfully buried at Westmynster. On whos soule God haue mercye.

How kinge Herry the vj biganne to regne. Alas þe sorow þat fille in his daies in the reme of Engelonde for so moche shedynge of blood and slaughter of lordis was neuer seyne in this londes bi no kinges regne sith Brute come firste into þis londe of Albion and callid it Breteyne aftir his owne name.

And aftir the deth of kinge Herry the vth regned his sone Herry the vj^{te} whiche was bore at Wyndesore in þe feste of Seynte Nicholas the bisshop. And whanne he was viij monthis iiij wokis and iij daies of age he bigan to regne.

Ends: As þe kinge was goynge to his bed beynge in his sherte þe said William Grame and oþer·hauynge in her handis spadis and fille vppon her kinge. And he for socoure fled out of his chambur for socour into a priuy sege and þer thei cursidly slowe him. And as it was seid the kinge had xxx woundes vpon him where-offe were vij dedly. In witnesse of þe which þe popis legate beynge in Scotlonde þat tyme bare þe kinges shirte with hym to Rome to þe pope. And so Englishmen ben moch bounde to yelde presynge laude and wurship to almyghty God the whiche of his infynyte godenesse full ofte tymes tho enemyes and peple that ar euell disposid he puttith hem vndir fote. [infynyte ... fote *repeated, with spelling variations, by another hand*]

Remarks: The text is a fusion of texts from two separate groups of the English *Brut* (which appears at the same time to have been influenced by texts from other groups), the ending of which is a translation from one type of the Latin *Brut* ending in 1437.

There are no EV/AV details in the prologue, but the chapter normally listing the kings of Britain may have been influenced by a text of the AV–1419:A(a) (cf. p. 208):

> How xxxiij kingis regned in pees eche aftir other aftir the deth of Hesidour. Capitulo xxxiij°.

> Aftir the deth of Hesidour regned xxxiij kinges eche aftir othir whos names ben expressid opinly in oþer places but the last of them alle was callyd Ely þe whiche regned but vij monthis. And this Ely had iij sones Lud Cassibulanne & Gemyoun.

The end of the passage on Engist's heptarchy is reminiscent of MSS. BL Harley 24 and Addit. 12030 of the EV–1419:A (see p. 187): "the vij kinge had Oxfordshire Gloucestre-shire Wurcestire-shire and Warwike-shire."

There is a curious break in the text after the death of Arthur that is probably of no greater significance than a missing leaf or two but which happens to resemble the majority of AV texts at this point, for instead of Constantine following Arthur, there seems to have been the loss of a few chapters and, as it stands, Conan follows:

> [fol. 93, foot] but certis this is the prophicie of Merleyn he sayd that his deth schulld be douteus and he said soth for men were not wheder he lyueth or dede. Arthur [fol. 94] moche honour and solempnite.

> Hou kyng [Arthur *del.*] Conan regnid in grete pride and slowe his vncles ij sonnes.

> After this Curan regnyd Conan [cf. Brie 90/22–26 and 92/29–31]

The combination of features, the end of the narrative to 1333, and the break in the narrative at the beginning of the continuation to 1377 suggest that the first part of the text has been based on a CV–1333 text and shortened to some extent by the compiler.

After 1333, the text has been taken from a text ending in 1419, although abbreviation continues throughout, especially from the beginning of Richard

II's reign on fol. 159v. This section of the narrative ends with the death of Henry IV (quoted above).

From the accession of Henry V (1413) to the murder of James I of Scotland (1437), the narrative corresponds to that found in those manuscripts of the Latin *Brut* ending in 1437 that contain the brief account of the reign of Henry V.[2] It is particularly, though not exclusively, close to the text of BL Cotton Domitian iv. The compiler appears to have translated his account from Latin, though the converse possibility should not be discounted that he took it from an English text that formed the basis for the Latin text (see further pp. 43, 46, 293). The chapter headings and their editorial apostrophes seem to be the compiler's personal contributions; that for Henry VI (quoted above) must date the compilation to the reign of Edward IV.

---

[1] See J. Conway Davies, *Catalogue of Manuscripts in the Library of the Inner Temple*, 2 vols. (Oxford, 1972), 1: 222–24. The manuscript has mid-sixteenth-century connections with Carnarvonshire, as marginal notes attest.
[2] See Kingsford, *English Historical Literature*, pp. 310–23.

The Peculiar Version to 1479/82 (PV–1479/82)

178. LAMBETH PALACE LIBRARY MS. 84[1]
Begins: In the noble land of Surre ther was a noble kyng and myhty and a worthy lord of name and a man of gret renoun
Contains: Cad, QIL, "5w" heading
Text to 1419 ends: And than þe kyng entryd ynto þe cite & restyd hym in þe castell tyl þe cite was sette in rewle & good gouernaunce.
Text from 1419 to ?1422 begins: And aftyr þat Roan was wonne Deepe & many oþer tounes in Baas Normandy gaf them ouer withoute strooke or syege [cf. Caxton, *Liber ultimus*, leaf cccix verso]
Text to ?1422 breaks off on fol. 200v: ffor euyr whan they of Syon rest they of þe Chartrehous begyn theyr servyce. And in lyke [wyse whanne *catchwords*]
Continuation to 1479/82 begins on fol. 201: [A]nd yn þe yer of our lorde M¹ CCCC & xxiij on þe last day of August Herry of Wyndelysore þe sone of Herry þe fyfthe began to reyne whan he was but ix monthis of age [Brie 598/32–599/1]
Continuation ends: & aftyr þat cam a gret dethe of pestilence þat lastyd iij

yer & peple dyed myhtely in euery p[l]ace man woman & chylde on whois soulys God haue mercy. Amen. [Brie 604/9–12]

Remarks: This elaborate expanded version of the *Brut* is the anonymous compiler's holograph copy, as the physical condition of the manuscript shows. The text fills not only the normal page, but is found written between the normal lines, in the margins, and in small notes written in the same hand that are inserted between the pages.

The manuscript was written in two stages at different times. The first stage was based on a *Brut* text ending in 1419, much expanded by the compiler by the insertion of material from a variety of historical and literary works. He seems also to have used a PV–1422 text, since a number of interpolated stories occur at points similar to where they occur in that group. Historical interpolations come from the compiler's own translation of sections of Higden's *Polychronicon* and William of Malmesbury's *Historia Regum Anglorum*; literary adaptations are based on the *Havelok* and *Arthur and Merlin* romances, Chaucer and Gower's versions of the Constance story, saints' lives such as Osbert's life of Dunstan, Lydgate's "Legend of St. Austin at Compton," and other literary works. A number of stories appear to be taken from works now lost.

At some point soon after the publication of Caxton's edition of the *Polychronicon* in 1482, the compiler thoroughly revised his book by using the printed edition as the source for further interpolations, added in the margins or on interleaved slips or written over original text that he washed out.

The original text may have ended on fol. 199 with the (r&g) ending, though the compiler may have added a few lines to the bottom of the page. Text at the foot of fol. 199 seems to have been erased, and as it stands the text continues with material copied from Caxton's *Liber ultimus* to the *Polychronicon*. This material breaks off with catchwords at the foot of fol. 200v, before the death of Henry V, and is now immediately followed by an apparently unique continuation that begins with the accession of Henry VI (see above). The Caxton continuation is written in a smaller hand than what precedes and follows it.

The unique continuation, which contains a ballad mocking the Flemish, takes the narrative first to Edward IV's French expedition of 1475 and then to what must be the plague of 1479.[2] Since the text notes that this "pestilence" lasted for three years, at least the final entries must have been written in or after 1482. However, a list of Edward IV's children (Brie 603/16–18) within the narrative on fol. 202v, the last page of the text, suggests that the date of writing of that section of the text was 1478–79.³ A possible explanation for this apparently contradictory chronological evidence is that the continuation originally ended after Edward IV's French expedition and that the concluding entries, rather vague in content, were added when the compiler revised the volume in or soon after 1482.

---

¹ See Matheson, "Printer and Scribe," pp. 607–609, and Lister M. Matheson, "The Arthurian Stories of Lambeth Palace Library MS 84," *Arthurian Literature V*, ed. Richard Barber (Cambridge, 1985), pp. 70–91; for full details of the compilation process and the interpolated material, see my *Literature and History in Late Medieval England: The Evidence of Lambeth Palace Library MS. 84* (in progress). Extracts from both stages of composition are printed in Brie 585–604, although he did not realize that the *Polychronicon* additions represented a later stage; for the Havelok narrative, see also Brie, "Zum Fortleben der Havelok-Sage," pp. 366–71.
² See Robert S. Gottfried, *Epidemic Disease in Fifteenth-Century England* (New Brunswick, 1978), pp. 44–45, 49–50.
³ See Kingsford, *English Historical Literature*, p. 125; the list includes George (born in 1478, died in March 1479) but not Catherine (born towards the end of 1479) or Bridget (born in 1480); Richard is called duke of York and Norfolk, having received the latter title in February 1478.

Sections of Longer *Brut* Texts

The Peculiar Version to 1431 (PV–1431)
The Peculiar Version to 1422: Group C (PV–1422:C)

The PV–1431 consists of closely related continuations, set down in civic chronicle form, to otherwise different *Brut* texts that are found in MSS. BL Egerton 650(2) and Bodl. Rawlinson B.173(2); Bodl. MS. Rawlinson B.166, now incomplete, may also have originally contained some version of this continuation. The continuation from 1419 to 1422 found in Pennsylvania State MS. PS. V–3A(2) is directly derived from the PV–1431 and is thus considered here.

179. BL MS. EGERTON 650(2)¹
Continuation begins on fol. 111v: In þat same yere þe Kyng lay at þe sege of Roon [Brie 444/1]
Ends on fol. 114v: And left þer þe Duke of Glaucestre, Leuetenaunte. Nicholas Watton maior. M. cccc. xxxi. [Brie 451/38–40]

Remarks: A folio has been lost between fols. 113 and 114, as comparison with the next manuscript shows (see Brie 449/34–35, 452/6–453/38). A final folio may also have been lost that would have brought the text to the same ending point as that found in the following manuscript.

---

[1] For (1), see item 29. The continuation is printed in Brie 444–51, whence it is quoted here.

180. BODLEIAN MS. RAWLINSON B.173(2)[1]

Continuation begins imperfectly on fol. 222: And in that yere oure kyng and dame Katerin his quene [cf. Brie 445/3]

Ends: and in that yere come to London the ambassiatours of Spayne to trete of pees. [Brie 455/14–15]

Remarks: The continuation, which follows immediately on the incomplete 1419(men) text, begins imperfectly since the manuscript has lost some leaves that contained the end of the 1419 text and the beginning of the continuation.

The manuscript is written in two hands of similar dialectal provenance, namely West Herefordshire, from close to the Welsh border.[2]

---

[1] For (1), see item 30. The text from 1422 to 1431 is printed in Brie 452–55, whence it is quoted here.
[2] See p. 102.

181. PENNSYLVANIA STATE UNIVERSITY MS. PS. V–3A(2)[1]

Continuation beyond 1419 begins on fol. 196: In the vij^{te} yere of þe same king lay atte sege of Roan. And the xvij day of Ianure it was yolden to oure king. And the tithinges come to London the vj day of Feuerer. And then þe duke of Bedford lieutenaunt of Englond and the chaunceler and mony other bisshopes and the mayre and shiriefes with the aldermen and al the comuners of the cite made a general procession ffrom Poules to Westmynster [cf. Brie 444/1–6]

Continuation to 1422 ends: And in the same yere died king Henre the v^{te} in Fraunce vpon the euen of the decollacion of Seint Iohn the Baptist. And than was his sone Henre made king. [cf. Brie 448/35–37]

Remarks: The continuation follows the 1419(men) ending without break and in the same hand.

---

[1] For (1), see item 32.

Remarks on the PV–1431 and the PV–1422:C
The continuations in BL Egerton 650 and Bodl. Rawlinson B.173 are very closely related,[1] as the beginning of the entry for 1429/30 shows:

The fi[f] day of Nouember, þe Kyng, wyth hys lordys, ryally rode frome Kyngstone ouer London Bryge, And so forth Fenchyrche strete, evyn vn-to the Toure, to hys mete. And þe Maire and þe Aldermen, all in Scarlete hodys, rode to mete the Kyng, And so rode forth with hym to þe Toure The Seterday next aftre; wher-of were þe Erle of Denshyre, þe Lord Spencer sone, the Erle of Warwyk, þe Lord Beamounde. And aftre none, þe Kyng, in a riall araye, with all hys lordys Ryally a-rayed in cloth of gold for þe most part, with the said xxiiij newe knyghtes all in blew, the prestes rode a-fore þe Kyng ij and ij, from þe Toure to Westmynstre. [BL Egerton 650: Brie 450/34–451/7]	The Friday, the iij^{de} day of Nouember, the King with his lordes, Rialli rode fro Kingeston ouer London Brige, And so forth Fanchirch strete, even to the Toure, to his mete. And the Maire and the Aldermen, all in scarlet hodes, Rode to mete the King, and rode forth with him to the Toure. the Saturday next after, the King made xxxiij knightes of the Bath, in the Toure of London; wherof were the Erle of Deuenysshshire, the Lorde Spencers sonne, the Erle of Warrewike, the Lorde Beaumond. and after none, the King, in riall aray, with all his lordes rialli arayed in clothes of golde for the most partie, with the saide xxxiij knightes all in blewe like prestes, rode a-fore the King ij and ij fro the Toure to Westminster. [Bodl. Rawlinson B.173: Brie 454/26–36]

The annual entries are in typical civic chronicle "note" form in both manuscripts, and the continuations are probably copied from the same exemplar. This exemplar may have been an independent London chronicle, or it may have been a continuation to the basic *Brut* text in Bodl. Rawlinson B.166, a now imperfect text of the CV–1419(men):A that agrees very well with the first part of the text of BL Egerton 650.[2] The Egerton text preserves a number of entries of local London interest that have been omitted from the text of Bodl. Rawlinson B.173.

The continuation from 1419 to 1422 in Pennsylvania State PS. V–3A(2) is an adaptation of part of the narrative represented in civic chronicle format in Egerton 650 and Rawlinson B.173 to the continuous narrative form typical of the *Brut*. Thus the names of the mayors and sheriffs are omitted. The initial transition is, however, awkwardly done (see the text above). The adaptor appears to have decided consciously to end the narrative in 1422 with the natural stopping-point of the death of Henry V and the accession of Henry VI.

---

[1] See McLaren, "Textual Transmission," p. 60.
[2] See pp. 102, 104. Kennedy, *Manual*, p. 2845, lists these sections of texts under London chronicles.

Very Brief Works Based on the *Brut*

The Peculiar Version to 1307 (PV–1307)

182. NLW MS. PENIARTH 343A[1]

Heading: Afore yat I will speake of Brute yt shalbe shewed how ye lond of Inglond was first named Albion & by what encheson yt so was named.

Begins: Off the noble lond of Surrye ther was a royal kyng & mightye & a man of greate renome yat called was Dioclesian

Contains: Cad

Ends on p. 58: Edward ye firste xxxii yeare & lyethe at Westminster.

Remarks: This text is a sixteenth- or seventeeth-century abstract of a *Brut* text and is probably the original compilation. The wording of the heading suggests that the source may have been one of the early printed editions to 1461 (cf. items 85, 204, 206, 207).

In the chapter on the British kings, the entries are set out in tabular form and only the name of the appropriate king and the length of his reign are given, for example, "Eldagan 15 Claten 12."

Constantine reigns after Arthur, and the text finally ends up by simply noting the names of the kings, the length of their individual reigns, and the place of their burial, as on page 45: "William Rouse his sonne xiij yere & is at Westminster."

After this reign follows an inserted passage on pages 45–57 entitled "De Natiuitate Domini nostri Ihesu Cristi" before the truncated *Brut* text recommences and ends with Edward I. Pages 59–60 contain a list of popes from Peter to Benedict, with notes on their reigns.

On the first page of the manuscript is the signature of "William White," who was probably the scribe, compiler, and owner of the manuscript.

---

[1] See Marx, "Middle English Manuscripts," pp. 361–62.

The Peculiar Version to 1400 (PV–1400)

183. LAMBETH PALACE LIBRARY MS. 306[1]
Heading: Cronycullys of Englonde.
Begins: In the noble londe off Surrye was some tyme a grete kynge and a myghty that was named Dioclesyan and he was the moste worthiest kynge than levinge on erthe as the story seythe. [Gairdner, ed., *Chronicles*, p. 1]
Contains: Cad (abbreviated)
Omits: QIL (see below), "5w" heading (see below)
Ends on fol. 17v: And thes lordes wiste wele that they were bewrayed and fled awaye and after they were taken and put to dethe. [Gairdner, ed., *Chronicles*, p. 28; cf. Brie 361/3–4ff.]

Remarks: The text, which ends in the first year of Henry IV, is extremely abbreviated, and the omission of Queen Isabella's letter and the "5w" heading may not be significant. It is based on a CV text, probably ending in 1419, with the addition of some chronological and other minor details. Unless it is a fair copy, the *Brut* text is not original to this manuscript, as scribal errors show.[2]

The *Brut* text is immediately followed, in the same hand, by Lydgate's verses on the kings of England, ending with Henry VI (who is said to have had reigned almost thirty-nine years) and by a chronicle of London from 1189 to 1465.[3]

[1] The text of the *Brut*, the version of Lydgate's verses on the kings of Englond, the London chronicle, and various historical memoranda (many by John Stow) are printed in James Gairdner, ed., *Three Fifteenth-Century Chronicles*, Camden Society n.s. 28 (1880), pp. 1–28 (*Brut* text), 28–147; the first three items form a booklet in the same fifteenth-century hand. For a description of the numerous other fifteenth- and sixteenth-century items in the manuscript, see James, *Descriptive Catalogue... Lambeth Palace*, pp. 421–26. See also Maldwyn Mills, ed., *Lybeaus Desconus*, EETS o.s. 261 (1969), pp. 2–3; Boffey, *Manuscripts of English Courtly Love Lyrics*, p. 21; and Mooney, "Lydgate's 'Kings of England'," pp. 256–63, 277–78.
[2] See, for example, the scribal correction in Gairdner, ed., *Chronicles*, p. 25 note.
[3] See McLaren, "Textual Transmission," pp. 40, 50–52.

The Peculiar Version to 1427 (PV–1427)
This small group consists of MSS. BL Harley 63, Edinburgh 184, and Bibl. Nat. fonds anglais 30.

184. BL MS. HARLEY 63
Heading: How this lond was ffirst called Albyon.
Begins: In the noble land of Surrey
Contains: Cad
Omits: QIL (see Remarks on the PV–1427 below)
Ends: that was oon of the wordieste knyghtes of the world and was buried at Burssham.

185. EDINBURGH UNIVERSITY LIBRARY MS. 184
Heading: How this lande was fyrst called Albyoun.
Begins: In the noble lande of Surrey there was a noble kyng called Dyoclesian which was a grete conquerour
Contains: Cad
Omits: QIL (see below)
Ends: And in the vj^{te} of his regne was the goode erle of Salysbury slayne atte the sege of Orliaunce with a gonne that was oon of the worthiest knyghtes of the world and was beryed at Burssham.

Remarks: Among many others, the folios are missing that might have contained Queen Isabella's letter and would have contained the Halidon Hill chapter.

186. BIBLIOTHÈQUE NATIONALE MS. FONDS ANGLAIS 30[1]
Begins imperfectly on damaged fol. 1: so he desyred of hur and [cf. Brie 8, ca. line 14]
Contains: Cad
Omits: QIL
Ends imperfectly: And he [hade *del.*] made euery archer to hafe a sharp stake afor hym for þer was [cf. Brie 378/7–9]

Remarks: This late fifteenth-century paper manuscript has early connections with Derbyshire, and the earliest known owner was Henry Lowe the Younger of Whittington.

---

[1] See James Simpson, *The Index of Middle English Prose, Handlist VII: A Handlist of Manuscripts Containing Middle English Prose in Parisian Libraries* (Cambridge, 1989), p. 2.

Remarks on the PV–1427
The text to 1419 is extremely abbreviated, but is apparently based on a CV–1419 of some type, to which some additional details have been added. A version of the Guy of Warwick story is found under the reign of Athelstan, and the CV story of Curan is transferred to Havelok to correspond to the popular legend.

Typical of the great shortening of the text is the chapter on the thirty-three British kings:

> The first hight Gorbodian & regned xij yere; Morgan ij yere; Eighnaus vj yere; Idwallon viij yere; Rowghgo xj yere [*etc.*] [Edinburgh 184]

The omission of Queen Isabella's letter may not be significant (cf. Lambeth 306) in view of the extreme abbreviation, which also marks the Halidon Hill passage:

> And they both came & lade sege to Berwyke. And as they lay at the sege þer come downe opon hom all the chyvalry of Scotland that is

to say lxv erles & barons C lx knyghtes ijM^l men of armes lxM^l comyners. And at Halydoun Hyll be syde Berwyke the hostes met & kyng Edward and Bayloyl hade the feld for the Scottes hade no mor fusyoun þat day ageyne the Englyssh men then hath xx shepe ageyne v wolfes for ther wer [*ins.*] slayne bot vij Englysch men and ther wer [*ins.*] slayne of the Scottes xxxvM^l vij^C. And then they of Berwyk did ȝeld vp the towne to kyng Edward. [Bibl. Nat. fonds anglais 30, p. 69; cf. Brie 281/25–286/9, 291/1–4]

Some extra details are added to (or were in the CV exemplar for) the account of the siege of Rouen, and the end of this section of narrative and the beginning of the short continuation to 1427 are as follows:

And there men mowth see childerin soke ther moderes when thei were deid and men layn in the dikes gnawyng grasse and eten childryn. And so ther dide in the dikes many thowsandes. And thei of the cyte were full fayn to yelde vp the cite & to have ther lyves and become the kyngis ligge men and of hym to holde for euer. And after in the vij yere of his regne ther was a trety taken bytwene the said owre kyng and the kyng of Fraunce and it was so acorded that owre kyng sholde wedde dame Kateryne. [BL Harley 63; cf. Brie 391/6ff.]

Texts Containing Brief King-Lists

Under this heading are grouped MSS. Bodl. Digby 196 (two texts), CUL Ff.1.6 (the Findern Manuscript), and Folger Shakespeare Library V.a.198 (1232.3).

These three related manuscripts (and the derivative early printed editions) contain brief lists of kings and reigning queens (primarily the monarch's name and the length of the reign) and other material that could be derived, at least in part, from *Brut* texts. Kennedy, while noting their possible debt to the much longer work, elected to treat these texts as two chronicles separate from the *Brut*; given the wide variety of treatments, often very abbreviated, of the *Brut*, I have chosen to include them here within the extended family of Peculiar Versions of the *Brut* since they may be to some degree abstracted from that source.[1] Such lists are often useful in dating the manuscripts in which they occur.

[1] See Kennedy, *Manual*, p. 2637, and cf. the present writer's review thereof in *Studies in the Age of Chaucer* 13 (1991): 212.

The Peculiar Version to 1396,
with a further text to 1422 (PV–1396/1422)

187. BODLEIAN MS. DIGBY 196[1]

First text begins on fol. 26: Brute come after the makyng of the world to þe lond of Albyon in the tyme þat Hely þe preste of þe law was in þe land of Israel iiijM lxxvij 3ere.

Newe Troye þat now ys cleped London was fownded by þe makyng of Brute after þe begynnyng of þe world iiijM^l C xxiiij 3ere.

Rome was fownded by Remo and Romolo iiijM^l iiij^C iiij^{xx} iiij 3ere.

First text ends on fol. 27: and fro þe incarnacion tyl þe fest of annunciacion of owre lady in þe xx of þe kynge Ricard þe secounde M^l CCC iiij^{xx} xvj 3ere: vjM^l D^C iiij^{xx} xv 3ere.

Second text begins on fol. 156v:
i   the first 3ere of kynge Ricard ii.
ii   the ii 3ere þe lord Latemer slow a squyer at þe shryne of Seynt Edward for þe erle of Dene wycche was prisoner.
iii   the iij 3ere [*ins.*] was þe commyng of þe galeys robbyng and brannyng vppe-on þe lande and tallage of childeren.

Second text ends on fol. 158:
ix   the ix 3ere he cam into Ingeland and crowned hys quene and so went into France a3ene and so he ended at Boys Vyncent and as a Cristen prynce to God passed owte of this wrecched world on whose sowle God have mercy. Amen.

Remarks: The first text is related to the texts in the two following manuscripts and is self-dated to 1396. The brief notices found in the second text could have been derived either from a PV *Brut* text ending in 1422 or from a chronicle of London.

---

[1] See Patrick J. Horner, *The Index of Middle English Prose, Handlist III: A Handlist of Manuscripts Containing Middle English Prose in the Digby Collection, Bodleian Library, Oxford* (Cambridge, 1986), pp. 59–61; Kennedy, *Manual*, p. 2637.

The Peculiar Version to 1436: Group B (PV–1436:B)
The Peculiar Version to 1475 (PV–1475)

188. CAMBRIDGE UNIVERSITY LIBRARY MS. FF.1.6 (THE FINDERN MANUSCRIPT)[1]
Heading on fol. 110: The cronekelys of seyntes & kynges of Yngelond.
Begins: Brute com after þe makyng of þe world into þys [wo *del.*] londe of Albyoun nowe Ynglande iiij^{Ml} lxxvij 3ere.
Ends in 1436 on fol. 113: And fro þe incarnacioun of Ihesu Crist til þe xx [*foll. by blank space*] of kyng Herre vj M^l iiij^C [xl *del.*] xlvj 3ere. And þe sum of all aboueseid vjM^l vj^C xlvj 3ere.

Remarks: After the introductory notice of Brutus are notices of the foundations of London and Rome and the conception and birth of Christ, all dated from the creation of the world. There follow notices of saints and martyrs, especially those of England, and of significant religious events in England dated from the incarnation of Christ, ending with the translation of Thomas Becket in 1220. The text then (fol. 111) returns to Brutus and the succeeding kings of England, generally noting only the relationship of each king to his predecessor and the length of his reign. The CV–1333 order is found for kings "Elfred & Kadwalader... Oswold & Kadwalyn."

The ending date suggests strongly that this section of the manuscript was written "in or immediately before 1446, and could not have been written after 1461."[2] The *terminus ad quem* is implied by the omission of the precise number of years for Henry VI's reign.

The manuscript was possibly compiled at the country seat of the Findern family in south Derbyshire.[3] The dialect of the texts in the manuscript is basically that of Derbyshire, "but with varying degrees of mixture."[4]

---

[1] A facsimile of the full manuscript is published in R. Beadle and A. E. B. Owen, introd., *The Findern Manuscript: Cambridge University Library MS. Ff.1.6* (London, 1977); for a complete list of contents, see pp. xix–xxx therein.
[2] L. F. Casson, ed., *The Romance of Sir Degrevant*, EETS o.s. 221 (1949), p. xii.
[3] For an account of several families associated with the manuscript, see Harris, "Origins and Make-Up of Cambridge University Library MS. Ff.1.6," pp. 302–307; see also George R. Keiser, "MS Rawl. A.393: Another Findern Manuscript," *Transactions of the Cambridge Bibliographical Society* 7 (1980): 445–49.
[4] See *LALME*, 1: 67.

189. FOLGER SHAKESPEARE LIBRARY MS. V.A.198 (1232.3)
Heading on fol. 1 of item 2: Here begynnythe the cronycles of sayntes and of the kyngys of Yngelonde.
Begins: Brute come in to thys londe of Albyon after callyd Bruteyne and now Inglonde ycallyd after the makyng of þe worlde iiijM¹ lxxvij 3ere.
Ends in 1475 on fol. 3v: Harry the vj^te reygnethe [d *add. above second* -e-] xxxix 3ere.
Kyng Edward the iiij^e raynethe [xxij yer *add. in a later hand; orig. left blank*]
The somme fro the begynnyng of þe worlde tyll the xv 3ere of kyng Edward vjM¹ viiC and lxxv [*second* x *over* v].

Remarks: On the page following this chronological list the same scribe begins a series of geographical notes in Latin and chronological entries in English on biblical and English religious and historical affairs. The text begins: "[T]res filij Noy diuuserunt [*sic*] orbem in tres partes post diliuium"; the Latin section ends: "Comitatus sunt in Anglia xxxvj & dj." The English begins: "Fro þe begynnyng of þe worlde vjMl vjC xlj [.. (*two letters, poss. the start of* 3e[re])] Adam lyued in erthe ixC xxxij 3ere"; the text ends: "And in the same 3ere was þe batel of Agyngkorte that ys to say xxv [the x *del.*] day of the monethe of October and A was dominicall letter that 3ere." Many of the entries that pertain to England may have been extracted from a chronicle of London.

The ending of the king-list suggests that the text was written in or soon after 1475.

Remarks on the PV–1396/1422, the PV–1436:B, and the PV–1475
A text of the type of these brief king-lists formed the basis for a series of sixteenth-century printed works, beginning with Richard Pynson's edition of ?1518, "the cronycle of all the kynges names that haue ben in Englande and how many yeres they reygned and how many sayntes & martyrs haue ben in this lande."[1] For his text up to the Norman Conquest, Pynson uses a king-list very similar to those found in the manuscripts described above, to which is then appended Lydgate's verse "Kings of England," supplemented to Henry VII.

Subsequent editions, by a variety of printers, include additional material such as "the compass of England" (road distances) or augment the historical annotations on the monarchs. The popularity of such *aides-mémoires* or simple historical cribs is shown by their frequent (sometimes annual) republication with minor additions to bring them up to date.

---

[1] For fourteen editions between ?1518 and 1557 (including Wynkyn de Worde's "Lytell Shorte Cronycle" [1530]), see STC 9983.3 to 9989.5. The "breuiat cronicle contaynynge all the kinges from Brute to this daye," published by John Mychell in 1552, was based in part on William Powell's 1552 edition of the preceding work; nine editions are listed as STC 9968 to 9976.

Appendages to Other Works

The Peculiar Version to 1066 (PV–1066)

190. MAYOR'S CALENDAR, CITY OF BRISTOL RECORD OFFICE, NO. 04720(1)[1]

Heading on fol. 3: Incipit primum principale a cronicula Brute.

Begins on fol. 3v: For asmoche as it is righte convenient and accordinge to euery bourgeis of the towne of Bristowe in especiall thoo that been men of worship for to knowe and vnderstande the begynnyng and first foundacion of the saide worshipfull toune: Therfore let hym rede the olde Cronycles of Brute and he shall fynde howe sone after that Brute had sette and billed the citee of Newe Troie whiche nowe is London in remembrans of the grete Troie that he and all his lynage came fro then Brute reigned xx winter and more and was beried in the newe Troie. [cf. Smith, ed., *Kalendar*, pp. 6, 8]

Omits: Cad

Ends on fol. 15: And in this wise lost Harold the reame of Englonde and reignid but fro the fest of Epiphanye vnto the saide feste of Seynt Calixt that is to say xl wekys and lieth buryed at Waltham.

Colophon: Expliciunt Cronicule ante Conquestum.

Remarks: The manuscript contains the *Bristowe Chronicle*, begun in the late fifteenth century by Robert Ricart, the town clerk of Bristol from 1479 to 1503, as an official town chronicle and document for the use of the civic officers. The language is, as one might expect, that of Gloucestershire.[2]

The first part of Ricart's compilation, from Brutus to the death of King Harold, is a much abbreviated version of a CV text, as the beginning of the text, quoted above, indicates; the CV text may have been of an early type, since it did not include the Cadwallader episode. Ricart's introduction to his work, in which he explains the contents of the six parts of his book, also describes the provenance and purposes of this first part:

> The first to shewe by cronicle the begynnyng and furst foundacioun of this saide worshipfull toune of Bristowe whiche was here furst sett and billed vpon a litill hille bytwene iiij yatis scilicet Seinte Nicholas yate Seint Johnes yate Seint Leonardes yate & the newe yate bi that noble prince Bryneus brother vnto kyng Bellynus tofore th'encarnacioun of Crist by recorde of Brutes Cronicles. And of al the kynges that were in Englonde affore the Conquest conveied in a bregement with the yeres of theire reigne and howe many of them were kinges anoynted. [cf. Smith, ed., *Kalendar*, p. 3]

True to his stated intention, Ricart inserts an account of the founding of Bristol by "Brynne" (see Smith, ed., *Kalendar*, p. 10, and the facsimile of the town plan opposite p. 10).

---

[1] See N. R. Ker, *Medieval Libraries of Great Britain: A List of Surviving Books. Supplement to the Second Edition*, ed. Andrew G. Watson (London, 1987), p. 4. The *Brut* section is edited, with introduction, notes, and plates, in Marcel Dikstra, "An Edition of the Brut Chronicle as Found in Ricart's Maior's Kalendar," M.A. diss., University of Bristol, 1992 (I am grateful to the author for a copy of his work). Short extracts from the early text are printed in Lucy Toulmin Smith, ed., *The Maire of Bristowe Is Kalendar, by Robert Ricart, Town Clerk of Bristol, 18 Edward IV*, Camden Society n.s. 5 (1872), pp. xv–xvi below, and 8–10. Smith erroneously describes the first part of the text as "taken from some version of Geoffrey of Monmouth" (p. xiv), followed by Kennedy, *Manual*, pp. 2655–56.
[2] *LALME*, 1: 62 ("in local language of a late type").

The Peculiar Version to 1419: Group D (PV–1419:D)

191. CAMBRIDGE UNIVERSITY LIBRARY MS. LL.2.14
Continuation begins on fol. 143: And in the meane tyme dyede kyng Henry at Westmynstre when he had bene kynge lv yere and xix wekes vppon Seynt Edmundes daye. [Brie 177/6-8]
Contains: QIL
Omits: "5w" heading (see below)
Ends imperfectly: And aryuede in Yorke-shire at Ravynsporne fast by Wydlyngtoun [*sic*]. And there he entred the londe. [Brie 357/25-26]

Remarks: The continuation follows an imperfect prose paraphrase of Robert of Gloucester's *Chronicle*,[1] and is written in the same hand; the ink, however, is lighter, suggesting that it was added at a later time by the scribe when a copy became available for him to use.

The continuation is a blend of *Brut* material with material from other sources. The text begins with the death of Henry III and contains the prophecy of Merlin regarding that king. The narrative of the reign of Edward I is abbreviated, while that of Edward II's reign follows the usual CV *Brut*.

The narrative on Edward III is considerably abridged; events are frequently rearranged and there are minor verbal correspondences with the London chronicles. The Halidon Hill campaign is highly abbreviated, as follows:

> And the vj yere of his regne kynge Edwarde besegede the towne and the castelle of Berwike. And vppon Seynt Margerettes evene the Scottes a huge nombre come hopynge to haue remevede the siege withom the kynge faught vppon Halydoun Hille and discomfited hem. And þer were slayne of the Scottes viij erles a M^l and iij hundred knyghtes and squiers and of fotemen xxxviijM^l. And of Englysshmen there were dede a knyght and a squier and xij fotemen. And vppon Seynt Margerettes day the towne and the castelle were yolden to the kynge in the yere of our lorde a M^l CCC xxxiij.

The reign of Richard II corresponds well to the normal *Brut* account, though there are some minor additions.

Dialectal analysis supports a reference in the Robert of Gloucester text that suggests that the manuscript should be associated with Leicestershire.[2]

---

[1] See Kennedy, *Manual*, pp. 2621–22, 2807. The text is edited in Andrew D. (Lan) Lipscomb, "A Fifteenth-Century Prose Paraphrase of Robert of Gloucester's *Chronicle*," Ph.D. diss., University of North Carolina at Chapel Hill, 1990.
[2] I thank Lan Lipscomb for this information.

The Peculiar Version to 1419: Group E (PV–1419:E)

192. HARVARD UNIVERSITY MS. ENG. 938[1]

Begins on fol. 91rb: Now speke we of the dethe of kyng Edwarde the secunde the whyche was put doun by the assent of quene Isabell [cf. Brie 252/21–23]

Next chapter begins: The yere of grace M¹ CCC xxvj Edwarde of Wyndesore the son of kyng Edwarde the secunde was crouned kyng and anoynted at Westmynster [cf. Brie 247/22–24]

Ends imperfectly on fol. 101vb: And there was dede on the kynges syde a worthy man called Spryngeys the whiche the kyng let bury in the abbey of Cane faste by Wyllyam Conquerour. And thus the kyng by manhode gette the toune of Cane and made [cf. Brie 384/6–8, and probably line 24]

Remarks: The *Brut* text, probably based on a CV–1419, has been used as a continuation to the incomplete translation of Nicholas Trevet's *Chronicle* (fols. 9ra–91rb), which it follows without break, beginning in the midst of a line.[2]

The *Brut* narrative has been reorganized and adapted in order to treat each king in a single chapter. Thus Edward II's death is treated before reverting to the coronation of Edward III and a similar reorganization occurs with the death of Richard II; in both instances, material is simply transferred to an earlier position.

Much material is omitted in favor of an outline of historical facts. Thus Edward III's Scottish campaign, including the battle of Halidon Hill (Brie 272/7–286/9, 291/1–291/9) is replaced by a single sentence: "Thys kyng Edwarde had grete worshyp in Scotlonde by warre in so moche that all Scottes had grete fere of hym" (fol. 92ra–rb).

One leaf of the last gathering is wanting, and it is probable that the original text ended in 1419.

An obit added beside November 18 in a calendar (fol. 8v) records the death of "Alicie Hungyrforthe," perhaps Alice Hungerford of London, widow, whose will dated 1 September 1491, directs that she be buried near her husband John in St. Michael's, Cornhill (BL Addit. 33412, fol. 153). Christine Rose reports that Jeremy J. Smith suggests very tentatively that the dialect might be Northwest Surrey.[3]

---

[1] See Voigts, "Handlist," pp. 39–43; Christine M. Rose, "The Provenance of the Trevet Chronicle (fMS Eng 938)," *Harvard Library Bulletin* n.s. 3, no. 4 (Winter, 1992–93): 38–55. Both the translation of Trevet and the continuation are edited in Christine M. Rose, "An Edition of Houghton Library fMS Eng 938: The Fifteenth-Century Middle English Translation of Nicholas Trevet's *Les Cronicles* with *Brut* Continuation," Ph.D. diss., Tufts University, 1985.

[2] See Kennedy, *Manual*, pp. 2666–68, 2881–82; Ruth J. Dean, "The Manuscripts of Nicholas Trevet's Anglo-Norman Chronicles," *Medievalia et Humanistica* 14 (1962): 97, 99 n. 10.
[3] Rose, "The Provenance of the Trevet Chronicle," p. 51 n. 33.

The Peculiar Version to 1419: Group F (PV–1419:F)

193. WOBURN ABBEY MS. 181[1]

Heading on fol. [100v]: Here enduth the cronycle of kyng Edwarde the furste aftur þe conqueste and begynneth þe cronycle of his sone Edwarde þe secounde borne at Carnarvan.

Brut *text begins*: And aftur þis Edwarde regned Edwarde his sone þat was borne in Carnariuan & þis Edwarde went into Fraunce & weddet Isabell þe kynges douȝtur of Fraunce þe xxv day of Ianyuere at þe churche of our lady at Boloigne in þe ȝere of our lorde M^l CCC & vij. [Brie 205/14–18]

Contains: QIL, "5w" heading

Brut *text to 1419 ends on fol. [202v]*: And þanne þe kyng entered into þe towne & restede hym in þe castell tyl þe towne was sette in rewle & in gouernaunce.

Remarks: The *Brut* text, based on a manuscript ending in 1419(r&g), is used as the conclusion of a compilation made by Richard Fox of St. Albans. Fox was a literate layman who was employed by the abbey of St. Albans, in whose records, by John of Amundesham, he appears in 1434 and 1435 described as "litteratus" and "Procurator religiosorum virorum."[2] Fox was also responsible for compiling CUL MS. Kk.1.6, which primarily contains Middle English devotional texts in verse and prose.[3] His will, dated 1454, includes a list of books, including Woburn 181.[4]

A preliminary six-page "table of all þe kynges that be comprehended withinne þis boke with mony incidences" begins with Alfred and ends with "þe wynnyng of Roone in þe vj ȝere of þe regne of kyng Harry of Munmouth."

The first part of Fox's chronicle is based on Pierre Langtoft's chronicle (possibly supplemented by Robert Mannyng's translation of Langtoft), Robert of Gloucester's chronicle, and other sources (for example, "anoþer cronyclere...").[5]

It would appear that Fox did not obtain a copy of the *Brut* until after he had composed a great part of the earlier section of his work, for immediately after the death of Edward III and before the accession of Richard II, Merlin's prophecy concerning Edward I is inserted, with the heading:

> Here endeth þe cronycle of kyng Edwarde off Wyndesore. And begyneth Merlynes prophecyee þat he prophesyed of kyng Edward with þe longe schankes wheche was graunfader to kyng Edward of Wyndesore and ffader to kyng Edwarde off Carnarvan. The cause þat þis prophesye is set here is þis for at þe wrytyng of þe seyd kyng Edward with þe longe schankes þe copy of þis prophecye was not hade.

The account of Richard II contains a number of additions: his premature birth "as somme croneclers wryte," after which he was wrapped in animal skins; a story of dishonorable treatment accorded the daughter of John Tyler (the true name of Jack Straw, according to Fox) by an officer of the king; and an account of the eighteenth and nineteenth years of the reign (printed in an appendix to *"Davies's" Chronicle*). Additions made to the reign of Henry IV include details on the capture and deaths of the duke of Surrey, the earl of Salisbury, and Sir "Raff Lompney." To the reign of Henry V are added details of a naval battle with the French in 1416.

An account of the deposition of Richard II, based on the "Record and Process" with some additions and omissions, and of the coronation of Henry IV (and subsequent parliamentary proceedings) appears as an appendix with a marginal note and *signe de renvoi* in the main *Brut* text:[6]

> Whoso liste to to [*sic*] loke on þe deposyng of kyng Rychard the secounde let hym turne to þe laste ende of þis booke & in þe too laste quayeris he schall fynde hit at þis same signe.

The colophon of this account names the author and dates the writing to 1448: "And thus enduth the Deposyng off kyng Rychard the secounde aftre the conqueste. Quod Rychard Fox off Seynt Albones. Anno domini M^l CCCC xlviij°." Fox's name appears throughout the manuscript, often in the phrase "Ghenade Fox Rychard" (or some variation thereof).

The "Deposing" is followed by accounts of the parliament at Bury and the death of Humphrey, duke of Gloucester (1446/7; printed in *"Davies's" Chronicle*); acts of the parliament of 27 Henry VI (1449); and, in different hands, five lines of alliterative verse on Richard, duke of York, and regulations concerning cooks' fees in London.

The bulk of the main text of the compilation is in a distinctive hand of unprofessional appearance, probably that of Fox himself since the text shows signs of immediate correction. In the reign of King John appear ten pages written by other hands.

Early names that occur in memoranda at the end of the manuscript include those of "Thomas Northlond grocer," possibly the sheriff of London in 1483 who died in 1484,[7] and "Elyssabeth Carpenter" (possibly fifteenth century); "John Ashe grocer" (1523); "Wylliam Stoddarde," son of one of the same name, and "Thomas Blackewell" (1543); Thomas Cantrell, William Hamyleen, and Henry Cantrell (sixteenth century).

---

[1] The accounts of the eighteenth and nineteenth years of Richard II and of the parliament at Bury St. Edmunds are printed in an appendix to *"Davies's" Chronicle*, pp. 111–18.

[2] See Henry T. Riley, ed., *Annales Monasterii S. Albani, a Johanne Amundesham, Monacho*, 2 vols., Rolls Series 28 (London, 1870, 1871), 2: 4, 90, 93, 94, and 97. For a discussion of the manuscript and the text of the Tyler story, see Lister M. Matheson, "The Peasants' Revolt through Five Centuries of Rumor and Reporting: Richard Fox, John Stow, and Their Successors," *Studies in Philology* 95 (1998): 124–28.

[3] See Alexandra Barratt, ed., *The Seven Psalms: A Commentary on the Penitential Psalms Translated from French into English by Dame Eleanor Hull*, EETS o.s. 307 (1995), pp. xiii–xl, especially pp. xix–xx (scribes, including Fox), xxii (later history of the manuscript), xxxiii–xl (dialect of South-West Norfolk/West Suffolk area); Alexandra Barratt, "Dame Eleanor Hull: A Fifteenth-Century Translator," in *The Medieval Translator: The Theory and Practice of Translation in the Middle Ages*, ed. Roger Ellis (Cambridge, 1989), pp. 87, 92; Tarvers, "English Women as Readers and Writers," p. 309.

[4] See G. R. Owst, "Some Books and Book-Owners of Fifteenth-Century St. Albans," *Transactions of the St. Albans and Hertfordshire Architectural and Archaeological Society* (1929): 179; Harris, "Patrons, Buyers, and Owners," pp. 164 and 184 n. 5.

[5] See Kennedy, *Manual*, pp. 2640–41. Robert of Gloucester is noted by name in the account of the sky's darkening after the battle of Evesham (1265): "a good clerke þat was called sir Robert sawe þis sy3t xxx^{ti} myle fro þe place wher þe batayle was. And for þis merveyle he labered fyrst þis booke."

[6] See Kennedy, *Manual*, pp. 2714–15, 2939–40. Cf. Given-Wilson, trans. and ed., *Chronicles of the Revolution*, pp. 168–89. A copy is also found in Lambeth 738 (item 33 and n. 2).

[7] BL MS. Cotton Vitellius A.xvi, in Kingsford, ed., *Chrons. London*, pp. 191, 193.

The Translation Attributed to John Mandeville (JM-1333)

Two medieval manuscripts have survived that contain all or part of a second translation into English of the Anglo-Norman *Brut*. The full text is found as the first part of BL MS. Harley 4690, while Coll. of Arms MS. Arundel 58 incorporates three passages from this translation in an elaborate historical compilation. A seventeenth-century transcript of Arundel 58 occurs in Magdalene College, Cambridge, Pepys 2833. The translation can be attributed on the basis of external evidence to a John Mandeville, rector of Burnham Thorpe in Norfolk, who made it in 1435.

194. BL MS. HARLEY 4690[1]

Heading on fol. 4: In nomine trino hoc opus incipio.
  Here a manne mey here how Englonde was cleped Albion and by wham itte received thate name and sine Britaine also & bi wham.
Begins: [Y]nne the nowble lond of Syrye
Omits: Cad, QIL, "5w" heading (see below)
Poem on Halidon Hill begins: And there men mighte see the nowbell king Edwarde off Englonde & his ffolke hough mannefully þei chaseden the Skottes were-off þis romance was made:
  There men mighte well see
  Many a Skotte lightely fflee [Brie 287/7–12]
Poem on Halidon Hill (and text to 1333) ends:
  Butt Godde þatte is heven king
  Sende vs pees and gode ending. [Brie 289/3–4]
Continuation to 1377 begins: Hough king Edwarde made a dewke off Corinwaile. And also of vj oþer erles thatte werren newe made. And off þe ffirste chalenge off the realme off Fraunce.

  In þe yeere of our lorde Ihesu Criste a M^l iijC & xxxvij and off king Edwarde þe xij [Brie 292/26–31]
Ends on fol. 108: and mannefully counterd wiþ our Englischemen.

Remarks: Mandeville's translation ended in 1333 with the poem on Halidon Hill, but is supplemented in this manuscript by a 1419(men) continuation taken from a CV text of the first translation. The change of exemplar is marked by a chronological and textual gap in the narrative from 1333 to 1337 (see Brie 291/1–292/25).
  Fols. 109–118 contain a copy, by the same scribe, of *Richard Coeur de Lion*.[2]
  The name of a Roger Newburgh occurs on a front flyleaf.

[1] The end of the prose text to 1333 and the poem on the battle of Halidon Hill are printed in Brie 287–89; also in Joseph Ritson, ed., *Poems, Written Anno MCCCLII by Laurence Minot* (London, 1825), pp. 55–64.

[2] See Karl Brunner, ed., *Der Mittelenglische Versroman über Richard Löwenherz*, Wiener Beiträge zur englischen Philologie 42 (Vienna, 1913).

195. COLLEGE OF ARMS MS. ARUNDEL 58[1]

Heading of first section on fol. 5ra (modern numbering): Here a man may hure how Yngelonde was ycleped Albyon and by wham hit receyued the name.

Begins: In þe noble londe of Syrye was a noble kynge myghty and of gret renoun

First section ends at foot of fol. 6ra (column b is left blank): Brute aryuede at Totynesse in þe same londe & þer conquered he þe gyauntis byfore yseyde. Here endith þe prologe of þe yle of Albyon.

Second section begins imperfectly on fol. 76ra: and shal the dragon & he bynde hure tailis togedre and than shal come a lyon out of Irlond [cf. Brie 75/33–34]

Second section ends on fol. 76rb: and thane this lond shal be cleped the lond of conquest and so shullen the rightfull eyris of Engelond end. [cf. Brie 76/17–19]

Third section begins on fol. 302va: And in that yere was Seynt Thomas of Cauntelbury [*sic*] itranslated in þe l yere of his martirdom [cf. Brie 173/9–10]

Omits: QIL, "5w" heading

Poem on Halidon Hill begins: and so men myght se þe worþy and noble kyng Edward of Engelond and his folk how manfully þey chastyde þe Scottes.
    There þan men myght se
    Many a Scott swiftly fle [Brie 289/5–6 (start of poem)]

Poem on Halidon Hill (and text) ends (imperfectly?) on fol. 334vb:
    & þe Englisshmen pursywid hem so
    Fort þe flood was al ago
    And þus þe Scottes discomfytyd were
    In lytil tyme wiþ gret fere. [Brie 287/27–30]

Remarks: A leaf is missing between fols. 75 and 76 that would have contained the end of the Arthur narrative and the beginning of the prophecies of Merlin, taken from the Mandeville translation (see the second section above).

The sections from the Mandeville translation of the *Brut* form part of an ambitious historical compilation in verse and prose finished in 1448, a narrative prospectus of which, followed by a list of contents, is given on fols. 1–4v:[2]

> *Heading*: The tabile of cronycul offe Engelonde fro quene Albion the furste erthely creature that entriede into this londe ynto kyng Richard the secunde.
> *Begins*: The fferste ether erthely creature that entred into this londe
> *Ends (page rubbed)*: This tabel kalender of [...] plennarly knowlich ffoluyng with a boke offe the fful text. Allso a petegrew ffro William Conquerour of the crowne of Engelonde lynnyally descendyng vnto kyng Henre the vj in the end of thys boke lymned in ffygurs. Thys boke with hys antecedens and consequens was ful ended the vj day offe August the 3ere of oure lorde a M^l CCCC xlviij and the [*blank*] yere of oure souerayn lorde kyng Harry the vj affter the conquest the xxvj.

The ensuing list of contents (probably imperfect at the end) is numbered by the medieval folio numbers and runs from "Albyon ffolio j°" to "Penda fo. C iiij" (a king of Sussex; a following reference to the "lettre of Boneface" is expuncted).

The basis of the compilation is the first recension of Robert of Gloucester's *Metrical Chronicle*, somewhat modernized in language and amplified and supplemented extensively by interpolations in prose and verse.[3]

These additions (indicated in the manuscript by being written in double columns) are translated or adapted from Geoffrey of Monmouth (to the end of his *Historia*, including Geoffrey's account of his sources [fol. 87]), William of Malmesbury's *Gesta Regum Anglorum*, John of Glastonbury's *Cronica sive Antiquitates Glastoniensis Ecclesie* (for the story of Joseph of Arimathea and the early history of Glastonbury [fols. 90–91v]), and Nicholas Trevet (as noted on fol. 300va),[4] among other, unidentifiable sources that the compiler has collated (for example, "here is a fallyng in of another cronicle of the same doyng" [fol. 240]).

The compiler has inserted a version of the romance of *Richard Coeur de Lion* (fols. 252ra–276ra), a copy of which is also found in BL Harley 4690.[5]

He has also preserved *passim* a series of extracts from a verse history similar in style (and literary quality) to the *Short English Metrical Chronicle*.

Fol. 335 contains a list of the burial places of the kings from Arthur to Harold. Fols. 335v to 342v contain a copy of the anonymous verse "Kings of England" (from William the Conqueror to Henry VI), illustrated with roundels containing full-length portraits of the individual kings and roundels with the names of their children.⁶ These are linked to show lines of succession; since the manuscript was completed in 1448, no issue is shown for Henry VI, whose son Edward was born in 1453.

The dialect of the manuscript is that of Wiltshire.⁷

Extracts transcribed from this manuscript are found in Magdalene College, Cambridge, Pepys 2833, pages 1–3 and fols. 485–518. They were made ca. 1685 for Sir William Hayward, after whose death the manuscript passed to Samuel Pepys.

---

[1] The poem on the battle of Halidon Hill is printed in Brie 289; also in Thomas Hearne, ed., *Robert of Gloucester's Chronicle*, 2 vols. (Oxford, 1724; rpt. as vols. 3 and 4 of *Works* [London, 1810]), 1: lxxxiii–iv.

[2] The manuscript also contains at its beginning an acephalous treatise on hunting and a list of terms of association.

[3] See Kennedy, *Manual*, pp. 2617–21, 2642.

[4] A notice of Thomas Trevet, justice of the eyre, is followed by the remark: "This Treuetes sone made cronicles icleped Triuetes Cronicles of whiche many thyngus of thes cronicles beth idrawe oute of."

[5] See Brunner, ed., *Der Mittelenglische Versroman über Richard Löwenherz*.

[6] See Mooney, "Lydgate's 'Kings of England'," pp. 263–73, 278–89. The Arundel text is published in Hearne, ed., *Robert of Gloucester's Chronicle*, 2: 585–95.

[7] *LALME*, 1: 117, 3: 547, where two hands, in similar language, are distinguished. It is possible, though, that only one scribe was involved.

Remarks on the JM–1333

In content the full text of BL Harley 4690 resembles the CV–1333, as might be expected, since both translations are based on texts of the Anglo-Norman Long Version. Stylistically and verbally, however, the versions differ considerably, and it appears that the translation exemplified by BL Harley 4690 must have been based on an Anglo-Norman text similar to that of Bibliothèque Mazarine 1860, a text as far removed as possible from that used for the first translation.¹

In the Halidon Hill passage in BL Harley 4690, the layout of the wards of the Scottish army is different from that found in the CV in that the names of the knights are given in list form; accordingly, the "5w" heading is not found. This layout is similar to that found in many of the Anglo-Norman manuscripts.² In Coll. of Arms Arundel 58, however, the wards and the Scots in them are presented as prose, in which the "5w" heading does not occur. Instead of the concluding prose description of the battle found in the Anglo-Norman texts (and followed in the first English translation), there appears a poem in rhyming couplets.

The translator of this version is not named in either BL Harley 4690 or Coll. of Arms Arundel 58. The evidence for ascribing the translation to John Mandeville is found in BL Harley 2279, which probably belongs to the CV–1377 f.c. Stage 1, but which breaks off in 1340.[3] At the end of this text a sixteenth-century hand has added the following lines:

>   This English booke that is present
>   was made to a good entent
>   ffor hem that Englishe understonde
>   of the Chronicles of Engelonde
>   This was translated by good avyse
>   owt of French into Englyse
>   By Sire Iohn the Maundeuyle
>   that hath ben person but a whyle
>   In Brunham Thorp that little toun
>   God graunt him hise benysoun
>   The yeer of Henry I understonde
>   the sexte kyng of Engelonde
>   After the conqueste soth to seyne
> 1435 the xiij yeere of hise reygne
>   He that sitt in Trynitee
>   one God and persons three
>   Save the kyng from all mischaunce
>   Bothen in Engelond and in Fraunce.

Beside these lines occur two comments. The first, in the same hand as the verses, reads "Thes verses written in the end of this mans translacioun which doth somwhat vary from this translacioun owt of ye first originall Frenche." The second, in a later, seventeenth- or eighteenth-century hand, reads "hic desunt 13 cap. que sunt in alio libro."

Brie has demonstrated that there are sufficient contemporary references to "John Maundevyle" to authenticate the existence of this person and that from 1427/28 to 1441 the rector of Burnham Thorpe in Norfolk was indeed so named.[4] The records suggest that Mandeville must have been born ca. 1380, and that he lived most of his life in obscure parishes in Norfolk, Lincolnshire, and apparently Worcestershire for a time. The series of parishes with which Brie associates him is Quidenham (Norfolk), Flegg (Norfolk), Brettenham's or Bridgeham's Manor (Norfolk), Hamburg (Worcester), Great Cressingham (Norfolk), Burnham Thorpe (Norfolk; 1427–1441), Ivenho (Lincoln), and Netherhall Manor (Norfolk). That he is called "Sir" John Mandeville is due to his clerical status.

The lines in BL Harley 2279 must have been copied from a manuscript of Mandeville's translation; however, the remark that thirteen chapters are missing that are in the other book shows that the later annotator was referring to a text that included a continuation to 1377, which would fit the number of missing chapters.

Although Brie apparently did not notice the later remark, he raises the question whether the evidence of BL Harley 4690 implies that the continuation to 1419 found therein was supplied by John Mandeville and was thereafter transferred to the first translation. The second marginal remark raises the question whether the 1377 continuation was first supplied by Mandeville. However, Brie's arguments for not ascribing the 1419 continuation to him can also be applied to the 1377 continuation:

1. Coll. of Arms Arundel 58 probably contained no more than the end of the poem on the battle of Halidon Hill in its original full state.
2. There is a gap in BL Harley 4690 between 1333 and 1337, suggesting hesitation on the scribe's part for some reason. This probably reflects a change of exemplar at this point.
3. A number of manuscripts of the CV–1377 were written *before* 1435, which is when John Mandeville apparently made his translation.

Textual comparison shows that neither of the surviving manuscripts is the original text of the translation, which must, in addition, have ended with the verses of ascription that were copied later into BL Harley 2279.[5] Nor can either manuscript be a copy of the other. Mandeville's translation does not seem to have had much circulation or any great popularity, and the extant manuscripts are probably close to the original, especially given the date of the translation (1435) and the date of compilation of Coll. of Arms Arundel 58 (1448).

---

[1] See Brie, *Geschichte und Quellen*, pp. 75–77.
[2] See pp. 86–87.
[3] See item 15.
[4] See Brie, *Geschichte und Quellen*, pp. 78–80.
[5] See Brie, *Geschichte und Quellen*, pp. 76–77.

V. Unclassified Texts

196. BIBLIOTHECA BODMERIANA, COD. BODMER 43
Begins on fol. 1: In the noble londe of Surrey there was a noble kynge and a myghti man and of grete renowne that men callede Dioclician that welle and wortheli gouernede hymself thrugh his noble chiualry

Ends on fol. 2v: and thei conceuede and broght forth geantes Gogmagogge and Laugheryan and so dwellede in Albyone to the tyme that Brute londe at Totnesse. [cf. Brie 4/26–32]

Remarks: The Albina prologue of a CV *Brut* has been used as a preface to a prose paraphrase of much of Robert of Gloucester's *Chronicle* (fols. 3–103v).[1]

---

[1] See Kennedy, *Manual*, pp. 2621–22. For an analogous use of *Brut* narrative (as a continuation) in conjunction with a prose version of Robert of Gloucester, one can compare CUL Ll.2.14 (see item 191); cf. also Coll. of Arms Arundel 58, where sections of John Mandeville's translation are interpolated in the verse form of Robert's *Chronicle* (see item 195) and BL Sloane 2027, where the *Brut* is used as a frame for Robert's *Chronicle* (see item 159).

197. LINCOLN CATHEDRAL MS. 70 (C.5.12)[1]
Heading on damaged and rubbed fol. 1: Here begynneth þe boke callyd Brute þ[. . .] tretith of þe kynges of Ingelonde.

Begins: In þe noble londe of Surre

Ends imperfectly: How Gurmonde drave kynge Cartyff to Chicester and killed the Bretons and þurgh queyntyse gate the towne. [Brie 94/15–17]

Remarks: Despite the heading, which is reminiscent of the heading and beginning of EV texts, there are no distinctive EV signs in, for example, the giant passages or the passages on Lud's naming of London and on Engist's heptarchy.

The chapter on the thirty-three kings is slightly abbreviated: "þe ffurst kynge off þe xxxiij^{ti} kynges men callyd Gorbodia; he reigned xij yere; þe ij^e kynge Morgan ij yere; Eighnaus vj yere [*etc.*]."

The text should be assigned to the CV, and, given the heading, it is possible that it represents a form of CV ending in 1377 that underlay the EV texts.

---

[1] See Thompson, *Catalogue*, p. 51, for sixteenth- and seventeenth-century names in the manuscript. (There are several misreadings in Thompson's description.)

198. CAMBRIDGE UNIVERSITY LIBRARY MS. KK.1.3

Begins imperfectly: after þat bataill Vter tooke his weye toward Wynchestre [Brie 64/29]

Ends imperfectly: And he sente before in to Scotlonde ser Aymer de Valaunce erl of Pembrook [Brie 200/14–15]

Remarks: The text consists of ten unnumbered folios inserted at the end of the manuscript that contain discontiguous pieces of text between Uther and Edward I. What remains corresponds well to the text of the earlier CV groups, but they could also be part of an EV text.

199. NLW MS. PENIARTH 396D(1)[1]

Heading on damaged p. 1: [. . .] may [.] m[. . .]s fyste called [*ins.*] Albion & thorugh [. . .] yt hadde that name. [Here may [.] man here how Englande was *marg.*]

Begins: In the noble londe of Surrey

Ends imperfectly on p. 16: but oon geaunte [*last word a catchword*]

Remarks: The text has been copied from a CV as far as chapter four before it breaks off imperfectly. The text then goes back to the third chapter and is thereafter a copy of the AV–1419:B.

---

[1] For (2), which is foliated rather than paginated, see item 138. See Marx, "Middle English Manuscripts," p. 362.

200. BROGYNTYN MS. 8 (LORD HARLECH; ON DEPOSIT AT NLW)[1]
Begins imperfectly: changed as the deuell wolde [Brie 70/30]
Contains: Cad
Ends imperfectly on fol. 18v: of tillers and this myschefe endured [Cad episode: see pp. 58–59]

Remarks: The manuscript consists of one gathering, perhaps preserved because it contains the section on King Arthur, including Merlin's prophecies. Constantine reigns after Arthur.
The text could be a CV, EV, or AV.

---

[1] See Marx, "Middle English Manuscripts," pp. 376–77; Rosalynn Voaden, ed. and trans., *Brogyntyn Manuscript No. 8*, introd. Felicity Riddy (Moreton-in-Marsh, 1991).

201. BL MS. ROYAL 11.B.IX
First fragment begins imperfectly on fol. 133: bene kynge xvij yere [Brie 142/16]
First fragment ends imperfectly in next chapter on fol. 133v.
Second fragment begins imperfectly on fol. 134 and ends on fol. 134v.

Remarks: The two fragments, which are very damaged and only partially legible, are bound into the *Registrum Cartarum Prioratus S. Andreae Northampton*. The fragments are from the reign of Henry I; the second comes from the chapter preceding the narrative of the first fragment (see Brie, chapter 135, 140/16–142/11). Kennedy notes that the manuscript is related to BL Harley 2182 but gives no evidence for the relationship.[1]

---

[1] See Kennedy, *Manual*, p. 2819.

202. LEHIGH UNIVERSITY (3 FRAGMENTS)[1]
Fragment A, recto, begins: kyng of moche Britaigne. Capitulum liij^m. [Brie 46/31–32]
Fragment A, verso, ends: and natheles he was somdel glad of his deth and [Brie 48/29]
Fragment B, recto, begins: herde telle that Engist was come aȝen [Brie 54/7–8]

Fragment B, verso, ends: Another kyng hadde Southsex where is now [Brie 55/8–9]

Fragment C, recto, begins: forto maken hym kyng [Brie 127/15]

Fragment C, verso, ends: & alle the lordes of Engelonde & heelde a grete par[. . .] [Brie 129/18–19]

Remarks: The three fragments come from a double-columned manuscript that was probably dismembered and cut up for its illustrated and decorated initials in the early 1930s. Fragments A and B preserve full columns, while Fragment C is the top part of a leaf. Fragment B has the modern foliation number 28 (25?); Fragment C is numbered 51.

---

[1] See John C. Hirsh, *Western Manuscripts of the Twelfth through the Sixteenth Centuries in Lehigh University Libraries: A Guide to the Exhibition* (Bethlehem, Penn., 1970), pp. 11–14. Hirsh prints the text of Fragment B on pp. 13–14.

203. GEELONG CHURCH OF ENGLAND GRAMMAR SCHOOL MS.[1]

Begins (imperfectly?): Afftre þe dethe of þis Eldrede knoght þat was a danoys bigan þo forto regne but Edmond Irensyde that was kyng Eldrede sonne bi his ferst wyf [Brie 119/5–7]

Omits: QIL (see below), "5w" heading (see below)

Ends imperfectly: Rebelles þat afore had done moche harme to oure English men marchauntes and to many Toynes [*sic*] and Poortes in Englonde upon þe [Brie 365/17–19 and cf. note 9]

Remarks: Sinclair's description indicates that, among many others, the folios are missing that might have contained QIL, the "5w" heading, and the changeover passages between 1333 and 1377 and 1377 and 1419. The information given in the published description concerning the contents of the remaining leaves suggests that the text was a CV, or possibly an EV, ending in 1419.

---

[1] The manuscript has been missing since the late 1960s. The present description is based on Sinclair, *Descriptive Catalogue*, pp. 306–307, from which quotations are taken and on which the Remarks are based.

VI. *The Early Printed Editions*

Thirteen printed editions of the English *Brut* appeared between 1480 and 1528 under the title *The Chronicles of England* or some variant thereof. William Caxton's *editio princeps* of 1480 was based on a manuscript text similar to that found in Huntington MS. HM 136(1), with the addition of a short prologue, a table of contents, and a continuation from 1419 to 1461 that was probably compiled by Caxton himself. The printed editions fall into two groups, here designated Types 1 and 2. Type 1 follows Caxton's text, while Type 2 follows the expanded edition published at St. Albans by the Schoolmaster-Printer. Both types end in 1461.

[85.] "The Cronicles of Englond." William Caxton, Westminster, June 10, 1480 (STC 9991).[1] Type 1.

Remarks: [See item 85 for a description and pp. 165–66 for discussion.] Later in 1480, Caxton published *The Description of Britain* (STC 13440a), consisting of geographical material from John Trevisa's translation of Ranulph Higden's *Polychronicon*. This small work was probably intended as a supplement to the *Chronicles of England*, with which a number of the extant copies are bound.[2] In certain later editions it became a regular part of the book.

---

[1] Available on microfilm in Early English Books 1475–1640 (University Microfilms), Reel 1573. For bibliographical details, see E. Gordon Duff, *Fifteenth-Century English Books* (Oxford, 1917), no. 97. The prologue and conclusion are printed in N. F. Blake, *Caxton's Own Prose* (London, 1973), pp. 68–69.
[2] See Duff, *Fifteenth-Century English Books*, no. 113; Blake, *Caxton's Own Prose*, p. 155. A modern rendering is available in Marie Collins, *Caxton: The Description of Britain* (New York, 1988).

204. "The Cronycles of Englond." William Caxton, Westminster, October 8, 1482 (STC 9992).[1] Type 1.

Preface begins: [I]n the yere of th'yncarnacyon of our lord Ihesu Crist M CCC lxxx and in the xx yere of the regne of kyng Edward the fourth

Heading: How the land of Englond was fyrst named Albyon and by what encheson it was so named.

Begins: In the noble land of Sirrie

Ends: and that after this present & short lyf we may come to the euerlastyng lyfe in the blysse of heuen. Amen.

Colophon: Thus endeth this present book of the Cronycles of Englond enprynted by me William Caxton in th'abbey of Westmestre by London. Fynysshed and accomplyssed the viij day of Octobre the yere of the incarnacyon of our lord God M CCCC lxxxij and in the xxij yere of the regne of kyng Edward the fourth.

Remarks: Caxton's second edition was set up from the first, retaining the same pagination, although the spelling system and punctuation marks have been altered.[2] Textually, only the colophon has been altered to reflect the new date.

---

[1] Early English Books 1475–1640 (University Microfilms), Reel 3. See Duff, *Fifteenth-Century English Books*, no. 98.
[2] Cf. N. F. Blake, *Caxton: England's First Publisher* (London, 1976), pp. 92-93.

205. "The Croniclis of Englonde with the Frute of Timis." [Schoolmaster-Printer,] St. Albans, [?1483] (STC 9995).[1] Type 2.

Table of contents begins: Here begynnys a schort & breue tabull on thes cronicles

Prologue begins: The Prolog. In so myche that it is necessari to all creaturis of Criston religyon or of fals religyon

Prologue ends: we vse most to nombnr [*read* nombur] fro the begynyng off the world vnto Crist wos borne and fro Crist wos borne vnto our tyme and this ordyr is kepyt in all the boke of euery thyng in his place as it is sayd afoor.

Heading to first part: Hic incipit Fructus Temporum.

First part begins: [B]e cause thys boke is mad to tel what tyme ony thyng notabull wos therfoor the begynyng of all tymes chortly shall be tochit.

Heading to Brut *text*: Incipit regnum Britanie nunc dicta Anglia. Afor þat I will speke of Brute it shall be shewed how þe londe of Englond was fyrst namd Albion & by what encheson it vos so namit.

Brut text begins: In the nobull land of Sirie

Brut text ends: And about Mydsomer after thee yere of our lord M CCC lx and thee frist yere of his regne he wos crouned at Westmynstre & anoynted kyng of Englond hauyng possession of all thee reame.

Seventh part ends: Ihon th'abbot of Habingdon was the popys legate to dispose thys godli tresure of the chirch to eueri faythfull man þat was disposed and that wolde habull him to resayue it.

Colophon: Here ende the Croniclis of Englonde with the Frute of Timis. Sanctus Albanus.

Remarks: This edition is based on Caxton's text (probably that of 1480), greatly augmented by material drawn from the popular *Fasciculus temporum* of Werner Rolewinck.[2]

There is a prologue on the use of history and on historical authorities that also contains an explanation of the seven parts into which the narrative has been divided and other matters thought necessary for understanding chronicles. The first part begins with a "Fructus Temporum" from the Creation to Homer, who "wrotte and fened gloriusli mony a lesyng." Interpolations on popes and foreign rulers are interspersed throughout the *Chronicles of England* text.

---

[1] Early English Books 1475–1640 (University Microfilms), Reel 161. See Duff, *Fifteenth-Century English Books*, no. 101. The edition, ascribed here to ?1483, is undated but is frequently ascribed to 1485 (as in the STC). However, the prologue assigns the compilation of the text to 1483, 23 Edward IV (March 4, 1483–April 9, 1483, the date of Edward's death, if the regnal year is used). The wording is similar to that of the colophon that gives 1486 as the date of compilation (but not necessarily that of printing) of the Schoolmaster-Printer's typographically related *Book of Hawking, Hunting, and Blasing of Arms*; see William Blades, introd., *The Boke of Saint Albans* (London, 1881), leaf fix^v, and Rachel Hands, ed., *English Hawking and Hunting in The Boke of St. Albans*, Oxford English Monographs (Oxford, 1975), pp. xvi–xvii. Near the end of the *Chronicles of England*, however, the Schoolmaster-Printer refers to Sextus IV, who died on August 12, 1484, as the current pope. Innocent VIII was elected his successor on August 29, 1484.

[2] The first official publication of the *Fasciculus temporum* was in Cologne in 1474; Johan Veldener, a former business associate of Caxton, published an edition at Louvain in 1475 that may have been used by Caxton in his compilation of the 1419–1461 continuation of the *Chronicles of England*. See Matheson, "Printer and Scribe," p. 599 and the references in nn. 25 and 29 therein.

206. ["CHRONICLES OF ENGLAND."] [WILLIAM DE MACHLINIA, LONDON, ?1486] (STC 9993).[1] TYPE 1.
Table of contents begins: Fyrst in the prologue is conceyued how Albyne with hir susters entrid into this ile and named yt Albyon.
Heading: How the lande of Englonde was fyrst namd Albyon and bi what encheson it was so namd.
Text begins: [I]n the noble lande of Surre
Text ends: & that after this present & short lyfe we may com to the euerlastyng lyfe in the blisse of heuen. Amen.

Remarks: This edition, probably printed by Machlinia, omits Caxton's short prologue and colophon but otherwise follows his edition of 1480 (though with some errors).

---

[1] Early English Books 1475–1640 (University Microfilms), Reel 3 (the British Library copy, which is imperfect at the end). See Duff, *Fifteenth-Century English Books*, no. 99.

207. "CRONYCLES OF THE LONDE OF ENGLOND." GERARD DE LEEW, ANTWERP, 1493 (STC 9994).[1] TYPE 1.
Heading to table of contents: Here begynneth the table of thys boke that men kalled Cronycles of the londe of Englond.
Table of contents begins: First in the prologue is conteyned how Albyne wyth hir sustres entrid into this ile & named it Albyon.
Heading: How the lande of Englonde was fyrst named Albion and by what encheson it was so named.
Text begins: Ther was in the noble lande of Surre
Text ends: & that after this present & short lyfe we may comen to the euerlasting lyfe in the blisse of heuen. Amen.
Colophon: Here ben endyd the Cronycles of the reame of Englond with their apperteignaunces. Enprentyd in the duchye of Braband in the towne of Andewarpe in the yere of owr lord M CCCC xciij by maistir Gerard de Leew a man of grete wysedom in all maner of kunnyng which nowe is come from lyfe vnto the deth which is grete harme for many a poure man. On whos sowle God Almyghty for hys hygh grace haue mercy. Amen.

Remarks: De Leew's edition, which is based on Caxton, has a title-page with the title "Cronycles of the londe of Englond."

EARLY PRINTED EDITIONS 343

---

[1] Early English Books 1475–1640 (University Microfilms), Reel 8. See Duff, *Fifteenth-Century English Books*, no. 100.

208. "Cronycle of Englonde wyth the Frute of Tymes." Wynkyn de Worde, Westminster, 1497 (STC 9996).[1] Type 2.
Table of contents begins: Tabula. Here begynneth a shorte and a breue table on these Cronycles
Prologue begins: The prologue. In so moche that it is necessary to all creatures of Crysten relygyon
Text ends: to euery faythfull man that was dysposyd & that wolde able hym to receyue it.
Colophon: Here endyth this present Cronycle of Englonde wyth the Frute of Tymes compiled in a booke & also enprynted by one somtyme scolemayster of Saynt Albons on whoos soule God haue mercy. And newely in the yer of our lord God M CCCC lxxxxvij enpryntid at Westmestre by Wynkyn de Worde.
Remarks: It is clear that this expanded text of the St. Albans type was intended to be issued with de Worde's 1498 edition of *The Description of Britain* (STC 13440b), since the latter work is listed at the end of the table of contents.
The colophon gives a *terminus ad quem* for the death of the Schoolmaster-printer of St. Albans.

---

[1] Early English Books 1475–1640 (University Microfilms), Reel 924. See Duff, *Fifteenth-Century English Books*, no. 102.

209. "Cronycle of Englonde wyth þe Fruyte of Tymes." Wynkyn de Worde, London, May, 1502 (STC 9997).[1] Type 2.
Table of contents begins: Tabula. Here begynneth a shorte & a breue table on these Cronycles
Prologue begins: The prologue. In so moche that it is necessary to all creatures of Crysten relygyon
Text ends: too euery faythfull man þat was dysposyd and that wolde able hym too receyue it.
Colophon: Here endeth this present Cronycle of Englonde wyth þe Fruyte of

Tymes compyled in a booke and also enprynted by one some tyme scolemayster of Saynt Albons vppon whoos soule God haue mercy. Amen. And newely in the yere of oure lorde God M CCCCC ii enprynted in Flete Strete in þe sygne of the Sonne by me Wynkyn de Worde.

Remarks: This is a reprint of de Worde's edition of 1497 and of the *The Description of Britain* of 1498, printed after his move from Westminster.

---

[1] Early English Books 1475–1640 (University Microfilms), Reel 3.

210. "CRONYCLE OF ENGLONDE WYTH ÞE FRUYTE OF TYMES." JULYAN NOTARY, LONDON, AUGUST, 1504 (STC 9998).[1] TYPE 2.

Table of contents begins: Tabula. Here begynneth a shorte and a breue table on these Cronycles

Prologue begins: The prologue. In so moche that it is necessary to all creatures of Crysten relygyon

Text ends: to euery feythfull man þat was disposed and that wolde able hym to receyue it.

Colophon: Here endeth this present Cronycle of Englonde wyth þe Fruyte of Tymes compyled in a booke & also enprynted by one somtyme scolemayster of Saint Albons vpon whos soule God haue mercy. Amen. And newely in the yere of our lorde God M CCCCC & iiii enprynted at Tempelbarre by me Julyane Nottary.

Remarks: The edition agrees with de Worde's editions of 1497 and 1502 and seems to have been taken from the latter; it also contains *The Description of Britain*.

---

[1] Early English Books 1475–1640 (University Microfilms), Reel 3.

211. "CRONYCLE OF ENGLONDE WITH THE FRUYTE OF TYMES." RICHARD PYNSON, LONDON, DECEMBER 19, 1510 (STC 9999).[1] TYPE 2.

Table of contents begins: Tabula. Here begynneth a shorte & a breue table on these Cronycles

Prologue begins: The Prologue. In so moche that it is necessary to all creatures of Cristen relygion

Text ends: to euery faythfull man that was dysposed and that wolde able hym to receyue it.

Colophon: Here endeth this present Cronycle of Englonde with the Fruyte of Tymes compyled in a boke & also enprynted by one some tyme scolemayster of Saint Albons vpon whos soule God haue mercy. Amen. And newely in the yere of oure lorde God M CCCCC x enprynted in Flete Strete at the sygne of the Gorge by Rycharde Pynson prynter vnto þe kynges noble grace.

Remarks: This edition appears to be a reprint of de Worde's edition of 1502, with *The Description of Britain*, which it resembles closely in typography and layout.

---

[1] Early English Books 1475–1640 (University Microfilms), Reel 3.

212. "CRONYCLE OF ENGLONDE WITH THE FRUYTE OF TYMES." JULYAN NOTARY, LONDON, 1515 (STC 10000).[1] TYPE 2.

Table of contents begins: Tabula. Here begynneth a shorte and a breue table on the Cronycles

Prologue begins: The Prologue. In soo moche that it is necessary to all creatures of Crysten relygyon

Text ends: to euery feythful man þat was diposed and that wolde able hym to receyue it.

Colophon: Here endeth this present Cronycle of Englonde with the Fruyte of Tymes compyled in I boke and also newely enprynted in the yere of our lorde God M CCCCC & xv by me Julyan Notary dwellynge in Powlys chyrche yarde besyde þe westedore by my lordes palyes.

Remarks: Notary's edition is presumably based on his earlier edition of 1504, with some minor changes. Thus, in his colophon to the chronicle Notary drops the attribution to the Schoolmaster-Printer; in the colophon to *The Description of Britain* he also drops Caxton's references to himself as the first printer thereof and to Trevisa as the translator.

---

[1] Early English Books 1475–1640 (University Microfilms), Reel 4.

213. "Cronycle of Englonde with the Fruyte of Tymes." Wynkyn de Worde, London, 1515 (STC 10000.5).[1] Type 2.

Table of contents begins: Tabula. Here begynneth a shorte and a breue table for to fynde lyghtly wherof ony man shall please hym to rede in this boke.

Prologue begins: The prologue. In so moche þat it is necessary to al creatures of Crysten relygyon

Text ends: to euery faythfull man that was dysposed & that wolde able hym to receyue it.

Colophon: Here endeth this present Cronycle of Englonde with the Fruyte of Tymes compyled in a boke and also enprynted by one somtyme scolemayster of Saynt Albons vpon whose soule God haue mercy. Amen. And newly enprynted in Flete Strete at the sygne of the Sonne by me Wynkyn de Worde in the yere of our lorde God M CCCCC and xv.

Remarks: This edition is based on de Worde's edition of 1502, with *The Description of Britain*, and provides a new system of reference by folio in the table of contents.

---

[1] Early English Books 1475–1640 (University Microfilms), Reel 4. The British Library copy filmed therein has a title-page imitated from de Worde's edition of 1528 (with the royal arms copied from Richard Pynson's version) and for that reason contains the title found in the later edition. Other copies contain de Worde's woodcut of the royal arms but no title.

214. "Cronycle of Englande with the Fruyte of Tymes." Wynkyn de Worde, London, 1520 (STC 10001).[1] Type 2.

Table of contents begins: Tabula. Here begynneth a shorte and a breue table

Prologue begins: The prologue. In so moche þat it is necessary to al creatures of Crysten relyg[y]on

Text ends: to euery faythful man that was dysposed & that wolde able hym to receyue it.

Colophon: Here endeth this presente Cronycle of Englande with the Fruyte of Tymes compyled in a boke & also imprynted by one sumtyme scolemayster of Seynt Albons vpon whose soule God haue mercy. Amen. And newly imprynted in Flete Strete at the sygne of the Sonne by me Wynkyn de Worde in the yere of oure lorde God M CCCCC and xx.

Remarks: This is a reset edition, with some spelling variation, of de Worde's edition of 1515.

[1] Early English Books 1475–1640 (University Microfilms), Reel 79.

215. "The Cronycles of Englonde with the dedes of popes and emperours and also the descripcyon of Englonde." Wynkyn de Worde, London, April 9, 1528 (STC 10002).[1] Type 2.
Table of contents begins: Tabula. Here begynneth a shorte and a breue table
Prologue begins: The prologue. In so moche þat it is necessary to all creatures of Chrysten relygion
Text ends: vnto euery faythfull man that was disposed and that wolde able themselfe to receyue it.
Colophon: Thus endeth the Cronycles of Englonde with the Fruyte of Tymes compyled in a boke and was fyrst imprynted by one somtyme scolemayster of Saynt Albons on whose soule God haue mercy. Amen. And now lately imprynted at London and dilygently amended in dyuers places where as ony faute was in Flete Strete at the sygne of the Sonne by me Wynkyn de Worde in the yere of our lorde God M CCCCC xxviij the ix daye of Apryll.

Remarks: The new title occurs on a title-page that also contains de Worde's woodcut of the royal arms. Generally, the text corresponds to de Worde's earlier edition of 1520 and is accompanied by *The Description of England*. Despite the claim in the colophon, the revisions are slight.

[1] Early English Books 1475–1640 (University Microfilms), Reel 4.

The new title and the exaggerated claim for diligent amendment in de Worde's edition of 1528, the last of the early printed editions, may be indications of a failing market. As the sixteenth century progressed, the salability of the *Chronicles of England* declined and they were superseded by the works of, *inter alia*, Richard Grafton, Edward Hall, Raphael Holinshed, and John Stow, most of whom, however, used the *Brut* or the *Chronicles of England* as a source. Continuing influence of the *Brut* can be seen in the succession of ever-augmented printed editions between ?1518 and 1557 (STC 9983.3 to 9989.5) of the short list of kings and saints (found in MSS. CUL Ff.1.6 and

Folger Shakespeare Library V.a.198) and in the similar *Breuiat Cronicle*, published between 1552 and 1561 (STC 9968 to 9976). The number of printers who were prepared to update and augment annually such ready-reference works suggests their widespread popularity and a continuing, indirect role for the *Brut* as a source of historical information for a popular audience.

Bibliography

Albano, Robert A. *Middle English Historiography.* New York: Peter Lang, 1993.

Allmand, Christopher. *Henry V.* Berkeley and Los Angeles: University of California Press, 1992.

Anglo, Sydney. "The British History in Early Tudor Propaganda." *Bulletin of the John Rylands Library* 44 (1961–62): 21–44.

Arnold, Ivor, ed. *Le Roman de Brut de Wace.* 2 vols. Société des anciens textes français. Paris, 1938, 1940.

Aungier, George J., ed. *Croniques de London depuis l'an 44 Hen. III jusqu'à l'an 17 Edw. III.* Camden Society o.s. 28. London: J. B. Nichols, 1844.

Babington, Churchill, ed. *Polychronicon Ranulphi Higden Monachi Cestrensis.* Vols. 1 and 2. Rolls Series 41. London: Longman, 1865, 1866. (See also Lumby.)

Barratt, Alexandra. "Dame Eleanor Hull: A Fifteenth-Century Translator." In *The Medieval Translator: The Theory and Practice of Translation in the Middle Ages,* ed. Roger Ellis. Pp. 87–101. Cambridge: D. S. Brewer, 1989.

——, ed. *The Seven Psalms: A Commentary on the Penitential Psalms Translated from French into English by Dame Eleanor Hull.* EETS o.s. 307. Oxford: Oxford University Press, 1995.

Beadle, R., and A. E. B. Owen, introd. *The Findern Manuscript: Cambridge University Library MS. Ff.1.6.* London: Scolar Press, 1977.

Beaven, Alfred B. *The Aldermen of the City of London Temp. Henry III–1908/1912.* 2 vols. London: Eden Fisher, 1908, 1913.

Bell, Alexander, ed. *L'Estoire des Engleis: By Geffrei Gaimar.* Anglo-Norman

Text Society 14–16. Oxford: B. Blackwell, 1960.
Bennett, Adelaide, Jean F. Preston, and William P. Stoneman. *A Summary Guide to Western Manuscripts at Princeton University.* Princeton: Princeton University Library, 1991.
Bennett, H. S. *The Pastons and Their England: Studies in an Age of Transition.* 2nd ed. 1932; rpt. Cambridge: Cambridge University Press, 1970.
Bishop, William W. *A Checklist of American Copies of 'Short-Title Catalogue' Books.* 2nd ed. Ann Arbor: University of Michigan Press, 1950.
Blades, William. *The Life and Typography of William Caxton.* 2 vols. 1863; rpt. New York: Burt Franklin, n.d.
———, introd. *The Boke of Saint Albans.* London: Elliot Stock, 1881.
Blaess, Madeleine. "L'abbaye de Bordesley et les livres de Guy de Beauchamp." *Romania* 78 (1957): 511–18.
Blake, N. F. *Caxton's Own Prose.* London: André Deutsch, 1973.
———. *Caxton: England's First Publisher.* London: Osprey, 1976.
———. "Manuscript to Print." In N. F. Blake, *William Caxton and English Literary Culture.* Pp. 275–303. London and Rio Grande: Hambledon, 1991. (Rpt. from *Publishing in Britain 1375–1475*, ed. Jeremy Griffiths and Derek Pearsall. Pp. 403–32. Cambridge: Cambridge University Press, 1989.)
Böddeker, Karl. "Die Geschichte des Königs Arthur." *Archiv* 52 (1874): 1–32.
Boffey, Julia. *Manuscripts of English Courtly Love Lyrics in the Later Middle Ages.* Woodbridge: D. S. Brewer, 1985.
———, and Carol M. Meale. "Selecting the Text: Rawlinson C.86 and Some Other Books for London Readers." In *Regionalism in Late Medieval Manuscripts and Texts*, ed. Felicity Riddy. Pp. 143–69. Cambridge: D. S. Brewer, 1991.
Bond, Edward A., ed. *Chronica Monasterii de Melsa, a Fundatione usque ad Annum 1396, Auctore Thoma de Burton, Abbate.* 3 vols. Rolls Series 43. London: Longmans, Green [etc.], 1866–1868.
Brandis, Tilo. *Die Codices in scrinio der Staats- und Universitätsbibliothek Hamburg, 1–110.* Hamburg: Ernst Hauswedell, 1972.
Breisach, Ernst. *Historiography: Ancient, Medieval, and Modern.* Chicago and London: University of Chicago Press, 1983.
Brereton, Georgine E., ed. *Des Grantz Geantz. An Anglo-Norman Poem.* Medium Ævum Monographs 2. Oxford: B. Blackwell, 1937.
Brie, Friedrich W. D. "Recovery of an Anglo-Norman Chronicle." *Notes and Queries* 10th ser., 2 (1904): 41.

———. *Geschichte und Quellen der mittelenglischen Prosachronik The Brute of England oder The Chronicles of England.* Marburg: N. G. Elwert'sche Verlagsbuchhandlung, 1905.

———. "Zum Fortleben der Havelok-Sage." *Englische Studien* 35 (1905): 359–71.

———, ed. *The Brut or The Chronicles of England.* 2 vols. Part I: EETS o.s. 131. 1906; rpt. London: Oxford University Press, 1960. Part II: EETS o.s. 136. 1908; rpt. Millwood: Kraus, 1987.

Brown, Peter. "The Seven Planets." In *Popular and Practical Science of Medieval England*, ed. Lister M. Matheson. Pp. 3–21. East Lansing: Colleagues Press, 1994.

———, and Elton D. Higgs. *The Index of Middle English Prose. Handlist V: A Handlist of Manuscripts Containing Middle English Prose in the Additional Collection (10001–14000), British Library, London.* Cambridge: D.S. Brewer, 1988.

Brunner, Karl, ed. *Der Mittelenglische Versroman über Richard Löwenherz.* Wiener Beiträge zur englischen Philologie 42. Vienna: W. Braumüller, 1913.

Bülbring, Karl D. "Über die Handschrift Nr. 491 der Lambeth-Bibliothek." *Archiv* 86 (1891): 383–92.

———. "Sidrac in England." *Beiträge zur romanischen und englischen Philologie: Festgabe für Wendelin Foerster.* Pp. 443–78. Halle: M. Niemeyer, 1902.

Carley, James P. "Polydore Vergil and John Leland on King Arthur: The Battle of the Books." *Interpretations* 15 (1984): 86–100.

———, and Julia Crick. "Constructing Albion's Past: An Annotated Edition of *De Origine Gigantum*." *Arthurian Literature XIII*, ed. James P. Carley and Felicity Riddy. Pp. 41–114. Cambridge: D. S. Brewer, 1995.

Carroll, Marion C., and Rosemond Tuve. "Two Manuscripts of the Middle English 'Anonymous Riming Chronicle'." *PMLA* 46 (1931): 115–54.

Casson, L. F., ed. *The Romance of Sir Degrevant.* EETS o.s. 221. 1949; rpt. London: Oxford University Press, 1970.

A Catalogue of the Manuscripts Preserved in the Library of the University of Cambridge. Cambridge: Cambridge University Press, 1857.

Childs, Wendy R., and John Taylor, eds. *The Anonimalle Chronicle, 1307 to 1334, From Brotherton Collection MS 29.* Yorkshire Archæological Society, Record Series 147. Leeds: for the Society, 1991.

Clarke, Maude V. *Fourteenth-Century Studies*, ed. L. S. Sutherland and M. McKisack. Oxford: Clarendon Press, 1937.

Colker, Marvin L. *Trinity College Library Dublin: Descriptive Catalogue of the Mediaeval and Renaissance Latin Manuscripts.* 2 vols. Aldershot: Scolar Press; Brookfield: Gower, 1991.
Collins, Marie. *Caxton: The Description of Britain.* New York: Weidenfeld and Nicolson, 1988.
Conybeare, John J. "On a Poem, Entitled the 'Siege of Rouen'," *Archaeologia* 21 (1827): 48–78.
Cooper, Helen. *The Canterbury Tales.* Oxford: Oxford University Press, 1989.
Cottle, Basil. *The Triumph of English 1350–1400.* London: Blandford, 1969.
Cox, D. C. "The French Chronicle of London." *Medium Ævum* 45 (1976): 201–208.
Crick, Julia C. *The 'Historia Regum Britannie' of Geoffrey of Monmouth, III: A Summary Catalogue of the Manuscripts.* Cambridge: D. S. Brewer, 1989.
Davies, J. Conway. *Catalogue of Manuscripts in the Library of the Inner Temple.* 2 vols. Oxford: Clarendon Press, 1972.
Davies, John Silvester, ed. *An English Chronicle of the Reigns of Richard II, Henry IV, Henry V, and Henry VI Written Before the Year 1471.* Camden Society o.s. 64. London: J. B. Nichols, 1856.
Dean, Ruth J. "The Manuscripts of Nicholas Trevet's Anglo-Norman Chronicles." *Medievalia et Humanistica* 14 (1962): 95–105.
de la Mare, Albinia. *Catalogue of the Collection of Medieval Manuscripts Bequeathed to the Bodleian Library, Oxford, by James P. R. Lyell.* Oxford: Clarendon Press, 1971.
The Dictionary of National Biography, ed. Leslie Stephen and Sidney Lee. 63 vols. London: Smith, Elder, 1885–1900 (and supplements).
Dikstra, Marcel. "An Edition of the Brut Chronicle as Found in Ricart's Maior's Kalendar." M.A. diss. University of Bristol, 1992.
Dobson, E. J. "The Affiliations of the Manuscripts of *Ancrene Wisse*." In *English and Medieval Studies Presented to J. R. R. Tolkien*, ed. Norman Davis and C. L. Wrenn. Pp. 128–63. London: Allen and Unwin, 1962.
Doyle, A. I. "More Light on John Shirley." *Medium Ævum* 30 (1961): 93–101.
Duff, E. Gordon. *Fifteenth-Century English Books.* Bibliographical Society Illustrated Monographs 18. Oxford: Oxford University Press, 1917.
Dupont, L. M. E., ed. *Anchiennes Cronicques d'Engleterre par Jehan de Wavrin.* 3 vols. Société de l'Histoire de France. Paris: for the Society, 1858–1863.
Dutschke, C. W. *Guide to Medieval and Renaissance Manuscripts in the Huntington Library.* 2 vols. San Marino: Huntington Library, 1989.

Eckhardt, Caroline D., ed. *The 'Prophetia Merlini' of Geoffrey of Monmouth: A Fifteenth-Century English Commentary*. Speculum Anniversary Monographs 8. Cambridge, Mass.: Medieval Academy of America, 1982.

Edwards, John. "History in the 'Chronicle of the Brute'." *Proceedings of the Royal Philosophical Society of Glasgow* 34 (1903): 272–81.

Ellis, Henry, ed. *Holinshed's Chronicles*. 6 vols. London: J. Johnson [etc.], 1807–1808; rpt., with an introduction by Vernon Snow, New York, 1965.

———, ed. *Hall's Chronicle*. London: J. Johnson, F. C. and J. Rivington, 1809.

———, ed. *The New Chronicles of England and France, by Robert Fabyan, Named by Himself the Concordance of Histories*. London: F. C. and J. Rivington, 1811.

———, ed. *The Chronicle of Iohn Hardyng*. London: F. C. and J. Rivington [etc.], 1812.

———, ed. *Three Books of Polydore Vergil's English History, Comprising the Reigns of Henry VI, Edward IV, and Richard III*. Camden Society o.s. 29. London: J. B. Nichols, 1844.

———, ed. *Polydore Vergil's English History, From an Early Translation. Vol. 1, Containing the First Eight Books, Comprising the Period Prior to the Norman Conquest*. Camden Society o.s. 36. London: J. B. Nichols, 1846.

Embree, Dan, ed. *The Chronicles of Rome* (forthcoming).

Emden, A. B. *A Biographical Register of the University of Oxford to A.D. 1500*. 3 vols. Oxford: Clarendon Press, 1957–1959.

Engel, Margaret H. "An Edition of MS. Nicholson 13: f. 161r–f. 177v." M.A. thesis. University of Sydney, 1981.

Fifth Report of the Royal Commission on Historical Manuscripts. London: HMSO, 1876.

Fisher, John H., R. Wayne Hamm, Peter G. Beidler, and Robert F. Yeager. "John Gower." In *A Manual of the Writings in Middle English*, ed. Albert E. Hartung. Vol. 7. Pp. 2195–2210, 2399–2418. Hamden: Archon Books for the Connecticut Academy of Arts and Sciences, 1986.

Fryde, E. B., D. E. Greenway, S. Porter, and I. Roy, eds. *Handbook of British Chronology*. 3rd ed. London: Royal Historical Society, 1986.

Fulman, William, ed. *Rerum Anglicarum Scriptorum Veterum Tom. I*. Oxford: e Theatro Sheldoniano, 1684.

Furnivall, Frederick J., ed. *Early English Meals and Manners*. EETS o.s. 32. 1868; rpt. Millwood: Kraus, 1973.

Gairdner, James, ed. *Historical Collections of a Citizen of London in the Fifteenth Century*. Camden Society n.s. 17. Westminster: J. B. Nichols, 1876.

———, ed. *Three Fifteenth-Century Chronicles*. Camden Society n.s. 28. Westminster: J. B. Nichols, 1880.

Galbraith, V. H., ed. *The Anonimalle Chronicle 1333–1381*. 1927; rpt. Manchester: Manchester University Press, 1970.

———. "The *Historia Aurea* of John, Vicar of Tynemouth, and the Sources of the St. Albans Chronicle." In *Essays in History Presented to Reginald Lane Poole*, ed. H. W. C. Poole. Pp. 379–93. Oxford: Clarendon Press, 1927.

———. "Extracts from the Historia Aurea and a French 'Brut' (1317–47)." *English Historical Review* 63 (1928): 203–17.

Gates, Robert J., ed. *The Awntyrs off Arthure at the Terne Wathelyne*. Philadelphia: University of Pennsylvania Press, 1969.

Gerould, Gordon H. "King Arthur and Politics." *Speculum* 2 (1927): 33–51.

Giffin, Mary E. "A Wigmore Manuscript at the University of Chicago." *The National Library of Wales Journal* 7 (1951–52): 316–25.

Giles, John A., ed. *Incerti Scriptoris Chronicon Angliae de Regnis Trium Regum Lancastrensium Henrici IV, Henrici V, et Henrici VI*. London: D. Nutt, 1848.

Given-Wilson, Chris, trans. and ed. *Chronicles of the Revolution, 1397–1400*. Manchester and New York: Manchester University Press, 1993.

Goldsmid, Edmund, trans. *The Chronicles of London from 44 Hen. III to 17 Edw. III*. 3 vols. Edinburgh: privately printed, 1885–1886.

Gooch, George P. *A History of Historical Writing*. 2nd rev. ed. New York: Dover, 1962.

Gottfried, Robert S. *Epidemic Disease in Fifteenth-Century England*. New Brunswick: Rutgers University Press, 1978.

Gransden, Antonia. *Historical Writing in England c. 550–c. 1307*. Ithaca: Cornell University Press, 1974.

———. *Historical Writing in England. II. c. 1307 to the Early Sixteenth Century*. Ithaca: Cornell University Press, 1982.

Graves, Edgar B., ed. *A Bibliography of English History to 1485*. Oxford: Clarendon Press, 1975.

Green, Richard F. "King Richard II's Books Revisited." *The Library* 5th ser., 31 (1976): 235–39.

Griscom, Acton, ed. *The Historia Regum Britanniæ of Geoffrey of Monmouth*. London: Longmans, Green, 1929.

Guide to the Location of Collections Described in the Reports and Calendars Series 1870–1980. Guides to Sources for British History 3. London: HMSO, 1982.

Hales, John W., and Frederick J. Furnivall, eds. *Bishop Percy's Folio Manuscript. Ballads and Romances.* 3 vols. London: N. Trübner, 1867–1868.
Hall, Edward. *The Union of the Two Noble Families of Lancaster and York, 1550.* Facsimile. Menston, Yorkshire: Scolar Press, 1970.
Halliwell, James Orchard, ed. *A Chronicle of the First Thirteen Years of the Reign of King Edward the Fourth, by John Warkworth, D.D.*, Camden Society o.s. 1. London: J. B. Nichols, 1839. (Rpt. in *Three Chronicles of the Reign of Edward IV*, introd. Keith Dockray. Gloucester: Alan Sutton, 1988. Also rpt. Lampeter, Dyfed: Llanerch, 1990.)
Hands, Rachel, ed. *English Hawking and Hunting in The Boke of St. Albans.* Oxford English Monographs. Oxford: Oxford University Press, 1975.
Hanna, Ralph III, ed. *The Awntyrs off Arthure at the Terne Wathelyn.* Manchester: Manchester University Press, 1974.
———. *The Index of Middle English Prose, Handlist I: A Handlist of Manuscripts Containing Middle English Prose in the Henry E. Huntington Library.* Cambridge: D. S. Brewer, 1984.
———. *William Langland.* Authors of the Middle Ages 3. Aldershot, Hants.: Variorum, 1993.
———. "Henry Daniel's *Liber Uricrisiarum* (Excerpt)." In *Popular and Practical Science of Medieval England*, ed. Lister M. Matheson. Pp. 185–218. East Lansing: Colleagues Press, 1994.
———. *Pursuing History: Middle English Manuscripts and Their Texts.* Stanford: Stanford University Press, 1996.
Hardy, William, and E. L. C. P. Hardy, eds. *Recueil des Croniques et Anchiennes Istories de la Grant Bretaigne.* 5 vols., with an English translation in 3 vols. Rolls Series 39. London: Longman, Green [etc.], 1864–1891.
Harris, Kate. "The Origins and Make-Up of Cambridge University Library MS. Ff.1.6." *Transactions of the Cambridge Bibliographical Society* 8 (1983): 299–333.
———. "Patrons, Buyers and Owners: The Evidence for Ownership and the Rôle of Book Owners in Book Production and the Book Trade." In *Book Production and Publishing in Britain 1375–1475*, ed. Jeremy Griffiths and Derek Pearsall. Pp. 163–99. Cambridge: Cambridge University Press, 1989.
Harriss, G. L., and M. A. Harriss, eds. *John Benet's Chronicle for the Years 1400 to 1462.* Camden Miscellany 24. Pp. 151–252. London: Royal Historical Society, 1972.
Hay, Denys, ed. and trans. *The Anglica Historia of Polydore Vergil A.D. 1485–1537.* Camden Society, 3rd ser., 74. London: Royal Historical Society, 1950.

Haydon, Frank S., ed. *Eulogium Historiarum sive Temporis: Chronicon ab Orbe condito usque ad Annum Domini M.CCC.LXVI, a Monacho quodam Malmesburiensi exaratum.* 3 vols. Rolls Series 9. London: Longman, Green [etc.], 1858–1863.

Hearne, Thomas, ed. *Joannis Rossi Antiquarii Warwicensis Historia Regum Angliae.* Oxford: e Theatro Sheldoniano, 1716.

———, ed. *Titi Livii Foro-Juliensis Vita Henrici Quinti.* Oxford: e Theatro Sheldoniano, 1716.

———, ed., *William Roper's Vita Thomae More.* Oxford: e Theatro Sheldoniano, 1716.

———, ed. *Robert of Gloucester's Chronicle.* 2 vols. Oxford: The Theater, 1724. (Rpt. as vols. 3 and 4 of *Works.* London: Samuel Bagster, 1810.)

———, ed. *Thomae de Elmham Vita et Gesta Henrici Quinti.* Oxford: e Theatro Sheldoniano, 1727.

———, ed. *Duo Rerum Anglicarum Scriptores Veteres viz. Thomas Otterbourne et Johannes Whethamstede.* 2 vols. Oxford: e Theatro Sheldoniano, 1732.

Hirsh, John C. *Western Manuscripts of the Twelfth through the Sixteenth Centuries in Lehigh University Libraries: A Guide to the Exhibition.* Bethlehem, Penn.: Rare Book Room, Linderman Library, Lehigh University, 1970.

Hog, Thomas, ed. *Adam Murimuthensis Chronica Sui Temporis . . . cum eorundem Continuatione (ad M.CCC.LXXX) a Quodam Anonymo.* 1846; rpt. Vaduz: Kraus, 1964.

Hooper, A. G. "The Lambeth Palace MS. of the 'Awntyrs off Arthure'." *Leeds Studies in English* 3 (1934): 37–43.

Horner, Patrick J. *The Index of Middle English Prose, Handlist III: A Handlist of Manuscripts Containing Middle English Prose in the Digby Collection, Bodleian Library, Oxford.* Cambridge: D. S. Brewer, 1986.

Huscher, Herbert, ed. *John Page's 'Siege of Rouen'.* Kölner Anglistische Arbeiten 1. Leipzig: B. Tauschnitz, 1927.

James, Montague Rhodes. *The Western Manuscripts in the Library of Trinity College, Cambridge. A Descriptive Catalogue.* 3 vols. Cambridge: Cambridge University Press, 1901–1903.

———. *A Descriptive Catalogue of the Manuscripts in the Library of Gonville and Caius College.* 2 vols. Cambridge: Cambridge University Press, 1907, 1908.

———. *A Descriptive Catalogue of the Manuscripts in the Library of Corpus Christi College, Cambridge.* 2 vols. Cambridge: Cambridge University Press, 1912. (Issued in 7 parts, 1909–1912.)

———. *A Descriptive Catalogue of the Manuscripts in the Library of Lambeth*

Palace: The Mediaeval Manuscripts. Cambridge: Cambridge University Press, 1932.

Jansen, Sharon L. "Prophecy, Propaganda, and Henry VIII." In *King Arthur through the Ages*, ed. Valerie M. Lagorio and Mildred Leake Day. 2 vols. New York and London: Garland, 1990. 1: 275–91.

Johnson, Lesley. "Return to Albion." *Arthurian Literature XIII*, ed. James P. Carley and Felicity Riddy. Pp. 19–40. Cambridge: D. S. Brewer, 1995.

Jones, Evan John, ed. *Medieval Heraldry: Some Fourteenth-Century Heraldic Works*. Cardiff: William Lewis, 1943.

Kane, George, ed. *Piers Plowman: The A Version*. Rev. ed. London: Athlone; Berkeley: University of California Press, 1988.

Keeler, Laura. *Geoffrey of Monmouth and the Late Latin Chroniclers, 1300–1500*. University of California Publications in English 17.1. Berkeley and Los Angeles: University of California Press, 1946.

Keiser, George R. "MS Rawl. A.393: Another Findern Manuscript." *Transactions of the Cambridge Bibliographical Society* 7 (1980): 445–48.

Kendrick, T. D. *British Antiquity*. London: Methuen, 1950.

Kennedy, Edward Donald. "Chronicles and Other Historical Writing." *A Manual of the Writings in Middle English 1050–1500*, ed. Albert E. Hartung. Vol. 8. Hamden: Archon Books for the Connecticut Academy of Arts and Sciences, 1989.

Ker, N. R. *Medieval Libraries of Great Britain: A List of Surviving Books*. 2nd ed. London: Royal Historical Society, 1964.

———. *Medieval Manuscripts in British Libraries. I. London*. Oxford: Clarendon Press, 1969.

———. *Medieval Manuscripts in British Libraries. II. Abbotsford–Keele*. Oxford: Clarendon Press, 1977.

———. *Medieval Manuscripts in British Libraries. III. Lampeter–Oxford*. Oxford: Clarendon Press, 1983.

———. *Medieval Libraries of Great Britain: A List of Surviving Books. Supplement to the Second Edition*, ed. Andrew G. Watson. London: Royal Historical Society, 1987.

Kingsford, Charles L., ed. *Chronicles of London*. Oxford: Clarendon Press, 1905.

———, ed. *The First English Life of King Henry the Fifth*. Oxford: Clarendon Press, 1911.

———. "The First Version of Hardyng's *Chronicle*." *English Historical Review* 27 (1912): 462–82, 740–53.

———. *English Historical Literature in the Fifteenth Century*. Oxford: Claren-

don Press, 1913; rpt. New York: Burt Franklin, 1972.
Legge, M. Dominica. "The Brut Abridged, A Query." *Medium Ævum* 16 (1947): 32–33.
———. *Anglo-Norman Literature and Its Background.* Oxford: Clarendon Press, 1963.
———, and Georgine E. Brereton. "Three Hitherto Unlisted MSS. of the French Prose *Brute Chronicle.*" *Medium Ævum* 7 (1938): 113–17.
Lester, Geoffrey A. *The Index of Middle English Prose, Handlist II: A Handlist of Manuscripts Containing Middle English Prose in the John Rylands and Chetham's Libraries, Manchester.* Cambridge: D. S. Brewer, 1985.
———, ed. *The Earliest English Translation of Vegetius' 'De Re Militari'.* Middle English Texts 21. Heidelberg: Carl Winter Universitätsverlag, 1988.
Lewis, Robert E., and Angus McIntosh. *A Descriptive Guide to the Manuscripts of the Prick of Conscience.* Medium Ævum Monographs n.s. 12. Oxford: Society for the Study of Mediæval Languages and Literature, 1982.
———, N. F. Blake, and A. S. G. Edwards. *Index of Printed Middle English Prose.* New York and London: Garland, 1985.
Lindberg, Conrad. "The Manuscripts and Versions of the Wycliffite Bible." *Studia Neophilologica* 42 (1970): 333–47.
Lipscomb, Andrew D. (Lan). "A Fifteenth-Century Prose Paraphrase of Robert of Gloucester's *Chronicle.*" Ph.D. diss. University of North Carolina at Chapel Hill, 1990.
Loomis, R. S. "Edward I, Arthurian Enthusiast." *Speculum* 28 (1953): 114–27.
Luard, Henry R., ed. *Annales Monastici.* Vol. 2. Rolls Series 36. London: Longman, Green [etc.], 1865.
Lumby, Joseph L., ed. *Polychronicon Ranulphi Higden Monachi Cestrensis.* Vol. 8. Rolls Series 41. London: Longman [etc.], 1882. (See also Babington.)
———, ed. *Chronicon Henrici Knighton vel Cnitthon Monachi Leycestrensis.* 2 vols. Rolls Series 92. London: HMSO, 1889, 1895.
MacCracken, Henry N., ed. *The Minor Poems of John Lydgate.* Part I: EETS e.s. 107. 1911; rpt. London: Oxford University Press, 1961. Part II: EETS o.s. 192. 1934; rpt. London: Oxford University Press, 1961.
MacDougall, Hugh A. *Racial Myth in English History: Trojans, Teutons, and Anglo-Saxons.* Montreal: Harvest House; Hanover: University Press of New England, 1982.
Madan, Falconer, H. E. Craster, Noel Denholm Young, et al. *A Summary*

Catalogue of Western Manuscripts in the Bodleian Library. 7 vols. Oxford: Clarendon Press, 1895–1953.

Madden, Frederic. "Old English Poem on the Siege of Rouen." *Archaeologia* 22 (1829): 361–84.

———. "Prose Chronicles of England Called the Brute." *Notes and Queries* 2nd ser., 1 (1856): 1–4.

Manly, John M., and Edith Rickert, eds. *The Text of the Canterbury Tales.* 8 vols. Chicago: University of Chicago Press, 1940.

Marx, C. W. "Middle English Manuscripts of the Brut in the National Library of Wales." *The National Library of Wales Journal* 27 (1991–92): 361–82.

Mather, Frank J., Jr., "King Ponthus and the Fair Sidone." *PMLA* 12 (1897): i–lxvii (introduction), 1–150 (text).

Matheson, Lister M. "The Prose *Brut*: A Parallel Edition of Glasgow Hunterian MSS. T.3.12 and V.5.13, with Introduction and Notes." 3 vols. Ph.D. diss. University of Glasgow, 1977.

———. "The Middle English Prose *Brut*: A Location List of the Manuscripts and Early Printed Editions." *Analytical and Enumerative Bibliography* 3 (1979): 254–66.

———. "A Fragment of *Sir Eglamour of Artois*." *English Language Notes* 17 (1980): 165–68.

———. "Historical Prose." In *Middle English Prose: A Critical Guide to Major Authors and Genres*, ed. A. S. G. Edwards. Pp. 209–48. New Brunswick: Rutgers University Press, 1984.

———. "The Arthurian Stories of Lambeth Palace Library MS 84." *Arthurian Literature V*, ed. Richard Barber. Pp. 70–91. Cambridge: D. S. Brewer, 1985.

———. "Printer and Scribe: Caxton, the *Polychronicon*, and the *Brut*." *Speculum* 60 (1985): 593–614.

———. "King Arthur and the Medieval English Chronicles." In *King Arthur through the Ages*, ed. Valerie M. Lagorio and Mildred Leake Day. 2 vols. New York and London: Garland, 1990. 1: 248–74.

———. Review of Edward Donald Kennedy, "Chronicles and Other Historical Writing," *A Manual of the Writings in Middle English 1050–1500*, ed. Albert E. Hartung. Vol. 8. *Studies in the Age of Chaucer* 13 (1991): 210–13.

———, ed. *Popular and Practical Science of Medieval England.* East Lansing: Colleagues Press, 1994.

———. "English Chronicle Contexts for Shakespeare's Death of Richard II."

In *From Page to Performance: Essays in Early English Drama*, ed. John A. Alford. Pp. 195–219. East Lansing: Michigan State University Press, 1995.

———. "The Peasants' Revolt through Five Centuries of Rumor and Reporting: Richard Fox, John Stow, and Their Successors." *Studies in Philology* 95 (1998): 121–51.

———, ed. *Death and Dissent: Two Fifteenth-Century Chronicles*. Cambridge: D. S. Brewer, 1998.

Maxwell, Herbert, trans. *Scalacronica. The Reigns of Edward I, Edward II, and Edward III As Recorded by Sir Thomas Gray*. Glasgow: James Maclehose, 1907.

Maxwell, Marcia L. "The Anglo-Norman Prose *Brut*: An Edition of British Library MS Cotton Cleopatra D.iii." Ph.D. diss. Michigan State University, 1995.

McIntosh, Angus, M. L. Samuels, and Michael Benskin. *A Linguistic Atlas of Late Mediaeval English*. 4 vols. Aberdeen: Aberdeen University Press, 1986.

McKisack, May. *Medieval History in the Tudor Age*. Oxford: Clarendon Press, 1971.

McLaren, Mary-Rose. "The Textual Transmission of the London Chronicles." *English Manuscript Studies 1100–1700*, ed. Peter Beal and Jeremy Griffiths. Vol. 3. Pp. 38–72. London: The British Library; Toronto: University of Toronto Press, 1992.

Meale, Carol M. "Patrons, Buyers and Owners: Book Production and Social Status." In *Book Production and Publishing in Britain 1375–1475*, ed. Jeremy Griffiths and Derek Pearsall. Pp. 201–38. Cambridge: Cambridge University Press, 1989.

———. "'... alle the bokes that I haue of latyn, englisch, and frensch': Laywomen and Their Books in Late Medieval England." In *Women and Literature in Britain 1150–1500*, ed. Carol M. Meale. Pp. 128–58. 2nd ed. Cambridge: Cambridge University Press, 1996.

Meyer, Paul. "De quelques chroniques anglo-normandes qui ont porté le nom de Brut." *Bulletin de la société des anciens textes français* (Paris, 1878): 104–45.

Millar, Eric G. "Les principaux manuscrits à peintures du Lambeth Palace à Londres." *Bulletin de la société française de réproductions des manuscrits à peintures* 9 (1925): 5–19.

Mills, Maldwyn, ed. *Lybeaus Desconus*. EETS o.s. 261. London: Oxford University Press, 1969.

Milton, John. *The History of Britain*, introd. Graham Parry. Stamford: Paul Watkins, 1991.

Mitchell, Rosamond J. *John Tiptoft, 1427–1470.* London: Longmans, Green, 1938.

Moe, Phyllis, ed. *The ME Prose Translation of Roger d'Argenteuil's Bible en François.* Middle English Texts 6. Heidelberg: Carl Winter Universitätsverlag, 1977.

Mooney, Linne R. "Lydgate's 'Kings of England' and Another Verse Chronicle of the Kings." *Viator* 20 (1989): 255–89.

———. *The Index of Middle English Prose, Handlist XI: Manuscripts in the Library of Trinity College, Cambridge.* Cambridge: D. S. Brewer, 1995.

Moran, Jo Ann Hoeppner. *Education and Learning in the City of York 1300–1560.* Borthwick Papers 55. [York]: University of York, Borthwick Institute of Historical Research, 1979.

———. *The Growth of English Schooling 1340–1548: Learning, Literacy, and Laicization in Pre-Reformation York Diocese.* Princeton: Princeton University Press, 1985.

Mynors, R. A. B., and R. M. Thomson. *Catalogue of the Manuscripts of Hereford Cathedral Library.* Cambridge: D. S. Brewer, 1993.

Nichols, R. E., Jr. "Sidrak and Bokkus, Now First Edited from Manuscript Lansdowne 793." Ph.D. diss. University of Washington, 1965.

Ogilvie-Thomson, S. J. *The Index of Middle English Prose, Handlist VIII: Manuscripts Containing Middle English Prose in Oxford College Libraries.* Cambridge: D. S. Brewer, 1991.

Owst, G. R. "Some Books and Book-Owners of Fifteenth-Century St. Albans." *Transactions of the St. Albans and Hertfordshire Architectural and Archaeological Society* (1929): 176–95.

Papworth, John W. *An Alphabetical Dictionary of Coats of Arms... Forming an Extensive Ordinary of British Armorials.* 1874; rpt. London: Tabard Publications, 1961.

Parkes, M. B. *English Cursive Book Hands 1250–1500.* 1969; rpt. Berkeley and Los Angeles: University of California Press, 1980.

Patterson, Annabel. *Reading Holinshed's 'Chronicles'.* Chicago and London: University of Chicago Press, 1994.

Piggott, Stuart. *Ancient Britons and the Antiquarian Imagination: Ideas from the Renaissance to the Regency.* New York: Thames and Hudson, 1989.

Pollard, A. W., and G. R. Redgrave, comps. *A Short-Title Catalogue of Books Printed in England, Scotland and Ireland, and of English Books Printed Abroad, 1475–1640.* 2nd ed., rev. and enlarged by W. A. Jackson, F. S.

Ferguson, and Katharine F. Pantzer. 2 vols. London: Bibliographical Society, 1976, 1986.

Powell, E. O. "From The Brute of the Chronicle of England." *Folklore* 48 (1937): 91–93.

Raine, James, Jr., ed. *Testamenta Eboracensia*. Vol. 1: Surtees Society 4. London: J. B. Nichols, 1855. Vol. 2: Surtees Society 45. Durham: for the Society, 1865.

Ramage, David. *A Finding-List of English Books to 1640 in Libraries in the British Isles*. Durham: Council of the Durham Colleges, 1958.

Reese, George H. "The Alderman *Brut*: A Diplomatic Transcript, Edited with a Study of the Text." Ph.D. diss. University of Virginia, 1947.

Reynolds, Susan. "Medieval *Origines Gentium* and the Community of the Realm." *History* 68 (1983): 375–90.

Rickert, Edith. "King Richard II's Books." *The Library* 4th. ser., 13 (1932): 144–47.

Riley, Henry T., ed. *Annales Monasterii S. Albani, a Johanne Amundesham, Monacho*. 2 vols. Rolls Series 28. London: Longmans, Green, 1870, 1871.

Ritson, Joseph, ed. *Ancient Englëish Metrical Romancees*. 3 vols. London: G. and W. Nicol, 1802.

———. ed. *Poems, Written Anno MCCCLII by Laurence Minot*. London: J. H. Burn, 1825.

Robbins, Rossell Hope. "Poems Dealing with Contemporary Conditions." In *A Manual of the Writings in Middle English 1050–1500*, ed. Albert E. Hartung. Vol. 5. Pp. 1385–1536, 1631–1725. Hamden: Archon Books for the Connecticut Academy of Arts and Sciences, 1975.

Rose, Christine M. "An Edition of Houghton Library fMS Eng 938: The Fifteenth-Century Middle English Translation of Nicholas Trevet's *Les Cronicles* with *Brut* Continuation." Ph.D. diss. Tufts University, 1985.

———. "The Provenance of the Trevet Chronicle (fMS Eng 938)." *Harvard Library Bulletin* n.s. 3, no. 4 (Winter, 1992–93): 38–55.

Rosenthal, Joel T. "The Estates and Finances of Richard, Duke of York (1411–1460)." *Studies in Medieval and Renaissance History* 2, ed. W. M. Bowsky. Pp. 115–204. Lincoln: University of Nebraska Press, 1965.

———. "Down the Up Staircase: Quondam Peers and Downward Mobility in Late Medieval England." *Medievalia* 15 (1993, for 1989): 299–319.

Ross, Charles. *Edward IV*. Berkeley and Los Angeles: University of California Press, 1974.

Rotuli Parliamentorum. 6 vols. [London, 1767–1777].

Rous, John. *The Rous Roll*, introd. Charles Ross. Gloucester: Alan Sutton, 1980.
Samuels, M. L. "Some Applications of Middle English Dialectology." *English Studies* 44 (1963): 81–94. (Rpt. in *Approaches to English Historical Linguistics*, ed. Roger Lass. Pp. 404–18. New York and Chicago: Holt, 1969.)
———. "Kent and the Low Countries." In *Edinburgh Studies in English and Scots*, ed. A. J. Aitken, Angus McIntosh, and Hermann Pálsson. Pp. 3–19. London: Longman, 1971.
———. "Spelling and Dialect in the Late and Post-Middle English Periods." In *So Meny People Longages and Tonges: Philological Essays in Scots and Mediaeval English Presented to Angus McIntosh*, ed. Michael Benskin and M. L. Samuels. Pp. 43–54. Edinburgh: for the editors, 1981. (Rpt. in *The English of Chaucer and His Contemporaries: Essays by M. L. Samuels and J. J. Smith*, ed. J. J. Smith. Pp. 86–95. Aberdeen: Aberdeen University Press, 1988.)
Scattergood, John. "Two Medieval Booklists." *The Library* 5th ser., 23 (1968): 236–39.
Schirmer, Walter F. *John Lydgate: A Study in the Culture of the XVth Century*, trans. Ann E. Keep. London: Methuen, 1961.
Seymour, M. C. "The English Manuscripts of *Mandeville's Travels*." *Edinburgh Bibliographical Society Transactions* 4 (1966): 167–210.
———. "The Manuscripts of Hoccleve's *Regiment of Princes*." *Edinburgh Bibliographical Society Transactions* 4 (1974): 253–97.
Shailor, Barbara A. *Catalogue of Medieval and Renaissance Manuscripts in the Beinecke Rare Book and Manuscript Library, Yale University*. 3 vols. Medieval & Renaissance Texts & Studies 34, 48, 100. Binghamton: MRTS, 1984–1992.
Shrader, Charles R. "A Handlist of Extant Manuscripts Containing the *De Re Militari* of Flavius Vegetius Renatus." *Scriptorium* 33 (1979): 280–305.
Simpson, James. *The Index of Middle English Prose, Handlist VII: A Handlist of Manuscripts Containing Middle English Prose in Parisian Libraries*. Cambridge: D. S. Brewer, 1989.
Sinclair, Keith V. *Descriptive Catalogue of Medieval and Renaissance Western Manuscripts in Australia*. Sydney: Sydney University Press, 1969.
Smith, Lucy Toulmin, ed. *The Maire of Bristowe Is Kalendar, by Robert Ricart, Town Clerk of Bristol, 18 Edward IV*. Camden Society n.s. 5. Westminster: J. B. Nichols, 1872.

Steele, Robert, ed. *Lydgate and Burgh's 'Secrees of Old Philisoffres'*. EETS e.s. 66. 1894; rpt. Millwood: Kraus, 1973.

Stevenson, Joseph, ed. *Scalacronica: By Sir Thomas Gray of Heton, Knight*. Maitland Club. Edinburgh, 1836.

Tarvers, Josephine Koster. "English Women as Readers and Writers." In *The Uses of Manuscripts in Literary Studies: Essays in Memory of Judson Boyce Allen*, ed. Charlotte Cook Morse, Penelope Reed Doob, and Marjorie Curry Woods. Pp. 305–27. Studies in Medieval Culture 31. Kalamazoo: Medieval Institute, 1992.

Taylor, Frank. "The Chronicle of John Strecche for the Reign of Henry V (1414–1422)." *Bulletin of the John Rylands Library* 16 (1932): 137–87.

Taylor, John. "The French *Brut* and the Reign of Edward II." *English Historical Review* 76 (1957): 423–37.

———. *The 'Universal Chronicle' of Ranulf Higden*. Oxford: Clarendon Press, 1966.

———. "The French Prose *Brut*: Popular History in Fourteenth-Century England." In *England in the Fourteenth Century: Proceedings of the 1985 Harlaxton Symposium*, ed. W. M. Ormrod. Pp. 247–54. Woodbridge: Boydell, 1986.

———. *English Historical Literature in the Fourteenth Century*. Oxford: Clarendon Press, 1987.

Third Report of the Royal Commission on Historical Manuscripts. London: HMSO, 1872.

Thomas, Arthur H., ed. *Calendar of Plea and Memoranda Rolls Preserved among the Archives of the Corporation of the City of London at the Guildhall, A.D. 1323–64*. Vol. 1. Cambridge: Cambridge University Press, 1926.

Thomas, A. H., and I. D. Thornley, eds. *The Great Chronicle of London*. London and Aylesbury: G. W. Jones, 1938; microprint rpt. Gloucester: Alan Sutton, 1983.

Thompson, Edward Maunde, ed. *Adae Murimuth Continuatio Chronicorum. Robertus de Avesbury de Gestis Mirabilibus Regis Edwardi Tertii*. Rolls Series 93. London: HMSO, 1889.

———, ed. *Chronicon Galfridi le Baker de Swynebroke*. Oxford: Clarendon Press, 1889.

Thompson, Rodney M. *Catalogue of the Manuscripts of Lincoln Cathedral Chapter Library*. Cambridge: D. S. Brewer, 1989.

Trimble, William R. "Early Tudor Historiography 1485–1548." *Journal of the History of Ideas* 11 (1950): 30–41.

Turville-Petre, Thorlac. *England the Nation: Language, Literature, and National Identity, 1290–1340*. Oxford: Clarendon Press, 1996.

Twelfth Report of the Royal Commission on Historical Manuscripts. London: HMSO, 1891.

Tyson, Diana B., ed. *Le Petit Bruit of Rauf de Boun*. Anglo-Norman Text Society. London: for the Society, 1987.

———. "Handlist of Manuscripts Containing the French Prose *Brut* Chronicle." *Scriptorium* 98 (1994): 333–44.

Tyson, Moses. "Hand-List of the Collection of English Manuscripts in the John Rylands Library, 1928." *Bulletin of the John Rylands Library* 13 (1929): 152–219.

Vale, Juliet. *Edward III and Chivalry: Chivalric Society and Its Context 1270–1350*. Woodbridge: Boydell, 1982.

Vale, M. G. A. *Piety, Charity and Literacy among the Yorkshire Gentry, 1370–1480*. Borthwick Papers 50. [York]: University of York, Borthwick Institute of Historical Research, 1976.

Venables, Edmund, ed., with a trans. by A. R. Maddison. *Chronicon Abbatie de Parco Lude: The Chronicle of Louth Park Abbey*. Lincolnshire Record Society. Horncastle: for the Society, 1891.

Vinaver, Eugène, ed. *The Works of Sir Thomas Malory*. 3 vols. Oxford: Clarendon Press, 1947.

Vising, Johan. *Anglo-Norman Language and Literature*. London and Oxford: Oxford University Press, 1923; rpt. Westport: Greenwood Press, 1970.

Voaden, Rosalynn, ed. and trans. *Brogyntyn Manuscript No. 8*, introd. Felicity Riddy. Moreton-in-Marsh, 1991.

Voigts, Linda Ehrsam. "A Handlist of Middle English in Harvard Manuscripts." *Harvard Library Bulletin* 33, no. 1 (Winter, 1985): 5–96.

Weiss, R. *Humanism in England during the Fifteenth Century*. 3rd ed. Medium Ævum Monographs n.s. 4. Oxford: B. Blackwell, 1967.

Wilson, R. M. *The Lost Literature of Medieval England*. 2nd ed. London: Methuen, 1970.

Woudhuysen, H. R. "Manuscripts at Auction January 1991 to December 1991." *English Manuscript Studies 1100–1700*, ed. Peter Beal and Jeremy Griffiths. Vol. 4. Pp. 287–98. London: The British Library; Toronto: University of Toronto Press, 1993.

Wright, Neil, ed. *The 'Historia Regum Britannie' of Geoffrey of Monmouth, I: Bern, Burgerbibliothek, MS. 568*. Cambridge: D. S. Brewer, 1984.

Zettl, Ewald, ed. *An Anonymous Short English Metrical Chronicle*. EETS o.s. 196. 1935; rpt. Millwood: Kraus, 1971.

Index of Manuscripts and Early Printed Editions

All references to manuscripts, whether of the *Brut* or of other works, and early printed editions of the *Chronicles of England* or other derivative works, are listed below. The order for manuscripts is alphabetical by the geographical location of library, repository, or collection. Early printed editions are arranged in a separate list under the printer's name. Those pages that include the formal descriptive entries for each text or portion of text are indicated by a preceding asterisk (*). Supplementary information on the manuscripts (for example, the names of previous owners and the number of folios) and early printed editions (STC references and the locations of copies) can be found in the lists given on pp. xviii–xx, xx–xxi, xxiii–xxxi, and xxxiii–xxxvi. A further listing of the manuscripts and early printed editions of the English *Brut*, arranged by version, group, and type, appears in the Synoptic Inventory of Versions on pp. 67–78.

Manuscripts

Aberystwyth, National Library of Wales
 442D: xxviii, 64–65, 72, 188, *194–95
 21608D: xxviii, 44, 75, 278, *290–93
 Brogyntyn 8: xxii, xxviii, 77, *337
 Peniarth 343A: xxviii, 27, 76, *314–15
 Peniarth 396D: xxviii, 73, 77, 215, *223–24, 226, 228, *336
 Peniarth 397C: xxviii, 75, 294, *294, 296 n.
 Peniarth 398D: xxviii, 68, 79, *83–84

Ann Arbor, University of Michigan, Hatcher Library
 225: xxix, 73, 215, *222, 226, 228, 241–42

Berkeley, University of California at Berkeley, Bancroft Library
 152: xxix, 69, 114, *115
Bern, Bürgerbibliothek
 568: 176
Bethlehem, Pennsylvania, Lehigh University Library
 3 fragments: xxix, 77, *337–38
Bradfer-Lawrence 11: *see* Tokyo, collection of Toshiyuki Takamiya, 67
Bristol, City of Bristol Record Office
 Mayor's Calendar, no. 04720 (1): xxii, xxiii, 76, *322–23
Brussels, Bibliothèque Royale
 IV.461: xxviii, 70, 114, *117
Buckinghamshire, Flackwell Heath, Allison collection
 MS.: 19 n.

Cambridge, Cambridge University Library
 Additional 2775: xxiii, 72, 188, *190
 Dd.14.2: 187
 Ee.1.20: xviii, 31, 34, 36
 Ee.4.31: xxiii, 71, 134, *137, 305 n.
 Ee.4.32: xxiii, 70, 124, *125–26
 Ff.1.6: xxii, xxiii, 12, 15, 76, 318, *320, 347
 Ff.2.26: xxiii, 15, 72, 188, *190–91
 Gg.1.1: xviii n., 32
 Gg.1.15: xviii, 34
 Hh.6.9: xxiii, 13, 71, 73, 150, *150–51, 153, 154–56, 230, *231, 232–33
 Ii.6.8: xviii, 36 and n.
 Kk.1.3: xxiii, 77, *336
 Kk.1.6: 326
 Kk.1.12: xxiii, 15, 48 n., 69, 107, *107–108
 Ll.2.14: xxiii, 76, *323–24, 335 n.
 Mm.1.33: xviii, 32–33
Cambridge, Corpus Christi College
 53: xviii n.
 98: xviii
 133: 18 n.
 174: xxiii, 68, 88, *88, 234

182: xxiii, 72, 197, *197
311: xx, 39 n., 43, 44, 305
Cambridge, Fitzwilliam Museum
　McClean 186: xxiii, 69, 107, *111
Cambridge, Gonville and Caius College
　72: xxi, 39 n., 43, 44
　82: 45 n.
Cambridge, Magdalene College
　Pepys 2833: xxii, xxiii, 27, 329, 332
Cambridge, Peterhouse
　190: xxiii, 13, 68, 71, 98, *99, 166, *169–70, 172
Cambridge, Trinity College
　O.9.1: xxiii, 13, 71, 72, 131, 150, *151–52, 152, 154–56, 197, *197–98, 235, 236, 238, 239
　O.10.34: xxiii, 69, 107, *108–109
　O.11.11: xxiii, 75, 278, *279–81, 285, 293
　R.4.26: xviii n., 30 n.
　R.5.32: xviii, 34
　R.5.43, Part II: xxiii, 70, 124, *126–27
　R.7.14: xviii, 11, 34
　R.7.23: xviii n.
　R.14.9: xviii n.
Cambridge, Mass., Harvard University, Houghton Library
　Eng. 530: xxix, 71, 74, 157, *164, 165, 166 n., *257–59
　Eng. 587: xxix, 69, 107, *112–13
　Eng. 750 (two texts): xxix, 75, 278, (first text) *282–83, 293 (second text) *283
　Eng. 938: xxix, 76, *324–26
　Richardson 35: xxix, 13, 72, 176, 177, *178–79, 184, 185, 186, 187, 212
Cambridge, Mass., Harvard University, Law School
　1: xviii n.
Chapel Hill, collection of Robert G. Heyneman
　MS.: xxix, 70, 98, 117, *119–21, 121
Charlottesville, University of Virginia Library
　38–173: xxix, 72, 188, *193
Chicago, University of Chicago Library
　224: 39 n.
　253: xxix, 68, 94, *96–97, 97
　254: xxix, 13, 70, 71, 131, *131–32, 150, *152, 153, 156 and nn.

INDEX OF MANUSCRIPTS

Cleveland, Cleveland Public Library
   W q091.92-C468: xxix, 74, 259, *259–60, 261, 262, 263
Cologny-Genève, Bibliotheca Bodmeriana
   Cod. Bodmer 43: xxix, 77, *335
Corio, Victoria, Geelong Church of England Grammar School
   MS.: xxxi, 77, *338

Dublin, Trinity College
   489: xxviii, 74, 259, *260–61, 262, 263
   490: xxviii, 13, 70, 79, 81, 84–86, 87, 117, *118–19
   500: xx, 11, 34
   501: xx, 36 and n.
   505: xxviii, 75, 98, 278, *285–87
   506: xxviii, 74, 272, *273–74, 276
   5895: xxviii, 74, 215, 226, 228, 268, *268, 269, 270

Edinburgh, National Library of Scotland
   6128: xxvii, 68, 94, *95, 97, 123, 128
Edinburgh, University of Edinburgh Library
   181: xx, 34
   184: xxvii, 76, 316, *316–17
   185: xxvii, 72, 188, *189

Glasgow, collection of John Edwards
   MS.: xxxi–xxxii
Glasgow, University of Glasgow Library
   Hunterian 61: xxvii, 70, 114, *116
   Hunterian 74: xxvii, 12, 15, 51, 70, 71, 129, *129, 130, 139, 141, 142, 157, *161, 165, 189
   Hunterian 83: xxvii, 15, 27, 71, 73, 166, *167–68, 170, 171–72, 181, 205, *205, 207–208, 235, 236, 241–42
   Hunterian 228: xxviii, 69, 71, 107, *112, 157, *162, 165
   Hunterian 230: xxviii, 12, 72, 188, *189–90, 190, 240
   Hunterian 443: xxviii, 15, 73, 215, *216, 220, 225, 226, 227, 228, 235, 236, 243, 244–46, 247–50

Hamburg, Staats- und Universitätsbibliothek Hamburg
   Cod. 98 in scrin: xxviii, 57–61, 68, 92, *93
Hereford, Hereford Cathedral
   O.v.12: 11 n.

Leeds, University of Leeds Library
  Brotherton 29: xviii, xviii n., 11, 34, 37
Leicester, University of Leicester Library
  47: xxiv, 70, 124, *127
Lincoln, Lincoln Cathedral
  70: xxiv, 77, *335–36
  98: xxiv, 72, 188, *193–94
London, Bedford Estates Office
  Woburn Abbey 181: xxiv, 14, 76, 105 n., *326–28
London, British Library
  Additional 6915: xxiv
  Additional 10099: xxiv, 71, 92, 104, 157, *159–60, 164, 165, 170, 171
  Additional 10622: xviii n.
  Additional 12030: xxiv, 72, 177, *179–80, 184, 185, 186, 187, 212, 237, 239, 241, 250, 308
  Additional 18462(a): xviii, 36 and n., 119
  Additional 18462(b): xviii, 34
  Additional 24859: xxiv, 72, 188, *192
  Additional 26746: xxiv, 69, 114, *115–16
  Additional 33242: xxiv, 69, 105, *106
  Additional 33412: 325
  Additional 34648: 267 n.
  Additional 35092: xviii, 30
  Additional 35113: xviii, 32
  Additional 35295: 18–19 n.
  Additional 70514: xxii, xxiv, 12, 74, *265–66
  Cotton Claudius A.viii: xxiv, 30 n., 71, 157, *161–62, 165
  Cotton Cleopatra C.iv: 263
  Cotton Cleopatra D.iii: xviii, 11, 31 n., 35, 36 and n., 84–85, 86–87
  Cotton Cleopatra D.vii: xix, 34
  Cotton Cleopatra D.ix: 33
  Cotton Domitian iv: xxi, 43, 309
  Cotton Domitian x: xix, 31 n., 34
  Cotton Galba E.vii: xxi, 38, 43
  Cotton Galba E.viii: xxiv, 71, 134, *134–35, 140, 141, 142–43, 149–50
  Cotton Julius A.i: xix, 33
  Cotton Julius B.ii: 105 n., 296
  Cotton Julius B.iii: xxi, 16, 37, 39, 41–42
  Cotton Tiberius A.vi: xix, 30, 36 n.
  Cotton Titus D.xv: 20 n.

INDEX OF MANUSCRIPTS 371

Cotton Vitellius A.x: 11
Cotton Vitellius A.xvi: 328 n.
Cotton Vitellius V.vi: 19 n.
Egerton 650: xxiv, 13, 14, 69, 75, 98, *100–101, 102, 103, 104, 311, *311–12, 313, 314
Egerton 672: 39 n.
Egerton 1995: 134 n., 144, 145 n.
Harley 24: xxiv, 72, 177, *179, 184, 185, 186, 212, 234, 235, 236, 237, 238, 239, 240, 241, 250, 308
Harley 53: xxiv, 12, 22, 75, 296, *296–98, 300, 301 and n.
Harley 63: xxiv, 76, 316, *316, 318
Harley 200: xix, 34
Harley 266: xxiv, 68, 71, 92, 94, *95–96, 97, 104, 123, 134, *137–38
Harley 540: 156 n.
Harley 753: xxiv, 71, 90, 92, 104, 145, *146–47, 148
Harley 902: 10
Harley 941: xxi, 38, 47
Harley 1337: xxiv, 73, 215, *217, 226, 227, 228
Harley 1568: xxiv, 70, 117, *121
Harley 2182: xxiv, 72, 188, *188–89, 240, 337
Harley 2248: xxiv, 69, 107, *109
Harley 2252: 160
Harley 2256: xxiv, 71, 134, *135–36
Harley 2279: xxiv, 68, 88, *89–90, 333, 334
Harley 3730: xxiv, 71, 73, 166, *170–71, 172, 205, *205–206, 207
Harley 3884: xxi, 16, 43
Harley 3906: xxi, 16, 43
Harley 3943: 92 n.
Harley 3945: xxiv, 68, 79, *83
Harley 4690: xxii, xxiv, 76, 87, 98, 329, *329–30, 331, 332, 333, 334
Harley 4827: xxv, 64–65, 72, 174–75, 176, 188, *188, 235, 236, 238, 239, 243, 244–46, 247–50, 252–53
Harley 4930: xxv, 70, 129, *130, 131
Harley 6097: 267 n.
Harley 6251: xxv, 73, 215, *217–18, 226, 227, 228
Harley 6359: xix, 33
Harley 7333: xxv, 13, 15, 74, 215, 226, 228, 268, *269, 269, 270–71
Lansdowne 204: 21
Lansdowne 212: xxi, 16, 43, 302 n.
Royal 11.B.ix : xxv, 77, *337

Royal 17.D.xxi: xxv, 13, 69, 107, *109–10
Royal 18.A.ix: xxv, 73, 211, *211–13, 213, 213–14, 235, 236, 240–41
Royal 18.B.iii: xxv, 12, 69, 114, *114–15
Royal 18.B.iv: xxv, 73, 208, *209–11, 235, 236
Royal 19.C.ix: xix, 12, 36 and n., 37, 116 n., 119
Royal 20.A.iii: xix, 36 and n., 80
Royal 20.A.xviii: xviii n., xix, 36 and n.
Royal 20.C.vi: xviii n.
Royal App. 85: xix, 36
Sloane 2027: xxv, 13, 15, 74, 272, *274–75, 335 n.
Stowe 68: xxv, 68, 88, *90
Stowe 69: xxv, 13, 69, 105, *105–106
Stowe 70: xxv, 73, 230, *230, 232, 233, 235, 236, 252–53
Stowe 71 : xxv, 73, 215, *218–19, 226, 227, 228

London, College of Arms
  Arundel 5: xxi, 16, 38 n., 43
  Arundel 8: xxv, 74, 271, *272–73
  Arundel 14: 32
  Arundel 31: xix, 32, 33
  Arundel 58: xxii, xxv, 15, 27, 77, 329, *330–32, 332, 333, 334, 335 n.
  Vincent 421: xxv, 69, 107, *111–12

London, Guildhall
  3313: 24
  Roll A 1b: 63 n.

London, Lambeth Palace Library
  6: xxv, 14, 22, 75, 296, 298 n., *298–99, 300, 301 and n.
  84: xxv, 3, 25 n., 75, 263 n., 296, 309
  99: xxi, 15, 37, 39–42
  259: xxv, 14, 70, 129, *130, 131
  264: xxv, 13, 69, 71, 98, *100, 157, *163, 165
  306: xxv, 13, 26 and n., 76, *315–16, 317
  331: xxv, 71, 90, 92, 104, 145, *147–48, 148
  386: 39 n.
  491: xxv, 68, 90, *91, 104, 133
  504: xix, 34
  738: xxv, 69, 92, 98, *104–105, 123, 328 n.
  751: xxxi n.

London, Library of the Inner Temple
  Petyt 511, Vol. XI: xxv, 75, *306–309
  Petyt 511, Vol. XIX: xix, 34

INDEX OF MANUSCRIPTS

London, Lincoln's Inn
   88: xix, 34, 35 n., 36 and n.
London, Public Record Office
   E154/1/19: 10 n.
   Exchequer 164/24: xviii n.
London, Sion College
   Arc. L.40.2/E.42: xxv, 69, 98, *99
London, Society of Antiquaries
   93: xxv, 68, 79, *82, 86, 87
   223: xxv, 72, 197, *201–202
London, Westminster Abbey
   25: xix, 34

Manchester, John Rylands University Library
   Eng. 102: xxvi, 68, 88, *88–89, 124
   Eng. 103: xxvi, 67, 68, 79, *81, 86, 87, 88, *89, 90
   Eng. 104: xxvi, 70, 114, *116
   Eng. 105: xxvi, 72, 177, *177–78, 184, 185, 186, 187, 212, 235, 236, 237, 239, 241, 252–53
   Eng. 206: xxvi, 68, 79, *83
   Eng. 207: xxvi, 74, *263–65

New Haven, Yale University, Beinecke Library
   86: xx
   323: xxix, 13, 69, 107, *110–11
   405: xx, 32
   494: xxx, 13, 14, 67, 79, *81–82, 86
   593: xx, 34
New York, Columbia University Library
   Plimpton 261: xxii, xxx, 46, 75, 302, *302–303
   Plimpton 262: xxx, 57–61, 62–63, 69, 98, *99
New York, collection of Mrs. J. D. Gordan
   63: xxx, xxxi, 67, 79, *80–81, 86
Norfolk, Holkham Hall
   210: xxxi n.
   236: xxxi n.
   669: xxii, xxvi, 75, 302 and n., *303–304
   670: xxvi, xxxi n., 71, 134, *136–37
   672: xxxi n.

Norfolk, Keswick Hall, Gurney collection
  116.13: xxxii
Northumberland, Alnwick Castle
  457A: xxvi, 73, 215, *222–23, 226, 228
Nottingham, Nottinghamshire County Council
  DDFS 3/1: xxvi, 75, 278, *278–79, 293

Oxford, Bodleian Library
  Arch. Selden B.24: 205
  Ashmole 791: xxii, xxvi, 27, 75, 302, *304–305
  Ashmole 793: xxvi, 73, 101 n., 225, 228, *228–29, 230, 235, 236, 251, 254
  Ashmole 1139.iv.2: xxii, xxvi, 27
  Ashmole 1804: xix, 36 and n.
  Bodley 231: xxvi, 69, 114, *114
  Bodley 754: xxvi, 75, 294, *294–95
  Bodley 840: xxvi, 15, 48 n., 70, 79, 86, 117, *118
  Digby 185: xxvi, 12, 15, 73, 205, *206–207, 207, 208, 254
  Digby 196 (two texts): xxii, xxvi, 76, 318, *319
  Douce 120: xix
  Douce 128: xix, 34
  Douce 290: xxvi, 70, 114, *116–17
  Douce 323: xxvi, 12, 67, 79, *80, 82, 84–86, 87
  e Musaeo 39: xxvi, 74, *267
  e Musaeo 108: xix, 33
  Eng. hist. b. 229: 10 n.
  Fairfax 24: 32
  Hatton 50: xxvi, 64–65, 73, 215, *217, 226, 227, 228
  Laud Misc. 550: xxvi, xxxi n., 74, 271, *272, 277, 286, 290
  Laud Misc. 571: xxvi, xxxi n., 13, 72, 197, *198–99
  Laud Misc. 733: xxvi, 12, 13, 74, *266–67
  Lyell 17: xix, 11, 34
  Lyell 34: xxvi, 15, 26, 44, 45, 75, 278, 283, *287–90, 292, 293, 293–94, 296
  Rawlinson B.147: xxi, 43
  Rawlinson B.166: xxvi, 15, 69, 98, *102, 311, 314
  Rawlinson B.169: xxi, 38, 43, 44, 305
  Rawlinson B.171: xxvi, 12, 15, 48 n., 67, 68, 79, *79–80, 81, 82, 84–86, 87, 90, *91, 187

INDEX OF MANUSCRIPTS 375

    Rawlinson B.173: xxvi, 13, 14, 15, 48 n., 69, 75, 98, *101–102, 103, 104, 311, *312, 313, 314
    Rawlinson B.187: xxvi, 72, 177, *180, 187, 238–39, 241
    Rawlinson B.190: xxvii, 73, 215, *224–26, 226, 227, 228
    Rawlinson B.195: xxi, 38, 43
    Rawlinson B.196: xxvii, 70, 129, *129–30, 131
    Rawlinson B.205: xxvii, 70, 124, *124–25
    Rawlinson B.216: xxvii, 69, 107, *112
    Rawlinson C.155: xxvii, 27, 68, 79, *82–83
    Rawlinson C.234: xxi, 38 n., 43
    Rawlinson C.398: xxi, 16, 38, 43, 44, 46, 303
    Rawlinson C.901: xxvii, 73, 215, *224, 226, 227, 228
    Rawlinson D.329: xix, 34
    Rawlinson poet. 32: xxvii, 71, 72, 74, 157, *162–63, 165, 188, *195–97, 240, 254, 272, *275–76
    Selden Supra 74: xviii n.
    Tanner 11: xxvii, 73, 215, *220–22, 226, 228
    Tanner 188: xxvii, 72, 177, *183–84, 187, 239, 254
    Wood empt. 8: xix, 31 n., 32
Oxford, Corpus Christi College
    78: xix, 31, 32 n., 37
    293: xix, 33
Oxford, Jesus College
    5: xxvii, 73, 215, *219–20, 226, 227, 228
Oxford, Lincoln College
    Lat. 151: xxvii, 74, *267–68
Oxford, Magdalen College
    200: xxi, 37, 39–40
Oxford, Queen's College
    304: 92 n.
Oxford, St. John's College
    78: xxi, 16, 43, 305
Oxford, Trinity College
    5: xxvii, 72, 188, *191–92
Oxford, University College
    154: xxvii, 73, 230, *230–31, 233, 253–54

Paris, Bibliothèque de l'Arsenal
    3346: xx, 11, 34

Paris, Bibliothèque Mazarine
    1860: xx, 36 and n., 332
Paris, Bibliothèque Nationale
    fonds anglais 30: xxviii, 76, 316, *317, 317–18
    fonds français 6761: 23
    fonds français 12155: xx, 12, 22, 36 and n., 37, 119
    fonds français 12156: xx, 12, 34
    fonds français 14640: xx, 30
    nouvelles acquisitions françaises 4267: xx, 30
Paris, Bibliothèque Ste. Geneviève
    935: xx, 12, 36 and n., 37
Philadelphia, Free Library of Philadelphia
    Lewis 238: xxx, 68, 88, *89
Princeton, Princeton University Library
    Garrett 150: xxx, 12, 72, 197, *199–200
    Taylor Medieval 3: xxx, xxxii, 68, 70, 93–94, *94–95, 97, 98, 118, 132, *132–33

Rennie 733: *see* New York, collection of Mrs. J. D. Gordan

San Marino, Henry E. Huntington Library
    HM 113: xxx, 70, 124, *128
    HM 114: 92 n.
    HM 131: xxx, 73, 211, *213–15, 235, 236
    HM 133: xxx, 72, 197, *202–203
    HM 136: xxx, 13, 70, 71, 92, 104, 117–18, *123, 128, 157, 158, *163–64, 165, 339
    HM 19960: xxi, 22 n., 39 n., 43
Suffolk, Beeleigh Abbey, Foyle collection
    MS.: xxxii
Sydney, University of Sydney Library
    Nicholson 13: xxxi, 70, 124, *127–28

Tokyo, collection of Toshiyuki Takamiya
    12: xxxi, 72, 177, *181–83, 187
    18: xxxi, 75, 278, *281–82, 293
    29: xxxi, 69, 98, *99–100
    67: xxxi, 69, 107, *113

University Park, Pennsylvania State University Library
  PS. V–3: 103
  PS. V–3A: xxx, 15, 69, 75, 98, *102–104, 104, 286, 287, 311, *312–13, 314
Urbana, University of Illinois Library
  82: xxx, 73, 75, 228, *229, 278, *283–85
  116: xxx, 71, 72, 145, *148–49, 197, *200–201

Washington, Folger Shakespeare Library
  V.a.198: xxii, xxx, 76, 318, *321, 348
  V.b.106: xxx, 62, 70, 117, *122
Wiltshire, Longleat House
  183A: xxvii, 13, 69, 107, *108
Worcestershire, Rhydd Court, collection of Sir Edward Lechmere
  MS.: xxxii

Yorkshire, Brough Hall, collection of Sir John Lawson
  MS.: xxxii

Early Printed Editions

Caxton, William, *Chronicles of England* (Westminster, 1480): xxxiii, 3, 7, 8, 14, 23, 30 n., 48, 71, 77, 92, 100, 104, 118, 157, *157–59, 159 n., 165, 166, 167, 170, 171, 172, 191, 258, 276, 290, 339, *339, 341, 342; (Westminster, 1482): xxxiii, 77, 162, 165, *340

Leew, Gerard de, *Chronicles of England* (Antwerp, 1493): xxxiv, 77, *342–43

[Machlinia, William de,] *Chronicles of England* [London, ?1486]: xxxiii–xxxiv, 77, *342

Mychell, John, "A breuiat cronicle" (London, [1552]): 322 n., 348

Notary, Julyan, *Chronicles of England* (London, 1504): xxxiv, 77, *344, 345; (London, 1515): xxxv, 78, *345

Powell, William, [*Chronicle of years*] (London, 1552): 322 n.

Pynson, Richard, *Chronicles of England* (London, 1510): xxxiv–xxxv, 77, *344–45, 346 n.; "The cronycle of all the kynges names" (London, ?1518): 321

[Schoolmaster-Printer,] *Chronicles of England* (St. Albans, [?1483]): xxxiii, 77, 168, 172, 339, *340–41, 343

Worde, Wynkyn de, *Chronicles of England* (Westminster, 1497): xxxiv, 77, *343, 344; (London, 1502): xxxiv, 77, *343–44, 344, 345, 346; (London, 1515): xxxv, 78, *346, 346; (London, 1520): xxxv, 78, *346–47, 347; (London, 1528): xxxv–xxxvi, 78, 346 n., *347, 347; "Lytell Shorte Cronycle" (London, 1530): 322 n.

Index of Persons, Places, and Texts Associated with Manuscripts and Early Printed Editions

Listed below are the names of persons and places and the titles or descriptions of texts that are directly or closely associated with the manuscripts and early printed editions of the *Brut*. The names of modern scholars and references to the *Brut* itself are excluded, though narrative references to the Cadwallader episode, Queen Isabella's letter, "The Description of Edward III," and John Page's "Siege of Rouen" are included. A number of early names of codicological interest that occur in the manuscripts are listed, generally through the sixteenth century but exceptionally into the seventeenth century and, in the case of transcribers of texts, even later. (It should be noted that such names and titles of works do not exhaustively cover all those that occur in the texts but only those of particular interest that are recorded in the present volume.)

Additional or further references to printers can be found in the preceding Index of Manuscripts and Early Printed Editions.

Adam through Roman rulers, genealogical chronicle from 287
Adam to Henry VI, genealogy from 297
Alen, Isabel (legatee) 13, 199; Eleanor, mother of 199; William, father of 199
Amundesham, John of 326
Anonimalle Chronicle, The 11, 34
archbishops of Canterbury, genealogi-

INDEX OF PERSONS, PLACES, AND TEXTS 379

cal chronicle of 287; from Augustine to William Whittesley, chronicle of 40, 41
Ardyn, John, son of (name in MS.) 281
arms, treatise on 266, 267 n.
Arrival of Edward IV, The 22
Arthur and Merlin 310
Ashe, John, grocer (name in MS.) 328
Autun, Honorius of, *Ymago mundi* 40
Avesbury, Robert of, *De Gestis Mirabilibus Regis Edwardi Tertii* 34 and n., 37
Awntyrs of Arthure, The 92 n.

Baker, Geoffrey le, of Swinbrook, Oxfordshire, *Chronicon* 17
Barret, William, of Sholton, Staffordshire (name in MS.) 198
Battle Abbey, Sussex (provenance?) 132; Roll 108
Baxter, John (owner) 183
Beauchamp, Guy, earl of Warwick (donor) 9
Becket, Thomas, life of 301 n.
Beckwith, Leonard 161
Belamy, S. (owner) 14, 82
Benet, John, *Chronicle* 21
Bentelee (Bentele, Bentyle), William (owner) 130
Berkshire 100
biblical and English religious and historical affairs, entries on 321
bishoprics, list of 40, 41
Blackwell, Thomas (name in MS.) 328
Bohun family 17
Bohun, John de, earl of Hereford (borrower) 10 n.
Bohun, Ralph de (abridger), *Le Petit Bruit* 10, 17, 18
Bordesley Abbey, Worcestershire (recipient) 9
Bourchier family 200 n.
Bourghier, Thomas, archbishop of Canterbury, 200 n.
Bourghier, Thomas, constable of Leeds Castle (owner) 12, 200; Anne, wife of 12, 200
Braundon, William, of Knowle, Warwickshire (owner) 13, 274–75
Bray, Berkshire (place name in MS.) 100
Brayne, Henry (owner) 147
Brice, Alice (owner) 13, 108
"Bridlington Prophecy" 123
Bristowe Chronicle xxii, 14, 322
Bromley(e), Thomas (owner?) 219
Bruges, Louis de, seigneur de Gruthuyse (owner) 22
Brut abrégé, Brut DEngletere abrege xviii n., 30 n., 187 n.
Burgh, Benedict 269 n.; *Parvus Cato* 137 n.; *see also* Lydgate, John
Burgundy, ducal library of 22
Burgundy, dukes of (owners?) 12
Burley, Sir Simon (owner) 10
Burton, Thomas (scribe) 160
Burton, Thomas, chronicle of the abbey of Meaux, Yorkshire 19 and n.
Bury St. Edmunds, account of parliament at 327
Button, Francis (owner) 99

Cadwallader episode xxxii, 3, 6, 7, 18 n., 22, 30, 40, 45, 49, 52, 53, 57, 84, 88, 91, 92, 93 and n., 94, 102, 105, 106, 107, 113, 114 and n., 116, 117, 124, 125, 133, 137, 149,

157, 173, 175, 176, 220, 223, 266, 274, 277, 283, 286, 289, 293, 300, 323; text of 58–61
Cantrell, Henry and Thomas (names in MS.) 328
Cardynall, William (scribe?) 222
Carnarvonshire (provenance) 309 n.
Carpenter, Elizabeth (name in MS.) 328
Caxton, William (owner? and compiler), 14, 14 n., 28 n., 164, 165, 166, 339, 341 n.; *Advertisement* 165; *Liber ultimus* of *Polychronicon* (1482) 23, 24, 25, 71, 166, 166–67, 167, 168, 170, 171, 172, 189, 310; *Polychronicon* (1482) 296 n., 310, 311 n.; see also *Description of Britain, The*
Cecil, William, Baron Burghley (owner?) 94
Central Midland Standard (dialect) 15, 191
Chadertun (-ton), Edmund and William (owners) 127
Charles the Bold, duke of Burgundy (owner?) 22
Charter of the Abbey of the Holy Ghost, The 80 n.
Chaucer, Geoffrey 269 n.; version of Constance story by 310
Chaworth, Thomas, of Wiverton, Nottinghamshire (testator) 14
Chelmsford, Essex (?), Dominican convent in (owner) 13, 82
Chicester family, notes on 287
Christ, notices of conception and birth of 320
Christianity, account of spread of 279
Chronicle of the Rebellion in Lincolnshire, The 22

Chronicles of England (printed editions) 23, 24, 27
Cokerych, John (name in MS.) 151
Cogman (scribe) 122
Colyer, Raynold, prior of St. Bartholomew's, Smithfield, London (name in MS.) 110
"compass of England, the" 321
Complaint of Christ, The 258
"Continuation of Murimuth" 92 and n.
Cooke, Hugh (owner) 137 n.
Cookham, Berkshire (place name in MS.) 100
cooks' fees in London, regulations concerning 327
coronation of Edward IV, note on 229
Creation to Brutus and of subsequent English history, account of world history from 279
Cronekelys of Seyntys and Kyngys of Yngelond, The xxii
"cronycle of kyng Henry the v, the" 30 n.
Cronicles d'Angleterre 11
"Cronicles of Englond, The" see Caxton, William
Croniques de London 17
Crowland, Lincolnshire, chronicle of abbey of 21

dates and events from 1042 to 1461, lists of 229
"Davies's" *Chronicle* 21, 26, 44, 46, 75, 278, 287–90
Dawbne, Elizabeth (owner?) 13, 266
"De Natiuitate Domini nostri Ihesu Cristi" 315
Denny, John, of Burnwood (name in MS.) 223

INDEX OF PERSONS, PLACES, AND TEXTS 381

Denny, Thomas (name in MS.) 223
"Deposition of Richard II, The" 105, 327
Derbyshire (scribal provenance) 15, 320; (provenance?) 317
Des Grantz Geanz 2, 33, 34, 299
Description of Britain, The (William Caxton, Westminster, 1480) 14 n., 159 n., 339, 345; (Wynkyn de Worde, Westminster, 1498; rpt. 1502) 343, 344, 345, 346, 347
"Description of Edward III, The" 52, 90, 92, 94, 96, 97, 98, 104, 107, 117–18, 123, 128, 133, 149, 157, 173, 265
Deuenysshe, Richard (name in MS.) 136
distance between earth and moon, item on 282
Dunstable, Bedfordshire, priory of 21
Dwnn, Lewis (writer and scribe), Welsh verses on the zodiac 287

Eadmer, *Historia Novorum in Anglia* 295, 296 n.
eclipses from 1384 to 1462, table of 130
Edinburgh Castle (provenance) 17–18
Edward I to Pope Boniface VIII, letter from 160
Edward III, king of England (legatee) 10; account of retinue of 283; genealogical narrative of descendants of 265
Edward IV, king of England (owner) 22; note on victories in 1471 of 229
Edward IV to Elizabeth, notes on accessions of monarchs from 160
Edward IV's claim to various crowns, treatise on 160
Edward Balliol to Edward III, charter from 160
election of Thomas Warthel to abbacy of Westminster, notes on 160
emperors and popes, genealogical chronicle of 287
Erdeswicke, Sampson (name in MS.) 27
Essex (scribal provenance) 15, 48 n., 118; Central South (scribal provenance) 15, 129; North-West (scribal provenance) 15, 129
Eulogium Historiarum 18, 38, 43, 44, 45, 274, 277; continuation to 290
Extended Version exordium, text of 64–65

Fabyan, Robert, *New Chronicles of England and France* 24, 25, 26
Fastolf, John (owner) 11
Fell, John, of York (testator) 14
Findern family of Derbyshire (owners) 12, 320
Flanders (provenance) 12
Fleming, Abraham 25, 26 and n.
Flemings, song against 301
Flemish, ballad mocking 310
Fortescue, John (owner) 16
Fountains Abbey, Yorkshire (owner) 11
Fox, Richard, of St. Albans (compiler and scribe) 326, 327, 328 and n.
France (provenance) 12
Frobyser, John (name in MS.) 183
Froissart, Jean, *Chroniques* 22
Frost, William (name in MS.) 109
Fytt, James (name in MS.) 151

INDEX OF PERSONS, PLACES, AND TEXTS

Gaguin, Robert, *Compendium super Francorum Gestis* 24
Gaimar, Geffrei, *Estoire des Engleis* 31 and n.
Gardenere, John (owner) 11 n.
Gaynesford family of Carshalton, Surrey (owners) 12, 115
Gaynesford, Erasmus, George, Mary, Ralph, and Thomas (names in MS.) 115
geography, notes on 321
George Lord Abergavenny (name in MS.) 266
Gesta Romanorum 269 n.
Gildas 45
Giles's Chronicle 20
Glastonbury Abbey, Somerset (owner) 16
Glastonbury, John of, *Cronica sive Antiquitates Glastoniensis Ecclesie* 331
Gloucester, Robert of, 328 n.; *Metrical Chronicle* 137, 274, 326, 331, 335 n.; prose paraphrases of 324, 335 and n.
Gloucestershire (scribal provenance) 322
Godstow Chronicle 43
Gogh, Matthew, epitaph on 292
Goodwyn, Edmond (name in MS.) 113
Governance of Princes, The 258
Gower, John 269 n.; version of Constance story by 310
Grafton, Richard 25 n., 347
Gray, Thomas, of Heaton, Northumberland, *Scalacronica* 17–18, 18 n.
Graystock, John (purchaser) 11
Great Chronicle of London, The 24, 189

Gruthuyse, seigneur de la (owner?) 12; *see also* Bruges, Louis de
Guisborough, Walter de, *Chronicle* 18

Hailes, Gloucestershire, abbey of (owner) 11
Halidon Hill, poem on battle of 52, 329, 330 n., 332 n.
Hall, Edward, *Union of the Two Noble Families of Lancaster and York* 25 and n., 26, 347
Hampshire (scribal provenance) 15, 269 and n.
Hamundson, John, of York (testator) 14, 15 n.
Hamyleen, William (name in MS.) 328
Hardyng, John, *Chronicle* 20–21, 25, 26, 172, 206
Havelok 310
Hayward, William (owner) 27, 332
Hearne, Thomas (transcriber) 225
Helbartun (-ton), Dorothy (owner) 13, 123
Henry VI and Richard, duke of York, accord between 261
Herdes, Robert (owner?) 147; Ellen, wife of 147
Hereford, Franciscan convent at (owner) 11 n.
Herefordshire (provenance) 15, 48; Central (scribal provenance) 15, 48 n., 108; South-West (scribal provenance) 15, 48 n., 79; West (scribal provenance) 14, 15, 48 n., 102, 312
"Heruest hath iij monethis" 198 n.
Higden, Ranulph, *Polychronicon* 18 and n., 21, 23, 40, 45 and n., 46, 92, 260, 261, 289, 295, 310, 311; extracts from, 160, 212, (English)

INDEX OF PERSONS, PLACES, AND TEXTS 383

260, 261; index to, 160; *see also* Caxton, William, and Trevisa, John

Hill family of Nettlecombe, Somersetshire (owners) 12

Hill, Egidius, of Nettlecombe, Somersetshire (owner) 266; Agatha, wife of 266

Hill, John (owner) 127

Hill, Robert, of Nettlecombe, Somersetshire, obit for 266

Hindley, J. H. (transcriber) xxiv

historical subjects, Latin verses on 123

Hobbes, Richard (owner) 178

Hoccleve, Thomas 269 n.; "Gerelaus" 206; "Jonathas" 206; *Regiment of Princes* 206

Holinshed, Raphael, *Chronicles of England, Scotland, and Ireland* 25, 25–26 n., 26, 27, 347

Hooker, John 25

Hopton family of Swillington, Yorkshire (owners) 12, 206

Hopton, Thomasin (legatee) 207 n.

Hopton, William (owner?) 206, 207 n.

"Hought'" (so in MS.), Thomas (owner) 178

Humphrey, duke of Gloucester (patron) 20; account of death of 327

Hungyrforthe, Alice (name in MS.) 325

hunting, poem on 92 n.

Huntingdon, Henry of 301

Ipotis 80 n.

Ipswich area (scribal provenance) 15, 129

Isabella of France, queen of Edward II (testator) 10 and n.; *see also* Queen Isabella's letter

Isham, Robert (owner) 11

Jones, William (owner?) 189

King Ponthus and the Fair Sidone 206

kings and their coronations from William the Conqueror to Henry III, note on 160

kings from Arthur to Harold, list of burial places of 331

"Kings of England" 331–32

kings of England, table of 197

Knighton, Henry, *Chronicon* 18

Knights Hospitallers of St. John, priory of, Clerkenwell, London (owner) 11

Knyvet, Edmund (name in MS.) 109

Lacy, Henry de (patron) 10

Langtoft, Pierre 301; *Chronicle* 32, 300, 301, 326; *see also* Mannyng, Robert

Lathum, Roland (owner?) 136

Leche, John, of Nantwich, Chester (owner) 13, 123

Leicestershire (provenance?) 324

Liber ultimus see Caxton, William

Livius, Titus, *Vita Henrici Quinti* 20, 24

Lokington, Walter (name in MS.) 151

London (provenance) 15, 17, 48; area of (provenance) 228; chronicle(s) of xxii, xxiv, xxv, 13, 16, 17, 18, 24, 26, 104, 105 n., 133, 142, 151, 152–53, 153–54, 156 nn., 166, 167, 263, 271, 296, 313, 314, 315, 316 n., 319, 321; *see also Croniques de London* and *Great Chronicle of London, The*

London and Rome, notices of foundations of 320
London, Thomas, of Teberton, Suffolk (owner) 115
Lorraine (provenance) 12
Louth Park, Lincolnshire, chronicle of the abbey of 19
Lowe, Henry, the Younger of Whittington, Derbyshire 317
Lydgate, John 258, 259, 269 n.; "Dietary" ("Doctrina sana") 160; *Guy of Warwick* 258; "Kings of England" 106, 135, 315, 316 n., 321; "Legend of St. Austin at Compton" 310; *Life of St. Edmund* 112 n.; *Serpent of Division* 258; and Benedict Burgh, *Secrees of Old Philosoffres* 275

Maidenhead, Berkshire (place name in MS.) 100
Malmesbury, William of 45, 301; *Gesta (Historia) Regum Anglorum* 310, 331
Malmesbury, Wiltshire, abbey of (provenance) 18
Mandeville, John, rector of Burnham Thorpe, Norfolk (translator) xxii, xxiii, xxiv, xxv, 5, 6, 8, 10, 27, 48–49, 52, 76–77, 87, 90, 98, 256, 328, 329, 330, 331, 333, 334, 335 n.
Mandeville's Travels 112 n.
Mannyng, Robert, *Chronicle* 326
Marche, counts of (owner) 22
Marianus Scotus 295
Martinus Polonus, *Chronicle of Popes and Emperors* 137 n., 305
memoranda, historical 316 n., 285
Mettham, Thomas, of Brayton, Yorkshire (owner) 183

Midlands, East (scribal provenance) 15; West (scribal provenance) 15, 103; central West (scribal provenance) 15
Milton, John, *History of Britain* 28–29
Mondeffeld, William, de Charre 130 n.
Monmouth, Geoffrey of, *Historia Regum Britannie* 18 n., 21, 23 and n., 24, 25, 27–28, 29, 30, 37, 41, 44, 57, 176, 211, 213, 252, 300, 301, 323 n., 331
Monstrelet, Enguerran de, *Chronique* 22, 24

Nasby, William, of London (owner) 14, 82
Naysbe, Robert (owner) 82
N(e)uton, John, prior of Battle Abbey, Sussex (owner) 13, 131–32, 152 n.
"New Croniclis" 305
New Cronicyls Compendyusly Idrawn of the Gestys of the Kynges of England, The xxii
Newburgh, Roger (name in MS.) 329
Newnham, Bedfordshire, prior of 130 n.
Noah to Edward IV, genealogical chronicle from 287
Norham, Master, chronicle of (writer or owner) 21
Northamptonshire (scribal provenance) 15, 103
Northlond, Thomas, grocer (name in MS.) 14, 328
notations and chronologies, historical 283
notes and extracts, historical 283
Noua Cronica, "Nova Cronica" 16, 305

INDEX OF PERSONS, PLACES, AND TEXTS 385

Ormonde, earl of 24
Osbert, life of St. Dunstan 310
Osburn, John (name in MS.) 275
Osney, Oxfordshire, abbey of 17 n.
Otterbourne, Thomas of, chronicle 19

Page, John, "The Siege of Rouen" 20 n., 52, 71, 133, 134 and n., 137, 142, 143–44, 144, 144–45, 145, 150, 153, 263
Pakington, William (supposed writer) 35, 36 n.
parliament of 27 Henry VI, acts of 327
Pat(s)all, John and Thomas (names in MS.) 92
Pawlyn, Thomas (owner) 178
Pepys, Samuel (owner) 332
Percyhay, John, of Swynton (testator) 10
Peterhouse, Cambridge (owner) 170, 172
Petit Bruit, Le see Bohun, Ralph de
Phelippus, John, of Mansell (borrower) 11 n.
Philip the Good, duke of Burgundy (owner?) 22
Picquigny, provisions of Treaty of 160
Piers Plowman 80 n.
Ponce, John (name in MS.) 188
popes from Peter to Benedict, list of 315
popes to Gregory XI, chronicle of 40, 41
Proverbs of Solomon, The 112 n.
pseudo-Elmham, *Vita et Gesta Henrici Quinti* 20
Purchas, William (owner?) 14, 299

Queen Isabella's letter 6, 17 and n., 49, 52, 53, 62, 63 and nn., 84, 88, 93, 94, 98, 101, 105, 106, 107, 113, 114 and n., 117, 122, 124, 133, 157, 173, 175, 176, 231, 262, 266, 315, 317; text of 62–63

Red, Robert (owner) 183
Rede, Richard (compiler, owner, or scribe) 16, 46, 303
Rede, William, bishop of Chichester (compiler?) 16, 42, 46
Registrum Cartarum Prioratus S. Andreae Northampton 337
religious events in England, notices of 320
religious sites, account of 279
Rendale, Richard (owner?) 135
Ricart, Robert, town clerk of Bristol (compiler) 14, 322, 323
Richard Coeur de Lion 329, 331
Richard, duke of York, verse on 327
Rither, Ryther (scribe) 113
"Roger [*sic*], monk of Chester," *Cosmographia* 40
Rolewinck, Werner, *Fasciculus temporum* 165, 341 and n.
Rolls of Parliament 261, 263
Roman and Holy Roman emperors from Julius Caesar to Charles IV, chronicle of 40, 41
Rotuli Parliamentorum see Rolls of Parliament
roundels, set of genealogical 111
Rous, John, *Historia Regum Anglie* 23 and n.
Russell, John, *Boke of Nurture* 275
Rydyng, Thomas (scribe and owner) 163

"St. Albans Chronicle" 299
St. Bartholomew, Smithfield, London, priory of (owner) 13, 109–10
St. George, Richard, Norroy Herald (owner) 272
St. George's Chapel, Windsor (owner) 15, 40 n.
St. James, prose life of 198 n.
St. Katherine, prose life of 198 n.
St. Mary de Pratis, Leicester, abbey of (provenance, owner?) 13, 269 and n.
St. Mary's Abbey, York (owner) 11
saints and martyrs, notices of 320
saints in England, catalogue of 40
Sarum use, calendar of 130
Scardeburgh, John de (legatee) 10
Schoolmaster-Printer of St. Albans, 343, 345; *Book of Hawking, Hunting, and Blasing of Arms* 341 n.
Shakerley, Rowland (owner) 147
Sheldwych (annotator) 22 n.
Shelley, William (name in MS.) 223
Sherborne, Dorset, abbey of (provenance) 16
shields of arms 179
Shirley, John 164, 258, 259, 269
Shirley, John, of Staunton Harold and Rakedale, Leicestershire 103
Short English Metrical Chronicle 7, 48, 53, 173, 176, 184, 185, 186, 186–87, 202, 203, 204, 238, 253, 300, 331
Shyrburne, John (owner or scribe) 16 and n.
Sidrak and Bokkus 94
Siege of Jerusalem, The 92 n.
Slegill, Thomas (temporary possessor of book) 10

Somerset, John (dedicatee) 20
South-West Norfolk/West Suffolk (scribal provenance) 328 n.
Speed, John (writer and owner) 26; *Historie of Great Britaine* 26
Spelman, Henry (transcriber and owner) xxvii, 27
Staffordshire (scribal provenance) 15
Staffordshire (scribal provenance) 102
Stokes family (owners) 12, 297, 298 n.
Stoddard, William (name in MS.) 328; William, son of 328
Stow, John (writer, transcriber, and owner) 25, 26 and n., 27, 156 n., 347; *Annales of England* 26 and n.; *Chronicles of England* 25, 26; *A Summarie of Englyshe Chronicles* 26 and n.; historical memoranda by 316 n.
Strecche, John, *Historia Regum Anglie* 19
Suffolk(?), Dominican convent in (owner) 13, 82
Suffolk, South-East (scribal provenance) 15, 129
Sulyard, John, justice of the King's Bench (owner) 12, 200 and n.; Anne, widow of 12, 200
Surrey (scribal provenance) 15, 145 n., 290; Central (scribal provenance) 15, 216; Northwest (scribal provenance?) 325
Symons, John (name in MS.) 109

"T[. . .]l, Sere I[.]h[.]" (so in MS.; owner?) 79
This(?), George (owner) 189
Thomas, Richard, of Neath, Glamorganshire (owner) 13, 179

INDEX OF PERSONS, PLACES, AND TEXTS 387

Thomas, William (owner) 109
Thornborough, Timothy (name in MS.) 115
Three Kings of Cologne, The 92 n., 126 nn., 258; (Latin) 135
Thynne, Francis 25; (owner) 108
Tiptoft, John, earl of Worcester, historical compilation by 21, 22 n.
Toddington, Bedfordshire, chapel and hospital at 21
Towers, Bartholomew (owner?) 218
Translator of Livius, English life of Henry V 24, 26
Trayfort, Edmund, Alexander, and Robert (names in MS.) 97
Trevet, Nicholas, *Chronicle* 283, 331, 332 n.; translation of 325
Trevisa, John, of Berkeley, Cornwall, translation of Ranulph Higden's *Polychronicon* 18 and n., 23, 25, 159 n., 339, 345; *see also* Caxton, William; *Description of Britain, The*; Higden, Ranulph
Trouthe, William, vicar, Salisbury (testator) 13, 199
Troyes, copy of Treaty of 112 n.
Turbantisville, John (name in MS.) 80
Tynemouth, John of, *Historia Aurea* 17, 18 n., 63 n.

Ughtred, Thomas (testator) 10; wife of (legatee) 10

Vegetius, *De Re Militari* (1408 English translation) 275
Veldener, Johan 165, 341
Vergil, Polydore, *Anglica Historia* 24–25, 28
Virgin, prose life of the 198 n.

Virgin Mary and St. Margaret, Dartford, Kent, priory of the (owner) 13, 119
Vmnor, William, of Sharrington, Norfolk (owner) 89

Wace, *Roman de Brut* 30, 31
Waleran, lord of Waurin (patron) 22
Walsby, Richard (name in MS.) 183
Walsingham, Thomas, chronicles 26
Walter Lord Hungerford (dedicatee) 20
Waltham, Essex, annals of abbey of 20
Warkworth, John, master of Peterhouse, Cambridge (owner) 13, 166, 170
"Warkworth's" *Chronicle* xxiii, xxvii, 71, 168, 170, 171, 172 and n., 205
Warwickshire (scribal provenance) 15, 274
Watson, Christopher (owner) 115
Watson, Thomas (name in MS.) 115
Wattsoun (Watson), Richard (owner) 183
Waurin, Jean de, lord of Forestal, *Recueil des Croniques et Anchiennes Istories de la Grant Bretaigne* 22
Wauton family of Great Staughton, Huntingdonshire, and Basmead, Bedfordshire (owners) 12, 129
Waveley, Surrey, annals of abbey of 31
Welles, Francis (name in MS.) 282
Wendover, Roger of, *Flores Historiarum* 283
Westmer to 1368, text on Scottish history from 40
Westminster 48
Whinkop, Mary (name in MS.) 115
White, William (scribe, compiler, and owner) 27, 315

Willeys, John, probably of Berkshire (owner) 13, 100

William the Conqueror, tractate and epitaphs on 40

Willoughby family of Nottinghamshire and Derbyshire (owners) 12, 189

Wiltshire (scribal provenance) 15, 332

Winkfield, Berkshire (place name in MS.) 100

Wise Book of Philosophy and Astronomy, The 137 n.

Wolston, Richard (owner) 99

Woods, W., clerk of the Privy Council (owner) 266

Worcester, Florence of, *Chronicon ex chronicis* 21, 295, 296 n.

Worde, Wynkyn de *see Description of Britain, The*

Wylloughbe, Richard (owner?) 189; *see also* Willoughby family

Wynnard, Hugo (owner) 178

Yorkshire, West Riding of (scribal provenance) 15, 206

Zouche family of Nottinghamshire and Derbyshire (owners) 12, 189